KIERKEGAARD AND THE ROMAN WORLD

Kierkegaard Research: Sources, Reception and Resources
Volume 3

Kierkegaard Research: Sources, Reception and Resources
is a publication of the Søren Kierkegaard Research Centre

General Editor
JON STEWART
Søren Kierkegaard Research Centre,
University of Copenhagen, Denmark

Editorial Board
KATALIN NUN
PETER ŠAJDA

Advisory Board
ISTVÁN CZAKÓ
FINN GREDAL JENSEN
DAVID D. POSSEN
HEIKO SCHULZ

This volume was published with the generous financial support
of the Danish Agency for Science, Technology and Innovation

Kierkegaard and the Roman World

Edited by
JON STEWART

ASHGATE

Published by
Ashgate Publishing Limited
Wey Court East
Union Road
Farnham
Surrey GU9 7PT
England

Ashgate Publishing Company
Suite 420
101 Cherry Street
Burlington, VT 05401-4405
USA

www.ashgate.com

British Library Cataloguing in Publication Data
Kierkegaard and the Roman world. – (Kierkegaard research :
  sources, reception and resources; v. 3)
  1. Kierkegaard, Soren, 1813–1855 – Knowledge – Classics
  2. Kierkegaard, Soren, 1813–1855
  I. Stewart, Jon (Jon Bartley)
  198.9

Library of Congress Cataloging-in-Publication Data
Kierkegaard and the Roman world / edited by Jon Stewart.
    p. cm. — (Kierkegaard research: sources, reception and resources; vol. 3)
  Includes bibliographical references and index.
  ISBN 978-0-7546-6554-0 (hardcover : alk. paper)
  1. Kierkegaard, Soren, 1813–1855. I. Stewart, Jon.

  198.9–dc22

ISBN 978-0-7546-6554-0

Cover design by Katalin Nun.

Mixed Sources
Product group from well-managed
forests and other controlled sources
www.fsc.org Cert no. SGS-COC-2482
© 1996 Forest Stewardship Council

Printed and bound in Great Britain by
TJ International Ltd, Padstow, Cornwall

Contents

List of Contributors

Stacey E. Ake, Department of English and Philosophy, 5040 MacAlister Hall, Drexel University, 3141 Chestnut Street, Philadelphia, PA 19104, USA.

Niels W. Bruun, Søren Kierkegaard Research Centre, Farvergade 27 D, 1463 Copenhagen K, Denmark.

Rick Anthony Furtak, Department of Philosophy, Colorado College, 14 E. Cache La Poudre, Colorado Springs, CO 80903, USA.

Sebastian Høeg Gulmann, Øregård Gymnasium, Gersonsvej 32, 2900 Hellerup, Denmark.

Mikkel Larsen, Søren Kierkegaard Research Centre, Farvergade 27 D, 1463 Copenhagen K, Denmark.

Thomas Miles, Philosophy Department, Boston College, 21 Campanella Way, Chestnut Hill, MA 02467, USA.

Thomas Eske Rasmussen, Søren Kierkegaard Research Centre, Farvergade 27 D, 1463 Copenhagen K, Denmark.

Steven P. Sondrup, Brigham Young University, Department of Germanic and Slavic Languages, Provo, UT 84602, USA.

Jon Stewart, Søren Kierkegaard Research Centre, Farvergade 27 D, 1463 Copenhagen K, Denmark.

Nataliya Vorobyova, Instytut Anglistyki Uniwersytetu Warzawskeigo, Nowy Swiat 4, Warsaw 00-497, Poland.

Preface

While Kierkegaard's use of the Greek authors, particularly Plato and Aristotle, has attracted considerable attention over the years, his use of the Roman authors has, by contrast, remained sadly neglected. There is to date not a single monograph-length study dedicated to the influence of the Roman thinkers and writers on his thought. This neglect is somewhat surprising given the fact that Kierkegaard was extremely well read in Latin and had a long list of Roman authors in his personal library. Moreover, his extensive and frequent use of writers such as Cicero, Horace, Terence, Seneca, Suetonius, and Ovid clearly warrants placing them in the select group of his major sources.

Kierkegaard's initial exposure to Latin was at the Borgerdyd School in Copenhagen, which he attended from 1821 to 1830.[1] At the time of his youth, Latin was the mainstay of the curriculum at the school. According to a report from 1815 by the school's headmaster Michael Nielsen (1776–1846), the students in the highest class had 13 hours of Latin instruction per week, which was far more than in any other discipline.[2] The report states that these 13 hours were distributed as follows: 7 hours were used to read the works of Virgil and Horace; 4 hours were spent on Cicero's *De oratore* and his speeches; and 2 hours were dedicated to the historian Livy.[3] Kierkegaard was thus exposed to a wide range of Latin literature, including different genres of poetry and prose.

There can be no doubt that the charismatic Nielsen played a central role in shaping the interests of generations of Danish school boys, including Søren Kierkegaard. According to another of his students, Orla Lehmann (1810–70), Nielsen's "ideal of scientificity was a Ciceronian style; his highest poetry was a Horacian ode." He continues, referring to Horace's lover in the *Odes* (I, 22; II, 5), "he even wanted to convince us that Lalage was virtue."[4] Here one can see the strong classical inspiration of the headmaster, who used the Latin classics as the foundation for the curriculum.

Given Kierkegaard's intensive occupation with the language in the classroom, the anecdote found in *Stages on Life's Way* about a group of students reading Terence is by no means surprising. The long passage begins, "When I attended grammar

---

[1]   See Valdemar Ammundsen, *Søren Kierkegaards Ungdom. Hans Slægt og hans religiøse Udvikling*, Copenhagen: Universitetsbogtrykkeriet 1912; Per Krarup, *Søren Kierkegaard og Borgerdydskolen*, Copenhagen: Gyldendal 1977.

[2]   Ibid., pp. 24–5.

[3]   Ibid., p. 25.

[4]   Holger Lund, *Borgerdydsskolen i Kjøbenhavn 1787–1887*, Copenhagen: Otto B. Wroblewskys Forlag 1887, pp. 150–1.

school as a boy I had a Latin teacher whom I frequently recall."[5] A wonderful description is given of the pupils' interaction with their demanding teacher. It is hard to avoid interpreting this story as in some way based on Kierkegaard's own personal experiences at the Borgerdyd School.

The strong emphasis on Latin grammar clearly made an impression on Kierkegaard, who frequently appeals to grammatical terms, often as metaphors, in his authorship. When he refers to Hans Christian Andersen's "indeclinability in life"[6] in *From the Papers of One Still Living* or when he talks about the use of the past tense in *Two Discourses at the Communion on Fridays*,[7] he is creatively drawing on his many hours of grammar instruction at the Borgerdyd School. Similarly, in the aforementioned story in *Stages on Life's Way*, Kierkegaard writes, "the teacher... thereupon began to explain that we were not to regard the subjunctive mood in an external way as if it were the particle as such that took the subjunctive. It was the internal and the psychical that determined the mood, and in the case at hand it was the optative passion, the impatient longing, the soul's emotion of expectancy."[8] The tedious and creative interpretation of the use of the moods in Latin testifies to Kierkegaard's personal experience of long-winded explanations of the subtleties of Latin grammar.

Kierkegaard's ability in Latin was recognized at an early stage. One of his classmates Frederik Peter Welding (1811–94) recalls that he "at an early age produced work in Latin composition...which showed signs of unusual maturity and meticulous preparation."[9] Kierkegaard's written Latin was so good that he helped another student, Hans Peter Holst (1811–93), by writing his assignments for him, in return for Holst writing the Danish assignments for Kierkegaard. Holst recalls:

> ...at the Borgerdyd School we had a regular practice whereby I wrote the Danish essays for him and he wrote the Latin ones for me. It is strange that he, who ended up writing such excellent Danish, had absolutely no grasp of it in his youth, but wrote a Latin-Danish, which was crawling with participials and the most complexly punctuated sentences.[10]

From this account it is clear that Kierkegaard allowed his well-cultivated Latin style to influence his writing in Danish. Traces of this influence can clearly be seen in Kierkegaard's first book, *From the Papers of One Still Living*. It is thus interesting to learn that Holst radically reworked this text stylistically before its publication. He writes, "I literally *rewrote* his first written work on Andersen—or rather, I translated it from Latin to Danish."[11] One can only imagine what the text looked like before Holst offered a helping hand. Holst also recalls that Kierkegaard's ability in Latin won him the confidence of the headmaster Nielsen: "After a while he got the reputation of

---

5   *SKS* 6, 191f. / *SLW*, 204–5.
6   *SKS* 1, 31 / *EPW*, 76.
7   *SV1* XII, 277 / *WA*, 175.
8   *SKS* 6, 192 / *SLW*, 205.
9   Quoted from Bruce H. Kirmmse (ed.), *Encounters with Kierkegaard: A Life as Seen by His Contemporaries*, Princeton: Princeton University Press 1996, p. 7.
10   Ibid., p. 12.
11   Ibid., p. 12.

being a good Latinist, and Prof. Nielsen made use of him to review and correct the Latin compositions in the classes in which he [sc. Nielsen] was the teacher."[12]

When Kierkegaard's studies at the school came to a close in 1830, Nielsen wrote a recommendation for him for the university. In addition to lauding Kierkegaard's character and ability, Nielsen also usefully gives an account of what works Kierkegaard studied during his period at the school. He lists the following for Kierkegaard's Latin readings:

> He has read and presents: In Latin: by Horace: the *Odes*, the first three books of the *Epistles*, and *Ars Poetica*; by Virgil: the first six books of the *Aeneid*; by Terence: *Andria* and *Phormio*; by Cicero: *De officiis*, the first two books of *De oratore*, the Catilinean orations, "Pro Roscio Amerino," "Lege Manilia," "Archia poeta," "Milone," "Ligario," "Dejotaro," the first forty letters in the Weiske edition; the first *Pentade* by Livy; *Bellum civile* by Caesar; both *Wars* by Sallust; Cornelius Nepos.[13]

Based on this account, one scholar has calculated that this would amount to some 11,000 verses of Latin poetry and some 1,250 pages of prose.[14] This list shows a solid familiarity with the main poets—Horace, Virgil, Terence—and prose writers—Cicero, Livy, Caesar, Sallust, and Nepos, with a clear weight placed on the historians. All of these writers appear in Kierkegaard's authorship. Somewhat striking is the absence of Ovid and Suetonius here, both of whom Kierkegaard clearly read and later used extensively. It is probable that these authors, for reasons having to do with their content, were not considered appropriate classroom material for adolescent boys. (One might also mention Apuleius in this category.)

Although the exact dates are a matter of some discussion, at some point during Kierkegaard's years as a student at the University of Copenhagen, he returned to the Borgerdyd School to teach Latin.[15] In a letter from November 1840, Nielsen explains the nature of Kierkegaard's employment:

> At my request he [sc. Kierkegaard] has therefore helped me for several years with students who were weak in Latin composition, and he has successfully motivated them to do the sort of thinking that is not merely directed at passing the examination but that will continue to have an effect in their later lives.[16]

He continues, "In accordance with his request, during one academic year he taught Latin to the students in the second form and helped them progress a great deal, both in their Latin and in their general intellectual development."[17] Nielsen concludes his letter, "As far as I can judge, he has an unusual command of the Latin language,

---

[12]   Ibid., p. 13.

[13]   *B&A*, vol 1, pp. 4–5 / *LD*, 5, Document V. (See also Kirmmse, *Encounters with Kierkegaard*, p. 273.)

[14]   See Krarup, *Søren Kierkegaard og Borgerdydskolen*, p. 27.

[15]   The Hongs claim, without documentation, that Kierkegaard held this position from 1837 to 1838. See *EPW*, p. xiv.

[16]   Kirmmse, *Encounters with Kierkegaard*, p. 28.

[17]   Ibid., p. 28.

both orally and in writing."[18] It should also be noted, as further evidence of his Latin skills, that from 1833 to 1836, while he was studying at the university, Kierkegaard worked on a translation of the New Testament into Latin.[19]

Kierkegaard's interest in the Roman authors is clearly evidenced by his book collection. In his private library he had a long list of Latin titles and Danish translations of the standard Roman authors in any number of different genres. Of the historians he owned an edition of and a commentary on Caesar's *Gallic Wars*,[20] two editions of Livy's *History of Rome*,[21] a German translation of Valerius Maximus,[22] a three-volume edition of the historian of the late Empire, Ammianus Marcellianus,[23] three complete works editions of Sallust along with a Danish translation,[24] an edition of Suetonius,[25] and finally four editions of Tacitus in Danish, German, and Latin.[26]

Kierkegaard was also fond of the Roman philosophers. He had two editions of the works of Marcus Aurelius,[27] three editions of the Stoic Seneca,[28] and numerous editions of Cicero's letters, speeches, and philosophical works.[29] Of the other prose writers, Kierkegaard possessed three editions of Apuleius,[30] and a two-volume edition of Quintilian.[31]

Kierkegaard seems to have particularly enjoyed different genres of Roman poetry. He owned a complete edition of Horace,[32] two editions of Juvenal's *Satires*,[33] an edition of Ovid,[34] a Danish translation of the satirist Persius,[35] five editions of the dramatist Terence in Danish and Latin,[36] and an edition of Virgil's *Aeneid*.[37] Given all this, there can be no doubt that Kierkegaard's collection of Roman authors filled a considerable amont of shelf space in his library.[38] In addition to all of these primary

---

[18]		Ibid., p. 29.
[19]		See *SKS* K17, 277–86 / *KJN* 1, 435–41.
[20]		*ASKB* 1220, 1221.
[21]		*ASKB* 1251–1255, 1256.
[22]		*ASKB* 1296.
[23]		*ASKB* 1257–1259.
[24]		*ASKB* 1269–1270, 1271, 1272, 1273.
[25]		*ASKB* 1281.
[26]		*ASKB* 1282, 1283–1285, 1286–1288, 1289.
[27]		*ASKB* 1218, 1219.
[28]		*ASKB* 1274, 1275–1279, 1280–1280c.
[29]		*ASKB* 1224–1229, 1230, 1231, 1232, 1233, 1234, 1235, 1236, 1237, 1238, 1239, 1240–1244, 1245, 1246.
[30]		*ASKB* 1215, 1216, 1217.
[31]		*ASKB* 1267–1268.
[32]		*ASKB* 1248.
[33]		*ASKB* 1249–1250.
[34]		*ASKB* 1265.
[35]		*ASKB* 1266.
[36]		*ASKB* 1290, 1291, 1292, 1293–1294, 1295.
[37]		*ASKB* 1298.
[38]		There are also various editions of Roman authors in the two appendices of the *Auction Catalogue*, which I omit here due to the disputed status of the books listed in these groups. One might also mention the "bundles" of unidentified school books listed at *ASKB* A II 27–28.

texts, Kierkegaard also owned a number of works by modern authors on Roman history, philosophy, and literature.

In this context it should also be noted that not all of Kierkegaard's school books are accounted for in this overview. We know, for example, from Nielsen's account that Kierkegaard read the historian Cornelius Nepos in the school, but no edition of Nepos' writings appears in the *Auction Catalogue*. In a letter from many years after Kierkegaard's death, his aforementioned classmate, Frederik Peter Welding asked about this: "Doesn't someone have S.K.'s school books, his Horace or his Cicero *de Oratore*? The underlining and the marginal notes would be enlightening. S.K. wrote what we called 'notes' about Horace in connection with Prof. M. Nielsen's interpretation."[39]

The articles in the present volume demonstrate that Kierkegaard made use of the Roman sources in a number of different ways. His readings from the school seem to have stuck with him as an adult. He constantly refers to Roman authors, such as Livy, Nepos, and Suetonius for colorful stories and anecdotes. In addition, he avails himself of pregnant sayings or formulations from the Roman authors, when appropriate. But his use of these authors is not merely as a rhetorical source. He is also profoundly interested in the Roman philosophy of Cicero, Seneca, and Marcus Aurelius. Similarly, just as he is fascinated by Tacitus' portrayal of the early Christians, so also he is amused by the humor of Terence and Apuleius. In short, the Roman authors serve to enrich any number of different aspects of Kierkegaard's authorship with respect to both content and form.

This volume overlaps in part with volume 4 of the present series, namely, *Kierkegaard and the Patristic and Medieval Traditions*. The overlap is primarily chronological and linguistic. As with the sources featured here, most of the sources featured in that volume also wrote in Latin. Moreover, some of the sources in the two volumes lived at the same time during the Roman Empire. The main point of distinction between these volumes is that while *Kierkegaard and the Patristic and Medieval Traditions* treats exclusively Christian sources, *Kierkegaard and the Roman World* treats exclusively pagan sources. Christianity is thus the connecting link among all of the authors featured in the very long period of time covered in the volume on the Patristic and Medieval authors. By contrast, the authors in the present volume share in common the fact that they were all pagans, writing in Latin, and living in some part of the Roman Republic or Empire. The period of time covered in this volume is about 400 years, running from Terence, who was born in the Republic in 185 BC to the death of the Emperor Marcus Aurelius in AD 180.

In its exploration of these Roman sources, the present collection represents a pioneering effort in Kierkegaard research. It is hoped that the articles featured here will inspire scholars to take up the question of Kierkegaard's Roman sources in more detail. The influence of other Roman authors such as Propertius, Ammianus Marcellianus, Persius, and Quintilian, is still waiting to be explored.

---

[39]   Kirmmse, *Encounters with Kierkegaard*, p. 9.

Acknowledgements

On behalf of the editorial and advisory board, I have the honor of gratefully acknowledging the financial assistance of the Danish Agency for Science, Technology and Innovation which has made this series possible. We would also like to recognize the Søren Kierkegaard Research Centre at the University of Copenhagen for making available to the project any number of resources in its capacity as the host institute. The great patience and highly professional efforts of the staff at Ashgate Publishing have been enormously appreciated.

The efforts of Niels W. Bruun and Finn Gredal Jensen have been particularly valuable in shaping the general conception of this volume. I am also very grateful for the many useful suggestions from the members of the project's editorial and advisory boards: István Czakó, Katalin Nun, David D. Possen, Peter Šajda, Heiko Schulz, and Brian Söderquist. The outstanding editorial and bibliographical work of Katalin Nun deserves a special word of appreciation. Her efforts have improved virtually every article in this series. A great debt of thanks is owed to Bjarne Laurberg Olsen for his all too often unacknowledged, behind-the-scenes work for this project.

I would like to thank the authors of the present volume for their willingness and cooperation in realizing this important and innovative collection. Their efforts will be appreciated by many Kierkegaard readers for years to come.

List of Abbreviations

Danish Abbreviations

B&A   *Breve og Aktstykker vedrørende Søren Kierkegaard*, ed. by Niels Thulstrup, vols. I-II, Copenhagen: Munksgaard 1953–54.

Bl.art.   *S. Kierkegaard's Bladartikler, med Bilag samlede efter Forfatterens Død, udgivne som Supplement til hans øvrige Skrifter*, ed. by Rasmus Nielsen, Copenhagen: C.A. Reitzel 1857.

EP   *Af Søren Kierkegaards Efterladte Papirer*, vols. 1–9, ed. by H.P. Barfod and Hermann Gottsched, Copenhagen C.A. Reitzel 1869–81.

Pap.   *Søren Kierkegaards Papirer*, vols. I to XI–3, ed. by Peter Andreas Heiberg, Victor Kuhr and Einer Torsting, Copenhagen: Gyldendalske Boghandel, Nordisk Forlag, 1909–48; second, expanded ed., vols. I to XI–3, by Niels Thulstrup, vols. XII to XIII supplementary volumes, ed. by Niels Thulstrup, vols. XIV to XVI index by Niels Jørgen Cappelørn, Copenhagen: Gyldendal 1968–78.

SKS   *Søren Kierkegaards Skrifter*, vols. 1–28, K1–K28, ed. by Niels Jørgen Cappelørn, Joakim Garff, Jette Knudsen, Johnny Kondrup, Alastair McKinnon and Finn Hauberg Mortensen, Copenhagen: Gads Forlag 1997ff.

SV1   *Samlede Værker*, vols. I–XIV, ed. by A.B. Drachmann, Johan Ludvig Heiberg and H.O. Lange, Copenhagen: Gyldendalske Boghandels Forlag 1901–06.

English Abbreviations

AN   *Armed Neutrality*, trans. by Howard V. Hong and Edna H. Hong, Princeton: Princeton University Press 1998.

AR   *On Authority and Revelation, The Book on Adler,* trans. by Walter Lowrie. Princeton: Princeton University Press 1955.

ASKB   *The Auctioneer's Sales Record of the Library of Søren Kierkegaard*, ed. by
        H.P. Rohde, Copenhagen: The Royal Library 1967.

BA   *The Book on Adler*, trans. by Howard V. Hong and Edna H. Hong, Princeton:
        Princeton University Press 1998.

C   *The Crisis and a Crisis in the Life of an Actress*, trans. by Howard V. Hong
        and Edna H. Hong, Princeton: Princeton University Press 1997.

CA   *The Concept of Anxiety*, trans. by Reidar Thomte in collaboration with
        Albert B. Anderson, Princeton: Princeton University Press 1980.

CD   *Christian Discourses*, trans. by Howard V. Hong and Edna H. Hong,
        Princeton: Princeton University Press 1997.

CI   *The Concept of Irony*, trans. by Howard V. Hong and Edna H. Hong,
        Princeton: Princeton University Press 1989.

CIC   *The Concept of Irony*, trans. with an Introduction and Notes by Lee M.
        Capel, London: Collins 1966.

COR   *The Corsair Affair; Articles Related to the Writings*, trans. by Howard V.
        Hong and Edna H. Hong, Princeton: Princeton University Press 1982.

CUP1   *Concluding Unscientific Postscript*, vol. 1, trans. by Howard V. Hong and
        Edna H. Hong, Princeton: Princeton University Press 1982.

CUP2   *Concluding Unscientific Postscript*, vol. 2, trans. by Howard V. Hong and
        Edna H. Hong, Princeton: Princeton University Press 1982.

EO1   *Either/Or*, Part I, trans. by Howard V. Hong and Edna H. Hong, Princeton:
        Princeton University Press 1987.

EO2   *Either/Or*, Part II, trans. by Howard V. Hong and Edna H. Hong, Princeton:
        Princeton University Press 1987.

EOP   *Either/Or*, trans. by Alastair Hannay, Harmondsworth: Penguin Books
        1992.

EPW   *Early Polemical Writings*, among others: *From the Papers of One Still
        Living*; *Articles from Student Days*; *The Battle Between the Old and the
        New Soap-Cellars*, trans. by Julia Watkin, Princeton: Princeton University
        Press 1990.

EUD   *Eighteen Upbuilding Discourses*, trans. by Howard V. Hong and Edna H.
        Hong, Princeton: Princeton University Press 1990.

FSE   *For Self-Examination*, trans. by Howard V. Hong and Edna H. Hong, Princeton: Princeton University Press 1990.

FT   *Fear and Trembling*, trans. by Howard V. Hong and Edna H. Hong, Princeton: Princeton University Press 1983.

FTP   *Fear and Trembling*, trans. by Alastair Hannay, Harmonds-worth: Penguin Books 1985.

JC   *Johannes Climacus, or De omnibus dubitandum est*, trans. by Howard V. Hong and Edna H. Hong, Princeton: Princeton University Press 1985.

JFY   *Judge for Yourself!*, trans. by Howard V. Hong and Edna H. Hong, Princeton: Princeton University Press 1990.

JP   *Søren Kierkegaard's Journals and Papers*, vols. 1–6, ed. and trans. by Howard V. Hong and Edna H. Hong, assisted by Gregor Malantschuk (vol. 7, Index and Composite Collation), Bloomington and London: Indiana University Press 1967–78.

KAC   *Kierkegaard's Attack upon "Christendom," 1854–1855*, trans. by Walter Lowrie, Princeton: Princeton University Press 1944.

KJN   *Kierkegaard's Journals and Notebooks*, vols. 1–11, ed. by Niels Jørgen Cappelørn, Alastair Hannay, David Kangas, Bruce H. Kirmmse, George Pattison, Vanessa Rumble, and K. Brian Söderquist, Princeton and Oxford: Princeton University Press 2007ff.

LD   *Letters and Documents*, trans. by Henrik Rosenmcicr, Princeton: Princeton University Press 1978 (A translation of *B&A*).

LR   *A Literary Review*, trans. by Alastair Hannay, Harmondsworth: Penguin Books 2001.

M   *The Moment and Late Writings*, trans. by Howard V. Hong and Edna H. Hong, Princeton: Princeton University Press 1998.

P   *Prefaces / Writing Sampler*, trans. by Todd W. Nichol, Princeton: Princeton University Press 1997.

PC   *Practice in Christianity*, trans. by Howard V. Hong and Edna H. Hong, Princeton: Princeton University Press 1991.

PF   *Philosophical Fragments*, trans. by Howard V. Hong and Edna H. Hong, Princeton: Princeton University Press 1985.

PJ   *Papers and Journals: A Selection*, trans. by Alastair Hannay, Harmondsworth:
            Penguin Books 1996.

PLR   *Prefaces: Light Reading for Certain Classes as the Occasion May Require*,
            trans. by William McDonald, Tallahassee: Florida State University Press
            1989.

PLS   *Concluding Unscientific Postscript*, trans. by David F. Swenson and Walter
            Lowrie, Princeton: Princeton University Press 1941.

PV   *The Point of View* including *On My Work as an Author*, *The Point of View
            for My Work as an Author*, and *Armed Neutrality*, trans. by Howard V.
            Hong and Edna H. Hong, Princeton: Princeton University Press 1998.

PVL   *The Point of View for My Work as an Author* including *On My Work as an
            Author*, trans. by Walter Lowrie. New York and London: Oxford University
            Press 1939.

R   *Repetition*, trans. by Howard V. Hong and Edna H. Hong, Princeton:
            Princeton University Press 1983.

SBL   *Notes of Schelling's Berlin Lectures*, trans. by Howard V. Hong and Edna
            H. Hong, Princeton: Princeton University Press 1989.

SLW   *Stages on Life's Way*, trans. by Howard V. Hong and Edna H. Hong,
            Princeton: Princeton University Press 1988.

SUD   *The Sickness unto Death*, trans. by Howard V. Hong and Edna H. Hong,
            Princeton: Princeton University Press 1980.

SUDP   *The Sickness unto Death*, trans. by Alastair Hannay, London and New York:
            Penguin Books 1989.

TA   *Two Ages: The Age of Revolution and the Present Age. A Literary Review*,
            trans. by Howard V. Hong and Edna H. Hong, Princeton: Princeton
            University Press 1978.

TD   *Three Discourses on Imagined Occasions*, trans. by Howard V. Hong and
            Edna H. Hong, Princeton: Princeton University Press 1993.

UD   *Upbuilding Discourses in Various Spirits*, trans. by Howard V. Hong and
            Edna H. Hong, Princeton: Princeton University Press 1993.

WA   *Without Authority* including *The Lily in the Field and the Bird of the Air,
            Two Ethical-Religious Essays, Three Discourses at the Communion on
            Fridays, An Upbuilding Discourse, Two Discourses at the Communion on*

Fridays, trans. by Howard V. Hong and Edna H. Hong, Princeton: Princeton University Press 1997.

WL   *Works of Love*, trans. by Howard V. Hong and Edna H. Hong, Princeton: Princeton University Press 1995.

Apuleius:

Direct and Possible Indirect Influences on the Thought of Kierkegaard

Stacey E. Ake

I. The Life and Works of Apuleius

Apuleius, also known as Lucius Apuleius by Renaissance writers, was regarded as the narrator of *Metamorphoses*,[1] and thus as the eponymously-named and silent ass, Lucian, from Corinth.[2] He is also known by medieval writers, such as his fellow countryman, Augustine of Hippo, as Apuleius Afer, due to his North African origins. He lived in the second century of the Common Era and was probably born around the year 125. His town of origin, Madouros in Numidia, now M'daourouch in Algeria, also gave rise to his being called Apuleius the Madouran or "of Madaura" by Augustine and subsequent writers.[3] In fact, aside from his own writings, the only other source of information on Apuleius is Augustine, who argues against him in several places in *City of God*.

Among the books found in the auction catalogue of Kierkegaard's library that discuss Apuleius was Carl Friedrich Flögel's (1729–88) *Geschichte der komischen Litteratur* from 1784 to 1787, which contains a section "On Satire" in which Apuleius appears.[4] Among the observations that Flögel makes is a criticism of Augustine that the story of Amor and Psyche is not intended as philosophy but as fable.

---

[1] In *City of God*, Book XVIII, Chapter 18, Augustine calls the books comprising Apuleius' *Metamorphoses* by the title *The Golden Ass* (*Asinus Aureus*). In this section, Augustine is arguing specifically about the nature of bodily and mental transformations (metamorphoses) in a demonic as opposed to human context. I would also suspect that the use of the name *Asinus Aureus* for the work of Apuleius would help the reader distinguish it from the earlier poetical work of the same name by Ovid (43 BC – AD 17). In his *Metamorphoses*, Ovid, too, speaks of the nature and mythology of the world, but he speaks as a poet and not a philosopher.

[2] There is also an extant Greek work by Lucian Africanus titled Λούκιος ἢ Ὄνος (*Lucius, or the Ass*) and a lost work titled *Metamorphoses* by Lucius of Patrae. It is thought that Apuleius relied on both of these texts as well as northern African myth in his own work. The story of Cupid and Psyche is believed to be Egyptian in origin.

[3] For example, in Book VIII, Chapter 14, of *City of God*.

[4] Carl Friedrich Flögel, *Geschichte der komischen Litteratur*, vols. 1–4, Liegnitz and Leipzig: David Siegert 1784–87, vol. 2 (*Von der Satire*) *Erstes Hauptstück*, pp. 48–52 (*ASKB* 1396–1399).

A well-educated and affluent Latin-speaking denizen of a Roman colony, Apuleius was also fluent in Greek and a self-described Platonist who took it as his mission to translate the thoughts of the Greeks into the language of the Romans.[5] His intellectual life and work coincided with the Second Sophistic revival and the spreading of Greek culture and thought throughout the Mediterranean, thus solidifying what would become Greco-Roman culture.

While a student in Athens in the early 150s, Apuleius shared rooms with a fellow North African, named Pontianus, from Oea (near modern-day Tripoli in Libya). About five years later, on a journey to Alexandria, Apuleius stayed with Pontianus and his family in Oea. This visit lasted a year and ended with the marriage of Apuleius and Pontianus' mother Pudentilla. Relatives accused the young Apuleius of using magic or sorcery to win Pudentilla's heart, and he was consequently tried before the proconsul Claudius Maximus. Apparently, Apuleius won the day, since a rhetorical tour-de-force of his defense, titled *Apologia* or *Pro Se De Magia*, appeared in the early 160s.

Along with several other early works, such as *De mundo* (a reworking of a text of the same name which is wrongly attributed to Aristotle) and *De Platone* as well as a set of fine art verses called *Florida*, Apuleius' career as a rhetorician and Platonist was established and also ended. The events in *Metamorphoses*, or *The Golden Ass*, while alluding to events during his trial for sorcery, imply that the text itself was not used against him. Thus, scholars agree that it was written after the above-mentioned works.[6]

II. The Metamorphoses

The lasting fame of Apuleius rests on his novel recounting of the adventures of one Lucius of Corinth after he has been converted or metamorphosed into a donkey. While the novel is titled *Metamorphoses*, it is more commonly known as *The Golden Ass* (*Aureus Asinus*). It is the only Latin novel to come down to us in its entirety, although there is a debate whether the preface to the work does not belong to *Florida*. It is also a prefiguring of the picaresque novels and tales of travel that we associate in later ages with Chaucer, Cervantes, Boccaccio, and Rabelais.

---

[5]   Augustine echoes this view in *City of God*, Book VIII, Chapter 12, where he notes: "A hardly less noble Platonist was the African Apuleius, who was a master of both Greek and Latin." In his work, Augustine does not concern himself with tales from the *Golden Ass*. Rather, he is combating Apuleian arguments advanced in *De mundo* (*On the World*) and *De Deo Socratis* (*On the God of Socrates*) about the nature of existence and the nature of God.

[6]   For a fuller discussion of the language, dating, and history of Apuleius' works, please consult Stephen Harrison's "General Introduction: Life and Writings of Apuleius" in *Apuleius: Rhetorical Writings*, trans. by Stephen Harrison, John Hilton, and Vincent Hunink, Oxford and New York: Oxford University Press 2001.

III. The Influence of Apuleius

As mentioned above, the tale of *The Golden Ass* had a considerable impact on the development of European literature. Within that tale, the fable of Psyche and Cupid (or Amor), of the Soul and Love, can be viewed as having an even larger, albeit subtler, impact on that literature. Whether we are considering the transformation of Bottom into an ass in Shakespeare's *A Midsummer's Night Dream*,[7] or the awakening of Sleeping Beauty from a curse by a kiss, or the relationship of love to the soul in Novalis' *Hymns to the Night*, we are encountering an often-unexamined cultural and literary appropriation of the Apuleian theme of Cupid and Psyche.

Theologically speaking, as allegory and parable, the relationship between love and the soul, whether it is the relationship between the Lover and Beloved from *The Song of Songs* or simply the New Testament notion of a God of love redeeming the human soul or Christ as Bridegroom to his Church, we begin to see how attributes from the tale of Cupid and Psyche can become entwined with these other stories to the point where it is almost impossible to tease the different strands apart.

But there is an aspect of Christianity that Apuleius' tale amplifies: namely, that "an incomprehensible happiness rests upon an incomprehensible condition. A box is opened, and all evils fly out. A word is forgotten, and cities perish. A lamp is lit, and love flies away....An apple is eaten, and the hope of God is gone."[8]

IV. Kierkegaard's Explicit Use of Apuleius

In his pseudonymous works, Kierkegaard's references to Apuleius are fleeting. It is known from the auction catalogue of his library that he owned a copy of *Appuleii Fabula de psyche et cupidine*.[9] The 1833 work was one of a series of classical texts edited by Johann Kaspar von Orelli (1787–1849) and Johann Georg Baiter (1801–77) of Zurich. This edition was intended especially for the use of adolescent students beginning *Gymnasium*. This version was edited from a text originally translated (or transliterated) from Classical, albeit Silver Age, Latin into Renaissance Latin by the Dutch poet and professor Bonaventura Vulcanius (1538–1614) in 1602.[10]

Although no mention is made of Kierkegaard's actually having read works by Apuleius during his years at the Borgerdyd School, a younger classmate, Frederik Peter Welding (1811–94), observed that Kierkegaard

> at an early age produced work in Latin composition and in Danish which showed signs of such unusual maturity and meticulous preparation that we others found it odd and

---

[7]   However, the tale of Pyramus and Thisbe in the same play is from Ovid's *Metamorphoses*.

[8]   Gilbert Keith Chesterton, *Orthodoxy*, New York and London: John Lane 1908, p. 55.

[9]   *Apuleii Fabula de psyche et cupidine*, ed. by Johann Caspar von Orelli, Turici: Orelli 1833 (*ASKB* 1217). Baiter is mentioned on the third page as having done the small favor of also being an editor.

[10]   Ibid., p. 6.

4   *Stacey E. Ake*

eccentric without being able to appreciate it. I was often surprised by his work, but did not really understand why the teachers were pleased with his written compositions.[11]

Perhaps the young Kierkegaard had access to Latin texts that his fellows did not? When one considers the "extravagant" nature of Apuleius' style in the *Metamorphoses*, with its "multifarious" vocabulary and picaresque content, along with the future works Kierkegaard would produce, one could certainly believe that the young Kierkegaard may indeed have had access to just such a book.[12]

Thus, we find in "The Seducer's Diary" that Johannes has used a German translation of *Amor and Psyche* as a weapon in his campaign to conquer Cordelia.[13] Yet, it is interesting to note that Johannes himself does not consider the story either poetry or poetical—at least not as poetical as Cordelia herself.[14] The book is a prop in his seduction of Cordelia, just as Cordelia is a prop in his own amusement. We see that Johannes considers her desire to finish the absently discarded, yet deliberately left book, as something akin to his desire to finish (with) her. "She wants to read this book, and with that the goal is reached. —When she opens it to the place where it was last read, she will find a little sprig of myrtle, and she will also find that this means a little more than to be a bookmark."[15]

In the same fashion, when Johannes has reached his goal with Cordelia, he laments: "Why cannot such a night last longer?...But now it is finished, and I never want to see her again....I do not want to be reminded of my relationship with her; she has lost her fragrance...."[16] What was once thought to be a flower, a sprig of myrtle, has lost its fragrance, and Cordelia is now nothing more than a bookmark.

In the "Diapsalmata," however, it is a couplet from the German translation that is quoted: "*Mit einem Kind, das göttlich, wenn Du schweigst / Doch menschlich, wenn Du das Geheimniß zeigst.*"[17] Here, Amor tells Psyche that her child will be divine if she keeps silent and does not divulge her state of happiness or the nature of her husband (and her lack of knowledge thereof) to her envious sisters. But the child will be a mere mortal if she divulges her secret, he warns her. From this, the writer of the "Diapsalmata" seems to derive a broader message: that everything (whatever that may entail) will be acquired and made well through silence and stillness.

---

[11]   *Encounters with Kierkegaard: A Life as Seen by his Contemporaries*, ed. by Bruce Kirmmse, Princeton, New Jersey: Princeton University Press 1996, p. 7.

[12]   Joseph G. DeFilippo, reviewing J. Arthur Hanson's *Apuleius: Metamorphoses* (vols. 1–2, Cambridge, Massachusetts: Harvard University Press 1989), in *The American Journal of Philology*, vol. 113, no. 2, 1992, pp. 300–303, with particular reference to p. 301.

[13]   I assume this would be the translation by Joseph Kehrein mentioned in *Pap.* III B 179.42 and *SKS* 24, 461F., NB25:38 [Apuleius], *Amor und Psyche, freie metrische Bearbeitung nach dem Lateinischen des Apuleius*, trans. by Joseph Kehrein, Giessen 1834 (*ASKB* 1216). It is of note that Kehrein was a philologist and historian of German literature as well as the director of the Catholic teachers' seminary at Montbaur.

[14]   *SKS* 2, 429–30 / *EO1*, 443.

[15]   *SKS* 2, 420 / *EO1*, 443.

[16]   *SKS* 2, 432 / *EO1*, 445.

[17]   *SKS* 2, 40 / *EO1*, 31.

But, oddly enough, what allows the birth of pleasure, the eventual immortality of Psyche, the soul, and the reconciliation of love (Amor), desire (Venus), and the soul (Psyche), is the simple fact that Psyche does *not* keep silent, and although both love and the soul have to pay dearly for her indiscretion, the final outcome is a happy ending. One wonders, then, when we read the person Kierkegaard into the author of the "Diapsalmata," had Kierkegaard had faith—had he perhaps spoken out and spoken out of turn—whether he might have in fact had a happy ending with Regine.

Johannes de silentio reiterates this peculiar Apuleian idea but with a twist of despair in Problema III of *Fear and Trembling*, where he notes that silence is not only divine but also demonic.[18] Johannes goes on to imply that it is through the discipline of despair and the power of dialectic that we shall perhaps be able to determine whether the silence in question is demonic or divine. Is our silence one that opens us up to something greater than ourselves—such as the mortal Psyche would have received in having an immortal child by keeping her own counsel—or does our silence isolate us in enclosing reserve and prevent our reception of something greater than ourselves? How might things have been different, for instance, if Abraham had spoken to Isaac on their way up the mountain?

Now, if we do read the person Kierkegaard into the pseudonymous author Johannes de silentio, are we seeing a revision of the true role silence might play in a relationship between love, desire, and the soul? In other words, was Kierkegaard's keeping silent, hoping with an almost superstitious belief in the power of passivity, the wrong kind of silence? Would a broken silence, something rather like an act of faith, have allowed him to stay with Regine?

V. A Major Implicit Theme in Kierkegaard: The Story of Love and the Soul

Apuleius' story of Psyche and Cupid as found in *The Golden Ass* is the story of the relationship between love, desire, and the soul. As such, it is the story of how the soul, by means of Love itself—a love empowered by the strength of the other immortal gods, most notably Mercury and Jupiter—overcomes its despair and alienation in pursuit of its irrevocably lost love—despite the often negative influence of desire. The soul, Psyche, undertakes this work because of her deliberate disobedience of the admonition of Love to not look upon him—a desire, arisen from doubt and a lack of trust, has destroyed love, and left Psyche, the soul, bereft. Thus, the moment of seeing love is the moment of losing love, and despair results.[19] In the introductory motto to *The Sickness Unto Death*, I think we are being shown that seeing, liking speaking, might be of uncertain moral value: "*Herr! gieb uns blöde Augen / für*

---

[18]   *SKS* 4, 177–8 / *FT*, 88.
[19]   Here an interesting parallel arises between seeing for the right reasons and speaking for the right reasons. In other words, Psyche must both stay silent and remain blind. She may not speak; she may not see, but she is allowed to hear. As a metaphor, this is extremely provocative. Consider the *Shema* (Deuteronomy 6:4): "Hear, O Israel, the Lord, your God, is One." Hearing is the medium of obedience; sight is the medium of understanding, and speech? It would seem to be the medium of unnecessary rebellion and senseless questioning.

Dinge, die nichts taugen, / und Augen voller Klarheit / in alle deine Wahrheit."[20] It would seem that in some way we can choose not simply what we see and how we see it, but *Deo volente* whether we shall see it at all.

In Apuleius' tale, Psyche, the soul, desires to have her love back in her arms, but she is at a loss as to how to go about this. She *needs* to find Amor again, despite the declared *impossibility* of such a reconciliation occurring. If we examine how she got herself into this predicament in the first place, we see that while she had no reason, no necessity, to act as she did, she was torn between two options: her desire to see her beautiful husband, for he was beautiful according to her experience, and her fear that he was a monster, as her sisters had warned her.

She is, to quote Kierkegaard, "lost in possibility....So it is with desire's possibility. Instead of taking the possibility back into necessity," i.e., instead of realizing that either one of those options mentioned above directly defy Amor's admonition that she *never* look at him, "she chases after possibility—and at last cannot find her way back to herself."[21] And this is the case, for when Psyche looks upon Cupid, she sees his beauty, and it overwhelms her. She flinches, and the oil from her lamp burns Cupid, awakening him, and immediately Psyche loses the self she had become: Cupid's wife. In the very instant of discovering that she was, in fact, exactly what she had hoped she was, she loses who and what she was and is.

Kierkegaard also points out that desire, melancholically enamored, that is, in a state of fear and not hope, "pursues one of anxiety's possibilities, which finally leads her away from herself so that she is a victim of anxiety or a victim of that about which she was so anxious lest she be overcome."[22] Thus, if we think of Psyche as being motivated to view Cupid out of fear that he be a monster, as evidenced, for instance, by the fact that he often leaves her alone and does not allow her to see him, we find that her anxious actions have brought about just the situation that she feared. Cupid has indeed become a monster, for he has left her alone, without his love, forever. Psyche in her fear, and in her desire to explore the possibilities of seeing Cupid without grounding them in necessity, namely, Cupid's injunction never to look at him, has lost possibility as well. And, now she must go and find him.

Thus we see that before she took the lamp and viewed Cupid, Psyche was suffering from possibility's despair—she lacked, or, in this case, ignored, necessity. Now, with Cupid gone, she suffers from necessity's despair, which is to lack possibility. How will she ever find Cupid again?

Another glimpse of the Apuleian story in *The Sickness Unto Death* is found with the challenges that confront Psyche in despair, which is the despair of weakness. She has enough of a self to know she is suffering, but she does not possess enough substance (quite literally) to move beyond her suffering. It surrounds her and

---

[20]   *SKS* 11, 116 / *SUD*, 3: "Lord, give us weak eyes / for things of little worth, / and eyes clear-sighted / in all of your truth."
[21]   *SKS* 11, 153 / *SUD*, 37. The change in the gender of the pronouns in this quotation reflects the intentions of the author of this present article.
[22]   *SKS* 11, 153 / *SUD*, 37. As before, the gender of the pronouns in this quotation has been changed.

permeates her as the suffering which is herself. She is living in the immediacy of despair. For this reason, she seeks out Venus, Cupid's mother, to help her find Cupid—despite the fact that Venus herself opposed the match. Numbly, Psyche moves from one mindless task to another, until she falls into a deep sleep.[23] She is the proverbial "Sleeping Beauty" awaiting anybody to help her:

> She claims she is in despair, she regards herself as dead, as a shadow of herself....If everything...were to change suddenly, and if her desire were fulfilled, then there would be life in her again....This is the only way immediacy knows how to strive, the only thing it knows: to despair and faint....[24]

This is exactly what Psyche does, but the fates are kind, and Cupid comes to awaken her. As Kierkegaard observes, when "help arrives from the outside, the person in despair comes alive again, she begins where she left off; a self she was not, and a self she did not become, but she goes on living, qualified only by immediacy."[25] This, too, is the case with Psyche. It is not Cupid's return *per se* that grants her immortality; rather, it is Love's return, Cupid *in tandem*, with the blessing of the gods.

There are other places in *The Sickness Unto Death* where the myth of Psyche and Cupid, of love and the soul, can be espied.[26] But, it is not present in an overt way; Apuleius is not even mentioned. However, glimpses of the myth, as a background motif, can be felt between the lines.

VI. A Minor Implicit Theme in Kierkegaard: De Deo Socratis

Although there is no record of Apuleius' work *De Deo Socratis* having been found in Kierkegaard's library, absence of proof is not necessarily proof of absence. However, this work, like the *Metamorphoses*, was a fairly common text in Latin Schools of the era.[27] Obviously, in this work Apuleius discusses the nature of the god of Socrates, which, in turn, is a kind of subtext of the *Philosophical Fragments*. Specifically, Apuleius puzzles over the nature of Socrates' daimon and whether such an entity was good or ill, or distinctly embodied or not. Apuleius raises even more questions about the nature of a superior god. For instance, is there not, in fact, so great a distance between the gods and human creatures so as to render communication and intercourse between them impossible?

It cannot be said, however, with any degree of certainty at this time whether this text influenced Kierkegaard's thinking in *Philosophical Fragments*. However, the similarity of the two authors in how they approach the question of the relationship

---

[23]   In part, this sleep results from the fact that even in the midst of despair, Psyche cannot overcome her vanity about her beauty. So, even though she may never find Cupid, it is still important that she look good for him.

[24]   *SKS* 11, 167 / *SUD*, 52.

[25]   *SKS* 11, 167–8. / *SUD*, 52.

[26]   See Stacey Ake, "Hints of Apuleius in *The Sickness Unto Death*," *Kierkegaardiana*, vol. 20, 1999, pp. 51–70.

[27]   Consider, for instance, *Apuleii Opera omnia ex editione Oudendorpiana cum notis et interpretatione in usum Delphini...accurate recensita*, vols. 1–7, London: A.J. Valpy 1825.

Stacey E. Ake

between Socrates and his god, and the implications of this relationship for the moral behavior of Socrates as well as his epistemological position concerning how and what he knows about the god, should well give us pause.

Due to the pervasiveness of Apuleian influence in Western Literature, it is, of course, impossible to pinpoint any further indirect influence on Kierkegaard's texts. Moreover, as a writer of myths, Apuleius' influence would be intentionally indirect. Thus, we are left with a mere hint, a mere glimpse, of the presence of Apuleius in Kierkegaard's work.

Bibliography

I. Apuleius' Works in The Auction Catalogue of Kierkegaard's Library

Madaurensis Opera omnia, ed. by Gustav Friedrich Hildebrand, editio minor, Leipzig: C. Cnobloch 1843 (*ASKB* 1215).
Amor und Psyche, freie metrische Bearbeitung nach dem Lateinischen des Apuleius, trans. by Joseph Kehrein, Giessen 1834 (*ASKB* 1216).
Apuleii Fabula de psyche et cupidine, ed. by Io. Casp. Orellius, Turici: Orellii 1833 (*ASKB* 1217).

II. Works in The Auction Catalogue of Kierkegaard's Library that Discuss Apuleius

Ast, Friedrich, *Grundriss einer Geschichte der Philosophie*, Landshut: bey Joseph Thomann 1807, p. 168 (*ASKB* 385).
Bähr, Johann Christian Felix, *Abriss der Römischen Literatur-Geschichte zum Gerbrauch für höhere Lehranstalten*, Heidelberg and Leipzig: Groos 1833 (*ASKB* 975).
Flögel, Carl Friedrich, *Geschichte der komischen Litteratur*, vols. 1–4, Liegnitz and Leipzig: David Siegert 1784–87, vol. 2 (*Von der Satire, Erstes Hauptstück*), pp. 48–52; p. 376 (*ASKB* 1396–1399).
[Møller, Poul Martin], *Efterladte Skrifter af Poul M. Møller*, vols. 1–3, ed. by Christian Winther, F.C. Olsen and Christen Thaarup, Copenhagen: C.A. Reitzel 1839–43, vol. 2, p. 413 (*ASKB* 1574–1576).
Ritter, Heinrich, *Geschichte der Philosophie alter Zeit*, vols. 1–4, 2nd revised ed., Hamburg: Friedrich Perthes 1836–39, pp. 556ff. (*ASKB* 735–738).
Schopenhauer, Arthur, *Die Welt als Wille und Vorstellung*, vols. 1–2, 2nd revised and enlarged ed., Leipzig: F.A. Brockhaus 1844 [1819], vol. 2, p. 153 (*ASKB* 773–773a).
Sulzer, Johann Georg, *Allgemeine Theorie der Schönen Künste, in einzeln, nach alphabetischer Ordnung der Kunstwörter auf einander folgenden, Artikeln abgehandelt*, vols. 1–4 and a Register Volume, 2nd revised ed., Leipzig: in der Weidmannschen Buchhandlung 1792–99, vol. 1, p. 202; p. 524; vol. 2, p. 134; p. 399; vol. 4, p. 147 (*ASKB* 1365–1369).

III. Secondary Literature on Kierkegaard's Relation to Apuleius

Ake, Stacey, "Hints of Apuleius in *The Sickness Unto Death*," *Kierkegaardiana*, vol. 20, 1999, pp. 51–70.

Cicero:

A Handy Roman Companion: Marcus Tullius Cicero's Appearance in Kierkegaard's Works

Thomas Eske Rasmussen

The Roman lawyer, politician and philosopher Marcus Tullius Cicero (106–43 BC) ranks among the major Latin classics of literature. His influence on the Western tradition, philosophy, and theology, as well as language cannot be overestimated. The following discussion presents an outline of the influence which Cicero had on Søren Kierkegaard.

I. Overview of Cicero's Life and Main Works

Marcus Tullius Cicero's life and works correspond with the fall of the Roman Republic, for which Cicero's writings are an important source. He came from a provincial family of knights, *equites*. After having completed military service, Cicero received the proper education of a young Roman aristocrat in philosophy and rhetoric in Rome, Rhodes, and Athens.

Cicero started his career in court. In 80 BC his breakthrough came about with the successful defense of young Sextus Roscius, who had been charged with the murder of his own father during Cornelius Sulla's dictatorship. Legal practice and politics were closely linked in Rome. Supported by his clients and contacts, Cicero was hereafter able to seek election for political posts. He quickly climbed the social ladder in terms of a political career and, in 63 BC, he reached the highest office in Rome, the consulship. In this same year Cicero also had to face a conspiracy led by a certain Lucius Sergius Catilina. The consulship and the successful suppression of Catilina's group was in a sense the highlight of Cicero's political career. He was a *homo novus*, that is, he did not belong to the noble elite, since he lacked the wealth and influence of people such as Julius Caesar, for instance. Moreover, he was politically sidetracked during the disturbed and bloody 50s and 40s BC. His political views were moderate. He maintained that the original republican constitution should ensure *concordia ordinum*, the concord of the classes. After the assassination of Caesar, Cicero made

I wish to thank Niels W. Bruun, philologist at the Søren Kierkegaard Research Centre for his assistance with the article. The process of writing in English has graciously been supervised by Christian Stage, M.A. in English, Copenhagen.

a comeback in politics by speaking in the senate against Marcus Antonius, whom he regarded as a public enemy. His idealism had great costs; in December 43 BC he was murdered. His head and hands, symbols of a long career, were cut off and exhibited in the rostrum on the Forum Romanum.

Nearly sixty speeches given by Cicero have survived. The speeches, which were edited for later publication, give a good impression of theoretical and practical politics in Rome. *In Catilinam*, the four speeches given against the conspirators in 63 BC became a masterpiece of Latin literature. Cicero also penned treatises on oratory, *De Oratore*, *Brutus*, and *Orator*, which deal with the concept of the perfect politician and lawyer. During the Middle Ages, *De Oratore* was used as a textbook for Latin in schools. A large collection of Cicero's letters to and from family members, friends, and political allies was published by his secretary, Tiro. However, in the present context, his philosophical treatises are most important. They were mainly written during the years of political troubles. Cicero's aim was not to create a system of philosophy, but to give a Roman audience access to Greek philosophy in the Latin language and with a Roman interpretation. Cicero employed the literary genre of writing dialogues between characters presenting their views in the sense of speaking *pro et contra*. The kind of dialogue resembles the manner known from Aristotle's now lost exoteric works. Cicero's most important works in this field are *De Legibus* (published in 52 BC) and *De Republica* (51 BC) on the ideal constitution, *De Finibus Bonorum et Malorum* (45 BC) and *De Officiis* (44 BC), which deal with practical moral philosophy, *Tusculanae Disputationes* (45 BC) on happiness and *De Natura Deorum* (44 BC) on the nature of the deities. Cicero had a skeptical view of Academic, Epicurean, and Stoic ways of thinking. He belongs to the Middle Stoa, the philosophical trend that flourished in the Mediterranean during the last two centuries BC. In his use of these thoughts, Cicero stresses human aspects and common responsibility, and these works are today our primary sources about the Middle Stoa. But important works have been lost as well. His *Hortensius*, for instance, the book that inspired Augustine to study philosophy, is only known to us through fragments.

In style and language Cicero represents the paradigm of classical Latin. As a well-educated man of his time, he wrote and spoke Greek as well as Latin. In his writings Cicero shows his skills in translating Greek technical terms into Latin, terms that have been used in the Western tradition ever since. In the correspondence, however, Cicero's style and language resemble the spoken Latin of his time.[1]

In Kierkegaard's time Cicero was still regarded as a great statesman. Cicero's reputation was questioned only a few years later by Kierkegaard's contemporary

---

[1]   For a general introduction to Cicero's works and literary outlook, see Michael von Albrecht, *A History of Roman Literature*, vols. 1–2, Leiden: E.J. Brill 1997, vol. 1, pp. 517–63. A good introduction to Cicero's philosophical views and methods is given in Karsten Friis Johansen, *A History of Ancient Philosophy*, London: Routledge 1998, pp. 484–97 (*Hellenistic Philosophy; Greece and Rome*). For general treatments of Cicero's career, see Elisabeth Rawson, *Cicero—A Portrait*, London: Allen Lane 1975; D.L. Stockton, *Cicero, a Political Biography*, Oxford: Oxford University Press 1971 and D.R. Shackleton Bailey, *Cicero*, London: Duckworth 1971.

Theodor Mommsen (1817–1903), professor of classics in Berlin from 1861. The image of Cicero as being a vain and conceited politician was presented in Denmark by Georg Brandes (1842–1927).[2]

II. Kierkegaard's Introduction to Cicero

Kierkegaard's knowledge of Cicero dates back to his school years 1821–30. It is evident from the Latin curriculum from the Borgerdyd School in Copenhagen that the emphasis of the historical subjects was put on Rome before the Emperors, i.e., from the end of sixth century until the 40s BC. Among the Latin authors, Cicero dominates:[3]

I. Speeches: The speeches against Catiline, the speeches in defence of Sextus Roscius, the poet Archias, Milo, Ligarius, the king Deiotarus and the speech held during the senatorial debates on the Manilian law.[4]

II. Philosophical works: *De Officiis* (one of three books, i.e. chapters).[5]

III. Rhetorical works: *De Oratore* (Two of three books).[6]

IV. Letters: 40 from the Weiske-collection.[7]

---

[2]   I.e., in Georg Brandes, *Cajus Julius Cæsar*, Copenhagen and Kristiania: Gyldendalske Boghandel 1918.

[3]   The curriculum appears in *Søren Kierkegaard truffet—et liv set af hans samtidige*, ed. by Bruce H. Kirmmse, Copenhagen: C.A. Reitzel 1996, p. 32 with note. (English translation, *Encounters with Kierkegaard: A Life as Seen by His Contemporaries*, Princeton, New Jersey: Princeton University Press 1996, pp. 14–15 with note.)

[4]   *Ciceronis Orationu*, tomi III, ed. by Dionysius Lambinus, [Geneva]: Aureliae Allobrogum 1609 (*ASKB* A II 48); *M. Tullii Ciceronis Orationes VII pro S. Roscio, pro lege Manilia, IV in Catilinam, atque pro Murena*, ed. by August Matthiae, 2nd ed., Leipzig: Vogel 1826 (*ASKB* 1231).

[5]   Marcus Tullius Cicero, *De Officiis libri tres: mit einem deutschen Kommentar besonders für Schulen*, ed. by Johann Friedrich Degen, 3rd revised ed., Berlin: Boicke 1825 (*ASKB* 1230); *M.T. Ciceronis libri tres de Officiis*, Hauniæ [Copenhagen]: Paullino 1679 (*ASKB* A II 49).

[6]   *M.T. Ciceronis Opera rhetorica*, vol. 2, *Libri tres ad Q. Fratrem de oratore*, ed. by Christianus Godofried Schütz, Leipzig: G.J. Goeschen 1805 (*ASKB* 1234).

[7]   M. Benjamin Weiske, *Erklärende Anmerkungen zur Auswahl der besten Briefe Ciceros*, 3rd ed., Braunschweig: Schulbuchhandlung 1824 (*ASKB* 1245). From the collection of letters to the family, *ad familiares*—Weiske and many before him called them *ad suos*—Kierkegaard according to the curriculum read fam. 5, 7; fam. 5, 1; fam. 5, 2; fam. 14, 4; fam. 14, 1; fam. 14, 3; fam. 5, 12; fam. 7, 1; fam. 7, 5; fam. 7, 17; fam. 7, 10; fam. 7, 15; fam. 2, 1; fam. 2, 2; fam. 2, 3; fam. 2, 4; fam. 2, 6; fam. 7, 2; fam. 3, 2; fam. 13, 1; fam. 2, 8; fam. 2, 7; fam. 2, 14; fam. 9, 25; fam. 3, 9; fam. 2, 11; fam. 2, 13; fam. 2, 12; fam. 3, 12; fam. 15, 4; fam. 15, 5; fam. 15, 6; fam. 3, 13; fam. 16, 1; fam. 16, 4; fam. 16, 11 and fam. 16, 12. Of letters to Atticus, Cicero's friend and publisher, Kierkegaard read Att. 9, 6A; Att. 3, 7 and Att. 3, 8.

Kierkegaard was thus given a broad knowledge of Cicero's career and literary style. Obviously the philosophical aspect was less important. The fact that Kierkegaard once refers in the journals to Cicero as *rhetor*, the Latin term for a teacher of rhetoric—which he was not—suggests how Cicero was perceived.[8]

In the *Auction Catalogue* of Kierkegaard's library we find two editions of Cicero's complete works: a 1646 edition by Denis Lambin (in Latin, Dionysius Lambinus, 1520–72) and a 1757 edition of Johann August Ernesti (1707–81), both with notes and commentary in Latin.[9] In addition, Kierkegaard had several editions of individual works of Cicero's production and translations into German and French. Some of the books were school editions, but it is difficult to tell exactly which editions Kierkegaard had during his time at the school. Only in the case of Cicero's letters are we told the specific edition used by the pupils. The translations of Cicero's works were probably bought later in Kierkegaard's life. We know that Kierkegaard bought Cicero in translation as late as 1852.[10] This suggests a more devoted study; the *opera omnias* were not handy and, certainly in the case of Lambin's edition, also difficult to read.

The earliest evidence from Kierkegaard himself on Cicero is a letter to his brother Peter Christian. The letter is dated March 15, 1829; Kierkegaard was not yet 16. It starts:

Dear Brother,

Your reply arrived long before I had expected it. I waited for your letter for less time than you had to be in suspense for mine, and I am pleased that you liked it. As to your belief that I have read Cicero's letters, this is not so at all; I have not read a single one of them. I suppose that I shall get to read them next year.[11]

From this, we learn first that Cicero's letters were read during the final years of school. Second, in this now lost letter, Peter Christian probably hints that his brother

---

[8]   *SKS* 24, 486, NB25:68.a. This is, by the way, the only time Kierkegaard ever presents Cicero. In one passage he is refered to as *en Hedning*, "a pagan" *SKS* 24, 481, NB25:64. Normally he merely refers to "Cicero."

[9]   *M. Tullii Ciceronis Opera omnia ex recensione Iacobi Gronovii, accedit varietas lectionis...cum singulorum librorum argumentis...*, vols. 1–6, 2nd ed., ed. by Io. Augusti Ernesti, Halle: Impensis Orphanotrophei 1757 (*ASKB* 1224–1229); *M.Tullii Ciceronis Opera omnia*, vols. 1–2, Geneva: Typis Jacobi Stoër 1646 (*ASKB* A I 149–150).

[10]   H.P. Rohde, "Om Søren Kierkegaard som bogsamler," in *Fund og Forskning i Det Kongelige Biblioteks Samlinger*, vol. 8 Copenhagen: Det Kongelige Bibliotek 1961, p. 126 lists *Über das höchste Gut und das höchste Uebel in fünf Büchern*, trans. by Carl Victor Hauff, Tübingen: Osiander 1822; *Von der Verachtung des Todes*, trans. by A.L.G. Krehl, Hannover: Hahn 1819; *Der Staat*, trans. and ed. by Friedrich von Kobbe, Göttingen: bei Vandenhoeck und Ruprecht 1824; *Paradoxieen. Mit erläuternden Inhaltsanzeigen und erklärenden Anmerkungen*, ed. by Christoph August Gottlieb Schreiber, Halle: Hendel 1799—in a single volume (*ASKB* 1237)—*Les lettres de Cicéron a sès amis*, tomes 1–4, trans. by Louis Maument, La Haye: Pierre Husson 1709 (*ASKB* A I 151).

[11]   *B&A*, vol. 1, p. 31 / *LD*, p. 39, Letter 2.

writes like Cicero in his letters or that he is somehow inspired by him.[12] Later, during the years of study at the University of Copenhagen, Kierkegaard had a part time job at the Borgerdyd School as a teacher of Latin.[13] His readings of Cicero thus continued.

That Kierkegaard had a thorough knowledge of Classical Latin is seen throughout his works. Only when quotations and references are Ciceronian with certainty, will they be treated in this article.

III. Cicero in Kierkegaard's Authorship 1841–46

Kierkegaard refers to Cicero only seven times in his published works; the first time in *The Concept of Irony* (1841) the last time in *Concluding Unscientific Postscript* (1846). Cicero's presence in Kierkegaard's journals is more frequent. References to Cicero or Cicero's works occur fifteen times between 1841 and 1854. From the correspondence we know of three references to Cicero.[14] Thus Cicero appears not only in the first part of Kierkegaard's authorship, but throughout Kierkegaard's life Cicero remains present in his mind.[15]

Not surprisingly Cicero is mentioned for the first time in Kierkegaard's authorship in his treatise *The Concept of Irony with Continual Reference to Socrates*. Cicero is one of the Latin and therefore Western sources of Socrates and his methods. In a chapter on Socrates' *daimon* or inner voice, Kierkegaard writes in a footnote, "Both Plutarch (*Plutarchi Chaeronensis opuscula*, ed. H. Stephanus, II, pp. 241, 231) and Cicero (*De divinatione*, I, 54) have preserved several stories about the activity of this daimonion, but in all of them it manifests itself only as warning."[16] The passage referred to in Cicero's *De Divinatione* reads:

> It is this purity of soul, no doubt, that explains that famous utterance which history attributes to Socrates, and his disciples in their books often represent him as repeating:

---

[12]   Kierkegaard's classmate H.P. Holst remembers Kierkegaard's letter, which although written in Danish was Latin in style; cf. Kirmmse, *Søren Kierkegaard truffet*, pp. 29–30. (*Encounters with Kierkegaard*, pp. 12–13.)

[13]   In his petition to the king, dated June 2, 1841, Kierkegaard informs that he has been teaching "a considerable period." Cf. Kirmmse, *Søren Kierkegaard truffet*, p. 377 note 9 / *LD*, p. 24, XV. Kirmmse suggests that Kierkegaard began his job at the Borgerdyd School about 1831 and taught until 1840. Cf. also Holger Lund, *Borgerdydsskolen i Kjøbenhavn 1787–1887*, Copenhagen: Otto B. Wroblewski's Forlag 1887, p. 236; Per Krarup, *Søren Kierkegaard og Borgerdydskolen*, Copenhagen: Gyldendal 1977, pp. 68–76.

[14]   Apart from the letter quoted above, the other references appear in letters addressed to F.C. Sibbern and Michael Nielsen.

[15]   In addition, Kierkegaard expresses himself in Latin terms throughout his works which *could* stem from Cicero. Instances like these, for example, a passage in *Journal JJ* (*SKS* 18, 271, JJ:392) including the Latin word *diffluentes* that probably, but not certainly is Ciceronian, will not be treated in this article.

[16]   *SKS* 1, 209 / *CI*, 159.

"There is some divine influence"—daimonion, he called it—"which I always obey, though it never urges me on, but often holds me back."[17]

Analyzing the sources on Socrates, Kierkegaard must, of course, consider their reliability. The two Athenians Xenophon and Plato, who were contemporaries of Socrates, disagree on the nature of the daimon. Therefore, Kierkegaard includes Cicero and the 150 years younger Plutarch to back up his argument that Xenophon's point of view is wrong. But it does not seem that Kierkegaard read Cicero's own words thoroughly in order to study Socrates. It is more likely that the German philologist Friedrich Ast (1778–1841) directed Kierkegaard's attention to the passage quoted. Ast's book on Plato's dialogues and their origin, published in 1816, is discussed throughout *The Concept of Irony*.[18] Ast refers to exactly these chapters in Plutarch and Cicero's works.[19] Kierkegaard got his knowledge from Ast's book. Later in *The Concept of Irony* Kierkegaard again concludes in a footnote:

> Although Socrates did not especially fetch philosophy down from the sky and bring it into the houses, as Cicero thinks, but rather brought people out of their houses and up from the netherworld in which they lived, it nevertheless may very well have happened that he himself, despite all his virtuosity, became bogged down sometimes and during a lengthy talk with every Tom, Dick, and Harry may even have lost the irony, lost sight of the ironic thread and momentarily wandered off into more or less triviality. So much for an earlier comment on Xenophon's view.[20]

Kierkegaard has the following passage in *Tusculanae Disputationes* in mind:

> But from that ancient day down to the time of Socrates, who had listened to Archelaus the pupil of Anaxagoras, philosophy dealt with numbers and movements, with the problem whence all things came, or whither they returned, and zealously inquired into the size of the stars, the spaces that divided them, their courses and all celestial phenomena; Socrates on the other hand was the first to call philosophy down from the heavens and set her in the cities of men and bring her also into their homes and compel her to ask questions about life and morality and things good and evil.[21]

---

[17]   Cicero, *De Divinatione*, 1.54.122; Ernesti, vol. 4: "*Hoc nimirum est illud, quod de Socrate accepimus, quodque ab ipso in libris Socraticorum saepe dicitur: esse divinum quiddam, quod* daimonion *appellat, cui semper ipse paruerit numquam impellenti, saepe revocanti.*" For the Latin text in this article, Ernesti's edition will be quoted. English translation quoted from Cicero, *De senectute, de amicitia, de divinatione*, trans. by W.A. Falconer, London: William Heinemann 1923 (*Loeb Classical Library*).

[18]   For example, *SKS* 1, 122–3 and passim / *CI*, 62–3 and passim.

[19]   Friedrich Ast, *Platon's Leben und Schriften. Ein Versuch, im Leben wie in den Schriften des Platon das Wahre und Aechte vom Erdichteten und Untergeschobenen zu scheiden, und die Zeitfolge der ächten Gespräche zu bestimmen. Als Einleitung in das Studium des Platon*, Leipzig: Weidmann 1816, pp. 484–5.

[20]   *SKS* 1, 228 / *CI*, 181.

[21]   Cicero, *Tusculanae Disputationes*, 5.4.10; Ernesti, vol. 4: "*Sed ab antiqua philosophia usque ad Socratem, qui Archelaum, Anaxagorae discipulum, audierat, numeri motusque tractabantur, et unde omnia orirentur, quove recederent: studioseque ab his siderum magnitudines, intervalla, cursus anquirebantur, et cuncta caelestia. Socrates autem primus*

In this particular instance, Kierkegaard discusses Socrates, expressing his view in Cicero's language by slightly changing the original Latin wording into his own expression: "brought people out of their houses and up from the netherworld." This is an imitation of Cicero and, as will be seen from his journals, the way Kierkegaard expresses personal views. This time Kierkegaard does not refer to the exact location of the Cicero statement. One might wonder, at this point, whether this derives from Kierkegaard's own studies of the *Tusculanae Disputationes*. The earliest references to Cicero in the journals date from this period. Hence an entry in *Notebook* 9 called "The Origin of Evil" (1841): "The biblical doctrine. Evil is posited in the body. Evil thoughts are ascribed the devil. It places the dominant sin in connection with the first sin. Aristotle calls evil, συγγενες. Plato says that children are not good φυσει also Cicero in the Tusculaners 3,1."[22] Kierkegaard refers to an earlier passage in *Tusculanae Disputationes* this time: "As things are, however, as soon as we come into the light of day and have been acknowledged, we at once find ourselves in a world of iniquity amid a medley of wrong beliefs, so that it seems as if we drank in deception with our nurse's milk."[23] Even though Cicero discusses ancient Stoic beliefs considering environmental influences on human beings, Kierkegaard is able to make a Christian interpretation of it and does so. There is a common link in both references to Cicero's treatise: the German theologian Philipp Konrad Marheineke (1780–1846), whose lectures Kierkegaard attended 1841–42 at the University of Berlin. In fact, a major part of *Notebook* 9 deals with Marheineke's lectures on Christian dogmatics.[24] This tends to be the way Kierkegaard reads Cicero, again a few years later in *The Concept of Anxiety* (1844):

> Such a procedure seems highly plausible to many, because to a great many thoughtlessness is the most natural thing, and in all ages their number is legion who regard as praiseworthy that way of thinking that through all centuries has in vain been labeled λογος αργος (Chryssipus), *ignava ratio* (Cicero), *sophisma pigrum*, *la raison paresseuse* (Leibniz).[25]

The Latin translation of the Greek concept comes from Cicero, who mentions it in one of his minor philosophical works *De Fato* or *On Fate*:

---

philosophiam devocavit e caelo, et in urbibus conlocavit, et in domos etiam introduxit, et coëgit de vita, et moribus, rebusque bonis et malis quaerere." English translation quoted from Cicero, *Tusculan Disputations*, trans. by J.E. King, London: William Heinemann (*Loeb Classical Library*) 1927.

[22] *SKS* 19, 256, Not. 9:1.

[23] Cicero, *Tusculanae Disputationes*, 3.1.2; Ernesti, vol. 4: "*Nunc autem, simul atque editi in lucem, et suscepti sumus, in omni continuo pravitate, et in summa opinionum perversitate versamur: ut paene cum lacte nutricis errorem suxisse videamur.*" (English translation quoted from Cicero, *Tusculan Disputation*, trans. by King.)

[24] *SKS* K19, 348–9. Niels Jørgen Cappelørn and Jon Stewart point out that Kierkegaard strictly followed the wording of Marheineke's lectures, which after his death were edited by S. Matthias and W. Vatke (*D. Philipp Marheineke's Theologische Vorlesungen*, vols. 1–4, Berlin: Duncker und Humblot 1847–49); *SKS* K19, 331–2.

[25] *SKS* 4, 415 / *CA*, 112–13.

Yet it does not immediately follow from the fact that every statement is either true or false that there are immutable causes, eternally existing, that forbid anything to fall out otherwise than it will fall out. The causes which bring it about that statements of the form "Cato will come into the Senate" are true statements, are fortuitous, and they are not inherent in the nature of things and the order of the universe; and nevertheless "he will come," when true, is as immutable as "he has come" (though we need not on that account be haunted by fear of fate or necessity), for it will necessarily be admitted that the statement "Hortensius will come to his place at Tusculum" is not true, and thus it follows that it is false. Our opponents hold that it is neither; which is impossible. Nor shall we for our part be hampered by what is called the "idle argument" [*ignavia ratio*]—for one argument is named by the philosophers the *Argos Logos*, because if we yielded to it we should live a life of absolute inaction. For they argue as follows: "If it is fated for you to recover from this illness, you will recover whether you call in a doctor or do not...."[26]

When Cicero discusses fate, he naturally must include a discussion of necessity and possibility. Especially the Stoics had a radical point of view here. Kierkegaard's knowledge of this passage derives from studies in 1842. Kierkegaard read Wilhelm Gottlieb Tennemann's (1761–1819) *Geschichte der Philosophie* (1803), in which the idle argument, *ignava ratio*, is treated. We know this from Kierkegaard himself since he wrote about it the *Journal JJ*.[27] Tennemann not only includes the Greek Stoic Chrysippos, but refers to the same Cicero passage in *De Fato*.

This approach to Cicero seems to be typical in Kierkegaard's authorship as well as his journals.[28] A journal entry written in 1846 reads: "Anaxagoras is supposed to have said: The senses are limited, the mind is feeble, life is short. Indeed, it is in Cicero, in *Quaestiones academicae*, 1.12."[29] Kierkegaard is not entirely sure of his

---

[26]   Cicero, *De Fato*, 12. 28; Ernesti, vol. 4: "*Nec si omne enuntiatum aut verum, aut falsum est, sequitur ilico, esse causas inmutabiles, easque aeternas, quae prohibeant quidquam secus cadere, atque casurum sit. fortuitae sunt causae, quae efficiant, ut vere dicantur, quae ita dicentur, Veniet Cato in senatum, non inclusae in rerum natura, atque mundo. Et tamen tam est inmutabile venturum, cum est verum, quam venisse: nec ob eam causam fatum, aut necessitas extimescenda est. Etenim erit confiteri necesse, si haec enuntiatio, Veniet in Tusculanum Hortensius, vera non est: sequitur, ut falsa sit. quorum isti neutrum volunt. quod fieri non potest. Nec nos impediet illa ignava ratio, quae dicitur. appellatur enim quidam a philosophis αργὸς λόγος, cui si pareamus, nihil omnino agamus in vita. Sic enim interrogant: Si fatum tibi est, ex hoc morbo convalescere; sive tu medicum adhibueris, sive non, convalesces.*" (English translation quoted from Cicero, *De Oratore in two volumes together with De Fato, Paradoxa Stoicorum, De partitione oratoria*, vols. 1–2, trans. by H. Rackham, London: William Heinemann 1948, vol. 2.)

[27]   *SKS* 18, 148, JJ:24 / *KJN* 2, 140: "It's excellent what Leibniz says about idle reason: '*la raison paresseuse.*' Cf. Erdmann's edition p. 470, second column.—Chrysippus has also used it, cf. Tennemann, Ges. d. Ph. vol. 4, p. 300." See Tennemann, Geschichte der Philosophie, vols. 1-11, Leipzig: Johann Ambrosius Barth 1798-1819, vol. 4, p. 300 *(ASKB 815-826); Cf. SKS* K4, 484.

[28]   Rick Anthony Furtak, *Wisdom In Love: Kierkegaard and the Ancient Quest for Emotional Integrity*, Notre Dame: University of Notre Dame Press 2005, pp. 42–3 has a few notes on Kierkegaard's admiration for Stoic ideas expressed in classic literature.

[29]   *SKS* 18, 291, JJ:452 /*KJN* 2, 2269.

reference, but it is true that one passage in Cicero's *Academica* (in the Ernesti edition called *Academicae quaestiones*) reads:

> "It was entirely with Zeno, so we have been told," I replied, "that Arcesilas set on foot his battle, not from obstinacy or desire for victory, as it seems to me at all events, but because of the obscurity of the facts that had led Socrates to a confession of ignorance, as also previously his predecessors Democritus, Anaxagoras, Empedocles, and almost all the old philosophers, who utterly denied all possibility of cognition or perception or knowledge, and maintained that the senses are limited, the mind feeble, the span of life short, and that truth (in Democritus' phrase) is sunk in an abyss...."[30]

One notes that the statement in Cicero's text is attributed not to Anaxagoras alone, but to nearly all the pre-Socratic philosophers in general. The Greek philosopher Anaxagoras captured Kierkegaard's interest more than Cicero and his testimony. We can trace this interest to *Geschichte der Philosophie alter Zeit* by the German philosopher Heinrich Ritter (1791-1869), which deals with Anaxagoras. Kierkegaard owned a copy of this book, in which the passage in *Academica* is mentioned.[31]

One should not be surprised if Kierkegaard even attributes to Cicero certain terms which he never had anything to do with. As seen in a journal entry written between 1842 and 1843: "Strangely enough, Aristotle gives no definition either (must be examined more closely). Κατηγορία (Cicero, *praedicamentum*; scholastics likewise.)"[32] Obviously, this entry is a sketch. Caught by a sudden idea, Kierkegaard quickly notes these two lines. The expression "must be examined more closely" confirms the presumption that Kierkegaard proceeds by guesswork that Cicero invented the Latin term from Greek κατηγορία, but this is incorrect. *Praedicamentum* is late Latin.[33]

Kierkegaard's approach to quotations of Cicero is more successful when it comes to subjects treated at school. In *Repetition* (1843) Constantin Constantius makes this outburst in a diary entry dated October 11:

> To whom shall I make my complaint? After all, life is a debate—may I ask that my observations be considered? If one has to take life as it is, would it not be best to find out how things go? What does it mean: a deceiver? Does not Cicero say that such a person can be exposed by asking: *cui bono*?[34]

---

[30] Cicero, *Academica*, 1.12.44; Ernesti, vol 4: "*Tum ego, Cum Zenone, inquam, ut accepimus Arcesilas sibi omne certamen instituit, non pertinacia, aut studio vincendi, ut quidem mihi videtur, sed earum rerum obscuritate, quae ad confessionem ignorationis adduxerant Socratem, et veluti amantes Socratem, Democritum, Anaxagoram, Empedoclem, omnes paene veteres: qui nihil cognosci nihil percipi nihil sciri posse [dixerunt]: angustos sensus, imbecillos animos, brevia curricula vitæ, et (ut Democritus) in profundo veritatem esse demersam.*" (English translation quoted from Cicero, *De natura deorum, academica*, ed. and trans. by H. Rackham, London: William Heinemann 1933.)

[31] Heinrich Ritter, *Geschichte der Philosophie alter Zeit*, vols. 1–4, 2nd revised ed., Hamburg: Friedrich Perthes 1836–39 (*ASKB* 735–738). Cf. *SKS* K18, 452.

[32] *SKS* 19, 406, Not13:41 / *JP* 2, 1597.

[33] Cf. *Thesaurus Lingvae Latinae*, vols. 1–10, Munich: B.G. Teubner 1900–2006, vol. 10, 2 fasc. IV, column 542. records ("praedicamentum") and *SKS* K19, 588.

[34] *SKS* 4, 68 / *R*, p. 200.

Constantius demands those rights in life that in antiquity, more exactly Rome, were granted persons charged with a crime. He speaks in forensic terms known from Cicero, for instance. From one of the speeches in Kierkegaard's school curriculum, *Pro Roscio Amerino*, the speech in defense of Sextus Roscius of Ameria, the following is said: "The illustrious Lucius Cassius, whom the Roman people considered the wisest and most conscientious of judges, was in the habit of asking repeatedly in trials, 'who had profited by it?' "[35] Kierkegaard's knowledge of Cicero has influenced his protagonist, for whom the Roman terminology is perfectly fit for a description of life's difficult conditions. Constantius knows his Cicero by heart as well as Kierkegaard does. The same year that *Repetition* was published Kierkegaard comforted his former principal, Michael Nielsen (1776–1846), in a letter. This time Kierkegaard quotes directly from Latin:

> If anyone should have self-confidence, rashness, and boldness enough to want to offer you consolation, then truly it is not I. But with your permission I should prefer to be the one who is no good at consoling, understood in the same sense as Cicero understands it when he writes to Titius: *unus ex omnibus <minime> sum ad te consolandum accommodatus, quod tantum ex tuis molestiis cepi doloris, ut consolatione ipse egerem.*[36]

The word *minime* Kierkegaard forgot to begin with but it was added afterwards. The source is a letter by Cicero to Lucius Titius, who lost his son:

> *Of all men I am the least suited to console you, since I am so grieved by your distress that I stand in need of consolation myself.* But seeing that my grief falls shorter that yours of the ultimate bitterness and sorrow, I have concluded that our friendship and my anxiety for your welfare make it wrong to be silent so long in your heavy affliction, and require me to proffer a measure of comfort, which may alleviate, if it cannot heal your pain.[37]

Evidently Kierkegaard has no difficulties finding a proper quotation for the occasion. Cicero's mentality is not old-fashioned, and his writings can serve to express a personal state of mind. The quotation is rendered correctly word for word.

---

[35]   Cicero, *Pro Roscio Amerino*, 30.84; Ernesti, vol. 2: "*Cassius ille, quem populus verissimum et sapientissimum iudicem putabat, identidem in causis quaerere solebat, cui bono fuisset.*" (English translation quoted from Cicero, *Pro Publio Quinctio, Pro Sexto Roscio Amerino, Pro Quinto Roscio Comoedo, De Lege Agraria*, ed. and trans. by J.H. Freese, London: William Heinemann 1967.) Kierkegaard read in school another speech by Cicero including the famous saying *cui bono*: *Pro Milone*, 12.32; Ernesti, vol. 2.
[36]   *B&A*, vol. 1, p. 133 / *LD*, Letter 107, p. 169.
[37]   Cicero, *Epistulae ad familiares* (Ernesti, *Ad diversos*) 5.16; Ernesti, vol. 3: "*Etsi unus ex omnibus minime sum ad te consolandum accommodatus, quod tantum ex tuis molestiis cepi doloris, ut consolatione ipse egerem: tamen, cum longius a summi luctus acerbitate meus abesset dolor, quam tuus, statui nostrae necessitudinis esse, meaeque in te benevolentiae, non tacere tanto in tuo maerore tamdiu, sed adhibere aliquam modicam consolationem, quae levare dolorem tuum posset, si minus sanare potuisset.*" (English translation quoted from Cicero, *Letters to his Friends*, vols. 1–3, ed. and trans. by D.R. Shackleton Bailey, Cambridge, Massachusetts: Harvard University Press 2001, vol. 2, letter 187.)

Another approach to Cicero is paraphrasing his statements. The story "In vino veritas" in *Stages on Life's Way* (1845) is almost a pastiche of the Greek *symposium* genre. A character in the story, a certain Young Man speaks:

> Who can comprehend this?...I feel blessedly bound in piety's beautiful bonds of love. I believe that it is the most sublime to owe life to another person; I believe that this debt cannot be settled or discharged by any reckoning, and this is why I feel that Cicero is right in saying that in relation to the father the son is always in the wrong, and it is precisely piety that teaches me to believe this, teaches me not even to want to penetrate what is hidden but rather to go on being hidden in the father.[38]

The context in which Kierkegaard makes use of Cicero resembles what was seen in *Repetition*: the protagonist shows his knowledge of Cicero. What is troubling at this point, though, is that it was probably never said by Cicero, at least not in any of his writings of which we know. Perhaps Kierkegaard mixes up the discussions of the father-and-son relationship from Cicero's *De Officiis* or *On Obligations*:[39]

> "Again, suppose a father were robbing temples or making underground passages to the treasury, should a son inform the officers of it?" "Nay; that were a crime; rather should he defend his father, in case he were indicted." "Well, then, are not the claims of country paramount to all other duties?" "Aye, verily; but it is to our country's interest to have citizens who are loyal to their parents." "But, once more—if the father attempts to make himself king, or to betray his country, shall the son hold his peace?" "Nay, verily; he will plead with his father not to do so. If that accomplishes nothing, he will take him to task; he will even threaten; and in the end, if things point to the destruction of the state, he will sacrifice his father to the safety of his country."[40]

Kierkegaard could have read this, which his book collection strongly suggests; he had at least three separate editions of *De Officiis* during his lifetime.[41] It is remarkable to note the way in which the Cicero passage is interpreted here. It is clearly wrong that—according to Cicero—the son "is always in the wrong." Obviously the terms "*pietas*, "father" and "son" are central, and Kierkegaard allows his young character to be negligent on his Cicero as long as it fits into the framework. A similar passage

---

[38]   *SKS* 6, 47 / *SLW*, 44 and Notes, p. 684.

[39]   So suggested by the editors of *Søren Kierkegaards Skrifter*; cf. *SKS* K6, 118.

[40]   Cicero, *De officiis*, 3.23.90; Ernesti, vol. 4: "*Quid? si pater fana expilet, cuniculos agat ad aerarium: indicetne id magistratibus filius? nefas id quidem est. quinetiam defendat patrem, si arguatur. non igitur patria praestat omnibus officiis? immo vero: sed ipsi patriae conducit, pios cives habere in parentes. Quid, si tyrannidem occupare, si patriam prodere conabitur pater? silebitne filius? immo vero obsecrabit patrem, ne id faciat. Si nihil proficiet, accusabit: minabitur etiam: ad extremum, si ad perniciem patriae res spectabit, patriae salutem anteponet saluti patris.*" (English translation quoted from Walther Miller, *Cicero: De officiis with an English translation*, London: William Heinemann 1913.)

[41]   *M.T. Ciceronis libri tres de Officiis*; Cicero, *Abhandlung über die menschlichen Pflichten in drei Büchern*, trans. by Christian Garve, 6th ed., Breslau: Wilhelm Gottlieb Korn 1819 (*ASKB* 1239); Cicero, *De Officiis libri tres: mit einem deutschen Kommentar besonders für Schulen*, ed. by Johann Friedrich Degen, 3rd revised ed., Berlin: Boicke 1825 (*ASKB* 1230).

is found on a more prominent place in *Stages on Life's Way*, concluding the diary "Guilty?/Not Guilty?":

> Here the diary ends for this time being. It deals with nothing, yet not in the sense of Louis XVI's diary, the alternating contents of which are supposed to have been: on one day, went hunting; the second day, *rien*; the third day, went hunting. It contains nothing, but if, as Cicero says, the easiest letters deal with nothing, then sometimes it is the hardest life that deals with nothing.[42]

The origin of this saying could indeed be Cicero, but it does not appear in Cicero's writings. One should be careful about implying that Kierkegaard's imagination leads him astray. However, it is interesting that the reference to Louis XVI has likewise not been linked to any source.[43] Still, the Ciceronian saying must have been one of Kierkegaard's favorites. Kierkegaard's nephew, Henrik Lund (1825–89) writes him a letter five years later in which he starts:

> Dear Uncle,
>
> It is entirely possible that Cicero once said "the most interesting letters deal with nothing," but that does not make every letter that deals with nothing—interesting. Therefore, if this letter, which deals with something that is as good as nothing, should fail to interest you, then please relegate it to the latter category and forgive me for having bored you![44]

Even though Lund alters the word "easiest" to "most interesting," this clearly derives from the same saying. The letter is dated March 8, 1850, which means Henrik Lund could have read *Stages on Life's Way* and thus makes an allusion to his uncle's book. On the other hand, chances are that he responds to something Kierkegaard has written in a now lost letter. One notices that even Lund himself is not sure that Cicero ever said it; it is but "entirely possible."[45]

A few funny approaches to Cicero are seen in puns or linguistic amusements. Kierkegaard writes in a journal entry 1846:

> When we say: While such and such took place, something else took place, we always think of the former as something that lasted longer and can thus be used to show that the latter occupies only a moment within the first "while." We say that while Cicero was

---

[42]   *SKS* 6, 368 / *SLW*, 397.
[43]   Cf. *SKS* K6, 328.
[44]   *B&A*, vol. 1, p. 272 / *LD*, Letter 251, pp. 346–7.
[45]   The editors of *Breve og Aktstykker*, p. 109 vol. 2, suggest a letter to Atticus as the source, IX, 10, 1: "I have nothing to write about, having heard no news and having replied to all your letters yesterday. But since my distress of mind is such that it is not only impossible to sleep but torment to be awake, I have started this scrawl without any subject in view, just in order as it were to talk to you, which is my only relief." (Cicero, *Letters to his Friends*, vol. 3, letter 177); Ernesti, vol. 3: *Nihil habebam, quod scriberem. neque enim novi quicquam audieram, et ad tuas omnes rescripseram pridie. sed cum me aegritudo non solum somno privaret, verum ne vigilare quidem sine summo dolore pateretur, tecum ut quasi loquerer, in quo acquiesco, hoc nescio quid, nullo argumento proposito, scribere institui.* A resemblance to Kierkegaard's paraphrase, though, is not really clear.

consul, thus and such took place; while Pitt was prime minister, etc. It thus produced a wonderfully comical effect some time ago when we could read in the newspaper about the festivities on Skamlingsbanken: *while* Grundtvig was speaking, the people from Funen arrived. The people from Funen are of course the insignificant part, but what is splendid and witty is the notion one gets of the fantastic length of Pastor Grundtvig's speech,—that *while* he was speaking (while Cicero was consul). One could say, e.g., *while* Grundtvig was speaking, a French fleet put to sea and conquered Algiers.[46]

Kierkegaard considers the syntax of the Danish language with respect to an incident that had taken place a couple of years prior to this.[47] But Cicero as such has nothing to do with the incident. In a letter to Frederik Christian Sibbern (1785–1872) dating from the same year, Kierkegaard says:

> Your Magnificence:
>
> I almost had forgotten this, and now I am annoyed that I did not remember it a few days ago when I sent you a copy of the book I have published. I would have liked to address you this way, and I am happy that my acknowledgement of the pseudonymous writings in the *Concluding Postscript* took effect in the very year (indeed that was the way the Romans put it: "In the year Cicero was Consul") Sibbern was Rector.[48]

Making use of the same expression, Kierkegaard imitates Roman chronology and thereby hints that Sibbern will make history as rector of the university like Cicero did in his consulship in 63 BC. This sentence obviously thrills Kierkegaard. The contrasts between Grundtvig and Cicero serve as an improvised satire; in the case of Sibbern it is a friendly eulogy. That Kierkegaard admires Cicero is certain.

Again in 1846 Cicero is mentioned—for the last time in Kierkegaard's books. He compares the methods of theology and philology in the *Concluding Unscientific Postscript*:

> When, for example, a philologist publishes a book by Cicero and does it with great acumen, with scholarly apparatus in noble obedience to the supremacy of the mind; when his ingenuity and his intimate knowledge of antiquity, obtained by indefatigable diligence, help his ferreting sensibility to remove difficulties, to prepare the way for the process of thought amid a confusion of variants, etc.— then it is safe to abandon oneself to admiration, for when he has completed his work, nothing follows from it except the admirable feat that through his skill and competence an ancient text has been made available in the most reliable form.[49]

Kierkegaard's example has a concrete basis. The passage probably refers to Johan Nicolai Madvig (1804–86), professor at the University of Copenhagen since 1829, and his renowned critical edition of Cicero's philosophical work *De finibus*,

---

46   *SKS* 18, 307–8, JJ:504 / *KJN* 2, 283.
47   Cf. *SKS* K18, 472.
48   *B&A*, vol. 1, p. 148 / *LD*, Letter 135, p. 188.
49   *SKS* 7, 33 / *CUP1*, 25–6.

published 1839.[50] Among the Latin classics Kierkegaard regards Cicero as being the absolute intellectual challenge. Also, the way in which Kierkegaard expresses himself indicates that he admires the results of this kind of work; Madvig, whom Kierkegaard knew personally, is an artist. Kierkegaard implicitly praises him.[51] From this time on, Cicero's name only appears in the journals.

IV. Cicero in the Journals after 1846

When one arrives at the end of Kierkegaard's authorship, one cannot decide with certainty whether he actually read Cicero's own texts in order to develop his thinking. This beginning of the journal entry called "That the Word of God is written in Poor Language," written sometime in 1851, has an interesting quotation from Calvin:

> It is with diligence or deliberation that the greatest secrets of the kingdom of God are given to us in very contemptible clothing. Read Demosthenes, Cicero, Plato—they will capture and transport you—....Holy Scripture will bore into your heart....*Ut promptum sit perspicere, divinum quiddam spirare sacras scripturas.*[52]

This is interesting because Kierkegaard's journals refer to Cicero a few months later. In fact, between November 29 and New Year's Eve 1851, Kierkegaard refers to Cicero's *De natura deorum* or *On the Nature of the Gods*, five times during his private controversy in the NB journals.[53] The first instance is an entry entitled "Immortality" written during Christmas 1851. It deals with immortality in Christianity and begins thus:

> Cicero says (in *De natura deorum*, bk II, near the end) that the gods have no advantage over man, except immortality, *but this is not necessary for living a happy life.* Surely the way in which mortality is shoved upon people in Christendom is very confusing, making them think that they feel a deep need for immortality.[54]

The second book of *De natura deorum* is an outline of the Stoic heaven and creatures presented by Cicero's character Balbus, who tries to prove the existence of wise gods:

> And contemplating the heavenly bodies, the mind arrives at a knowledge of the gods, from which arises piety, with its comrades' justice and the rest of virtues, the sources of a

---

[50]   *De finibus bonorum et malorum libri quinque*, recensuit et enarravit Io. Nicolaus Maduigius, Copenhagen: Gyldendal 1839.

[51]   Unfortunately we do not know whether Kierkegaard ever owned a copy of Madvig's *De officiis*; the *Auction Catalogue* bears no witness to this.

[52]   *SKS* 24, 361, NB24:64 / *JP* 3, 2328. Kierkegaard got Calvin's statement from Paul Emil Henry, *Das Leben Johann Calvins des grossen Reformators: mit Benutzung der handschriftlichen Urkunden, vornehmlich der Genfer und Züricher Bibliothek, entworfen; nebst einem Anhang bisher ungedruckter Briefe*, vols. 1–3, Hamburg: Friedrich Perthes 1835–44.

[53]   According to the arrangement of the entries by the editors of the *Papirer* edition. Kierkegaard has dated the beginning of the journal NB25, November 29, 1851.

[54]   *SKS* 24, 448–9, NB25:17 / *JP* 2, 1952.

life of happiness that vie with and resemble the divine existence and leave us inferior to the celestial beings in nothing else save immortality, which is immaterial for happiness.[55]

Kierkegaard, who shows no interest in the first book or the better part of the second book of *De natura deorum*, apparently finds the Stoic statement suitable for his point. In the context it opposes the Epicurean concept of world order as created by atoms without any influence from the gods. However, this particular discussion has no relevance for Kierkegaard. Shortly after, in *De natura deorum*, Kierkegaard met another statement from Cicero, which is commented upon in the journal entry entitled "Paganism":

> At the very end of Book II of *De natura deorum* Cicero articulates the essence of paganism: There is a providence which is concerned about the whole and also about individual men—but, note well, superior men. He says the gods are concerned about weighty matters, not insignificant matters.[56]

In this single entry Kierkegaard is referring to a long passage in *De natura deorum*. Through this Kierkegaard is equipped with arguments in his analysis of Christian and non-Christian concepts of God. That is, Cicero's definition of his own, heathen god serves as an example to Kierkegaard of how the Christian God is *not* to be defined. Again, it is Cicero's character, the Stoic Balbus, who articulates it:

> We may narrow down the entirety of the human race and bring it gradually down to smaller and smaller groups, and finally to single individuals. For if we believe, for the reason that we have spoken before, that the gods care for all human beings everywhere in every coast and region of the lands remote from this continent in which we dwell, then they care also for the men who inhabit with us these lands between the sunrise and the sunset....Therefore they also cherish the divisions of those divisions, for instance Rome, Athens, Sparta, and Rhodes; and they cherish the individual citizens of those cities regarded separately from the whole body collectively, for example, Curius, Fabricius and Coruncanius in the war with Pyhrrus....[57]

Cicero continues:

> The gods attend to great matters; they neglect small ones. Now great men always prosper in all their affairs, assuming that the teachers of our school and Socrates, the prince of

---

[55] Cicero, *De natura deorum*, 2.61.153; Ernesti, vol. 4: "*Quae contuens animus, accipit ab his cognitionem deorum; ex qua oritur pietas: cui conjuncta justitia est reliquaeque virtutes: e quibus vita beata exsistit par et similis deorum; nulla re, nisi immortalitate, quae nihil ad bene vivendum pertinet, cedens caelestibus.*" (Cicero, *de natura deorum, academica*)
[56] *SKS* 24, 450, NB25:19 / *JP* 3, 3062.
[57] Cicero, *De natura deorum*, 2.65.164–2.66.165; Ernesti, vol. 4: "*Licet enim contrahere universitatem generis humani, eamque gradatim ad pauciores, postremo deducere ad singulos. Nam si omnibus hominibus, qui ubique sunt, quacumque in ora ac parte terrarum, ab hujusce terrae, quam nos incolimus, continuatione distantium, deos consulere censemus ob has causas, quas ante diximus: his quoque hominibus consulunt, qui has nobiscum terras ab oriente ad occidentem colunt....Ergo et earum partes diligunt, ut Romam Athenas, Spartam, Rhodum: et earum urbium separatim ab universis,singulos diligunt, ut Pyhrri bello Curium Fabricium, Coruncanium.*" (Cicero, *de natura deorum, academica*)

philosophy, have satisfactorily discoursed upon the bounteous abundance of wealth that virtue bestows.[58]

It is noteworthy that Kierkegaard does not take the context into account, but merely browses through Cicero, as if he were searching for philosophical arguments—or, as seen previously, as if he knows Cicero from an indirect source. The analysis of the intimate relations between man and God continues in the following third journal entry dealing with *De Natura Deorum*, titled "Solidarity." To this entry Kierkegaard has added a note in the margin. It begins:

> Paganism has no concept of God's majesty, which is the case with Judaism, too, although to a lesser degree. This explains how paganism (for example, Cicero in *de natura deorum*, III, end) claimed to disprove the existence of a God on the grounds that evil men prosper in the world just as Diogenes did in saying of a robber, Harpalus, who was regarded as lucky: Your existence disproves the existence of gods. This is the shallow concept of human gods, who are believed to strike immediately, presumably because they are unsure of themselves.[59]

Now, it is the third book of *De natura deorum*, that provides Kierkegaard with examples of pagan thinking.[60] The character Cotta in this part of the treatise criticizes his Stoic counterpart, Balbus, using the the Greek Cynic Diogenes and his happiness as an example of the lack of divine interference with mankind: "Indeed Diogenes the Cynic used to say that Harpalus, a brigand of the day who passed as fortunate, was a standing witness against the gods, because he lived and prospered as he did for so long."[61]

For Kierkegaard, too, the anecdote is a perfect paradigm. Though he still keeps mentioning the title of the work by Cicero he has in mind, he never distinguishes between the character and the author. The fourth reference to the treatise is found previously in the Cicero work:

> *Cicero* says (in *De natura deorum*, third book, at the end) that it does not matter that no one is wise or that no one can be wise.

---

[58]   Cicero, *De natura deorum*, 2.66.166–7; Ernesti, vol. 4: "*Magna dii curant, parva neglegunt. Magnis autem viris prospere semper eveniunt omnes res: si quidem satis a nostris et a principe philosophorum Socrate dictum est de ubertatibus virtutis et copiis.*" (Cicero, *De natura deorum, academica*)

[59]   *SKS* 24, 451, NB25:20.a / *JP* 3, 2558.

[60]   Cicero, *De natura deorum*, 3.34.83; Ernesti, vol. 4: "*Diogenes quidem Cynicus dicere solebat, Harpalum, qui temporibus illis praedo felix habebatur, contra deos testimonium dicere, quod in illa fortuna tam diu viveret.*" (Cicero, *de natura deorum, academica*: "Indeed Diogenes the Cynic used to say that Harpalus, a brigand of the day who passed as fortunate, was a standing witness against the gods, because he lived and prospered as he did for so long.")

[61]   Cicero, *De natura deorum*, 3.34.83; Ernesti, vol. 4: "*Diogenes quidem Cynicus dicere solebat, Harpalum, qui temporibus illis praedo felix habebatur, contra deos testimonium dicere, quod in illa fortuna tam diu viveret.*"

Thank-you. Thus we also receive the conclusion: it does not matter that no one is pure, blameless and that no one can be so. It is also in this way that people in our time will do away with the ethical. One says: none of us is ethical—ergo no one of us can be it, or one says that these two statements are one and the same.[62]

Again Kierkegaard has found a useful expression, and again it is not exactly said by Cicero, but by the character Cotta, who in fact opposes the Stoic religious outlook through a Stoic maxim. In the Cicero text, we read:

For just as it makes no difference whether no one *is* in good health or no one *can be* in good health, so I do not understand what difference it makes whether no one *is* wise or no one *can be* wise. However, we are dwelling too long on a point that is perfectly clear. Telamo dispatches the whole topic of proving that the gods pay no heed to man in a single verse: *For if they cared for men, good men would prosper and bad men come to grief; but this is not so.* Indeed the gods ought to have made all men good, if they really cared for the human race; or failing that, they certainly ought at all events to have cared for the good.[63]

Kierkegaard has initiated a comparison between ancient and contemporary views. Making use of an academic argument from analogy, Kierkegaard again shows his linguistic and academic interest. Moreover, Kierkegaard finds that the philosophical issues have been dealt with long ago. Two journal entries follow, also undated, after which the last reference to *De natura deorum* is found:

Paganism

said (see *De natura deorum,* end of book III, also Horace: *aequam mentem mihi ipsi praestabo*): We should thank God for good fortune; wisdom is to one's own credit.

Christianity teaches that the Pharisee sinned most deeply by thanking God that he was righteous. Yet it automatically follows (something Luther points out in the sermon on the Pharisee and the publican) that one is not to ascribe sins falsely to himself but simply avoid confusing the merely human criterion with God's criterion.[64]

Cotta says in Cicero's treatise:

Did anyone ever render thanks to the gods because he was a good man? No, but because he was rich, honored, secure. The reason why men give to Jupiter the titles of Best and Greatest is not that they think that he makes us just, temperate and wise, but safe, secure wealthy and opulent. Nor did anyone ever vow to pay a tithe to Hercules if he became a wise man! It is true there is a story that Pythagoras used to sacrifice an ox to the Muses

---

62   *SKS* 24, 451, NB25:21.

63   Cicero, *De natura deorum,* 3.32.79; Ernesti, vol. 4: "*Nam ut nihil interest, utrum nemo valeat, an nemo possit valere: sic non intellego, quid intersit, utrum nemo sit sapiens, an nemo esse possit. Ac nos quidem nimis multa de re apertissima. Telamo autem uno versu locum totum conficit, cur di homines neglegant:* Nam si curent, bene bonis sit, male malis: quod nunc abest. *Debebant illi quidem omnes bonos efficere, si quidem hominum generi consulebant. Sin id minus: bonis quidem certe consulere debebant.*" (Cicero, *de natura deorum, academica*).

64   *SKS* 24, 453, NB25:24 / *JP* 3, 3063.

when he made a new discovery in geometry! But I don't believe it, since Pythagoras refused even to sacrifice a victim to Apollo of Delos, for fear of sprinkling the altar with blood. However, to return to my point, it is the considered belief of all mankind that they must pray to god for fortune but obtain wisdom for themselves.[65]

According to Cotta the gods exist, but they are not responsible for anything human, such as wisdom. That Kierkegaard names Horace implies that he does not argue against Cicero, but focuses on the relationship with God in pagan sources, or more specifically, those who do not believe in the God of Christianity. Kierkegaard simply applies Cotta's skepticism on Stoic thought to stress his own point. This journal entry is the last reference to *De natura deorum*; at the same time the entry concludes the year 1851 in the *Journal NB25*. The journal entries from January 1852 do not deal with the treatise.

However, the increased interest in Cicero has not faded. We know that on January 13, 1852 Kierkegaard bought a German translation of the philosophical treatises *De divinatione*, *De finibus bonorum et malorum*, *Tusculanae disputationes* (two editions),[66] *Paradoxa stoicorum*, and *De re publica*.[67] To find out whether this is just a coincidence, one must read further into Kierkegaard's journals in 1852. The next journal entry that can be dated is written in May,[68] so it is impossible to compare the purchases with an exact journal entry. The subjects treated, though, are the same, and some quotations of references to ancient writers follow.[69] Kierkegaard criticizes the theology of his day and attacks contemporary clergymen, which he calls *Declamateurs*.[70] Suddenly Cicero's name appears again: "Cicero (in *Tusculan Disputations*) says it splendidly: He (Socrates) drinks the poison as if he were

---

[65]   Cicero, *De natura deorum*, 3.36.87–8; Ernesti, vol. 4: "*Num quis, quod bonus vir esset, gratias diis egit umquam? At quod dives, quod honoratus, quod incolumis. Jovemque optimum et maximum, ob eas res appellant, non quod nos justos, temperantes, sapientes efficiat, sed quod salvos, incolumes, opulentos, copiosos. Neque Herculi quisquam decumam vovit umquam, si sapiens factus esset. Quamquam Pythagoras, cum in geometria quiddam novi invenisset, Musis bovem inmolasse dicitur. sed id quidem non credo, quoniam ille ne Apollini quidem Delio hostiam inmolare voluit, ne aram sanguine adspergeret. Ad rem autem ut redeam, judicium hoc omnium mortalium est, fortunam a deo petendam, a se ipso sumendam esse sapientiam.*" (Cicero, *de natura deorum, academica*)
[66]   August Ludwig Gottlob Krehl's *Von der Verachtung des Todes: erstes tusculanisches Gespräch* (Hannover: Hahn 1819) is a translation of *Tusculanae disputationes*, first book (*ASKB* 1237).
[67]   Rohde, *Om Søren Kierkegaard som bogsamler*, p. 126. From this large number of texts *De natura deorum* is missing. Kierkegaard supposedly had a copy of this book already; by the time of his death, at least he had an old translation from 1787 (*ASKB* 1238).
[68]   I.e. the entry "About Her," which Kierkegaard himself has dated May 1852 (*SKS* 24, 521-3, NB25:109 / *JP* 6, 6800). Having no reason to doubt the chronological arrangement in *SKS* 24, 454, NB25:25. I suppose the entries leading up to "About Her" from *SKS* 24, 454ff., NB25:25ff. and onwards are written between January and May 1852. See *SKS* 24, 521–3, NB25:109, see also, p. 358 with editors' note.
[69]   For example, *SKS* 24, 461–2, NB25:38–41.
[70]   *SKS* 24, 463, NB25:42.

drinking to quench his thirst. I would add (this appears in *Phaedo*): He drinks it festively as if it were a delight."[71]

Yet another anecdote captured Kierkegaard's interest. He refers to *Tusculanae disputationes*, a book he recently bought. If he ever read it, he read it quickly; what Cicero in fact writes is:

> How charmed I am with Theramenes! How lofty a spirit is his! For though we shed tears as we read, nevertheless a notable man dies a death that is not pitiable: he was flung into prison by order of the thirty tyrants, and when he had swallowed the poison like a thirsty man he tossed the remainder out of the cup to make a splash, and with a laugh at the sound it made, "I drink," said he, "to the health of the fair Critias," the man who had treated him abominably.[72]

Though the trial and death of Socrates are mentioned a few lines later, Cicero refers not to Socrates, but Theramenes as the thirsty person. A third reference to one of Kierkegaard's newly purchased books we find in the long journal entry "Suffering":

> A pagan (Cicero, in *De finibus*) relates that the greatest sensualist in the Orient (Sardanapalus) put on his tombstone: I took all the pleasures of the world with me to the grave—to which another pagan (Aristotle) is supposed to have said: How so? You could not even hold on to a single one of them while you were living.[73]

In Cicero's text we read:

> Yet if bodily pleasure even when past can give delight, I do not see why Aristotle should be so contemptuous of the epitaph of Sardanapalus. The famous Syrian monarch boasts that he has taken with him all the sensual pleasures that he has enjoyed. How, asks Aristotle, could a dead man continue to experience a feeling which even while alive he could only be conscious of so long as he was actually enjoying it?[74]

Corrections in Kierkegaard's manuscripts—the words "in *De finibus*" are added to the text afterwards—leave the impression that he was in a hurry at the time of writing.

---

[71]   *SKS* 24, 464, NB25:43 / *JP* 4, 4288.
[72]   Cicero, *Tusculanae disputationes*, 1.40.96; Ernesti, vol. 4: "*quam me delectat Theramenes! quam elato animo est! etsi enim flemus, cum legimus, tamen non miserabiliter vir clarus emoritur. qui cum conjectus in carcerem triginta jussu tyrannorum, venenum ut sitiens obduxisset, reliquum sic e poculo ejecit, ut id resonare; quo sonitu reddito arridens,* Propino, *inquit,* hoc pulchro Critiae, *qui in eum fuerat taeterrimus.*" (English translation quoted from Cicero, *Tusculan Disputations*, trans. by King.) As mentioned above, Kierkegaard referred to *Tusculanae disputationes* in *The Concept of Anxiety*.
[73]   *SKS* 24, 481, NB25:64 / *JP* 6, 6794.
[74]   Cicero, *De finibus*, 2.32.106; Ernesti, vol. 4: "*Corporis autem voluptas si etiam praeterita delectat, non intellego, cur Aristoteles Sardanapali epigramma tantopere derideat: in quo ille rex Assyriae glorietur, se omnis secum libidinum voluptates abstulisse. quod enim ne vivus quidem, inquit, diutius sentire poterat, quam dum fruebatur; quo modo id potuit mortuo permanere.*" (English translation is quoted from Cicero, *De finibus bonorum et malorum*, trans. by H. Rackham, London: William Heinemann 1914.)

Perhaps his intention was to use the references to check later. In 1854 Kierkegaard in the journals refers to the story again. This time he does not tell where or by whom it is written.[75]

The reading of Cicero, if that is the question, peaks in the long journal entry "Mynster's Preaching of Christianity," again including Stoicism. The entry is undated, but with certainty written before May 1852.[76] In section 3 he describes his relationship with Bishop J.P. Mynster stressing that the enmity is not personal, but based on principles. Kierkegaard continues in section 4:

> Let me take an analogous case. The most rigorous ethics in paganism was, as is well known, Stoicism. It claims the ideal; merely interested in the idea in a qualitative respect, it claims the ideal, the ideal of the Sage, of whom Stoicism itself consequently says: such a person has never lived. [77]

The wise man who never lived, is the Stoic maxim that Kierkegaard through the Ciceronian interpretation argued against previously in the *Journal NB25*. As a note in the margin Kierkegaard has added:

> *Note.* Therefore, they called their own statements paradoxes, and they were so called by others: paradoxes—short, laconic, qualitatively tightened, and intended to be followed by action. But antiquity, also, shows a confusion, resembling the continuous one in Christendom, in which the same thing happened to the Christian paradox. The great, world famous rhetor Cicero has also written Paradoxes, a short work in which he gives an account of some Stoic doctrines, but in which, as he believes, he goes further than the Stoics, for he adorns them rhetorically, thereby proudly managing to make them less repelling. Perhaps! But perhaps exactly in this way the Stoics wanted to find them repelling.[78]

The comparison is evident. Mynster's interpretation of Christianity is like Cicero's interpretation of Stoic thoughts. This is the first instance of Kierkegaard directly criticizing Cicero. Prior to this he merely repeated what Cicero wrote. He might have read the introductory comments in Cicero's *Paradoxa stoicorum*, translated in one of Kierkegaard's new books:

> For Cato at all events follows the Stoic practice of employing the embellishments of eloquence when he is discoursing on the grandeur of mind, or self-control, or death, or the glory of virtue in general, or the immortal gods, or love of country; but I for my part have amused myself by throwing into common form, for your benefit, even those doctrines which the Stoics scarcely succeed in proving in the retirements of the schools of philosophy. These doctrines are surprising, and they run counter to universal opinion—the Stoics themselves actually term them *paradoxa*; so I wanted to try whether it is possible for them to be brought out into the light of common daily life and expounded in a form to

---

[75]   *Pap.* XI–1 A 449 / *JP* 4, 4303: "It is said that Sardanapalus had the following put on his grave: 'I took all the pleasures of life along with me,' about which even a pagan has brilliantly observed: How was it possible; even while you lived you could not hold fast to a single one."

[76]   *SKS* 24, 521-3, NB25:109; see also *Pap.* X–4 A 540 with editors' note.

[77]   *SKS* 24, 486, NB25:68.

[78]   *SKS* 24, 486, NB25:68.a.

win acceptance, or whether learning has one style and discourse and ordinary life another; and I wrote with the greater pleasure because the doctrines styled *paradoxa* by the Stoics appear to me to be in the highest degree Socratic, and far and away the truest.[79]

The language and the style are, according to Kierkegaard, deeply connected with the philosophy explained. Therefore, a comparison between Mynster and Cicero is obvious. Kierkegaard accuses Mynster for having flattened the language, that is, the expression of Christianity, without which it is no longer Christianity, but merely academic and rhetorical formulas. However, this is not an original analysis by Kierkegaard—who got his knowledge of the Stoa from Cicero—but a reaction solely to Cicero's own introductory words in *Paradoxa*. Cicero is never mentioned again in Kierkegaard's works.

We have seen examples in this article of Kierkegaard's various approaches to the Latin author Cicero. To begin with, Cicero is primarily regarded as a writer of historical significance. Throughout Kierkegaard's life, the impact of Cicero reverberates in the usage of Latin expressions and proverbs. Kierkegaard's use of Cicero is connected with the Latin readings from his school-days. This is seen at least in his earliest writings. During Kierkegaard's studies at the university, he gains more knowledge of Cicero, as Cicero becomes an introduction to classical philosophy and one of the founders of traditional philosophical terms. Kierkegaard's references to Cicero move from taking pleasure in making puns and sayings based on Cicero's writings to a more mature reading of the Ciceronian texts. For example, Cicero's wisdom of life comes in handy when Kierkegaard writes a letter of compassion to Michael Nielsen. Kierkegaard is cultivated and so become the characters of his books. They are able to quote Cicero, and their points of view are not too complex to find expression through ancient Latin terms. What Kierkegaard regards as paganism has already been clearly defined in Cicero's philosophical writings. Moreover, in Cicero's writings Kierkegaard finds terms and definitions applicable to how he perceives the tendencies of nineteenth-century clergy in Copenhagen. In this sense Kierkegaard is deeply inspired by Cicero.

A close reading of Kierkegaard's books, journals, and letters shows a superficial approach to Cicero from time to time. Although some of Kierkegaard's Latin terms might stem directly from Cicero's writings, there is no evidence of this. In terms of theology or philosophy, Kierkegaard regards Cicero as being fundamental for the European tradition, but Kierkegaard's main focus is elsewhere. Seldom does he quote Cicero *ad fontes*. Instead, he cites from secondary, contemporary sources.

---

[79]   Cicero, *Paradoxa stoicorum*, 1 Ernesti, vol. 4 (here called *Paradoxa ad M. Brutum*): "*Cato enim duntaxat de magnitudine animi, de continentia, de morte, de omni laude virtutis, de diis immortalibus, de caritate patriae, Stoice solet, oratoriis ornamentis adhibitis, dicere. Ego vero illa ipsa, quae vix in gymnasiis, et in otio Stoici probant, ludens conjeci in communes locos. quae, quia sunt admirabilia, contraque opinionem omnium, ab ipsis etiam παράδοξα appellantur, tentare volui, possentne proferri in lucem, id est, in forum, et ita dici, ut probarentur, an alia quaedam esset erudita, alia popularis oratio: eoque scripsi libentius, quod mihi ista, παράδοξα quae appellant, maxime videntur esse Socratica, longeque verissima.*" (English translation quoted from Cicero, *De Oratore in two volumes together with De Fato, Paradoxa Stoicorum, De partitione oratoria*, vols. 1–2, trans. by Rackham.)

This is evident from the errors in Kierkegaard's quotations of Cicero. Cicero is even credited for terms and sayings that he probably never had anything to do with. Only from 1851–52 can we trace a more serious interest in the writings of Cicero. On the other hand, it seems as if this interest is only short term. The frequent occurrence of Cicero's name in the journals peaks just before Kierkegaard buys translations of Cicero in 1852. What catches Kierkegaard's interest is Stoic philosophy, but Kierkegaard does not go into details with the Stoic tradition. In fact he only refers to the Stoic views as general expressions of pagan notions of God. Kierkegaard never distinguishes between what Cicero's characters say and what might be Cicero's own opinion. In that way, Kierkegaard's approach to the Latin texts suits his own purpose as a writer. In 1852 Kierkegaard finds arguments in Cicero's writing that enable him to criticize Mynster and the practices of contemporary theology.

In conclusion, we may argue that Cicero's direct influence on Kierkegaard is limited to a certain extent. However, as a learned man of his time, Kierkegaard draws on this Latin scholar in his writings as a source of inspiration. While Cicero's writings have been used as a stepping stone for Kierkegaard to develop new ideas, his language has inspired him in regard to his own literary ways of expression.

Bibliography

I. Cicero's Works in The Auction Catalogue *of Kierkegaard's Library*

M. Tullii Ciceronis Opera omnia ex recensione Iacobi Gronovii, accedit varietas lectionis...cum singulorum librorum argumentis..., vols. 1–6, 2nd ed., ed. by Io. Augusti Ernesti, Halle: Impensis Orphanotrophei 1757 (*ASKB* 1224–1229).

De Officiis libri tres: mit einem deutschen Kommentar besonders für Schulen, ed. by Johann Friedrich Degen, 3rd revised ed., Berlin: Boicke 1825 (*ASKB* 1230).

M. Tullii Ciceronis Orationes VII pro S. Roscio, pro lege Manilia, IV in Catilinam, atque pro Murena, ed. August Matthiae, editio altera, Leipzig: Vogel 1826 (*ASKB* 1231).

M. Tullii Ciceronis de claris oratoribus liber qui dicitur Brutus: für den Schulgebrauch erläutert, ed. by Reinhard Stern, Hamm 1837 (*ASKB* 1232).

M. Tullii Ciceronis Laelius, sive de amicitia dialogus, mit erklärenden Anmerkungen, 3rd revised edition, Leipzig: Schwickert 1829 (*ASKB* 1233).

M.T. Ciceronis Opera rhetorica, vol. 2, *Libri tres ad Q. Fratrem de oratore*, ed. by Christianus Godofried Schütz, Leipzig: G.J. Goeschen 1805 (*ASKB* 1234).

Cicero's Rede für den Milo, trans. and ed. by J.P. Brewer, Düsseldorf: Schreiner 1830 (*ASKB* 1235).

Cicero's zwei Bücher von der Vorhersehung in einer teutschen Uebersetzung, Leipzig 1784 (*ASKB* 1236).

Marcus Tullius Cicero's Tusculanische Untersuchungen, trans. and ed. by Johann David Büchling, Halle: Johann Christian Hendel 1799 (*ASKB* 1236).

Über das höchste Gut und das höchste Uebel in fünf Büchern, trans. by Carl Victor Hauff, Tübingen: bei Chr. Fr. Osiander 1822 (*ASKB* 1237).

Von der Verachtung des Todes: erstes tusculanisches Gespräch, trans. by August Ludwig Gottlob Krehl, Hannover: Hahn 1819 (*ASKB* 1237).

Der Staat, trans. and ed. by Friedrich von Kobbe, Göttingen: bei Vandenboeck und Ruprecht 1824 (*ASKB* 1237).

Paradoxieen. Mit erläuternden Inhaltsanzeigen und erklärenden Anmerkungen, ed. by Christoph August Gottlieb Schreiber, Halle: Hendel 1799 (*ASKB* 1237).

Gespräche über das Wesen der Götter in drey Büchern. Aus dem Lateinischen des Marcus Tullis Cicero übersetzt, Zürich: bey Drell, Geßner, Füßli und Comp. 1787 (*ASKB* 1238).

Abhandlung über die menschlichen Pflichten in drei Büchern, trans. by Christian Garve, 6th ed. Breslau: Wilhelm Gottlieb Korn 1819 (*ASKB* 1239).

Marcus Tullius Cicero's Vermischte Briefe, vols. 1–5, trans. by A.C. Borheck, 2nd ed., Frankfurt am Main: Hermann 1789–1801 (*ASKB* 1240–1244).

Auswahl der besten Briefe Cicero's, ed. by Benjamin Weiske, 3rd ed., Braunschweig: Schulbuchhandlung 1824 (*Encyclopädie der lateinischen Classiker*, Abtheilung 2, Theil 2) (*ASKB* 1245).

Erklärende Anmerkungen zur Auswahl der besten Briefe Cicero's, ed. by Benjamin Weiske, Braunschweig: Schulbuchhandlung 1796 (*ASKB* 1246).

M.Tullii Ciceronis Opera omnia, vols. 1–2, Geneva: Typis Jacobi Stoër 1646 (*ASKB* A I 149–150).

Les lettres de Cicéron à ses amis, tomes 1–4, trans. by Louis Maument, La Haye: Pierre Husson 1709 (*ASKB* A I 151).

Von dem Redner. Drei Gespräche, trans. and ed. by Friedrich Carl Wolff, Altona: Johann Friedrich Hammerich 1801 (*ASKB* A I 152).

Ciceronis Orationum, tomi III, ed. by Dionysii Lambini, [Geneva]: Aurel. Allobr. 1609 (*ASKB* A II 48).

M.T. Ciceronis libri tres de Officiis, Hauniæ [Copenhagen]: Paullino 1679 (*ASKB* A II 49).

II. Works in The Auction Catalogue *of Kierkegaard's Library that Discuss Cicero*

Ast, Friedrich, *Grundriss einer Geschichte der Philosophie*, Landshut: Joseph Thomann 1807, p. 157 (*ASKB* 385).

Bähr, Johann Christian Felix, *Abriss der Römischen Literatur-Geschichte zum Gebrauch für höhere Lehranstalten*, Heidelberg and Leipzig: Groos 1833 (*ASKB* 975).

[Becker, Karl Friedrich], *Karl Friedrich Beckers Verdenshistorie, omarbeidet af Johan Gottfried Woltmann*, vols. 1–12, trans. by J. Riise, Copenhagen: Fr. Brummers Forlag 1822–29, vol. 3, p. 422; p. 440; p. 444; p. 548; p. 563; p. 611 (*ASKB* 1972–1983).

Buhle, Johann Gottlieb, *Geschichte der neuern Philosophie seit der Epoche der Wiederherstellung der Wissenschaften*, vols. 1–6 (in 10 tomes), vols. 1–2, Göttingen: Johann Georg Rosenbusch's Wittwe 1800; vols. 3–6, Göttingen: Johann Friedrich Röwer 1802–05 [Abtheilung 6 in *Geschichte der Künste und Wissenschaften seit der Wiederherstellung derselben bis an das Ende des achtzehnten Jahrhunderts. Von einer Gesellschaft gelehrter Männer ausgearbeitet*, Abtheilungen 1–11, Göttingen: Röwer and Göttingen: Rosenbusch 1796–1820], vol. 1, pp. 578–84 passim; vol. 2, p. 563 (*ASKB* 440–445).

Dyck, Johann Gottfried and Georg Schatz (eds.), *Charaktere der vornehmsten Dichter aller Nationen; nebst kritischen und historischen Abhandlungen über Gegenstände der schönen Künste und Wissenschaften, von einer Gesellschaft von Gelehrten*, vols. 1–8, Leipzig: Dyk 1792–1808, vol. 1, pp. 13–14; p. 28 (*ASKB* 1370–1377).

Flögel, Carl Friedrich, *Geschichte der komischen Litteratur*, vols. 1–4, Liegnitz and Leipzig: David Siegert 1784–87, vol. 1, p. 4; p. 8; p. 11; p. 42; p. 216; p. 218 (*ASKB* 1396–1399).

Hagen, Johan Frederik, *Ægteskabet. Betragtet fra et ethisk–historiskt Standpunct*, Copenhagen: Wahlske Boghandels Forlag 1845, p. 128; p. 136n; p. 141n (*ASKB* 534).

Hahn, August (ed.), *Lehrbuch des christlichen Glaubens*, Leipzig: Friedrich Christian Wilhelm Vogel 1828, p. 2; p. 13; p. 40; p. 75; p. 166; p. 185; p. 191; p. 313; p. 315; p. 335 (*ASKB* 535).

[Hamann, Johann Georg], *Hamann's Schriften*, vols. 1–8, ed. by Friedrich Roth, Berlin: G. Reimer 1821–43, vol. 1, p. 15; p. 20; p. 387; p. 404; vol. 3, p. 134; vol. 4, p. 107; vol. 5, p. 25; p. 206; vol. 6, p. 11; p. 15; p. 25; pp. 37–8; p. 41; vol. 7, p. 19; pp. 76–7; p. 123 (*ASKB* 536–544).

[Hegel, Georg Wilhelm Friedrich], *Georg Wilhelm Friedrich Hegel's Vorlesungen über die Philosophie der Religion*, vols. 1–2, ed. by Philipp Marheineke, 2nd revised ed., Berlin: Duncker und Humblot 1840 (vols. 11–12 in *Georg Wilhelm Friedrich Hegel's Werke. Vollständige Ausgabe*, ed. by Philipp Marheineke et al., Berlin: Duncker und Humblot 1832–45), vol. 2, pp. 174–7; p. 401 (*ASKB* 564–565).

Jäger, Josef Nikolaus, *Moral-Philosophie*, Vienna: Im Verlage von J.G. Heubner 1839, p. 95 (*ASKB* 582).

[Leibniz, Gottfried Wilhelm], *God. Guil. Leibnitii Opera philosophica, quæ exstant latina gallica germanica omnia*, vols. 1–2, ed. by Johann Eduard Erdmann, Berlin 1839–40, p. 554; p. 600; p. 609 (*ASKB* 620).

Longin, Dionysius, *Dionysius Longin vom Erhabenen Griechisch und Teutsch, Nebst dessen Leben, einer Nachricht von seinen Schriften, und einer Untersuchung, was Longin durch das Erhabene verstehe*, trans. and ed. by Carl Heinrich Heineken, Leipzig and Hamburg: Conrad König 1738, p. 125; p. 127; p. 299; p. 322 (*ASKB* 1129).

Meierotto, Johann Heinrich Ludwig, *Ueber Sitten und Lebensart der Römer in verschiedenen Zeiten der Republik*, vols. 1–2, 3rd revised and enlarged ed., Berlin: in der Myliussischen Buchhandlung 1814 (*ASKB* 656).

Meiners, Christoph, *Geschichte des Verfalls der Sitten und der Staatsverfassung der Römer*, Leipzig: bey Weidmanns Erben und Reich 1782 (*ASKB* 660).

[Møller, Poul Martin], *Efterladte Skrifter af Poul M. Møller*, vols. 1–3, ed. by Christian Winther, F.C. Olsen and Christen Thaarup, Copenhagen: C.A. Reitzel 1839–43, vol. 2, p. 76; p. 341; p. 396; p. 413; p. 460; pp. 525–7; vol. 3, p. 173; p. 195; p. 203; p. 229; p. 238; p. 254; p. 304 (*ASKB* 1574–1576).

[Montaigne, Michel de], *Michael Montaigne's Gedanken und Meinungen über allerley Gegenstände, ins Deutsche übersetzt*, vols. 1–7, Berlin: F.T. Lagarde 1793–99, vol. 1, p. 74; p. 118; p. 199; p. 207; p. 262; p. 324; vol. 2, p. 190; p. 195; pp. 199–212; vol. 3, pp. 199ff.; pp. 204–5; p. 380; p. 411; p. 518; vol. 4, p. 159; p. 391; p. 411 (*ASKB* 681–687).

Mynster, Jakob Peter, *Den hedenske Verden ved Christendommens Begyndelse*, Copenhagen: Schultz 1850, p. 20; p. 25; pp. 31–2; p. 47 (*ASKB* 693).

—— *Blandede Skrivter*, vols. 1–3, Copenhagen: Den Gyldendalske Boghandlings Forlag 1852–53 (vols. 4–6, Copenhagen: Den Gyldendalske Boghandlings Forlag 1855–57), vol. 1, p. 41n; p. 84n; p. 96; p. 111n; p. 114n; p. 115n; p. 116; p. 127; vol. 2, p. 135; p. 191; vol. 3, p. 42n (*ASKB* 358–363).

[Richter, Johann Paul Friedrich], Jean Paul, *Vorschule der Aesthetik nebst einigen Vorlesungen in Leipzig über die Parteien der Zeit*, vols. 1–3, 2nd revised ed., Stuttgart and Tübingen: J.G. Cotta'sche Buchhandlung 1813, vol. 1, p. 179; vol. 2, p. 576; p. 772; vol. 3, p. 836 (*ASKB* 1381–1383).

Ritter, Heinrich, *Geschichte der Philosophie alter Zeit*, vols. 1–4, 2nd revised ed., Hamburg: Friedrich Perthes 1836–39, vol. 4, pp. 106–75 (*ASKB* 735–738).

Ritter, Heinrich and L. Preller, *Historia philosophiae graeco-romanae ex fontium locis contexta*, ed. by L. Preller, Hamburg: Perthes 1838, pp. 416–33 (*ASKB* 726).

Rötscher, Heinrich Theodor, *Die Kunst der dramatischen Darstellung. In ihrem organischen Zusammenhange*, vols. 1–3, Berlin: Verlag von Wilhelm Thome 1841–46, vol. 1, 1841, p. 40n; p. 75n; p. 138n; pp. 140–2; p. 150; p. 237 (*ASKB* 1391; for vols. 2–3, also entitled *Cyclus dramatischer Charaktere. Nebst einer einleitenden Abhandlung über das Wesen dramatischer Charaktergestaltung*, cf. *ASKB* 1802–1803).

Schmidt, W. Adolf, *Geschichte der Denk- und Glaubensfreiheit im ersten Jahrhundert der Kaiserherrschaft und des Christenthums*, Berlin: Verlag von Veit und Comp. 1847, passim (*ASKB* 771).

Schopenhauer, Arthur, *Die Welt als Wille und Vorstellung*, vols. 1–2, 2nd revised and enlarged ed., Leipzig: F.A. Brockhaus 1844 [1819], vol. 1, p. 100n; p. 341; p. 580; p. 583; vol. 2, p. 151; pp. 157–8; p. 382; p. 600; p. 622 (*ASKB* 773–773a).

Stäudlin, Carl Friedrich, *Geschichte und Geist des Skepticismus vorzüglich in Rücksicht auf Moral und Religion*, vols. 1–2, Leipzig: Siegfried Lebrecht Crusius 1794, vol. 1, pp. 346–56 (*ASKB* 791).

[Sulzer, Johann George], *Johann George Sulzers vermischte philosophische Schriften. Aus den Jahrbüchern der Akademie der Wissenschaften zu Berlin gesammelt*, vols. 1–2, Leipzig: bey Weidmanns Erben und Reich 1773–81 [the title of the second volume is modified and reads as follows, *Johann George Sulzers vermischte Schriften. Eine Fortsetzung der vermischten philosophischen Schriften desselben. Nebst einigen Nachrichten von seinem Leben, und seinen sämtlichen Werken*], vol. 1, p. 131; vol. 2, Vorbericht, p. 120; vol. 2, main text, p. 193 (*ASKB* 807–808).

——*Allgemeine Theorie der Schönen Künste, in einzeln, nach alphabetischer Ordnung der Kunstwörter auf einander folgenden, Artikeln abgehandelt*, vols. 1–4 and a Register Volume, 2nd revised ed., Leipzig: in der Weidmannschen Buchhandlung 1792–99, vol. 1, p. 146; p. 166; p. 171; p. 174; p. 177; p. 259; p. 263; p. 276; p. 279; p. 362; p. 366; p. 373; pp. 380; p. 381; p. 390; p. 392; p. 393; p. 400; p. 477; p. 499; p. 518; p. 600; p. 603; vol. 2, p. 25; p. 77; p. 78; p. 86; p. 95; p. 100; p. 115; p. 118; p. 244; p. 314; p. 317; p. 670; p. 699; vol. 3, p. 54; p. 74; p. 129; p. 140; p. 141; p. 168; p. 246; p. 284; p. 286; p. 317; p. 428; p. 535; p. 670; vol. 4, p. 33; p. 34; p. 47; p. 48; p. 49; p. 71 (*ASKB* 1365–1369).

Tennemann, Wilhelm Gottlieb, "Cicero," in his *Geschichte der Philosophie*, vols. 1–11, Leipzig: Johann Ambrosius Barth 1798–1819, vol. 5, pp. 110–34 (*ASKB* 815–826).

Thiersch, Friedrich, *Allgemeine Aesthetik in akademischen Lehrvorträgen*, Berlin: G. Reimer 1846, pp. 38–9; p. 58 (*ASKB* 1378).

Thomsen, Grimur, *Om den nyfranske Poesie, et Forsøg til Besvarelse af Universitetets æsthetiske Priisspørgsmaal for 1841: "Har Smag og Sands for Poesi gjort Frem-eller Tilbageskridt i Frankrig i de sidste Tider og hvilken Aarsagen?,"* Copenhagen: Paa den Wahlske Boghandlings Forlag 1843, p. 7 (*ASKB* 1390).

Tiedemann, Dieterich, *System der stoischen Philosophie*, vols. 1–3, Leipzig: bey Weidmanns Erben und Reich 1776 (*ASKB* 833–835).

Wirth, Johann Ulrich, *Die speculative Idee Gottes und die damit zusammenhängenden Probleme der Philosophie. Eine kritisch-dogmatische Untersuchung*, Stuttgart and Tübingen: J.G. Cotta'scher Verlag 1845, p. 137; p. 145; pp. 228–9; p. 237 (*ASKB* 876).

Zeuthen, Ludvig, *Om den christelige Tro i dens Betydning for Verdenshistorien. Et Forsøg*, Copenhagen: Gyldendalske Boghandels Forlag 1838, p. 39 (*ASKB* 259).

—— *Om Ydmyghed. En Afhandling*, Copenhagen: Gyldendalske Boghandel 1852, p. 18; pp. 42–3 (*ASKB* 916).

Zimmermann, Johann Georg, *Ueber die Einsamkeit*, vols. 1–4, Leipzig: bey Weidmanns Erben und Reich 1784–85, vol. 1, p. 59 (*ASKB* 917–920).

III. Secondary Literature on Kierkegaard's Relation to Cicero

Burgess, Andrew J., "Kierkegaard and the Classical Oratorical Tradition," in *Kierkegaard and the Word(s): Essays on Hermeneutics and Communication*, ed. by Poul Houe and Gordon D. Marino, Copenhagen: C.A. Reitzel 2003, pp. 228–39.

Furtak, Rick Anthony, *Wisdom in Love: Kierkegaard and the Ancient Quest for Emotional Integrity*, Notre Dame: University of Notre Dame Press 2005, p. 20; p. 42; p. 43.

Krarup, Per, *Søren Kierkegaard og Borgerdydskolen*, Copenhagen: Gyldendal 1977, pp. 68–76.

Lund, Holger, *Borgerdydsskolen i Kjøbenhavn 1787–1887*, Copenhagen: Otto Wroblewskys Forlag 1887.

Horace:

The Art of Poetry and the Search for the Good Life

Thomas Miles

The Roman poet Quintus Horatius Flaccus, known in English as Horace, seems to have been one of the earliest and longest lasting of Kierkegaard's influences. As a boy, Kierkegaard was a gifted Latin scholar, and we know from multiple sources that he had read and written on Horace from an early age. Kierkegaard would go on to quote Horace in most of his published works. Often Kierkegaard simply borrows a nicely crafted phrase or image from Horace, but there are several interesting points, especially in Kierkegaard's early authorship, where he turns to Horace for important insights on ethical or aesthetic matters.

Quintus Horatius Flaccus was born on December 8, 65 BC in the Roman colonial town of Venusia (now Venosa) in Italy. Horace's father had been a slave at some point in his life but had been freed, and Horace was born a free man.[1] Like Kierkegaard, Horace was not ashamed of his father's humble origins. In his first published book of poems, Horace declared "I shall never regret such a father"; he even credits his father with instilling in him any personal merits he might have.[2] Horace's father rose from being a *coactor*, a collector of money and goods for a small town auctioneer, to being an auctioneer and businessman in his own right, and he eventually became a wealthy man.[3] He spared no expense in educating his son. When Horace was a teenager, his father brought him to Rome and enrolled him in a school that would provide the young man with the best education available. Later, his father sent him to Athens for further study.

After the assassination of Julius Caesar in 44 BC, Horace enlisted as an officer in the army of Brutus, which fought in the name of preserving the Roman Republic against Caesar's heir, Octavius Caesar (later Emperor Augustus) and Mark Antony. At the age of 22, Horace took part in the battle of Philippi in which Brutus' army was decisively defeated. The vanquished soldiers were given amnesty, but Horace returned to Italy to find his father's farm confiscated; lands of defeated soldiers had

[1]   *The Complete Works of Horace,* trans. and ed. by Charles Passage, New York: Frederick Ungar Publishing Co. 1983, p. 1.
[2]   Horace, *Satires*, I, 6, 89, 65–71 as translated in *Complete Works*, p. 39.
[3]   Peter Levi, *Horace: A Life*, New York: Routledge 1998, p. 23.

been taken and given as payment to the soldiers of the victors.[4] Horace would later attribute his first undertaking in poetry to his poverty at this time:

> After Philippi my service was over, but I was in want, my
> Wings had been clipped, I was destitute, left without home and deprived of
> Land that my father had owned, until poverty gave me sufficient
> Boldness to start writing poems.[5]

This autobiographical account is not entirely accurate, however. Horace seems to have written some poetry even before his military service.[6] Also, we know that he was not completely destitute, since he had the means to purchase a position as treasury clerk after returning to Italy.[7] But it was at this time that Horace's poems began to be noticed, most importantly by his fellow poets Virgil and Varius. They befriended Horace and introduced him to a wealthy statesman and close advisor to Octavius named Maecenas. Maecenas became Horace's patron and five years later gave Horace a tract of land in the Sabine country thirty miles north-east of Rome. Horace prudently sublet most of the land to tenant farmers, but the rest became his beloved and frequently invoked "Sabine farm."[8] Horace's first published works were the two books of the *Satires*, published in 35 BC and 30 BC respectively, and the *Epodes*, also published in 30 BC. In the next seven years, Horace composed the three books of the *Odes*, often considered his masterworks. These were followed by a collection of twenty letters written in verse, the first book of the *Epistles*, published in 20 BC.

Having produced a number of excellent works in a short number of years Horace, like Kierkegaard, expressed a wish to end his authorship. But like Kierkegaard, Horace found that he could not retire from literature so easily. At the request of Emperor Augustus, Horace composed the hymn for the centennial rites of 17 BC and a poem celebrating the Roman victories of 15 BC. This latter poem was collected with a number of others into the fourth book of *Odes*, published around 13 BC. At this time, Horace also published a verse letter solicited by Augustus, together with two other verse letters written years earlier, as a second book of *Epistles*.[9] The last of these epistles is the famous *Ars Poetica*, a name acquired only after the poet's death.[10] Little is known about the last five years of Horace's life; although by this time he was widely acknowledged as Rome's greatest living poet, in these final years he apparently composed nothing more. He died on November 27, 8 BC and was buried beside his patron Maecenas, who had died two months earlier, in the gardens of Maecenas' mansion on the Esquiline Hill in Rome.[11]

---

4   Horace, *Complete Works*, p. 2.
5   Horace, *Epistles*, II, 2, 49–52 as translated in *Complete Works*, p. 352.
6   Levi, *Horace A Life*, p. 29.
7   Ibid., p. 44.
8   Horace, *Complete Works*, p. 3.
9   Ibid., pp. 3–4.
10   Ibid., p. 340.
11   Ibid., p. 4.

By AD 60 the work of Horace had become a standard subject of Latin study in schools. This remained true in Kierkegaard's day and is still true today. The curriculum of the Borgerdyd School, which Kierkegaard attended from 1821 until 1830, had a strong emphasis on Latin. Students in the higher grades had 45 hours of instruction per week, and 13 of them were devoted to Latin, more than twice that of any other subject.[12] We know from accounts of his schoolmates that Kierkegaard showed an early talent for Latin compositions, and Horace may have been the first author to receive Kierkegaard's attention. In response to a request for information about Kierkegaard's school days by Hans Peter Barfod (1834–92), the first editor of Kierkegaard's papers, one of his classmates, Frederik Peter Welding (1811–94), asked "Doesn't someone have S.K.'s school books, his Horace or his Cicero *de Oratore*? The underlining and the marginal notes would be enlightening. S.K. wrote what we called 'notes' about Horace in connection with Prof. M. Nielsen's interpretation."[13] There is some evidence that Kierkegaard's skill in writing Latin was better than his skill in writing Danish. Another fellow classmate, Hans Peter Holst (1811–93), recalls that he and Kierkegaard regularly cheated by swapping assignments:

> [A]t the Borgerdyd School we had a regular practice whereby I wrote the Danish essays for him and he wrote the Latin ones for me. It is strange that he, who ended up writing such excellent Danish, had absolutely no grasp of it in his youth, but wrote a Latin-Danish, which was crawling with participials and the most complexly punctuated sentences.[14]

Because he developed a reputation for being a "good Latinist," Kierkegaard was honored with the responsibility of helping the school's headmaster Michael Nielsen (1776–1846) correct the other students' Latin compositions. Upon graduation, this same M. Nielsen wrote an official testimony of Kierkegaard's academic merits. This included a certification that Kierkegaard "has read and presents for examination," among other works in Latin, "Horace, *The Odes*, the first three books of the *Epistles*, and the *Ars Poetica*."[15] Thus we have sound evidence that Kierkegaard was well-versed in Horace from an early age, and that some of his first attempts at writing concerned interpretations of Horace. Later, as a university student, Kierkegaard taught Latin at the Borgerdyd School in 1837 and 1838.[16] According to accounts from his students and from M. Nielsen, Kierkegaard was an engaging, "extraordinarily capable" teacher with "an unusual command of the Latin language," and it is highly probable that Kierkegaard taught his students Horace.[17] Throughout his life Kierkegaard would continue to quote Horace in Latin, and at the time of his death the *Auction Catalogue* of his books included two works by Horace: *Q. Horatii Flacci*

---

[12]   Joakim Garff, *Søren Kierkegaard: A Biography*, Princeton: Princeton University Press 2005 [2000], pp. 21–2.

[13]   Bruce H. Kirmmse (ed.), *Encounters with Kierkegaard*, Princeton: Princeton University Press 1996, p. 9.

[14]   Ibid., p. 12.

[15]   Ibid., p. 13; p. 15; p. 273.

[16]   *EPW*, p. xiv.

[17]   Kirmmse, *Encounters with Kierkegaard*, p. 23; p. 29.

Opera, published in Leipzig in 1828[18] and a two-volume German edition, *Horazens Briefe*, translated and edited by C.M. Wieland, and published in 1816.[19]

Kierkegaard quotes Horace only once and in an off-hand way in his first book, his critique of Hans Christian Andersen (1805–75), entitled *From the Papers of One Still Living*. In a footnote to a passage ridiculing the political meetings of his day, Kierkegaard quotes Horace's line "*Sed nimis arta premunt olidae convivia caprae*,"[20] or "But the reek of goats makes too crowded feasts unpleasant." In Kierkegaard's dissertation, *On the Concept of Irony*, he turns to Horace for more serious insights, mainly on the aesthetic communication of ideas. In a discussion of the Socratic method of questioning, which he calls "the art of conversing," Kierkegaard discusses how Socrates "points out to the Sophists that they do indeed know how to speak but do not know how to converse."[21] Kierkegaard contrasts the meaningful beauty of Plato's dialogues with what he calls "abstract beauty," quoting Horace's critique in his *Ars Poetica* of *versus rerum inopes nugaeque canorae* or "verses void of thought, and sonorous trifles."[22] Kierkegaard says that such "abstract beauty" venerates "the expression itself, dissociated from its relation to an idea," whereas the beauty of Socratic conversing makes for a "concentricity of conversation" in which questions and answers remain centered on some meaningful idea or concept.[23] Interestingly, in the passage quoted, Horace is recommending that the aspiring poet study the "Socratic philosophers."[24]

Later in his dissertation, when contrasting ironic and straightforward forms of speaking, Kierkegaard turns to Horace while discussing the speaker's freedom in relation to what is said. When speaking straightforwardly in the sense that I mean what I say and I assume the speaker grasps my meaning, "then I am bound in what has been said—that is, I am positively free therein." Kierkegaard quotes an expression from Horace to explain this idea: "Here the old verse is appropriate: *semel emissum volat irrevocabile verbum* [the word once let slip flies beyond recall]."[25] Whereas Horace uses this phrase to simply warn against speaking too freely or to gossips ("Watch what you say at all times, and about whom and to whom you say it"[26]), Kierkegaard finds in it an expression for a speaker's responsibility and ownership of what is said.[27] As we see here, Kierkegaard often invested new weight and greater meaning to phrases he borrowed from Horace. To give another example of this, in a journal entry about writing the preface for his dissertation, Kierkegaard expresses his "indescribable joy in giving up all objective thought and really pouring [himself] out

---

18   *Q. Horatii Flacci Opera*, Leipzig: Tauchnitz 1828 (*ASKB* 1248).
19   *Horazens Briefe*, vols. 1–2, trans. and ed. by C.M. Wieland, Leipzig: in der Weidmannschen Buchhandlung 1816 (*ASKB* A I 164–165).
20   *SKS* 1, 27n / *EPW*, 72n. Horace, *Epistles*, I, 5, 29.
21   *SKS* 1, 94 / *CI*, 33.
22   *SKS* 1, 94 / *CI*, 33. Horace, *Epistles* II, 3, 322.
23   *SKS* 1, 94–5 / *CI*, 34.
24   Horace, *Epistles* II, 3, 310 as translated in *Complete Works*, p. 367.
25   *SKS* 1, 286 / *CI*, 247. Horace, *Epistles* I, 18, 71.
26   Horace, *Epistles* I, 18, 68 as translated in *Complete Works*, p. 292.
27   For other references to Horace in *On the Concept of Irony* see: *SKS* 1, 96 / *CI*, 35; *SKS* 1, 241 / *CI*, 195.

in [his] wishes and hopes, in secretly whispering to the reader, a Horatian *sussuratio* [low whisper] in the evening twilight."[28] In Horace's poem, this phrase describes evening trysts between young lovers, but Kierkegaard uses it to express an author's most intimate communication with his readers. In the later book entitled *Prefaces*, Kierkegaard repeats the notion that a preface is like such a Horatian "low whisper" in the evening.[29]

In the first volume of *Either/Or*, Kierkegaard has the esthete A quote Horace by name on multiple occasions. This has the effect of emphasizing A's character as a brilliant and learned wit. For example, in his critique of Mozart's opera *The Magic Flute*, A uses a reference to Horace to illustrate his point that the character Tamino's flute playing is "boring and sentimental": "every time he takes out his flute and blows a piece on it one thinks of the peasant in Horace (*rusticus exspectat, dum defluat amnis* [the bumpkin waiting for the river to run out]), except that Horace did not give his peasant a flute for pointless pastime."[30] This is another example of Kierkegaard putting Horace's words to a very different use than Horace did. Whereas A uses this humorous image to sharpen A's witty aesthetic remarks, Horace uses this image in giving ethical advice: "Begin working. Postponing the time for right living is only / Aping the rustic who waits for the river to finish its flow."[31]

A also employs references to Horace to explain his central distinction between those who live for immediate pleasure and those who live for reflective pleasure. Immediate esthetes seek to escape boredom by indulging in the satisfaction of their desires in immediate experience, for example, in the pleasure of a good meal or an entertaining concert. This method of escaping boredom is made ever more difficult by the fact that whatever entertains this esthete one moment bores him the next. As a result, he must continually scramble for new sources of enjoyment. To illustrate this dilemma, both A and Judge Wilhelm use the legendary figure of Nero. Nero has the whole Roman world at the disposal of his aesthetic desires, and yet his all-consuming appetite is never satisfied. "One is weary of eating on porcelain and eats on silver; weary of that, one eats on gold; one burns down half of Rome in order to visualize the Trojan conflagration."[32] In a draft for this passage, A turns to Horace to emphasize the desperation of immediate esthetes who attempt to escape boredom in this way: "With regard to boredom, they do what according to Horace the merchant does with regard to poverty and with the same restlessness, as the verse so excellently depicts: *per mare pauperiem fugiens per saxa per ignes* [fleeing poverty through sea, through rocks, through flames]."[33] Here Kierkegaard's use of Horace's words is very

28   *SKS* 18, 30, EE:73 / *KJN* 2, 25–6. Horace, *Odes*, I, 9, 19. Note that the word in Horace is "*susurri.*"
29   *SKS* 4, 469 / *P*, 5. See also the reference to Horace in the draft for the preface of *Stages on Life's Way*: *Pap.* V B 191.
30   *SKS* 2, 88 / *EO1*, 82. Horace, *Epistles* I, 2, 42. For a similar example of A's use of Horace, see *SKS* 2, 66 / *EO1*, 59. The demonic esthete Johannes the Seducer also quotes Horace playfully. See *SKS* 2, 414 / *EO1*, 427.
31   Horace, *Epistles* I, 2, 41–2 as translated in *Complete Works*, p. 263.
32   *SKS* 2, 281 / *EO1*, 292.
33   *Pap.* III B 122:6. Horace, *Epistles* I, 1, 46. Another reference to Horace in the drafts for this volume of *Either/Or* can be found in *Pap.* III B 122:11.

close to Horace's original meaning. In the passage quoted Horace exhorts his reader to listen to "philosophy's mandates" and not "care for the things that you crave and admire in your folly" such as wealth and social position. He warns that the pursuit of such things leads to the desperate, reckless actions: "with anguish of mind and at risk to your life...you go, business obsessed, as a trader to the farthermost Hindus, / Fleeing poverty ever by sea and through fire and at cliff's brink."[34] For Kierkegaard, this image "excellently depicts" the despair of those who seek satisfaction in such worldly aims; his fondness for this image is evident not only here, but in the fact that he repeats it in several other places.[35]

A also employs Horace's words to explain the life of reflective enjoyment, which A recommends as a way of escaping the problems that plague the life of immediate enjoyment. Rather than seeking to immerse oneself in enjoyable experiences while avoiding boring or painful experiences, A recommends a kind of reflective detachment from one's actual experiences in which one forgets what actually happened but then remembers them in a creatively reconstructed way. This life employs a kind of poetic recollection in which actual experiences are poetically altered in their recollection, thereby allowing for infinite variety and enjoyment. This requires that one be willing and able to "forget" every experience as it actually happened. In what may be the best-known reference to Horace in Kierkegaard's works, A concludes: "Thus *nil admirari* [marvel at nothing] is the proper wisdom of life. No part of life ought to have so much meaning for a person that he cannot forget it any moment he wants to."[36] At first glance it seems that A has here distorted the original meaning of Horace's famous phrase, which Horace actually borrows from Pythagoras.[37] Horace does offer this advice as the proper wisdom of life, but for Horace this phrase describes an almost Stoic attitude toward life that is very different from any version of the aesthetic life of enjoyment. Horace's meaning is that one should maintain a kind of ethical self-composure and self-control and not become enthralled with worldly goods like wealth and fame. Yet there is an odd sort of Stoicism or asceticism at work in the way of life A recommends. Being able to control one's attachments to things in life in order to have the freedom to enjoy them reflectively constitutes a certain kind of self-control and self-denial, what A calls "the principle of limitation, the sole saving principle in the world."[38]

In the second volume of *Either/Or*, Judge Wilhelm also makes frequent use of Horace. It may even be that Horace's *Epistles* served as a literary model for Kierkegaard while constructing the second volume of *Either/Or*. Horace pioneered the art of publishing letters in verse, sometimes addressed to imaginary characters. Moreover, some of Horace's epistles are addressed to a young hedonist and offer the kind of passionate exhortations to give up the life of pleasure and live an ethical life that we find Judge Wilhelm offering to A. Occasionally, the judge quotes Horace's *Epistles* when offering ethical advice. Judge Wilhelm quotes the line discussed above,

---

34   Horace, *Epistles*, I, 1, 40–46 as translated in *Complete Works*, p. 260.
35   See *SKS* 3, 195 / *EO2*, 202. *SKS* 6, 322 / *SLW*, 347. *Pap.* V B 135:4.
36   *SKS* 2, 282 / *EO1*, 293. Horace, *Epistles* I, 6, 1.
37   Horace, *Complete Works*, p. 270n.
38   *SKS* 2, 281 / *EO1*, 292.

acknowledging that A has "composure only by contrast with the person who is still pursuing phantoms of enjoyment *per mare pauperiem fugiens*" but asserting that A lacks "a secure and revitalizing confidence in life."[39] In contrast to the desperation of the aesthetic life, the judge asserts that living ethically "gives life peace, safety, and security, because it continually calls to us: *Quod petis, hic est* [What you are seeking is here]."[40] This line comes from a letter in which Horace addresses a busy world traveler and advises him that the goal of his wanderings is at home, that "if your mind is at peace" a simple village can provide contentment.[41] Judge Wilhelm also makes use of Horace's aesthetic advice in making an ethical point about A's conception of love. The judge accuses A of "the very deepest profaning of the eternal power of erotic love" by reducing love to isolated, unrepeatable moments such as when lovers see each other for the first time.[42] Focusing on such "accidental circumstances" the judge explains that "it is no wonder that you are uneasy and that you classify these symbols and 'gesticulations' with the things about which one does not dare to say: *decies repetita placebunt* [they will please even when repeated ten times]."[43] Here Judge Wilhelm borrows Horace's advice on writing poetry of lasting value, but the judge employs this advice in the service of making an ethical point.

Yet not all of the judge's references to Horace are immediately aimed at making ethical points. The judge also quotes Horace when describing A, especially when emphasizing A's wit and aesthetic sophistication. For example, Judge Wilhelm says of A "you are indeed a virtuoso, you, *cui di dederunt formam, divitias, artemque fruendi* [to whom the gods gave beauty, wealth, and the art of enjoyment].[44] Later the judge adds, "but you also have pathos, courage, an *os rotundum* [round mouth] from which eloquence gushes."[45] Like A, Judge Wilhelm is fond of Horace for the grace and beauty of his expressions, and not just for his ethical insights. Thus, we can see that it is not simply the case that Kierkgaard's aesthetic pseudonyms turn to Horace for his aesthetic advice and sophistication and his ethical pseudonyms turn to Horace for his ethical advice. We see that Kierkegaard, expressing himself in both the aesthetic and the ethical pseudonyms of *Either/Or*, consistently turns to Horace for the beauty and sophistication of his language as well as for his insights into how to live.

This pattern remains largely true for the works that immediately followed *Either/Or*. Kierkegaard continues to turn to Horace for ethical insights in other works published in 1843, namely, *Fear and Trembling* and its accompanying *Three Upbuilding Discourses*. In *Fear and Trembling* Kierkegaard's pseudonymous author, Johannes de silentio, uses a quotation from Horace at a key place in his discussion of the strangely repelling nature of faith and the hero of faith. Describing

---

[39] *SKS* 3, 195 / *EO2*, 202. Horace, *Epistles* I, 1, 46.

[40] *SKS* 3, 305 / *EO2*, 323. Horace, *Epistles* I, 11, 29.

[41] Horace, *Epistles* 1, 11, 30 as translated in *Complete Works*, p. 279.

[42] *SKS* 3, 139 / *EO2*, 141.

[43] *SKS* 3, 140 / *EO2*, 141. Horace, *Epistles* II, 3 (*Ars Poetica*), 365.

[44] *SKS* 3, 32 / *EO2*, 24. Horace, *Epistles* I, 4, 6.

[45] *SKS* 3, 122 / *EO2*, 122. Horace, *Epistles* II, 3 (*Ars Poetica*), 323.

the sympathy one can feel toward the ethical hero in contrast to the strangeness and incomprehensibility of faith and the knight of faith, Johannes says:

> I am not unfamiliar with what the world has admired as great and magnanimous. My soul feels its kinship with it and in all humility is certain that the cause for which the hero strives is also my cause, and when I consider it, I cry out to myself: *jam tua res agitur* [now your cause is at stake.] I *think* myself *into* the hero; I cannot think myself into Abraham.[46]

This reference comes from one of the didactic epistles discussed above. In addition to his advice to avoid gossips and loose talk, Horace uses an analogy to exhort his reader to come to the defense of a friend being slandered since one's own reputation is imperiled when one's friends are attacked: "*You* are in danger whenever the house of a neighbor is burning, / And, if the fire is not checked, its intensity only increases."[47] In another place in *Fear and Trembling* Johannes borrows a phrase from Horace to describe how the "movement" of infinite resignation must be freely taken upon oneself. He expresses exasperation at "the various misunderstandings, the awkward positions, the botched up movements" he has encountered, and he insists that since the movement of resignation is properly a movement of spirit, it must be made freely rather than as a result of necessity: "It is essential that it not be a unilateral result of a *dira necessitas* [cruel constraint of necessity], and the more this is present, the more doubtful it always is that the movement is normal."[48] Likewise, in one of the *Upbuilding Discourses* that was published on the same day as *Fear and Trembling* and *Repetition*, Kierkegaard employs one of his favorite images from Horace to illustrate an ethical insight on the nature of care: "an ancient pagan has already said: It does not help a person to ride away from care; it is sitting behind him on the horse."[49] Kierkegaard was so fond of this image that he repeated it in a later discourse[50] and in a letter from 1848.[51]

In the works from 1844 and after, Kierkegaard continues to quote Horace often, but he seldom turns to Horace for meaningful insights into ethical or aesthetic matters. Sometimes he borrows witty, satirical lines from Horace to humorous effect. For example, in *Prefaces*, the eighth preface begins with a humorous epigraph: "What I predict will either happen or it will not happen—Apollo has granted me the gift of prophecy.—Tiresias."[52] In this preface, Kierkegaard's pseudonym Nicolaus Notabene makes a satirical call for a new philosophical journal, and this quotation

---

[46]   *SKS* 4, 128 / *FT*, 33. Horace, *Epistles* I, 18, 84. Note that in Horace's Latin the phrase begins "*nam tua...*"
[47]   Horace, *Epistles* 1, 18, 84–5 as translated in *Complete Works*, p. 293.
[48]   *SKS* 4, 140 / *FT*, 46. Horace, *Odes*, III, 24, 6.
[49]   *SKS* 5, 83 / *EUD*, 74. Horace, *Odes*, III, 1, 40.
[50]   *SV1* XII, 285 / *WA*, 183.
[51]   *B&A*, vol. 1, 203 / *LD*, 256, Letter 185 (to J.L.A. Kolderup-Rosenvinge, August 8, 1848). Kierkegaard makes another reference to Horace in a different letter to this same acquaintance written a few months later. See *B&A*, vol. 1, 232 / *LD*, 294, Letter 211 (to J.L.A. Kolderup-Rosenvinge, July 1849).
[52]   *SKS* 4, 508 / *P*, 47. Horace, *Satires*, II, 5, 59–60. Another reference to Horace in *Prefaces* can be found in the fifth preface, *SKS* 4, 492 / *P*, 30.

from Horace's satirical dialogue between Odysseus and Tiresias sets the mood. Notabene acknowledges the difficulty of starting a new journal of this sort, and the reference to Tiresias' "prophecy" presumably points to Notabene's ambivalence about whether or not he will succeed. Kierkegaard also uses this satirical "prophecy" in his witty critique of modern life in his *Literary Review of Two Ages*, although here he mistakenly attributes the quotation to Thales rather than Tiresias.[53] In *Stages*, he also implants a reference to Horace's (fictional) lover Lalage in the speech of the esthete known as "the Young Man" in much the way he did for *Either/Or*'s A, as a way of showing his aesthetic sophistication.[54]

In *Stages* and the works that follow Kierkegaard occasionally repeated images or phrases he had referenced earlier. However, in these works we see a general shift in the way Kierkegaard makes use of Horace. Although *Stages* contains more references to Horace than any other work, and although Kierkegaard continued to pepper his later works with references to Horace, most of the references to Horace in *Stages* and in later works consist of inconsequential stock phrases in Latin that just happen to be borrowed from Horace. For example, Kierkegaard employs phrases like *"adhuc sub judice lis"*[55] [the case is still before the court], *"poscimur"* [we are called upon],[56] *"tenax propositi"*[57] [tenacious of purpose] and *"in verba magistri"*[58] [to the master's words] in various contexts. Kierkegaard no longer mentions Horace by name, and it seems largely incidental that these phrases come from Horace. These references reflect no serious engagement with Horace's ideas on Kierkegaard's behalf. Examples of this sort of usage are not entirely absent from earlier works,[59] but they are rare; in contrast, this sort of usage becomes the norm throughout *Stages on Life's Way*[60] and in later works.[61]

What explains this shift in Kierkegaard's usage of Horace? It may simply be that over time Kierkegaard became less and less familiar with the details of Horace's thought and remembered only these simple phrases. But there is also evidence that Kierkegaard had a change of heart with respect to Horace, as he did with "pagan" authors more generally. In his later writings, Kierkegaard sought to put some

---

[53]   *SKS* 8, 100 / *TA*, 106.

[54]   *SKS* 6, 38–9 / *SLW*, 34. Horace, *Odes*, I, 22, 10–11. Kierkegaard also makes reference to these lines in a draft for his *Book on Adler*: *Pap.* VII–2, B 235, p. 132.

[55]   *SKS* 6, 198 / *SLW*, 211. Horace, *Epistles* II, 3 (*Ars Poetica*), 78. Kierkegaard also references this phrase at *SV1* VII, 52 / *COR*, 13 and *SV1* XII, 463 / *JFY*, 196.

[56]   *SKS* 6, 108 / *SLW*, 114. Horace, *Odes*, I, 32. Kierkegaard also references this phrase at *SKS* 6, 258 / *SLW*, 277.

[57]   *SV1* XIII, 417 / *COR*, 23.

[58]   *SKS* 7, 70 / *CUP1*, 68. Horace, *Epistles* I, 1, 14.

[59]   For example, Kierkegaard borrows Horace's phrase *"disjecta membra"* [separated members] in a journal entry from 1842 and again in *Stages on Life's Way*. See *SKS* 18, 309, JJ:505 and *SKS* 6, 65 / *SLW*, 64.

[60]   For instances of this kind of usage in the text and drafts of *Stages*, see *SKS* 6, 71 / *SLW*, 71. *SKS* 6, 126 / *SLW*, 132. *SKS* 6, 129 / *SLW*, 133. *SKS* 6, 163 / *SLW*, 175. *SKS* 6, 440 / *SLW*, 478. *Pap.* V B 175:6. *Pap.* V B 191.

[61]   See *SV1* XIV, 194 / *M*, 182. *SV1* XIV, 244 / *M*, 229. *SV1* XIV, 251 / *M*, 236. *Pap.* VII–2 B 235, p. 209 / *BA*, 121.

distance between "pagan" teachings of Greek and Roman antiquity and specifically Christian teachings. For example, in *The Sickness Unto Death*, Kierkegaard's pseudonym talks about the "spiritless" despair inherent in all pagan thinking: "That is what the ancient Church Fathers meant when they said that the virtues of the pagans were glittering vices: they meant that the heart of paganism was despair."[62] There are a few passages in which Kierkegaard makes reference to Horace in a way that is unmistakably critical. For example, Kierkegaard more than once explicitly condemns Horace's call of *nil admirari*.[63] He also criticizes the view of guilt, and repentance, he suggests, we can find in Horace if we "understand the poet's words *nulla pallescere culpa* [no wrongdoing to turn us pale] to refer to the brazenness that does not turn pale at guilt" since "in that case the principle is extremely unethical."[64] Of course, it is quite possible that anyone who interprets *nulla pallascere culpa* in this way misreads Horace. From the passage from which this line is taken, it is clear that Horace is urging his reader to have a clear conscience by remaining virtuous. Of course Kierkegaard, writing from a Christian perspective, may doubt whether remaining virtuous is possible, but in any case it is clear that Horace does *not* urge us to be brazenly unremorseful while continuing to commit vice. Likewise, Kierkegaard may misread Horace if he interprets *nil admirari* as A does in *Either/Or*. In any case, whether or not Kierkegaard outgrew or decisively renounced his earlier admiration for Horace as a purveyor of wise aesthetic and ethical advice, the words of Horace that he learned as a child and taught as a young man remained with him throughout his life.

---

[62]   *SKS* 11, 161 / *SUD*, 46.
[63]   *SKS* 5, 224 / *EUD*, 225–6 and *SKS* 6, 437 / *SLW*, 474.
[64]   *SKS* 6, 438 / *SLW*, 475. Horace, *Epistles* I, 1, 61.

Bibliography

I. Horace's Works in The Auction Catalogue *of Kierkegaard's Library*

Q. Horatii Flacci Opera, Leipzig: Tauchnitz 1828 (*ASKB* 1248).
Q. Horatii Flacci Opera Omnia, vols. 1–2, ed. by Friedericus Guil. Doering, Leipzig: Hahn 1815–24 (*ASKB* A I 162–163).
Horazens Briefe, vols. 1–2, trans. and ed. by C.M. Wieland, Leipzig: in der Weidmannschen Buchhandlung 1816 (*ASKB* A I 164–165).

II. Works in The Auction Catalogue *of Kierkegaard's Library that Discuss Horace*

Adler, Adolph Peter, *Optegnelser fra en Reise*, Copenhagen: C.A. Reitzel 1849, p. III (*ASKB* 2041).
Bähr, Johann Christian Felix, *Abriss der Römischen Literatur-Geschichte zum Gebrauch für höhere Lehranstalten*, Heidelberg and Leipzig: Groos 1833 (*ASKB* 975).
Döring, Heinrich, *Joh. Gottfr. von Herder's Leben*, 2nd enlarged and revised ed., Weimar: Wilhelm Hoffmann 1829, p. 271; p. 290 (*ASKB* A I 134).
Dyck, Johann Gottfried and Georg Schatz (eds.), *Charaktere der vornehmsten Dichter aller Nationen; nebst kritischen und historischen Abhandlungen über Gegenstände der schönen Künste und Wissenschaften, von einer Gesellschaft von Gelehrten*, vols. 1–8, Leipzig: Dyk 1792–1808, vol. 1, p. 6; pp. 10–11; p. 23; p. 31; p. 33; vol. 4, pp. 409–96; vol. 5, pp. 301–34; vol. 6, pp. 395–450 (*ASKB* 1370–1377).
Flögel, Carl Friedrich, *Geschichte der komischen Litteratur*, vols. 1–4, Liegnitz and Leipzig: David Siegert 1784–87, vol. 1, p. 9; vol. 2, pp. 23–30 (*ASKB* 1396–1399).
[Hamann, Johann Georg], *Hamann's Schriften*, vols. 1–8, ed. by Friedrich Roth, Berlin: G. Reimer 1821–43, vol. 2, p. 267; p. 392; p. 417; vol. 3, p. 69; vol. 4, p. 70; p. 75; p. 79; p. 87; p. 91; p. 96; p. 114; p 173; p. 217; p. 281; p. 424; vol. 5, p. 129; vol. 7, p. 76; p. 254; p. 261 (*ASKB* 536–544).
[Hegel, Georg Wilhelm Friedrich], *Georg Wilhelm Friedrich Hegel's Vorlesungen über die Aesthetik*, vols. 1–3, ed. by von Heinrich Gustav Hotho, Berlin: Duncker und Humblot 1835–38 (vols. 10.1–10.3 in *Georg Wilhelm Friedrich Hegel's Werke. Vollständige Ausgabe*, vols. 1–18, ed. by Philipp Marheineke et al., Berlin: Duncker und Humblot 1832–45) (*ASKB* 1384–1386).
Longin, Dionysius, *Dionysius Longin vom Erhabenen Griechisch und Teutsch, Nebst dessen Leben, einer Nachricht von seinen Schriften, und einer Untersuchung, was*

Longin durch das Erhabene verstehe, trans. and ed. by Carl Heinrich Heineken, Leipzig and Hamburg: Conrad König 1738, p. 109 (*ASKB* 1129).

Meierotto, Johann Heinrich Ludwig, *Ueber Sitten und Lebensart der Römer in verschiedenen Zeiten der Republik*, vols. 1–2, 3rd revised and enlarged ed., Berlin: in der Myliussischen Buchhandlung 1814 (*ASKB* 656).

Meiners, Christoph, *Geschichte des Verfalls der Sitten und der Staatsverfassung der Römer*, Leipzig: bey Weidmanns Erben und Reich 1782, p. 178; p. 200 (*ASKB* 660).

[Møller, Poul Martin], *Efterladte Skrifter af Poul M. Møller*, vols. 1–3, ed. by Christian Winther F.C. Olsen and Christen Thaarup, Copenhagen: C.A. Reitzel 1839–43, vol. 2, p. 28; p. 385; vol. 3, p. 3; p. 79 (*ASKB* 1574–1576).

[Montaigne, Michel de], *Michael Montaigne's Gedanken und Meinungen über allerley Gegenstände, ins Deutsche übersetzt*, vols. 1–7, Berlin: F.T. Lagarde 1793–99, vol. 3, p. 191; vol. 5, p. 224 (*ASKB* 681–687).

Mynster, Jakob Peter, *Den hedenske Verden ved Christendommens Begyndelse*, Copenhagen: Schultz 1850, p. 20 (*ASKB* 693).

—— *Blandede Skrivter*, vols. 1–3, Copenhagen: Den Gyldendalske Boghandlings Forlag 1852–53 [vols. 4–6, Copenhagen: Den Gyldendalske Boghandlings Forlag 1855–57], vol. 2, p. 308; p. 360; vol. 3, p. 284 (*ASKB* 358–363).

Schlegel, August Wilhelm, *Ueber dramatische Kunst und Litteratur. Vorlesungen*, vols. 1–2 (vol. 2 in two Parts), Heidelberg: Mohr und Zimmer 1809–11, vol. 2.1, p. 18 (*ASKB* 1392–1394).

Schmidt, W. Adolf, *Geschichte der Denk--und Glaubensfreiheit im ersten Jahrhundert der Kaiserherrschaft und des Christenthums*, Berlin: Verlag von Veit und Comp. 1847, p. 112; p. 116; p. 119; pp. 122–7; p. 135; p. 144; pp. 147–8; pp. 256–8; p. 261; p. 265; pp. 267–8; p. 276; pp. 286–7; pp. 292–301; pp. 307–12 passim; p. 423 (*ASKB* 771).

Schopenhauer, Arthur, *Die Welt als Wille und Vorstellung*, vols. 1–2, 2nd revised and enlarged ed., Leipzig: F.A. Brockhaus 1844 [1819], vol. 1, p. 21; p. 359; p. 582; vol. 2, p. 409; p. 426 (*ASKB* 773–773a).

[Solger, Karl Wilhelm Ferdinand], *K.W.F. Solger's Vorlesungen über Aesthetik*, ed. by K.W.L. Heyse, Leipzig: F.A. Brockhaus 1829, p. 19; p. 288; p. 302 (*ASKB* 1387).

[Sulzer, Johann George], *Johann George Sulzers vermischte philosophische Schriften. Aus den Jahrbüchern der Akademie der Wissenschaften zu Berlin gesammelt*, vols. 1–2, Leipzig: bey Weidmanns Erben und Reich 1773–81 [the title of the second volume is modified and reads as follows, *Johann George Sulzers vermischte Schriften. Eine Fortsetzung der vermischten philosophischen Schriften desselben. Nebst einigen Nachrichten von seinem Leben, und seinen sämtlichen Werken*], vol. 1, p. 131; vol. 2, main text, p. 82; p. 119 (*ASKB* 807–808).

—— *Allgemeine Theorie der Schönen Künste, in einzeln, nach alphabetischer Ordnung der Kunstwörter auf einander folgenden, Artikeln abgehandelt*, vols. 1–4 and a Register Volume, 2nd revised ed., Leipzig: in der Weidmannschen Buchhandlung 1792–99, vol. 1, p. 27; p. 38; p. 73; p. 113; p. 127; p. 140; p. 145; p. 169; pp. 204–5; p. 223; p. 259; pp. 398ff.; p. 407; p. 465; p. 487; p. 493; p. 497;

pp. 521–2; pp. 608–9; p. 612; p. 700; vol. 2, pp. 651ff.; vol. 3, p. 182; p. 211; p. 261; p. 551; vol. 4, pp. 144ff.; p. 416 (*ASKB* 1365–1369).

Thiersch, Friedrich, *Allgemeine Aesthetik in akademischen Lehrvorträgen*, Berlin: G. Reimer 1846, p. 11; p. 87; p. 166 (*ASKB* 1378).

Thomsen, Grimur, *Om den nyfranske Poesie, et Forsøg til Besvarelse af Universitetets æsthetiske Priisspørgsmaal for 1841: "Har Smag og Sands for Poesi gjort Frem-eller Tilbageskridt i Frankrig i de sidste Tider og hvilken Aarsagen?,"* Copenhagen: Paa den Wahlske Boghandlings Forlag 1843, p. 10; p. 58; p. 116; p. 155 (*ASKB* 1390).

Zimmermann, Johann Georg, *Ueber die Einsamkeit*, vols. 1–4, Leipzig: bey Weidmanns Erben und Reich 1784–85, vol. 1, p. 59 (*ASKB* 917–920).

III. Secondary Literature on Kierkegaard's Relation to Horace

None.

Livy:

The History of Rome in Kierkegaard's Works

Nataliya Vorobyova

I. The Author of The History of Rome from Its Foundation

"The Roman historian does not have a history of his own."[1] These words by the French philosopher Hippolyte Adolphe Taine (1828–93) offer the best summary of how much we know about Titus Livius, more commonly known as Livy. He did not leave any accounts of his own life, nor did he include abstracts of personal experience in his monumental work. What we know today about Livy comes from a few anecdotes found in the works of later Roman authors. He was born in Patavium in 59 BC, today's Padua in Italy, into a prosperous family of native citizens.

Knabe calls attention to an unusual coincidence. The life of a Roman, before he reached full maturity as a man and citizen, was divided into a number of seven-year cycles.[2] If one looks at these cycles of Livy's life, it becomes apparent that they match particular phases of the historical crisis of the Roman Republic, and each seventh year was a milestone in the story.[3] The life of the historian unfolded in the same rhythm as that of his motherland. Livy witnessed the transformation of the Republic into an empty name without a body, as Augustus allowed his army to enter

---

[1]   Hippolyte Adolphe Taine, *Essai sur Tite Live*, Paris: L. Hachette 1874 [1856], p. 1. See also Will Durant, *Caesar and Christ: A History of Roman Civilization and of Christianity from their Beginnings to A.D. 325*, New York: Simon and Schuster 1944 (vol. 3 of Will Durant, *The Story of Civilization*, vols. 1–10, New York: Simon and Schuster 1939–67), p. 272.

[2]   At first, a man was "devoid of words" and considered *infans*, always at home and under the strict and loving eye of his mother. Between the ages of 7 and 14, he would become *puer*, or a boy. In this period of his life the attention would be focused on developing physical fitness and vigor, as well as on getting a proper education either at school or from private tutorials. Becoming 15 marked a turning point in the life of a young man. A medallion with incense, a sign of childhood, was exchanged for a toga, which symbolized maturity and allowed the boy to become *iuvenis*—someone who is already allowed to participate in public life, but only as an observer, a companion to a political or public leader. The end of the third cycle was traditionally marked either by marriage or entrance into the army. Finally, from the ages of 21 to 28, the young man was seen as *adulscens*—someone who became a rightful citizen, and could obtain low positions at the magistrates, yet without great public or political influence.

[3]   G.S. Knabe, "Rome of Titus Livy—Image, Myth and History," in Titus Livy, *History of Rome from its Foundation*, vols. 1–3, Moscow: Ladomir 2002, vol. 3, p. 661.

the city, creating a new ruling apparatus and transforming the empire into his own private household. Livy's regret and the feeling of nostalgia towards the values of the old Rome would emerge between the lines of his *History*.

The political upheavals that took place in Rome in the 30s BC. did not, however, disturb the flow of Livy's life, which seemed untroubled at that time. Livy moved to Rome and started a family. It is not known who his wife was, but he had at least two sons—the elder one died in childhood,[4] and the younger one became famous as the author of works on geography. He also had a daughter who later married Lucius Magius, who is mentioned in Seneca the Elder's *Controversies* (X, 2) as his son-in-law.

It seems that Livy's education and family fortune made it possible for him to fully devote himself to his studies. Around the year 27 BC he started writing his epic work. We do not have any accounts of Livy's public speeches or participation in politics, which has led scholars to believe that his work consumed all his time and energy. In the year AD 14 he returned to his hometown, where he worked presumably until his death at the age of 76 in AD 17.

Livy was a well-known person, and there is a famous anecdote told by Pliny the Younger that once a man came all the way from Cadiz in Andalusia from the legendary edges of the earth to see the historian.[5] Yet, Livy was not a very popular man. There was, it is said, never a large audience when he recited his work. Compared to his more popular contemporary, the elegant poet Ovid, the serious historian from Padua lacked charm, irony, and other cosmopolitan qualities. His world-view was in contradiction with that of the Roman literary elite; he always remained a provincial. It comes as no surprise that Livy probably died in Padua, though he possibly owned a house somewhere to the northeast of Rome because he gives remarkably accurate descriptions of the valley of the river Anio.

Livy's work, *The History of Rome from its Foundation* or *Ab urbe condita*, altogether contained 142 books. This number is quite impressive, especially taking into account that it probably took him 45 years to finish the work. The original only partly survives, as the books 11–20 and 46–142 were never found. However, it is possible to reconstruct their content thanks to the existence of the *Periochae*, summaries of the work from the fourth century. Livy arranged his material according to pentades and decades. These organizational categories are named after the number of scrolls on which the book was originally written: pentades were groups of five scrolls, and decades were the groups of ten. Unfortunately, there is no information about the publishing history of the work. Critics have noticed that, paradoxically, the books of *The History* which present Rome in the most unpleasant light are missing.

Livy drew his information about Roman history almost entirely from the published works of earlier annalists, and so a study of the annalistic tradition becomes an essential prerequisite for an assessment of his reliability as a historian. In the introduction to his monograph Luce suggests:

4   *Inscriptiones Latinae Selectae*, ed. by H. Dessau, Rome: Instituto Italiano per la Storia Antica 1954, 2919.
5   Pliny, *Epistulae*, Book II, 3. (English translation: *The Letters of the Younger Pliny*, trans. by Betty Radice, Harmondsworth: Penguin 1963, pp. 60–1)

Livy is a stylist, not an interpreter—a writer concerned with producing a dignified, stimulating history of his people that would rival those of the great historians of Greece.... Scholars believe that Livy also saw himself in this light, and when he declares in the Preface that new writers invariably believe they can either bring new and more reliable facts to light or surpass their predecessors in the eloquence of their presentation, it was the second goal he chose for himself, not the first.[6]

This conclusion disqualifies Livy as a historian in the contemporary sense of the word, but it makes of him a historical writer, as a literary critic might say. His goal was not to tell any final truth about events; it was not to unfold the real reasons for what happened in a long history of his country. His aim was rather to tell the story anew, to tell it beautifully and to make it memorable.

After Latin disappeared from the school curriculum, the significance of Livy's creation diminished, for he only used different methods of factual adaptations and did not offer new interpretations. Therefore, for a long time the prevailing opinion was that Livy's only merits were his style, narration and rhetoric, while looking at Livy in terms of an organizer or a historian was rather unpopular. Scholars have frequently accused him of providing no original groupings of his material or combining various accounts of the same event found in various sources, or focusing on a new, reactionary interpretation of the most significant events contemporary to him. For example, Luce writes:

> Kurt Witte at the end of his study on Livy's use of Polybius stated flatly that Livy did not look beyond the single episode or attempt to combine the *Einzelerzählungen* into larger, integrated units. Since Livy generally preferred to follow a single source over longer stretches, the subject matter as well as its order and arrangement derived largely from his sources.[7]

This view only supports the idea that Livy's work lacks what we call today scientific objectivity. However, Livy scholars agree and admit that eloquence is his strong point.

Relying heavily upon the annalist's tradition, as has been already mentioned, he took from it two important aspects: the focus on virtue and ethics which makes his tone rather moralistic, and the incorporation of examples. Besides, as Luce suggests, the historian used two essential methods in designing the narrative. First of all, the text has a visible thematic unity. For instance: a close look at Book II, which covers a period 509–468 BC, shows that Livy, instead of narrating the events chronologically, decided to add to his presentation a slight moralistic overtone and draws the main attention to the motif of *libertas*.[8] Luce claims that it is quite easy to find similar themes, which represent one of the virtues of early Rome, around which the books were revolving. So, if Book II is devoted to *libertas*, Book V is focused on *pietas*, etc. The second traceable method is architectonic, which was achieved "by placing important and carefully developed episodes at certain preferred points within books

---

6   Torrey James Luce, *Livy: The Composition of His History*, Princeton, New Jersey: Princeton University Press 1977, p. xvii.
7   Ibid., p. 25.
8   Ibid., p. 26.

or pentades." In this way "special focus, balance, and even symmetry could be achieved."[9] Luce's claim contradicts the opinion which argues for the insignificance of *The History*, for it shows that the interpretation of the events was not the prevailing method in historical studies of the time.

Luce in his study of Livy outlines the probable way in which the historian worked. Without doubt Livy used later sources since they very conveniently represented previous research, thereby saving himself the trouble of going back to earlier authorities. He completely relied on those accounts, and, as noted by Chaplin, "often associated the use of *exempla* with 'voices of experience,' men who lived long enough to offer advice based on personal knowledge."[10] According to Luce, Livy had three preparatory steps before beginning writing. The first one was extensive reading on long periods of Roman history, which helped him to produce the outline for the work and give it a structure. "After this stage Livy went back to the start once more. The second step was to read through the main blocks of the core material for periods of at least a consular year in the later books."[11] At this step he produced his own adaptations. And finally, he went to the start once again to write up the material section by section. This is how the material got broken into small episodes or units. In the case of the foreign sources, such as for instance Polybius' text, Livy did not translate word for word, but read the original and then wrote down the passage from memory.

For some reason Livy avoided admitting his presence as a writer in the text. There are very few asides in Livy's own person and very few generalized comments. He preferred to retell simple stories which praised Roman virtues and their opposites. Luce claims, "To a large extent this approach caused him to treat history as a panorama—a series of episodes embodying moral virtues."[12]

Another interesting issue concerning *The History of Rome from its Foundation* is the question of who was the intended audience, the addressees of this epic? Chaplin suggests that Livy had

> three voices for articulating *exempla* within *The History*. The least frequent of these is that of the historian in his role as narrator: explicit moralising, editorialising or the introduction of an exemplary episode can call out this voice. Much more often, Livy introduces *exempla* through either the speeches or the thoughts of historical characters.[13]

As Solodow points out,[14] one of Livy's narrative techniques is "to depict an internal audience responding to a person or an event in the very way the historian wants his contemporary audience to do."[15] Consequently, it is possible to speak about the

---

9   Ibid., p. 27.
10   Jane D. Chaplin, *Livy's Exemplary History*, New York: Oxford University Press 2000, p. 37.
11   Luce, *Livy: The Composition of His History*, p. 228.
12   Ibid., p. 231.
13   Chaplin, *Livy's Exemplary History*, p. 50.
14   Joseph. B. Solodow, "Livy and the Story of Horatius," *Transcriptions of the American Philological Association*, vol. 109, 1974, pp. 251–68.
15   Chaplin, *Livy's Exemplary History*, p. 51.

so-called "internal audience," who generate the response of the spectators, that is, observers, but from within the text.

There can be no doubt, that Livy's monumental work presents an illustrative and exciting narrative, which, even though lacking historical merits, offers rather entertaining and educational reading. It demonstrates an entirely different perspective on history itself, where the attention is directed not to the organization of facts into a comprehensive and even ideological narrative, but to the ethical values which shaped society and history.

II. Livy at the Borgerdyd School

It is most likely that Livy's text, like other works which Kierkegaard studied in his Latin classes at the Borgerdyd School, made a significant impact on the later works of the philosopher. There is a school evaluation dating from 1830, which represents the general assessment of Kierkegaard as a student and also includes a summary of the texts he studied at the school, and on which he had chosen to be tested at the exam. There we find: "He has read and presented: In Latin:...the first Pentade by Livy."[16] Livy's name thus can be found in the curriculum among Latin authors such as Horace, Virgil, and Cicero.

A closer reading of the memoirs of some of Kierkegaard's friends or acquaintances indicates that Latin was a special subject for the young Søren, mainly because of the professor Michael Nielsen (1776–1846). Although the recollections of events which occurred during Kierkegaard's school years may be somewhat twisted, since the narrators wanted to fit them into their later image of the philosopher, the stories nonetheless presumably have a grain of truth, such as an incident told by Martin Attrup.[17] The anecdote recalls a history class and illustrates professor Nielsen's special talent for story-telling and the extent to which he influenced young minds:

> One day he had spoken with special warmth about the famous naval battle at Salamis, ca. 500 B.C., when the brave little Greeks defeated the mighty Persian fleet. The next day he examined us boys on the Battle of Salamis....First he asked number one: "Were you there at the Battle of Salamis?" But when P.C.K. [sc. Peter Christian Kierkegaard] answered, "No!" he got a well-directed slap on the head....The question then passed to number three. "Were you there at the Battle of Salamis?" to which Søren Kierkegaard answered, "Yes! I

---

[16]   *B&A*, vol. 1, p. 4 / *LD*, Document V, p. 5. In Bruce H. Kirmmse (ed.), *Encounters with Kierkegaard. A Life as Seen by His Contemporaries* (Princeton, New Jersey: Princeton University Press 1996), School Reports are presented, which were made by the headmaster of the school Michael Nielsen. These "were submitted annually with respect to each group of pupils who intended to matriculate into the University of Copenhagen." (See ibid., p. 273.)
[17]   Kirmmse, *Encounters with Kierkegaard*, p. 271 note: "Martin Attrup (born 1854) was parish clerk and schoolteacher in Hørby on Tuse Næs in northern Zealand....Peter Christian Kierkegaard had graduated from the school in 1822 and Søren Kierkegaard in 1830. Therefore none of the three who are mentioned in this story were in the same class. But one should not necessarily conclude from this that the recollection has merely been fabricated by Attrup, because much of it appears to bear the mark of authenticity. Since Attrup seems to have remembered other things very well...."

was there in spirit, Herr Professor!" The strict headmaster smiled, stroked him on the chin, and exclaimed: "You will be a source of joy and honor to me."[18]

What is impressive in this account is Kierkegaard's sensitivity and imagination. Assuming that this story is representative of the Danish philosopher's true nature, it is easy to trace the significance of such extraordinary impressionability to his written works. For much later he would regularly return to the classical stories, weaving summaries of them into his narrative in the most remarkable fashion.

The next story worth mentioning in the present context is the one told by Hans Peter Holst (1811–93), another of Kierkegaard's classmates, who reveals the philosopher's lack of eloquence in the Danish language in the early years. Referring to Kierkegaard's first book, *From the Papers of One Still Living*, Holst writes:

> I literally *rewrote* his [sc. Kierkegaard's] first written work on Andersen—or rather, I translated it from Latin to Danish. It was quite natural that he turned to me for this help, because at the Borgerdyd School we had a regular practice whereby I wrote the Danish essays for him and he wrote the Latin ones for me.[19]

These anecdotes only confirm the relevance of the Latin language, the classical literary tradition, and the extraordinary role played by professor Nielsen in the whole educational process at the school.

According to the *Auction Catalogue*, Kierkegaard owned three different editions of Livy's *History*, all in Latin.[20] One of these was published in Germany, which is a rather important fact since in the nineteenth century Livy's work received a great deal of attention particularly in German classical studies. For a long while, the German school was considered to be one of the most influential regarding *The History*. German scholars focused on identifying the sources, which recurred in the text, consequently neglecting its other aspects. Therefore, it was not until recently that Livy was studied as an organizer or a historian, but there are a number of detailed treatises about his eloquent style, narration and rhetoric. As Luce comments on the scholarly work done by Germans:

> Study of the historian's sources dominated the field, although valuable work was also done on topics such as his Latinity and style. But after a time the spate of *Quellenforschung* began to abate, partly because the *Quellenforscher* began to bicker among themselves, and partly because some began to have misgivings about the validity of some of their methods and results.[21]

---

[18]   Ibid., p. 12.

[19]   Ibid.

[20]   [Livy], *Titi Livii operum omnium*, vols. 1–2, ed. by Rasmus Möller, Copenhagen: Gyldendal 1815–19. (*ASKB* A II 31–32); *T. Livii Patavini Historiarum libri qui supersunt omnes*, vols. 1–5, ed. by Augusto Guil. Ernesti, Leipzig: Weidmann 1801–04 (*ASKB* 1251–1255); Titi Livii Historiarum Libri I–X. Ad fidem optimarum editionum Strothii præcipue et Doeringii; textum exhibuit, horum aliorumque animadversiones excerpsit suasque adiecit Erasmus Möller, ed. by Christian Frederik Ingerslev, Gyldendal 1831, vol. 1 (containing Books I-V) (*ASKB* 1256).

[21]   Luce, *Livy: The Composition of His History*, p. xv.

We do not know whether Kierkegaard was familiar with any of these German achievements; however, it is likely that his editions had detailed commentaries to the original text, which without doubt, influenced and modified both the reading and understanding of *The History.*

The last piece of evidence worth mentioning supports the claim that Kierkegaard not only read Livy's texts, but knew them quite well. This can be found in a letter from Kolderup-Rosenvinge (1792–1850)—a prominent professor of law at the University of Copenhagen, who developed the study of Danish legal history and published widely on old Danish jurisprudence. On Monday afternoons Kierkegaard and Kolderup-Rosenvinge took walks around Copenhagen. From the reading of their correspondence, it becomes clear that the two discussed quite a range of topics. In the aforementioned letter, dated August 20, 1848, Kolderup-Rosenvinge writes:

> I shall add to my apropos about Canaignac an apropos about the French, which Livius (V. 37) gives in the following apt characterization, which I happened to come upon in the course of some work I am doing at present on the oldest French system of justice (I cannot be bothered with the most recent justice or injustice). He calls the French "*nata in vanos tumultus gens*" [a people born for futile tumult]. Is that not marvelous? One has to believe that regardless of all their commotion the French have not progressed much beyond those days with this exception: they have managed to get other people to run along with them or after them.[22]

Unfortunately we will never find out what the topic of this conversation was, but the passage makes it clear that Livy's *History* was a well-known source. It provided scholars with possibilities for illuminating their points on various occasions just by drawing parallels with the ancient text, which was generally familiar to educated people.

Another passage from Kierkegaard's journals shows how he was inspired by Latin history. He noted down quotations, adding comments to the text itself. It is already here we can observe the prevailing tendency to provide a bright and widely recognized illustration of the discussed concept: "*Ea non media sed nulla via est, velut eventum exspectantium, quo fortunae suae consilia applicent.* Livius 32, 21. Splendidly spoken of those who 'have to see results first' before they pass judgments."[23]

III. The History of Rome from Its Foundation *in Kierkegaard's Writings*

A reference to *The History of Rome* appears as early as Kierkegaard's master's thesis, *The Concept of Irony,* where he, while making a remark about Hegel's views on Socrates, writes the following:

> The difficulty implicit in the establishment of certainty about the phenomenal aspect of Socrates' life does not bother Hegel. He generally does not acknowledge such trivial

---

[22]   *B&A,* vol. 1, p. 210 / *LD,* p. 266, Letter 187.

[23]   *SKS* 24, 22, NB21:20 / *JP* 3, 3358. Translation of this passage: "...that is not a middle course, it is no course at all, to play the part of men who have been merely awaiting the event with the intention of adapting our counsels to the decisions of fortune."

concerns. And when the troubled augurs report that the sacred hens will not eat, he replies with Appius Claudius Pulcher, "Then they must drink,"—and so saying throws them overboard. Although he himself observes that with respect to Socrates it is a matter not so much of philosophy as of the individual life, there is nothing at all in his presentation of Socrates in *Geschichte der Philosophie* to illuminate the relations of the three different contemporary views of Socrates. He uses one single dialogue from Plato as an example of the Socratic method without explaining why he chose this particular one.[24]

One of the disputed issues between Kierkegaard and Hegel was the status of the particular human subject and its individual existence in the temporal world. Kierkegaard undertook the task of advocating and restating Socratic categories, adopting them to the Christian context.

One of the paramount conclusions offered in his master's thesis was the development of the character of an ironist—an individual who realizes the absence of all values in the immediate world and, through this, gains superiority. A direct dismissal of Socrates, as it is claimed in the passage quoted above, provoked Kierkegaard, who straightforwardly criticized opinions of this kind. The remark becomes even more bitter after one reads the relevant passage in Livy's *History*, Book XIX (which covers the years 254–241 BC and the text of which we know only from *Periochae*):

> When a certain consul (Publius Claudius Pulcher, son of Appius Claudius) who was anxious to conduct a campaign was prevented from departing by a tribune of the commons, the consul ordered the chickens to be brought. When these failed to eat the grain scattered before them, the consul, mocking the omen, said: "Let them drink, then," and flung them into the Tiber. After that as he was triumphantly returning in his fleet to Africa he lost his life at sea, along with all his men.[25]

Kierkegaard's point in using this anecdote in this context is presumably that Hegel fails to notice and appreciate the genius of Socratic irony. Failing to believe in the predictions, Hegel's fate is to perish, in the same manner as did Pulcher's fleet.

The next reference to Livy's monumental work can be found in *Fear and Trembling*, published in 1843. Its author, Johannes de silentio, in "Problema I," entitled "Is there a Teleological Suspension of the Ethical?" after comparing Jephthah, Agamemnon, and Brutus, enigmatically concludes that "the difference between the tragic hero and Abraham is very obvious. The tragic hero is still within the ethical."[26] In this way he merges the figures from ancient history and the Old Testament. Even though he is moved by the story of Abraham, he insists that there is nothing tragic in the situation of the biblical character, not in the Greek sense of the term at least, adding that the heroism of Jephthah, Agamemnon, and Brutus is comprehensible—they

---

[24]   *SKS* 1, 265–6 / *CI*, 221.

[25]   *CI*, 534 notes. See Livy, *Ab urbe condita*, Book XIX, 12. (English translation quoted from *Livy with and English Translation*, trans. by B.O. Foster, Cambridge, Massachusetts: Harvard University Press 1965–84 (*Loeb Classical Library*), vol. XIV, p. 181.) However, the origin of this passage in Kierkegaard's text might be problematic, as the same account appears in the texts of Valerius Maximus, Suetonius and Cicero.

[26]   *SKS* 4, 152 / *FT*, 59.

sacrificed their children because their moral virtue, devotion to their nation, state or gods were placed higher than parental love. The paradox of this statement lies in the author's view of the ethical and faith *per se*. Even though the author begins the investigation of the problem by saying that "the ethical as such is the universal,"[27] he concludes that "faith is namely this paradox that the single individual is higher that the universal."[28] Therefore, Abraham can appear simultaneously as a murderer and the father of faith. The story of his sacrifice represents an act which puts on one side of the scale personal faith and on the other, a father's love, in this way juxtaposing the ethical and the religious, and letting the religious win out. But a reference to ancient history, for instance to Brutus, opens a slightly different perspective on the whole matter:

> When a son forgets his duty, when the state entrusts the sword of judgment to the father, when the laws demand punishment from the father's hand, then the father must heroically forget that the guilty one is his son, he must nobly hide his agony, but no one in the nation, not even the son, will fail to admire the father, and every time the Roman laws are interpreted, it will be remembered that many interpreted them more learnedly but no one more magnificently than Brutus.[29]

In this case the ethical is in fact the universal, the *telos*, for there is nothing more beyond it. This is why paganism is tragic: it forces the ethical on a human being and makes it the ultimate goal. Being ethical towards the law is valued higher than being ethical towards one's family. It determines the tragic and excludes Abraham from this category, because he had faith or the religious; he does what he does "for God's sake and...for his own sake."[30]

The account devoted to Brutus (Junius) comes from Book II of the *History*, where Livy places the story next to the *exempla* about Mucius Scaevola. In this narrative what is reported is doubly significant, as one of the political consequences of the event is the birth of the Republic. However, de silentio is not touched by the story of the rape of Lucretia, nor by the later expelling of Tarquins from Rome. (Brutus already appears as a key character in this part, as he takes his vengeance on Tarquinus for the death of his father.) After the expulsion of the Etruscan dynasty and the substitution of the monarchy in favor of the rule of aristocracy, there was an attempt to restore the monarchy. Ironically, two of Brutus' sons were caught together with the conspirators. Brutus, being the first consul had to set an example for coming generations of Roman citizens.[31] He sentenced his children to flagellation and decapitation. Stoic norms and values won over the ethical

---

[27]   *SKS* 4, 148 / *FT*, 54.
[28]   *SKS* 4, 149 / *FT*, 55.
[29]   *SKS* 4, 151–2 / *FT*, 58. See Livy, *Ab urbe condita*, Book II, 3–5. (English translation: Livy, *The Early History of Rome*, trans. by Aubrey de Sélincourt, Harmondsworth: Penguin 1960, pp. 108–10.)
[30]   *SKS* 4, 153 / *FT*, 59.
[31]   Will Durant speculates that this story could be of mythological origin; see Durant, *Caesar and Christ*, p. 25.

duty of the father to his sons, and, as de silentio explains, it could not have been otherwise.

A very short reference to Livy's text can be found in *Stages on Life's Way*,[32] a work edited by Hilarius Bogbinder and published in 1845. However, the note is rather insignificant. In a footnote one finds the following passage: "And B. imagined himself persecuted as a demagogue! He is so aristocratic that here he is obviously ridiculing the tribune's speech about the whole body's suffering when one member suffers."[33] This refers to a descriptive passage in *The History*, which describes a famous chapter in the so-called struggle of the orders, that is, the long struggle for political power between the plebians and the patricians. At a particularly tense time when the plebians were threatening armed revolt due to the political inequalities from which they suffered, the plebians sent Menenius Agrippa as their spokesman to go to them and attempt to reason with them. He argued by means of an analogy, comparing the state with the human body, the parts of both of which must work together for the whole to continue to exist. He explained:

> Long ago when the members of the human body did not, as now they do, agree together, but had each its own thoughts and the words to express them in, the other parts resented the fact that they should have the worry and trouble of providing everything for the belly, which remained idle, surrounded by its ministers, with nothing to do but enjoy the pleasant things they gave it. So the discontented members plotted together that the hand should carry no food to the mouth, that the mouth should take nothing that was offered it, and that the teeth should accept nothing to chew. But alas! while they sought in their resentment to subdue the belly by starvation, they themselves and the whole body wasted away to nothing. By this it was apparent that the belly, too, has no mean service to perform: it receives food, indeed; but it also nourishes in its turn the other members, giving back to all parts of the body, through all its veins, the blood it has made by the process of digestion; and upon this blood our life and our health depend.[34]

In the current political crisis, it was clear that the belly represented the patricians, who seemed to do nothing, and the rest of the body represented the plebians, who had to work hard apparently for no reward to keep the patricians satisfied. The analogy demonstrated that, in fact, the plebians, like the belly, did perform an important service, and that both classes had to work together in harmony if the state were to continue to exist.

Lengthy and elaborate references to *The History* can be found in the *Concluding Unscientific Postscript*, signed by the name of Johannes Climacus and published in February 1846. A passage in the chapter which discusses subjective truth and inwardness is devoted to the recurring theme of sin and its forgiveness through faith. The author classifies forgiveness as a Socratic paradox, since in forgiveness the relationship between the "eternal truth" and "an existing person"[35] is at stake. In forgiveness the finite and infinite are in unity. For the subject, the first step to

---

[32]   *SLW*, 740 notes.
[33]   *SKS* 6, 442n / *SLW*, 480n.
[34]   Livy, *Ab urbe condita*, Book II, 32. (*The Early History of Rome*, trans. by Aubrey de Sélincourt, pp. 141–2.)
[35]   *SKS* 7, 204 / *CUP1*, 224.

understanding forgiveness is to realize, with the deepest pain, the fact that he or she has sinned. Faith, being the "resilience of inwardness," assists in the comprehension and grasping of forgiveness, even though it has to "battle in just this way, as the Romans once did, blinded by the light of the sun."[36] This poetic and rather conspicuous comparison in this case, is inspired by Livy's *History*, as the commentators affirm:

> The Romans, under Cornelius Scipio Africanus, were victorious over Hannibal's army at Zama in northern Africa (202 B.C.) in the Second Punic war. Climacus apparently confuses the report of this battle and conditions with some other account, perhaps that of the battle at Cannae in South Italy (216 B.C.), where, however, the Romans were defeated by Hannibal's army.[37]

Even though the reference has a degree of inaccuracy, the precision of the parallel Kierkegaard draws between the episode and the characteristics of faith is undeniable. This is the passage from Livy which Climacus must have had in mind:

> The Roman line faced south, the Carthaginian north; and luckily for both the early morning sun (whether they had taken up their positions by accident or design) shone obliquely on each other; but a wind which had got up—called locally the Volturnus—was a disadvantage to the Romans as it carried clouds of dust into their eyes and obscured their vision.[38]

This is one of the passages where Livy stands out as a prominent stylist and rhetorician, as his depiction of the battle strikes with vividness, creating an unforgettable mood and atmosphere of the actual battlefield. In the text of the *Postscript*, there is a longer explanatory comment, added by Johannes Climacus, which develops the above mentioned comparison:

> That one can battle in this way, blinded by the sun, and yet see to battle, the Romans demonstrated at Zama. That one can battle in this way, blinded and yet see to conquer, the Romans demonstrated at Zama. And now the battle of faith, is that supposed to be tomfoolery, a tagged swordplay of gallantry, this battle that is longer than a Thirty Years' War, because one does not fight merely to acquire but fights even more vehemently to preserve, this battle in which every day is just as hot as the day of battle at Zama! While the understanding despairs, faith presses forward victoriously in the passion of inwardness.[39]

This elaboration signifies the degree to which Climacus was inspired by the original description, and even though there is a confusion of the historical facts, his parallel is enlightening. On the one hand, we Christians are obviously blinded by the sun, the wind, and dust and do not see the blessedness and grace of the forgiveness offered to us, while, on the other hand, faith has to carry out the most vicious battle, in the same manner as the Romans did, in order for us to realize the advantages given to us by Christianity.

---

[36]   Ibid.

[37]   *CUP2*, 230 notes. *SKS* K7, 221.

[38]   See Livy, *Ab urbe condita*, Book XXII, 46. (English translation quoted from Livy, *The War with Hannibal*, trans. by Aubrey de Sélincourt, Harmondsworth: Penguin 1965, p. 146.)

[39]   *SKS* 7, 205n / *CUP1*, 224–5 note.

The History appears one more time in the *Postscript* and is included in the broader discussion of the distinction between the humorous and the religious. However, its primary function is to illustrate religious suffering. Climacus looks back at the suffering of the apostles which is mentioned in the New Testament, and adds the following comment: "...and I do not doubt that the apostles have the power of faith to be joyful even in physical pain and to thank God, just as even among pagans we find examples of fortitude, like Scaevola, for instance, who were joyful even in the moment of physical pain."[40] Climacus claims though that such an experience of physical pain cannot be defined as truly religious suffering. This particular reference to Roman history can hardly be considered commonplace nowadays.

In order to gain a full understanding of the differences between religious suffering and ordinary suffering, it is worth remembering the story reported by Livy. The example with Mucius Scaevola was included in *The History* only because it was a very popular story. Therefore, it had a specific purpose—to show how Romans expose their national character to foreigners and to remind the reader of true Roman virtues. The story itself portrays Gaius Mucius, a young nobleman remembered for his prominent deed during the siege of Rome in 500 BC by the Etruscans: "His first thought was to make his way, on his own initiative, into the enemy lines."[41] Mucius received permission from the consuls to assassinate the king Lars Porsena who led the army of the enemy. Unfortunately, Mucius was caught and had to stand before the royal tribunal, but when, upon interrogation, he told of a secret plot against Porsena, the king became terrified: "Porsena in rage and alarm ordered the prisoner to be burnt alive unless he at once divulged the plot thus obscurely hinted at."[42] But Mucius' reaction to the prospect of punishment astonished everyone, as he

> thrust his right hand into the fire which had been kindled for a sacrifice, and let it burn there as if he were unconscious of the pain. Porsena was so astonished by the young man's almost superhuman endurance that he leapt to his feet and ordered his guards to drag him from the altar. "Go free," he said; "you have dared to be a worse enemy to yourself than to me. I should bless your courage, if it lay with my country to dispose of. But, as that cannot be, I, as an honorable enemy, grant you pardon, life, and liberty."[43]

After this incident Mucius was called Scaevola, or "Left-handed." Livy's narrative focuses on how virtues, so much praised in the past and almost forgotten in his day, produced and shaped history. In the *Postscript*, however, the focus of the example shifts from the representation of the ethical value to the evocative presentation of the suffering. Climacus points out that "when the individual is secure in his relationship with God and suffers only in the external, this is not religious suffering," but "esthetic-dialectical."[44]

The final allusion to the text of *The History* can be found in the posthumously published *The Point of View for My Work as an Author*, in the chapter on "Personal

---

[40] *SKS* 7, 411 / *CUP1*, 452–3.
[41] Livy, *Ab urbe condita*, Book II, 12. (*The Early History of Rome*, p. 118.)
[42] Livy, *Ab urbe condita*, Book II, 12. (*The Early History of Rome*, p. 119.)
[43] Livy, *Ab urbe condita*, Book II, 12. (*The Early History of Rome*, p. 119.)
[44] *SKS* 7, 412 / *CUP1*, 453.

Existing in Relation to the Religious Writing," where Kierkegaard compares himself with Marcus Curtius:

> Ah, yes, surely that was just what the contemporaries thought of that Roman who made his immortal leap to save his country, a kind of insanity—ah, yes, and once again, ah, yes, since dialectically it was exactly Christian self-denial—and I, the poor master of irony, became the sorry object of the laughter of a highly cultured public.[45]

This refers to another well-known story from Livy, who recounts what in his consideration was a monumental legend of Roman virtue and military valor, a story of the self-sacrifice of Marcus Curtius.[46] Once, an enormous crack appeared in the middle of the Forum. Though the citizens tried to fill it with dirt, the crack continued to grow into the endless abyss. According to prophecies, if Rome were to last, the gods demanded a sacrifice which had to represent what was considered to be the male power of the Romans. So, Marcus Curtius asked the citizens whether Rome had anything more powerful and virtuous than weapons and valor. The citizens stood in silent recognition, as the young warrior threw himself into the chasm. The "immortal leap" saved the nation.

There is one feature which Kierkegaard and Livy have in common: both possessed a profound ability to retell and by that to reinterpret well-known stories. Livy focused on the shift in the ethical values, which in his eyes separated his contemporaries from what he considered truly Roman nature. Kierkegaard, in his turn, used ancient history as a counterargument in the discussion of Christianity. A consistent thought runs though most of his pseudonymous works: the attempt to find concepts which would, on the one hand, show the similarity and, on the other, the clear-cut distinction between paganism and Christianity. His purpose was to eliminate an ignorant opinion that "a light shines over the Christian world, whereas a darkness enshrouds paganism,"[47] and to show that paganism treated many Christian concepts differently (suffering, the ethical) and did not know about the existence of others (faith, sin, forgiveness). This is how Livy's work became a source of examples, which was well known to Kierkegaard's contemporaries. With the help of these passages, so familiar from school readings, the philosopher made an attempt to form vivid and appealing explanations of complex theoretical distinctions between what was considered typically pagan and Christianity.

---

[45]   *SV1* XIII, 553 / *PV*, 67.
[46]   Livy, *Ab urbe condita*, Book VII, 6. (English translation: Livy, *Rome and Italy*, trans. by Betty Radice, Harmondsworth: Penguin 1982, pp. 103–4.)
[47]   *SKS* 4, 149 / *FT*, 55.

Bibliography

I. Livy's Works in The Auction Catalogue *of Kierkegaard's Library*

T. Livii Patavini Historiarum libri qui supersunt omnes, vols. 1–5, ed. by Augusto Guil. Ernesti, Leipzig: Weidmann 1801–04 (*ASKB* 1251–1255).
Titi Livii Historiarum Libri I–X. Ad fidem optimarum editionum Strothii præcipue et Doeringii; textum exhibuit, horum aliorumque animadversiones excerpsit suasque adiecit Erasmus Möller, ed. by Christian Frederik Ingerslev, Gyldendal 1831, vol. 1 (containing Books I-V).
T. Livii Patavini Historiarum libri qui supersunt omnes, vols. 1–3, editio nova, Halle: Orphanotropheum 1811–12 (*ASKB* A I 167–169).
Titi Livii operum omnium, vols. 1–2, ed. by Rasmus Möller, Copenhagen: Gyldendal 1815–19 (*ASKB* A II 31–32).

II. Works in The Auction Catalogue *of Kierkegaard's Library that Discuss Livy*

[Becker, Karl Friedrich], *Karl Friedrich Beckers Verdenshistorie, omarbeidet af Johan Gottfried Woltmann*, vols. 1–12, trans. by J. Riise, Copenhagen: Fr. Brummers Forlag 1822–29, vol. 3, p. 611 (*ASKB* 1972–1983).
Dyck, Johann Gottfried and Georg Schatz (eds.), *Charaktere der vornehmsten Dichter aller Nationen; nebst kritischen und historischen Abhandlungen über Gegenstände der schönen Künste und Wissenschaften, von einer Gesellschaft von Gelehrten*, vols. 1–8, Leipzig: Dyk 1792–1808, vol. 1, pp. 6–7; (*ASKB* 1370–1377).
Hagen, Johan Frederik, *Ægteskabet. Betragtet fra et ethisk-historiskt Standpunct*, Copenhagen: Wahlske Boghandels Forlag 1845, p. 135n (*ASKB* 534).
Meierotto, Johann Heinrich Ludwig, *Ueber Sitten und Lebensart der Römer in verschiedenen Zeiten der Republik*, vols. 1–2, 3rd revised and enlarged ed., Berlin: in der Myliussischen Buchhandlung 1814 (*ASKB* 656).
Meiners, Christoph, *Geschichte des Verfalls der Sitten und der Staatsverfassung der Römer*, Leipzig: bey Weidmanns Erben und Reich 1782 (*ASKB* 660).
[Montaigne, Michel de], *Michael Montaigne's Gedanken und Meinungen über allerley Gegenstände, ins Deutsche übersetzt*, vols. 1–7, Berlin: F.T. Lagarde 1793–99, vol. 1, p. 21 (*ASKB* 681–687).
Mynster, Jakob Peter, *Blandede Skrivter*, vols. 1–3, Copenhagen: Den Gyldendalske Boghandlings Forlag 1852–53 (vols. 4–6, Copenhagen: Den Gyldendalske Boghandlings Forlag 1855–57), vol. 3, p. 43 (*ASKB* 358–363).

Schopenhauer, Arthur, *Die Welt als Wille und Vorstellung*, vols. 1–2, 2nd revised and enlarged ed., Leipzig: F.A. Brockhaus 1844 [1819], vol. 2, p. 156; p. 162 (*ASKB* 773–773a).

Schmidt, W. Adolf, *Geschichte der Denk- und Glaubensfreiheit im ersten Jahrhundert der Kaiserherrschaft und des Christenthums*, Berlin: Verlag von Veit und Comp. 1847, p. 168; p. 405 (*ASKB* 771).

III. Secondary Literature on Kierkegaard's Relation to Livy

None.

Marcus Aurelius:

Kierkegaard's Use and Abuse of the Stoic Emperor

Rick Anthony Furtak

I. A Profile of the Life and Writings of Marcus Aurelius

Marcus Aurelius, born in AD 121, was the Roman emperor from 161 until the time of his death in 180. His *Meditations*, written in Greek and organized into twelve books, were published posthumously by an unknown editor: the only title given to them by their author was *To Himself*, which indicates their inward and reflective orientation. Although his writings "give us very little information about his personal experiences," as Pierre Hadot has pointed out, they do show him struggling to cope with the ups and downs of what we know to have been a "tormented reign" that was filled with military and political tumult as well as personal upheaval.[1] His method of coping was largely shaped by the influence of Epictetus, whose teachings were introduced to Marcus Aurelius by his own teacher Junius Rusticus.[2] For this reason, Marcus is the last great representative of Stoic ethics in the ancient world. Time and time again, he advises himself to remember the Stoic principle that what lies outside of one's own mind is of no importance, so that he can remain unperturbed in the face of any worldly occurrence: "If you are disturbed by something outside yourself," he writes, "it is not the thing which troubles you but what you think about it, and it is within your power to obliterate this [conception] immediately."[3]

Marcus is fully in accord with Stoic orthodoxy when he claims that practical wisdom lies in the peace of mind that follows upon recognizing that external circumstances are not a factor in determining a person's happiness. Right reason and moral virtue are thus one and the same, and they consist in recognizing what is truly of value—namely, the integrity of the soul—and being vigilant in refusing to ascribe value to anything else. If we succeed at checking our tendency to be affected by

---

[1]   Pierre Hadot, "Marcus Aurelius," in *Philosophy as a Way of Life*, ed. by Arnold I. Davidson, Oxford: Blackwell 1995, pp. 179–205; p. 184. See also Pierre Hadot, *The Inner Citadel: The "Meditations" of Marcus Aurelius*, trans. by Michael Chase, Cambridge, Massachusetts: Harvard University Press 1998, p. 3.

[2]   This is made evident by his own account: see Marcus Aurelius, *Meditations* I.7.

[3]   *Meditations* VIII.47; see also *Meditations* VII.2. Cf. Hadot, *The Inner Citadel*, p. 114.

things that do not really matter, then we will subsequently repose in a state of calm, untroubled by any of the passions that are suffered by ordinary mortals.[4]

This idea enables Marcus Aurelius to claim that it would in theory be possible for a person to remain happy even while his flesh is being torn apart by wild animals, since bodily injury is among the contingent events that supposedly do not affect our well-being.[5] By using an especially morbid example to illustrate the point, however, Marcus shows a side of his intellectual temperament which sets him apart from other Stoics: that is, he calls attention to the most extreme implications of Stoicism, painting a bleak or even nihilistic vision of the world in which everything under the sun is devoid of value. "All that is prized in life is vain, rotten, and worthless," he claims, and human life itself is a hollow procession of transitory events leading from the cradle to the grave.[6]

Marcus is not departing from earlier Stoic doctrine when he advises us to raise ourselves to a lofty standpoint and look down on human affairs with the disdain of an adult toward the ridiculous games that are taken seriously by children.[7] Nevertheless, he does place an unusual emphasis on the project of abstracting from a human point of view and stripping things of their ordinary significance, and this often leads him to speak with an air of severe alienation and disgust. Some commentators, including Pierre Hadot, applaud Marcus for regarding objects with such clinical detachment; others, such as Julia Annas, argue that his radically austere position may be at odds with the more humane goals of Stoic ethics.[8] Clearly, other ancient Stoics do not tend to adopt such a weary and embittered tone, or to describe the world as putrid and miserable rather than simply indifferent. But it could be that Marcus Aurelius is only bringing classical Stoicism to its logical conclusion when he makes it sound as if life is utterly vacuous and revolting.

A more likely interpretation of those moments when Marcus emphasizes the absurdity of existence is that he is shifting his rhetorical strategy throughout the *Meditations*. A passage in which he tells himself that nothing matters may be therapeutically geared toward the times when he finds himself troubled by certain things that *do* matter to him. This would also explain what appears to be an incoherence: alongside his litany of how everything is contemptible, Marcus continually pauses to remark upon the beauty and order of the universe. In one instance, he cites the way that bread cracks open as it is baking, pointing to this as an example of how even what might seem like an imperfection actually makes the bread look more attractive to us.[9] Calling to mind this kind of detail is unlikely to help us view the bread as yet another worthless item, but it may enable us to become reconciled to what we cannot change in a world that is mostly out of our control.

---

[4]   See, for example, *Meditations* VI.52 and XI.11.

[5]   This vivid example is from *Meditations* VII.68.

[6]   Marcus Aurelius, *Meditations* V.33 and IV.48; see also *Meditations* VII.3 and VIII.24.

[7]   See *Meditations* XII.24 and V.36.

[8]   Hadot, "Marcus Aurelius," pp. 185–7; Julia Annas, *The Morality of Happiness*, Oxford: Oxford University Press 1993, pp. 175–6.

[9]   *Meditations* III.2. See also, for example, *Meditations* IV.50.

And the Stoic sage, according to Marcus Aurelius, is someone who has learned to accept whatever is necessary, rather than wishing that anything be different than it is.[10] Whether this embrace of fate depends upon a conviction that the cosmos is guided by divine providence, as opposed to being a random collection of atoms in the void, is a question that Marcus prefers to leave open.[11] Whether or not human rationality is mirrored by a divine reason that governs the universe, it is best for us to orient ourselves by the dictates of reason, since this can be identified as our highest faculty—with or without an appeal to Stoic cosmology.

If he is a less consistent philosopher by virtue of claiming at one moment that the universe is a beautiful arrangement of things realizing their proper end and, at another moment, that it is thoroughly absurd or even atrocious, he has a memorable personality as an author for the same reason. Marcus Aurelius comes across in his writings as an intensely sensitive thinker who finds in himself a depressive tendency to wonder if life is worth living and an equally powerful capacity to be overwhelmed by all-too-human emotions. In the former state of mind, he counsels himself that everything is exactly as it ought to be; in the latter mood, he affirms that nothing really matters.

II. Kierkegaard's Use of Marcus Aurelius and Its Significance

In one journal passage, Kierkegaard praises Epictetus with the *ad hominem* remark that "it takes a slave to write with the loftiness of Stoicism," and he adds that Marcus Aurelius was only a pampered emperor whose writings are comparatively "insignificant" as a result.[12] Although this is the sort of biographical critique that could be made by someone who had not studied the works of either Stoic author, Kierkegaard was better acquainted with Marcus Aurelius than one might assume from hearing his crude generalizations about the emperor and the slave. In addition to Wilhelm Gottlieb Tennemann's (1761–1819) *Geschichte der Philosophie*, which introduced him to many of the basic themes of Stoic ethics, Kierkegaard's library also included the *Meditations* of Marcus Aurelius in volumes edited by the same Johann Matthias Schultz (1771–1849) whom he knew as the German translator of Epictetus.[13] That he read this text with some care is demonstrated by the fact that he uses it as a source of information about Socrates and his wife, having discovered the lone place in the *Meditations* where this topic is mentioned.[14] Other unpublished

---

[10]   On *amor fati* see *Meditations* IV.10, VIII.50, and X.35. See also F.H. Sandbach, *The Stoics*, 2nd ed., Indianapolis: Hackett 1989, pp. 79–82; p. 173.

[11]   See *Meditations* IV.3, VI.10, IX.28, and X.6. Regarding this issue, see also Gretchen Reydams-Schils, *The Roman Stoics*, Chicago: University of Chicago Press 2005, pp. 42–3.

[12]   *Pap.* X–4 A 576 / *JP* 4, 4516.

[13]   *D. Imperatoris Marci Antonini Commentariorum Quos Sibi Ipsi Scripsit Libri XII: Ad Optimorum Librorum Fidem Diligenter Recogniti*, ed. by Johann Matthias Schultz, Leipzig: Tauchnitz 1829 (*ASKB* 1218).

[14]   See *Pap.* IV A 202 / *JP* 4, 4249. Kierkegaard cites *Meditations* XI.28 as the source of a story about what Socrates said to his embarrassed friends after Xanthippe had taken his cloak and left him wearing only a loincloth.

references to the Stoic emperor are more philosophically significant, such as the 1848 notebook entry in which Kierkegaard takes issue with Marcus Aurelius on the topic of suicide. As opposed to the dramatic and passionate martyrdom of the early Christians, Marcus argues that a Stoic ought to meet death with a reasonable demeanor—but this, according to Kierkegaard, only shows the isolation of the Stoic self from any purpose higher than the satisfaction of his own desire for tranquillity of mind.[15] More favorable is the mention in an 1849 letter to Janus Lauritz Andreas Kolderup-Rosenvinge (1792–1850) of a passage in the *Meditations* where Marcus is talking about the possibility of reviving one's life by seeing things in a different light, which Kierkegaard quotes in the original Greek.[16] In this letter, he also uses the title *ad se ipsum*, or *To Himself*, to refer to the book written by Marcus Aurelius.

This same title appears on the cover of Kierkegaard's 1839 *Journal EE* and at the start of the "Diapsalmata" section that opens the first volume of *Either/Or*. This overt allusion to Marcus Aurelius confirms that the "Diapsalmata" are directly related to some of Kierkegaard's own early journal entries, and it also provides a hermeneutic aid to the reading of *Either/Or I*, which is where the bulk of Kierkegaard's published references to Marcus Aurelius can be found. It is "Victor Eremita," the pseudonymous editor of *Either/Or*, who claims to have found "*ad se ipsum*" written on some of the papers of "A" with which the first volume begins: so he used this phrase as "a kind of motto" to the "Diapsalmata," adding that it is "by me and yet not by me."[17] Our editor says no more about the significance of this quotation, but the fact that it is borrowed from Marcus Aurelius makes it a suitable epigraph for the aesthete's fragments. This is because one characteristic of these fragments is their repeated oscillation from moments in which the aesthete is almost overcome with passion to moods in which he is remarkably apathetic. Among the former are his comments on how he felt after seeing "a person standing utterly alone in the world," and his remarks on "the first period of falling in love."[18] On the other hand, he reports having the harrowing impression that life is "empty and meaningless," and complains that he does not "feel like doing anything."[19] Although he seems to be capable of momentary emotional sensitivity, even to the point of being "painfully moved" on some occasions, at other times he finds himself in an unemotional void.[20] This state of torment is diagnosed in the second volume of *Either/Or* as the inevitable result of the aesthete's tentative and inconsistent participation in moral life—in other words, his failure to become a coherent self.

---

[15]   *SKS* 21, 137, NB7:112 / *JP* 4, 3898. In this entry, Kierkegaard refers to *Meditations* XI.3. Merold Westphal comments on Kierkegaard's understanding of the "relational, intersubjective nature of the self" in *Becoming a Self*, West Lafayette: Purdue University Press 1996, p. 143. By contrast, Martha Nussbaum discusses some of the self–isolating effects of Stoic autonomy, especially as advocated by Marcus Aurelius: see *Upheavals of Thought*, Cambridge, Massachusetts: Cambridge University Press 2001, pp. 207 and 324–5.

[16]   See *B&A*, 214 / *LD*, 302. The letter is dated July 28, 1849, and the passage quoted is from *Meditations* VII.2.

[17]   *SKS* 2, 16 / *EO1*, 8.

[18]   See *SKS* 2, 29–33 / *EO1*, 21–4.

[19]   *SKS* 2, 39 / *EO1*, 29. *SKS* 2, 28 / *EO1*, 20.

[20]   See *SKS* 2, 32–4 / *EO1*, 24–5.

Late in the "Rotation of Crops" section of *Either/Or I*, "A" uses the above-quoted phrase by Marcus Aurelius about seeing things in a new light in the process of explaining his method of recollection, which involves forgetting the ways in which one has been moved in the past while making sure that one is not affected too strongly by any new emotion. It is a way of existing on the surface of life, entering into passionate experience briefly and then retreating to a standpoint of passionless detachment not unlike that of a Stoic sage. After perfecting this method, a person "is then able to play shuttlecock with all existence."[21] Consequently, the aesthete is "incapable of genuine relationships,"[22] unable to keep a promise or to make a commitment to another person. Once again, the aesthete's affinity for Stoic ethics reveals much about the defects of character from which he suffers. Emotional attunement to particular situations is an essential part of moral agency, according to *Either/Or II*, and it allows a person to live in a moment filled with meaning instead of a pointless, evanescent moment. From this point of view, emotional ties are not hindrances to be cut away, but necessary threads that bind a person to the world, enabling him or her to lead a virtuous life. Kierkegaard's portrait of what an ethical person looks like relies upon an implied contrast with Stoicism, which is set up by the aesthete's mercuric emotions as well as his attitude toward them. Due to the unique version of Stoicism he represents, in addition to his occasional inconsistencies, Marcus Aurelius is a valuable resource for the characterization of the aesthete in *Either/Or I*.[23]

---

[21]   *SKS* 2, 281–4 / *EO1*, 292–5. The passage by Marcus Aurelius is appropriated from *Meditations* VII.2.

[22]   George Pattison, *Kierkegaard: The Aesthetic and the Religious*, New York: St Martin's Press 1992, p. 58.

[23]   For a more extensive discussion of Kierkegaard's relation to classical Stoic philosophy in general, and to Marcus Aurelius in particular, see my book *Wisdom in Love: Kierkegaard and the Ancient Quest for Emotional Integrity*, Notre Dame: University of Notre Dame Press 2005. In addition to everyone thanked therein, I also owe a debt of gratitude to Jon Stewart and Richard Purkarthofer, for their helpful editorial suggestions with respect to this article.

Bibliography

I. Marcus Aurelius' Works in The Auction Catalogue *of Kierkegaard's Library*

D. *Imperatoris Marci Antonini Commentariorum Quos Sibi Ipsi Scripsit Libri XII: Ad Optimorum Librorum Fidem Diligenter Recogniti*, Editio Stereotypa, ed. by Johann Matthias Schultz, Leipzig: Tauchnitz 1829 (*ASKB* 1218).
Marc. Aurel. Antonin's Unterhaltungen mit sich selbst. Aus dem Griechischen übersetzt. Mit Anmerkungen und einem Versuche über Antonin's philosophische Grundsätze begleitet, trans. and ed. by Johann Matthias Schultz, Schleswig: bei Johann Gottlob Röhß 1799 (*ASKB* 1219).

II. Works in The Auction Catalogue *of Kierkegaard's Library that Discuss Marcus Aurelius*

Ast, Friedrich, *Grundriss einer Geschichte der Philosophie*, Landshut: bey Joseph Thomann 1807, pp. 159–60 (*ASKB* 385).
[Becker, Karl Friedrich], *Karl Friedrich Beckers Verdenshistorie, omarbeidet af Johan Gottfried Woltmann*, vols. 1–12, trans. by J. Riise, Copenhagen: Fr. Brummers Forlag 1822–29, vol. 3, pp. 751–3 (*ASKB* 1972–1983).
Ritter, Heinrich and L. Preller, *Historia philosophiae graeco-romanae ex fontium locis contexta*, ed. by L. Preller, Hamburg: Perthes 1838, pp. 450–2 (*ASKB* 726).
Schmidt, W. Adolf, *Geschichte der Denk- und Glaubensfreiheit im ersten Jahrhundert der Kaiserherrschaft und des Christenthums*, Berlin: Verlag von Veit und Comp. 1847, pp. 231–2 (*ASKB* 771).
Schopenhauer, Arthur, *Die Welt als Wille und Vorstellung*, vols. 1–2, 2nd revised and enlarged ed., Leipzig: F.A. Brockhaus 1844 [1819], vol. 2, p. 156; p. 162 (*ASKB* 773–773a).
Tennemann, Wilhelm Gottlieb, *Geschichte der Philosophie*, vols. 1–11, Leipzig: Johann Ambrosius Barth 1798–1819, vol. 5 (1805), pp. 180–1 (*ASKB* 815–826).

III. Secondary Literature on Kierkegaard's Relation to Marcus Aurelius

Furtak, Rick Anthony, *Wisdom in Love: Kierkegaard and the Ancient Quest for Emotional Integrity*, Notre Dame: University of Notre Dame Press 2005, p. 17; p. 21; p. 23; p. 27; p. 32; p. 37; p. 43; p. 60; p. 123.
—— "Kierkegaard and the Passions of Hellenistic Philosophy," *Kierkegaardiana*, vol. 24, 2007, pp. 68–85.

Nepos:

Traces of Kierkegaard's Use of an Edifying Roman Biographer

Jon Stewart

Cornelius Nepos ranks as one of Rome's lesser historians, well behind familiar giants such as Livy or Tacitus. His surviving works are not extensive, and they are of little actual historical value. His work has a moralistic or eulogizing tone, presenting celebrated figures primarily from Greek and Roman history and holding them forth as moral exemplars for others to follow. The intent is that their virtues and vices should serve for the edification of the reader.

It was natural that Kierkegaard, as a lover of Latin literature, would take some interest in Nepos. There are references to the Roman historian in a couple of places in the early authorship. It is possible that Kierkegaard was inspired by the moralistic treatment of some of the generals and orators whom Nepos discusses. Like Nepos, Kierkegaard also likes to present specific characters, such as Johannes Climacus, Johannes the seducer, the young man in *Repetition*, or Judge William as examples of specific positions or world-views. These figures are painted in vivid colors so that the reader can examine and evaluate them with great scrutiny. Given this similarity, it is possible that Kierkegaard's methodology in this regard was in part inspired by Nepos, or minimally that he found in him a kindred spirit.

I. The Life and Work of Nepos

Little is known about the life of Cornelius Nepos.[1] He was born in Cisalpine Gaul, today's northern Italy, sometime around 99 BC. He later moved to Rome, where he soon entered the capital's literary circles. He was on friendly terms with a number

---

[1]   For the life of Nepos, see the introduction in *Cornelius Nepos*, with an English translation by John C. Rolfe, Cambridge, Massachusetts: Harvard University Press, London: William Heinemann 1984, pp. vii–xiii; Joseph Geiger, *Cornelius Nepos and Ancient Political Biography*, Stuttgart: Franz Steiner Verlag Wiesbaden 1985, pp. 67–78; Arnaldo Momigliano, *The Development of Greek Biography*, Cambridge, Massachusetts: Harvard University Press 1971, pp. 97–9; Edna Jenkinson, "Nepos—An Introduction to Latin Biography," in *Latin Biography*, ed. by T.A. Dorey, London: Routledge & Kegan Paul 1967, pp. 1–15; Friedrich Leo, "Cornelius Nepos" in his *Die griechisch-römische Biographie nach ihrer litterarischen Form*, Leipzig: B.G. Teubner 1901, pp. 193–218.

of well-known Romans such as Cicero (with whom he corresponded), Atticus (whose biography he writes), and the poet Catullus (who dedicated a book to him). In addition to his historical writings, Nepos is also said to have been a publisher. He died sometime around 24 BC, although the exact date is uncertain. Pliny the Elder mentions merely that he died under the reign of Augustus.[2]

Although Nepos wrote a vast number of works, only a small part survives. The Younger Pliny mentions that Nepos wrote a volume of love poems.[3] In the aforementioned dedication, Catullus refers to a work, known from other sources as *Chronica*, which was a history of the world from the earliest times in three books: "To whom should I present this / little book so carefully polished / but to you, Cornelius, who have always / been so tolerant of my verses, / you who of us all has dared / to take the whole of human history / as his field / —three doctoral and weighty volumes!"[4] The writer Aulus Gellius quotes from a lost work called *Exempla*, which was apparently a series of anecdotes intended for rhetorical use.[5] In addition to his short extant account of Cato, Nepos himself mentions a more detailed biography, which is now lost.[6] Gellius also refers to a lost *Life of Cicero*.[7] Finally, the Elder Pliny implies that Nepos authored a work on geography.[8]

The sole work by Nepos which survives, albeit only in part, is his *De Viris Illustribus* or *On Illustrious Men*, which is thought to have originally contained sixteen books. This work describes the lives of famous Roman and foreign kings, historians, generals, poets and orators. Given the fact that the work appeared before the death of Atticus in 32 BC, scholars conjecture that it was probably published around 34 BC. Of this work only two sections survive; the first is the book *De Excellentibus*

---

[2]   Pliny, *Natural History*, Book IX, 137 and X, 60.

[3]   Pliny, *Epistles*, Book V, 3, 6.

[4]   Catullus, *Carmina*, I: "*Cui dono lepidum nouum libellum / Arido modo pumice expolitum? / Corneli, tibi; namque tu solebas / Meas esse aliquid putare nugas, / Iam tum cum ausus es unus Italorum / Omne aeuum tribus explicare chartis, / Doctis, Iuppiter, et laboriosis!*" (English translation quoted from *The Poems of Catullus*, trans. by Peter Whigham, Harmondsworth: Penguin 1966, p. 49.) For an account of the *Chronica*, see Geiger, *Cornelius Nepos and Ancient Political Biography*, pp. 68–73.

[5]   Aulus Gellius, *Attic Nights*, Book VI, 18. 11: "Furthermore Cornelius Nepos, in the fifth book of his *Examples*, has recorded also that many of the senators recommended that those who refused to return should be sent to Hannibal under guard, but that the motion was defeated by a majority of dissentients. He adds that, in spite of this, those who had not returned to Hannibal were so infamous and hated that they became tired of life and committed suicide." (English translation quoted from *The Attic Nights of Aulus Gellius*, vols. 1–3, trans. by John C. Rolfe, Cambridge, Massachusetts: Harvard University Press, London: William Heinemann 1967–70, vol. 2, p. 77.) For an account of the *Exempla*, see Geiger, *Cornelius Nepos and Ancient Political Biography*, pp. 73–6.

[6]   Nepos, Book XXIV, 3: "Concerning this man's life and character I have given fuller details in the separate book which I have devoted to his biography at the urgent request of Titus Pomponius Atticus." (English translation quoted from *Cornelius Nepos*, with an English translation by John C. Rolfe, p. 287.)

[7]   Aulus Gellius, *Attic Nights*, XV, 28, 2.

[8]   Pliny, *Natural History*, Book V, 4. For this, see Geiger, *Cornelius Nepos and Ancient Political Biography*, pp. 76–7.

Ducibus Exterarum Gentium or *On Excellent Leaders of Foreign Peoples*, which survives *in toto*. This text contains accounts of the careers of Greek generals such as Miltiades, Cimon, and Epaminondas as well as other foreign generals such as the Persian, Datames, and the Carthaginians, Hamilcar and Hannibal. The second text is a part of a book called *De Historicis Latinis*, of which two brief biographies of the Romans, Marcus Porcius Cato and Titus Pomponius Atticus, survive.

Nepos' favored genre is the biography. Indeed, he is hailed as the first author of biography in history. As one scholar puts it, "Cornelius Nepos is the originator of political biography as a literary form and the earliest writer of any sort of biography in Greek or Latin from whom whole Lives survive."[9] Nepos tells of the successes and failures of great leaders, highlighting the conditions that contributed to their greatness. He is not a scholarly writer, but rather his goal is to appeal to a general public and to edify the reader by means of examples of well-known historical figures. He belongs to a tradition of authors including Plutarch, who compare the lives of famous Romans with Greek and foreign counterparts. Another scholar explains Nepos' importance in contrast to his forerunners Varro and Atticus:

> With Nepos, indeed, biography acquired a new dimension. It became the means by which Greek and Roman men and achievements could be compared. Valerius Maximus and Plutarch are unthinkable without Cornelius Nepos; and Cornelius Nepos must also have helped to familiarize the Romans with the Hellenistic distinction between history and biography.[10]

While this positive view does have its detractors,[11] there can be no doubt that Nepos, for all his shortcomings as a historian, played an important role in the development of the biography as a genre.

Stylistically Nepos is not known as a great writer.[12] This judgement may, however, be somewhat harsh given the high standard set by contemporary authors with whom he is inevitably compared. He uses a limited vocabulary, and his sentences are relatively short—features that have made him well suited for elementary Latin instruction in later ages. He does now and then depart from this simple style, but these occasional rhetorical flairs have been often criticized. His sentences are said to lack balance, and he is purportedly overly fond of alliteration.

Nor is he known as a great historian. His accounts cannot be trusted for historical accuracy. As one scholar puts it, "All the *Lives* afford a happy hunting-ground for those in quest of historical errors."[13] There are confusions of persons, mistaken dates and distances, particularly in Nepos' treatment of the Greek figures. Understandably enough, his accounts of Roman and Carthaginian matters are more accurate. In

---

9   Geiger, *Cornelius Nepos and Ancient Political Biography*, p. 66.
10   Arnaldo Momigliano, *The Development of Greek Biography*, pp. 98–9.
11   B. Baldwin, "Biography at Rome," in *Studies in Latin Literature and Roman History I*, ed. by Carl Deroux, Brussels: Latomus 1979 (*Collection Latomus*, vol. 164), pp. 100–18; p. 114.
12   See Bernhard Lupus, *Der Sprachgebrauch des Cornelius Nepos*, Berlin: Weidmannsche Buchhandlung 1876; Edna Jenkinson, "Nepos—An Introduction to Latin Biography," in *Latin Biography*, pp. 11–13.
13   Jenkinson, "Nepos—An Introduction to Latin Biography," in *Latin Biography*, p. 10.

his treatment of foreign peoples, Nepos tends to Romanize customs and habits, transposing onto them Roman political or religious institutions.

Some of these criticisms would probably seem to Nepos himself to miss the point. He is consciously aware of his genre as biography, which he distinguishes from history. Right away in his Preface he is quick to defend himself against the critics who regard biography as unworthy and of little value. Writing in Latin for a people known for its *gravitas*, he notes that some of the personal character traits of or anecdotes about the figures portrayed may appear fatuous in comparison to serious history; for example, he notes that he describes how the Theban general Epaminondas in his youth was taught dancing and singing to the flute. However, Nepos argues that those who make these criticisms do not understand the different customs of foreign peoples. Thus, while some things may seem silly to the Roman reader, to the Greeks of the age, they were perfectly accepted customs. The larger point is that in biography there is room for such things, in contrast to the more sober historical writing. In any case it is clear that his goal is to entertain and edify the reader, and the accuracy of his accounts is subordinated to this end.

II. Kierkegaard's Knowledge of Nepos

Kierkegaard learned Latin at an early age at the Borgerdyd School in Copenhagen.[14] In 1830 the headmaster of the school, Michael Nielsen (1776–1846), wrote for him both a school evaluation and a testimony, which functioned as a letter of recommendation for Kierkegaard's application to enter the University of Copenhagen. The purpose of the former document was in part to give an overview of Kierkegaard's studies at the school. In this context Nielsen provides a list of both the Latin and the Greek authors that were covered in the school. Here Nepos is mentioned among the Roman authors whom Kierkegaard read.[15] He appears together with a handful of Roman historians, that is, Livy, Caesar, and Sallust, who were presumably standard reading in the Latin courses at the time.

Given that we know that Kierkegaard read Nepos in the school, it is odd that there are no editions of Nepos in his book collection. However, in Appendix II of the *Auction Catalogue*, entry 27 is described merely as "various schoolbooks in a bundle,"[16] and entry 28 is apparently the same.[17] It is tempting to think that Kierkegaard's school edition of Nepos was among the works in this group, but unfortunately there is no way to confirm this. There does seem to have been some confusion at a fairly early stage about what happened to Kierkegaard's schoolbooks. In 1869 Frederik Peter Welding (1811–94), a former schoolmate of Kierkegaard, in a

---

[14]   For this period of Kierkegaard's life, see Valdemar Ammundsen, *Søren Kierkegaards Ungdom. Hans Slægt og hans religiøse Udvikling*, Copenhagen: Universitetsbogtrykkeriet 1912; Per Krarup, *Søren Kierkegaard og Borgerdydskolen*, Copenhagen: Gyldendal 1977.
[15]   *B&A*, vol 1, pp. 4–5 / *LD*, Document V, p. 5. (See also Bruce H. Kirmmse (ed.), *Encounters with Kierkegaard: A Life as Seen by His Contemporaries*, Princeton: Princeton University Press 1996, p. 273.)
[16]   *ASKB* A II 27: "*Forskjellige Skolebøger i 1 Bundt.*"
[17]   *ASKB* A II 28: "*Dito dito i 1 dito.*"

correspondence with Hans Peter Barfod (1834–92), writes, "Doesn't someone have S.K.'s schoolbooks, his Horace or his Cicero's *de Oratore*? The underlining and the marginal notes would be enlightening."[18]

While a student at the University of Copenhagen, Kierkegaard himself later taught Latin at the Borgerdyd School.[19] He thus was presumably either reusing his old textbooks or making use of new ones that had been adopted in the interim. Unfortunately no record survives of what exactly he read in these courses or what textbooks he used, and thus we cannot know if Nepos belonged to his favorite instructional material.

There was, however, no shortage of editions of Nepos' works at the time. In his overview, Marshall lists some 9 different works that appeared between 1750 and 1850.[20] There were also a number of Danish editions (not listed by Marshall), which Kierkegaard might have known. One of these, published in Copenhagen in 1776, was designed especially for classroom use in Danish and Norwegian schools.[21] In 1778 there appeared in Copenhagen a critical work on Nepos with the title *Observationes criticae et historicae in Cornelium Nepotem* by Johann Heinrich Schlegel (1724–80).[22] Another edition of the primary text appeared in Copenhagen in 1811 and was edited by Børge Riisbrigh Thorlacius (1775–1829), professor of Latin at the University of Copenhagen.[23] A further edition followed in 1829, edited by Carl Wilhelm Elberling (1800–70).[24]

In addition to these editions of the primary texts, there were also, somewhat surprisingly, at least three different contemporary Danish translations that Kierkegaard might have come across. A certain Mathias Rathje, about whom nothing is known, published the first in 1796.[25] A second translation was published in 1819 by the Latinist and jurist, Carl Frederik Gerdsen (1798–1856),[26] who was also responsible

---

18   "Letter F. Welding to H.P. Barfod," October 23, 1869, in Kirmmse, *Encounters with Kierkegaard*, p. 9.

19   The exact dates of his employment at the school are disputed. The estimates range from the beginning of the 1830s until 1840. See Kirmmse's illuminating discussion in the note apparatus to *Encounters with Kierkegaard*, p. 276.

20   See "Conspectus editionum," in *Cornelii Nepotis Vitae cum Fragmentis*, ed. by Peter K. Marshall, Leipzig: Teubner 1977, pp. X–XII.

21   *Cornelii Nepotis Vitae excellentium imperatorum et alia, quae supersunt omnia. Ad exemplar Keuchenianum in usum scholarum Daniae et Norvegiae*, Copenhagen: A.H. Godiche 1776.

22   J.H. Schlegel, *Observationes criticae et historicae in Cornelium Nepotem cum chronologica rerum graecarum et persicarum, carthageniensium et romanarum ad eundem auctorem illustratandum*, Copenhagen: Philibert 1778.

23   *Cornelii Nepotis Vitae & fragmenta. Textum ad optimarum editionum fidem constituit & lectionum maxime memorabilium varietatem adjecit*, ed. by M. Birgerus Thorlacius, Copenhagen: Brünnich 1811.

24   *Cornelii Nepotis quae exstant*, ed. by Carolous Guil. Elberling, Copenhagen: Soldenfeldt 1829.

25   *Kornelius Nepos Om store Generalers Liv og Levenet*, trans. by Mathias Rathje, Copenhagen: P.M. Liunge 1796.

26   *Cornelius Nepos's Store Hærføreres Levnetsbeskrivelser*, trans. by C.F. Gerdsen, Copenhagen: H. Soldin 1819.

for some Danish translations of Cicero's works. A third translation, containing only the first eleven Lives, appeared in 1839, the work of Carl Ludvig Jensen (1810–?), a teacher and later parish pastor.[27] These translators do not seem generally to be well-known figures in Golden Age Denmark.

Although there are no editions of Nepos' works in Kierkegaard's library, he had at least some ancient texts which mention Nepos, such as Cicero's letters, which contained Nepos' correspondence with the famous orator,[28] and Pliny's letters, an edition of which appears in the first appendix of the *Auction Catalogue*.[29] Moreover, he owned a few books by modern authors who mention or discuss Nepos. Johann Heinrich Ludwig Meierotto's (1742–1800) *Ueber Sitten und Lebensart der Römer in verschiedenen Zeiten der Republik*, from 1814, refers frequently to Nepos as a source.[30] There are also a few references to Nepos in the German philosopher Christoph Meiners' (1747–1810) *Geschichte des Verfalls der Sitten und der Staatsverfassung der Römer*.[31] Finally, the Hegelian philosopher Carl Ludwig Michelet (1801–93) refers to Nepos' account of Themistocles in his *Vorlesungen über die Persönlichkeit Gottes und Unsterblichkeit der Seele oder die ewige Persönlichkeit des Geistes* from 1841.[32]

III. References to Nepos in Kierkegaard's Writings

The first mention of Nepos in Kierkegaard's *corpus* appears in his *Journal EE*, which he wrote in during the time when he was studying for his theological examination. There is little continuity or defining theme in this journal, which instead consists of 197 rather heterogeneous entries. This said, some clear continuous traces of his theological studies are present. Kierkegaard mentions Nepos explicitly in an entry dated May 10, 1839, where he writes:

> Cornelius Nepos tells the story of a general who was besieged in a stronghold with a substantial body of cavalry and who, in order to prevent the horses from becoming sick

---

[27]   *Cornelius Nepos's udmærkede Feltherrers Levnetsbeskrivelser*, trans. by C.L. Jensen, 1. Hefte, Copenhagen: J.H. Schubothes Boghandling 1839.

[28]   *Markus Tullius Cicero's Vermischte Briefe*, vols. 1–5, trans. by August Christian Borheck, 2nd ed., Frankfurt am Main: Hermann 1789–1801 (*ASKB* 1240–1244); M.B. Weiske, *Auswahl der besten Briefe Ciceros*, 3rd printing, Braunschweig: Schulbuchhandlung 1824 (*ASKB* 1245). M.B. Weiske, *Erklärende Anmerkungen zur Auswahl der besten Briefe Ciceros*, Braunschweig: Schulbuchhandlung 1796 (*ASKB* 1246).

[29]   C. Plinius Caecilius Secundus, *Epistolae et Panegyricus*, Halle: Orphanotropheum 1789 (*ASKB* A I 182).

[30]   Johann Heinrich Ludwig Meierotto, *Ueber Sitten und Lebensart der Römer in verschiedenen Zeiten der Republik*, vols. 1–2, 3rd revised and enlarged ed., Berlin: in der Myliussischen Buchhandlung 1814 (*ASKB* 656).

[31]   Christoph Meiners, *Geschichte des Verfalls der Sitten und der Staatsverfassung der Römer*, Leipzig: bey Weidmanns Erben und Reich. 1782, p. 69; p. 160 (*ASKB* 660).

[32]   Carl Ludwig Michelet, *Vorlesungen über die Persönlichkeit Gottes und Unsterblichkeit der Seele oder die ewige Persönlichkeit des Geistes*, Berlin: Verlag von Ferdinand Dümmler 1841, p. 207 (*ASKB* 680).

through having to be stationary for so long, had them whipped every day in order thus to get them moving—so I live in my room like one under siege—I don't care to see anyone, and every moment I am afraid that the enemies will mount an assault, i.e., that someone will come and visit me; I don't care to go out; but in order not to take any harm from having to be stationary for so long—I cry myself into a state of exhaustion.[33]

In the context of the journal, this strikes one as a rather off-handed anecdote. It seems doubtful that Kierkegaard had just reread Nepos at this time. Instead, the tone of the entry suggests that he is citing it from memory. However, it is worthy of note that he explicitly identifies Nepos as the source of the story.

This is a reference to Nepos' account (Book XVIII, 5) of the Greek general Eumenes of Cardia, who lived from ca. 362 to 316 BC. Although a Greek, Eumenes lived in Macedonia during its most glorious period. He was the secretary first of Philip of Macedon and then of Alexander the Great. Upon the death of the latter as the kingdom was divided, Eumenes was put in charge of the satrapy of Cappadocia, although it still remained to be conquered. There he waged a series of campaigns, doing his best to keep Alexander's empire in tact. When the other generals revolted, he remained loyal to Perdiccas, whom Alexander had appointed as his successor. When Perdiccas was ultimately killed by his enemies and Antipater assumed power, Eumenes was condemned *in absentia*. Since he had limited resources and inexperienced soldiers, Eumenes was forced to use a defensive strategy, avoiding pitched battles. Ultimately his fortunes turned, and after the battle of Paraecene in 317 BC he saw his best troops desert. Due to the resentment among the Macedonians caused by him, as a foreigner, holding such great power over them, he was betrayed to his enemy Antigonus. He was ultimately executed in 316 BC.

The story Kierkegaard refers to relates how Eumenes was on the run, being pursued by the army of general Antigonus. He was forced to take refuge in a fortress in a place called Nora. Nepos writes:

Being besieged there and fearing that by remaining in one place he might ruin the horses of his army, because there was no room for exercising them, Eumenes hit upon a clever device by which an animal standing in one place might be warmed and exercised, so that it would have a better appetite and not lose its bodily activity. He drew up its head with a thong so high that it could not quite touch the ground with its forefeet, and then forced it by blows of a whip to bound and kick out behind, an exercise which produced no less sweat than running on a race-track. The result was that, to the surprise of all, the animals were led out of the fortress after a siege of several months in as good condition as if he had kept them in pasture.[34]

In the context of the overall narrative, this anecdote is by no means striking. It is merely one of the many examples that Nepos gives to illustrate the intelligence and ingenuity of Eumenes, often under trying circumstances.

The reader is naturally inclined to read Kierkegaard's entry from *EE* as an autobiographical statement: it seems to be a self-description of Kierkegaard's lonely

---

[33]   *SKS* 18, 26, EE:59 / *KJN* 2, 21.
[34]   *Corneli Nepotis Vitae*, ed. by E.O. Winstedt, Oxford: Oxford University Press 1962, Book XVIII, 5. (English translation quoted from *Cornelius Nepos*, trans. by Rolfe, p. 217.)

life during a time when he was obliged to focus intensely on his studies and for this reason did not have the opportunity to go out or meet with people. Thus, he feels as if he were under siege since he cannot leave his books. Moreover, he fears that an unexpected visitor will come by and distract him from his studies. According to this interpretation, Kierkegaard recalls an anecdote from Nepos that he interprets so as to fit with his then current situation.

This autobiographical interpretation of the entry takes on a new twist, when one sees that this same text appears in a slightly shortened version as one of the "Diapsalmata" in *Either/Or*, Part One. There this anecdote is attributed not to Kierkegaard himself but to his anonymous esthete A. Here one reads:

> Cornelius Nepos tells of a general who was kept confined with a considerable cavalry regiment in a fortress; to keep the horses from being harmed because of too much inactivity, he had them whipped daily—in like manner I live in this age as one besieged, but lest I be harmed by sitting still so much, I cry myself tired.[35]

Kierkegaard modifies the original passage from *EE* by eliminating the apparently main self-referential part: "I don't care to see anyone, and every moment I am afraid that the enemies will mount an assault, i.e., that someone will come and visit me."[36] However, he keeps the line "in like manner I live in my room as one besieged." This can be taken as evidence that he identified with the esthete in some aspects since he could, with only minor modification, revise the originally self-referential statement to fit the esthete. Indeed, as has been noted, a number of journal entries, especially from *EE*, appear later in the "Diapsalmata."[37]

In any case, in the context of *Either/Or*, Kierkegaard is interested in portraying the esthete as someone isolated from the rest of society, someone who shuns established social customs and habits and instead prefers to live in his own subjectivity. Thus, the anecdote from Nepos represents this metaphorically with the image of general Eumenes under siege. Despite being cut off from the outside world, Eumenes nonetheless attempts to keep up with the physical training of the horse by the mentioned device. In the same way the esthete tries to keep fit by crying until he has grown tired.

The esthete returns to Nepos at the end of "The Tragic in Ancient Drama Reflected in the Tragic in Modern Drama." There in the analysis of Sophocles' *Antigone*, he explains the tragic conflict between Antigone, the loyal daughter of Oedipus, and her beloved Haemon, in whom she cannot confide the tormenting secret of her family: "Only in the moment of her death can she confess the fervency of her love; only in the moment she does not belong to him can she confess that she belongs to him."[38] In short, if she reveals the secret, she must die, for she cannot continue to live with the knowledge that she has betrayed the crimes of her father. However, if she does not reveal this secret to Haemon, then she betrays her love for him by keeping such

[35]   *SKS* 2, 30 / *EO1*, 21.
[36]   *SKS* 18, 26, EE:59 / *KJN* 2, 22.
[37]   See Leon Jaurnow and Steen Tullberg, "Tekstredegørelse" to the *Journal EE* in *SKS* K18, 17.
[38]   *SKS* 2, 162 / *EO1*, 164.

an important secret from her beloved. The esthete then recalls another story from Nepos: "When Epaminondas was wounded in the battle at Mantinea, he let the arrow remain in the wound until he heard that the battle was won, for he knew that it was his death when he pulled it out."[39] This is then used as a parallel to the account of Antigone: "In the same way, our Antigone carries her secret in her heart like an arrow that life has continually plunged deeper and deeper, without depriving her of her life, for as long as it is in her heart she can live, but the instant it is taken out, she must die."[40] In this account Nepos is not mentioned by name, and Kierkegaard leaves it to the reader to identify the source.

The printed passage was actually revised from an earlier draft, in which the parallel with Epaminondas is recounted in the first person by Antigone herself. In this draft, the passage reads: "I feel that my life must soon end—it goes with me as with Epaminondas after the battle at Mantinea; my secret is an arrow sticking in my heart; as long as it remains sticking there I can no doubt live, but as soon as I pull it out, I must die. Now I have revealed myself; now I must die."[41] One reason for the reformulation of this passage might have been that, for reasons of chronology, it would have been impossible for Antigone to utter it. While the story of Oedipus and Antigone belongs to the distant legendary past, the battle of Mantinea in fact belongs to historical times, taking place in 362 BC. Thus, it would be anachronistic to have Antigone recall an event that took place centuries *after* her time.

This passage refers to Nepos' treatment of the aforementioned Theban general Epaminondas (Book XV, 9). Epaminondas played an important role in Thebes' brief rise to power among the Greek states. He became famous for defeating an invading army of Spartans and later aiding the subjugated states in the Peloponnesus win their freedom from Sparta. In his portrayal Nepos depicts primarily Epaminondas' moral character and not so much his biography as such.

The account of Epaminondas' death that Kierkegaard recalls, appears as follows in Nepos' narrative:

> Finally, when commander at Mantinea, in the heat of battle he charged the enemy too boldly. He was recognized by the Lacedaemonians, and since they believed that the death of that one man would ensure the safety of their country, they all directed their attack at him alone and kept on until, after great bloodshed and the loss of many men, they saw Epaminondas himself fall valiantly fighting, struck down by a lance hurled from afar. By his death the Boeotians were checked for a time, but they did not leave the field until they had completely defeated the enemy. But Epaminondas, realizing that he had received a mortal wound, and at the same time that if he drew out the head of the lance, which was separated from the shaft and fixed in his body, he would at once die, retained it until news came that the Boeotians were victorious. As soon as he heard that, he cried: "I have lived long enough, since I die unconquered." Then he drew out the iron and at once breathed his last.[42]

---

[39]   *SKS* 2, 162 / *EO1*, 164.

[40]   *SKS* 2, 162 / *EO1*, 164.

[41]   *Pap.* III B 179:40 / *EO1*, Supplement, p. 544.

[42]   *Corneli Nepotis Vitae*, ed. by E.O. Winstedt, Book XV, 9. (English translation quoted from *Cornelius Nepos*, trans. by Rolfe, pp. 181–2.)

Like the previous anecdote, this one is in no way outstanding in the narrative. In fact Nepos mentions others that are more striking and more entertaining. The point of this narrative is clearly to show the virtue and noble-mindedness of the Theban general, whose sole interest was the safety of the homeland and not his own welfare.

Once again Kierkegaard seems to recall this passage from memory. There is no reference to Nepos, and the allusion has only been identified by commentators. As in the passage before, Kierkegaard seems simply to recall an anecdote suitable for the given situation, here for illustrating something in the text he is working on. The image fits well with the description he gives of Antigone's situation in the retelling of the story in the version the esthete presents.

IV. Kierkegaard's Use and Understanding of Nepos

Comparatively speaking, Kierkegaard's use of Nepos was minimal. He presumably knew Nepos' biographies from having read them as a schoolboy. Then, as he was beginning his authorship, he recalled individual stories and anecdotes that served by way of illustration to things that he was trying to describe and analyze. It should be noted that his appropriations of the anecdotes found in Nepos are rather far-fetched from their original context as is most clearly illustrated by comparison of the contraption conceived to keep the horses fit with Kierkegaard's or the esthete's lonely, isolated situation. While Kierkegaard has an eye for an odd or striking story, he is most interested in reworking it by putting it into his own context and universe of thought. Thus Nepos is, for Kierkegaard, a ready source of anecdotal material that he draws upon when he wishes, regardless of whether or not the appropriation is a natural or obvious one in the context in which he wishes to use it. It is not out of the question that other appropriations of Nepos await our discovery in Kierkegaard's authorship.

It is possible that Kierkegaard was attracted to the "edifying" element in Nepos' biographies. In Nepos the anecdotes are supposed to illustrate the moral virtue of the figure being described in a way that invites the reader to imitation. In his authorship Kierkegaard also wanted to have a similar effect on his readers. He hoped that by problematizing certain issues about, for example, Christianity, his readers would of their own accord be obliged to reflect on their own relation to faith, sin, and the Christian message. Thus it is possible that one can regard Nepos as a kind of pagan edifying author in a way that Kierkegaard appreciated. It must, however, be conceded that the cleverness of Eumenes or the patriotic virtue of Epaminondas are not the main focus in Kierkegaard's use of these stories, although these are clearly the elements that Nepos wished to illustrate with the stories. In the absence of the identification of other appropriations of Nepos in the authorship, the notion of the influence of Nepos as a kind of edifying author must remain a mere suggestion or tentative working hypothesis awaiting more definitive confirmation or contradiction.

Bibliography

I. Nepos' Works in The Auction Catalogue *of Kierkegaard's Library*

None.

II. Works in The Auction Catalogue *of Kierkegaard's Library that Discuss Nepos*

Meierotto, Johann Heinrich Ludwig, *Ueber Sitten und Lebensart der Römer in verschiedenen Zeiten der Republik*, vols. 1–2, 3rd revised and enlarged ed., Berlin: in der Myliussischen Buchhandlung 1814 (*ASKB* 656).
Meiners, Christoph, *Geschichte des Verfalls der Sitten und der Staatsverfassung der Römer*, Leipzig: bey Weidmanns Erben und Reich 1782, p. 69; p. 160 (*ASKB* 660).
Michelet, Carl Ludwig, *Vorlesungen über die Persönlichkeit Gottes und Unsterblichkeit der Seele oder die ewige Persönlichkeit des Geistes*, Berlin: Verlag von Ferdinand Dümmler 1841, p. 207 (*ASKB* 680).

III. Secondary Literature on Kierkegaard's Relation to Nepos

None.

Ovid:

Of Love and Exile: Kierkegaard's Appropriation of Ovid

Steven P. Sondrup

In spite of his troubled relationship with the Emperor Caesar Augustus and his family, Ovid (Publius Ovidius Naso) was among the most illustrious poets to grace the Augustan age. He was recognized during his life as a highly accomplished poet in spite of the fact that he gave up the effort to write an epic with the claim that the form was beyond his skill. He addressed his poetry to the cultivated society living in Rome during the years of relative peace that Augustus had brought to the empire and was appreciated for the wit, levity, and sparkling brilliance of well-turned phrases. Although well-educated and possessed of an extensive knowledge of Greek literature, he avoided any ostentatious display of his erudition. He has long been praised for his sensitivity to beauty and his singular ability to portray it with lightness, grace, and elegance. His influence persisted through the Middle Ages and Renaissance to this day, when renewed attention is being paid particularly to the dynamics of change portrayed in his work of most lasting fame, the *Metamorphoses*.

I. Survey of Ovid's Life and Work

Ovid was born in 43 BC into a socially and politically well-situated family in Sulmona, a small town of the Paelignians—today the Abruzzo—and enjoyed the advantages that birth into a respected and prosperous family afforded.[1] He was sent to Rome for his education where he studied rhetoric and law without much enthusiasm and completed his studies in Athens. Although sensing his vocation as a poet, he briefly adhered to his father's advice to choose a more financially promising course and served in relatively unimportant public offices. He was a friend of the poet Propertius and heard

---

[1]   Among the most important modern studies of Ovid's life are Niklas Holzberg, *Ovid: Dichter und Werk*, Munich: C.H. Beck 1997, published in English as *Ovid: The Poet and his Work*, trans. by G.M. Goshgarian, Ithaca, New York: Cornell University Press 2002; Sara Mack, *Ovid*, New Haven, Connecticut: Yale University Press 1988; John Barby, *Ovid*, Oxford: Clarendon Press 1978; L.P. Wilkinson, *Ovid Recalled*, Cambridge: Cambridge University Press 1955; Herman Fränkel, *Ovid: A Poet between Two Worlds*, Berkeley, California: University of California Press 1945 (*Sather Classical Lectures*, vol. 18).

recitations by Macer and Horace. He also enjoyed a brief friendship with Tibullus, whose death he lamented in moving verse, and claims only to have seen Virgil.

Comfortably situated in Rome, he was in a position to devote himself to his poetic interests. His composition of the *Amores* brought him not only fame and public appreciation but also established the thematic orientation for his next several books. The love poems that constitute the *Amores* portray the fragile beauty and allure of a fictitious woman named Corinna, who is a composite of traits Ovid observed in many women. The *Heroides*, a more accomplished work, consists of amorous letters addressed by aristocratic ladies of the legendary past to husbands or lovers from whom they were separated and offers readers an early view of Ovid's deep interest in mythology. Originally known as the *Epistulae Heroidum*, this collection of verse love letters, whose composition extended over several years, signals Ovid's originality and brought him renewed appreciation and fame. Ovid's masterpiece in the erotic vein is surely the *Ars Amatoria*, in which he presents himself as a *"praeceptor amoris,"* a professor of love who offers instruction on how to seduce women in three books in the elegiac meter. The conclusion of the didactic cycle devoted to love is the *Remedia Amoris*, which as a kind of counter to the *Ars Amatoria* suggests remedies for any afflicted with the sickness of love.

The concept of love that Ovid presents is blatantly seductive and erotic and in stark contrast to the traditional Roman views of marital fidelity that Augustus was endeavoring to re-establish. In AD 8 while away from Rome, Ovid learned that he had been banished ostensibly as a result of the salacious nature of his poetry but more probably because of an error in judgement that may have involved some knowledge of, or role in, the adultery of Julia, the granddaughter of Augustus.

Before Ovid left for exile, he had written but not polished the masterpiece for which he is best remembered: the *Metamorphoses*, a compendium of Greek and Latin mythology in fifteen books of hexameters. Epic in scope—despite Ovid's disclaimers—it is a work united by the theme of change of form or shape from the initial transmutation of primal chaos into order down to the transformation of Julius Caesar into a star. The *Metamorphoses* are certainly Ovid's most influential book, which with Virgil's *Aeneid* stand as a pinnacle of Latin culture with traces appearing in the works of numerous writers from Dante through Chaucer and Shakespeare to Kafka. Although the renown and influence of the *Metamorphoses* in championing Roman culture are undeniable, the *Fasti* are his most clearly civic-minded poems in their projection of the ancient customs and values of Latium onto the first six months of the year.

Ovid went into exile in November of AD 8 and in the summer of AD 9 arrived in Tomi (sometimes spelled Tomis) on the Black Sea (today Costanza). In stark contrast to the culture and luxury of Rome, life in this frontier fortress was harsh, uncultivated, and cold. Since Latin was all but unknown in this remote region, Ovid learned the indigenous languages but continued to address his poetry in Latin to his reading public in Rome. The most important work written during his banishment was the *Tristia*, a work in five books sent back to Rome with some trepidation bitterly lamenting the harshness of his life in exile and appealing to his wife and friends for remediation of his circumstances. He hoped to find complete restoration of his former status, but failing that resolution, he at least would have liked a more congenial place in which to spend his declining years. Ovid also assembled in four books a collection of elegies written clearly in epistolary form collectively known as the *Epistulae ex Ponto*. Although the *Tristia* and these letters represent a highly noteworthy revival of the supposed Greek sense of the elegy—poetry of lament and desolation—they were of no avail in gaining restitution of his former status in Rome. Ovid died in AD 17 or 18 while still in exile among those he considered barbarians.

II. Kierkegaard and Ovid

Ovid's works so completely permeated Western culture generally and particularly the curriculum of Latin instruction throughout the world at least through the nineteenth century that it is inconceivable that someone with Kierkegaard's extraordinary proficiency in Latin would not be intimately familiar with the vast majority of the corpus almost from boyhood on.[2] But evidence of his knowledge

---

[2]   The number of studies of Ovid's influence is vast. A highly selective list of contemporary book-length investigations includes Richard J. King, *Desiring Rome: Male Subjectivity and Reading Ovid's Fasti*, Columbus, Ohio: Ohio State University Press 2006; Marilynn Desmond, *Ovid's Art and the Wife of Bath: The Ethics of Erotic Violence*, Ithaca, New York: Cornell University Press 2006; Theodore Ziolkowski, *Ovid and the Moderns*, Ithaca, New York: Cornell University Press 2005; Syrithe Pugh, *Spenser and Ovid*, Aldershot: Ashgate 2005; Suzanne C. Hagedorn, *Abandoned Women: Rewriting the Classics in Dante, Boccaccio, and Chaucer*, Ann Arbor, Michigan: University of Michigan Press 2004; Gregory M. Sadlek, *Idleness Working: The Discourse of Love's Labor from Ovid through Chaucer and Gower*, Washington, DC: Catholic University of America Press 2004; Sun Hee Kim Gertz, *Echoes and Reflections: Memory and Memorials in Ovid and Marie de France*, Amsterdam: Rodopi 2003; Mariantoniette Acocella, *L'Asino d'oro nel Rinascimento: Dai volgarizzamenti alle raffigurazioni pittoriche*, Ravenna: Longo 2001; Lynn Enterline, *The Rhetoric of the Body from Ovid to Shakespeare*, Cambridge: Cambridge University Press 2000; Sarah Annes Brown, *The Metamorphosis of Ovid: From Chaucer to Ted Hughes*, New York: St Martin's Press 1999; Patrick Cheney, *Marlowe's Counterfeit Profession: Ovid, Spenser, Counter-Nationhood*, Toronto, Ontario: University of Toronto Press 1997; M.L. Stapleton, *Harmful Eloquence: Ovid's Amores from Antiquity to Shakespeare*, Ann Arbor, Michigan: University of Michigan Press 1996; Michael A. Calabrese, *Chaucer's Ovidian Arts of Love*, Gainesville: University Press of Florida 1994; Pieropaolo Fornaro, *Metamorfosi con Ovidio: Il classico da riscrivere sempre*, Florence: Olschki 1994; Eric Downing, *Artificial I's: The Self as Artwork in Ovid, Kierkegaard, and Thomas Mann*, Tübingen: Niemeyer 1993 (*Studien zur deutschen Literatur*, vol. 127); Jonathan Bate, *Shakespeare and Ovid*, Oxford: Clarendon Press 1993; Peter L. Allen, *The Art of Love: Amatory Fiction from Ovid to the Romance of the Rose*, Philadelphia: University of Pennsylvania Press 1992; Madison U. Sowell (ed.), *Dante and Ovid: Essays in Interpretation*, Binghamton: State University of New York Press 1991 (*Medieval Texts and Studies*); Kathleen Anne Perry, *Another Reality: Metamorphosis and the Imagination in the Poetry of Ovid, Petrarch, and Ronsard*, New York: Peter Lang 1990; Marina Scordilis Brownlee, *The Severed Word: Ovid's Heroides and the novela sentimental*, Princeton, New Jersey: Princeton University Press 1990; Deborah S. Greenhut, *Feminine Rhetorical Culture: Tudor Adaptations of Ovid's Heroides*, New York: Peter Lang 1988; Kathleen Wall, *The Callisto Myth from Ovid to Atwood: Initiation and Rape in Literature*, Kingston, Quebec: McGill-Queen's University Press 1988; Vanna Lippi Bigazzi,

rests on an even more secure foundation: *The Auctioneer's Sales Record of the Library of Søren Kiekegaard* lists as item 1265 in the main collection *P. Ovidii Nasonis, quae exstant.*[3] Kierkegaard also owned two important guides to classical mythology that would have served him well with information about the classical past in general and Ovid in particular. The first is the important early nineteenth-century two-volume guide to classical mythology, the *Neues mythologisches Wörterbuch: für studirende Jünglinge, angehende Künstler und jeden Gebildeten überhaupt* by Paul Friedrich Achat Nitsch (1754–94).[4] The edition in Kierkegaard's library was the second, revised and expanded edition. These two volumes list both well-known and relatively obscure figures from classical mythology and identify their various sources. For example, the entry on Argus Pantoptes notes that he is mentioned in the first book of Ovid's *Metamorphoses* as well as earlier in the earlier work of Apollodorus also dealing with the mythology. While the edition of Ovid and this guide to classical mythology are standard early-nineteenth-century publications, *Le Grand dictionnaire historique, ou le Mélange curieux de l'histoire sacrée et profane Qui Contient en Abregé l'Histoire Fabuleuse des Dieux & des Héros de l'Antiquité Payenne* has a much longer history.[5] Louis Moréri (1643–80) began work on the dictionary in 1674, and the first edition was published in Basel by Pierre Roques and a second important edition in Lyon in 1681. The work was widely disseminated and went through several editions during the late seventeenth and eighteenth centuries.

I volgarizzamenti trecenteschi: Dell'Ars Amandi e dei Remedia Amoris, vols. 1–2, Florence: Accademia della Crusca 1987; Leonar Barkan, *The Gods Made Flesh: Metamorphosis & the Pursuit of Paganism*, New Haven, Connecticut: Yale University Press 1986; Jonathan Goldberg, *Voice Terminal Echo: Postmodernism and English Renaissance Texts*, New York: Methuen 1986; Richard J. DuRocher, *Milton and Ovid*, Ithaca and New York: Cornell University Press 1985; G.F.C. Plowden, *Pope on Classic Ground*, Athens, Ohio: Ohio University Press 1983; Ron Thomas, *The Latin Masks of Ezra Pound*, Ann Arbor, Michigan: University Microfilms International Research Press 1983; John M. Fyler, *Chaucer*, New Haven, Connecticut: Yale University Press 1979; Annegret Dinter, *Der Pygmalion-Stoff in der europaischen Literatur: Rezeptionsgeschichte einer Ovid-Fabel*, Heidelberg: Winter 1979; Richard L. Hoffman, *Ovid and The Canterbury Tales*, Philadelphia: University of Pennsylvania Press 1966; Otis Brooks, *Ovid as an Epic Poet*, New York: Cambridge University Press 1966; Karl Bartsch, *Albrecht von Halberstadt und Ovid im Mittelalter*, Amsterdam: Rodopi 1965; W.H.D. Rouse (ed.), *Shakespeare's Ovid: Being Arthur Golding's Translation of the Metamorphoses*, London: Centaur Press 1961; and Franco Munari, *Ovid im Mittelalter*, Zürich: Artemis 1960.

[3]   *P. Ovidii Nasonis*, vols. 1–3, ed. by Anton Richter, Editio Stereotypa, Leipzig: Tauchnitz 1828 (*ASKB* 1265).

[4]   Paul Friedrich Achat Nitsch, *Neues mythologisches Wörterbuch: für studirende Jünglinge, angehende Künstler und jeden Gebildeten überhaupt*, 2nd revised and enlarged ed. by Friedrich Gotthilf Klopfer, Leipzig: F. Fleischer 1821 (*ASKB* 1944–45).

[5]   Louis Moréri, *Le Grand dictionnaire historique, ou le Mélange curieux de l'histoire sacrée et profane Qui Contient en Abregé l'Histoire Fabuleuse des Dieux & des Héros de l'Antiquité Payenne*, vols. 1–6, Basel: Jean Brandmuller 1731–32 (*ASKB* 1965–69).

A. Ovid and Love

Although Kierkegaard's published works and papers make frequent allusions to Ovid, he is mentioned directly by name relatively rarely and not surprisingly in his published works only in *Either/Or*'s "Diary of a Seducer" in the context of his being an expert on the dynamics of erotic love.[6] In "The Diary of a Seducer," for example, Kierkegaard cites but does not provide specific identification of a passage in which Ovid explicitly identifies his narrator—and implicitly himself—as the poet of love.[7] In the beginning of *Remedia Amoris*, the narrator counters the suggestion that wars were in store by insisting rather that he is by nature a lover who has taught Cupid's art of erotic love and how what was once impulse has become science, "*quod nunc ratio est, impetus ante fuit*" (1.10).[8] In thus arguing that what in the youth is the raw erotic drive, under the tutelage of Ovid's narrator—one of Cupid's most ardent followers—becomes method: Kierkegaard's seducer, Johannes, is not only counseling patience in his own amorous pursuits but identifying himself as similarly expert in the art of erotic love. To wit, he recognizes that Cordelia

> must be spun into my web in a totally different way, and then suddenly I shall let the full force of love burst forth....I am pulling the bow of love tighter in order to wound all the deeper. Like an archer, I slacken the string, pull it tight again, listen to its song; it is my martial music, but as yet I do not aim—as yet I do not place the arrow to the string.[9]

Although one might recall the source of this citation or recognize the sequence of typically Ovidian images, the identification of Ovid as the source of a quotation is by no means always left to the reader. Later in "The Diary of a Seducer," an entry begins with the proclamation that Johannes is engaged but continues explaining at some length how the amorous relationship will nonetheless continue.[10] Then with specific reference to Ovid, Johannes notes, "The more the conflict in a love relationship

---

[6]   Downing, *Artifical I's: The Self as Artwork in Ovid, Kierkegaard, and Thomas Mann*, gives particular attention to Ovid's and Kierkegaard's erotic agendas as extensions of the literary constructions of the self, "All three feature protagonists who are at once seducers, aesthetes, and fiction-making artists, who individually undertake to live 'by art,' 'poetically,' and '*im Gleichnis*' and who in doing so all undertake to fashion something of a literary artwork out of the self. Kierkegaard and Ovid also present a variation on the project that I consider for comparative purposes, namely the attempt to fashion literary artwork out of another, out of the woman who in each case is the object of the protagonist's aesthetic and erotic designs" (p. 1).

[7]   Passages that are not specifically designated as having been derived from Ovid but nonetheless have clear and convincing analogues in the works of Ovid will be discussed even though they may have resonance or play an important role in the works of other classical authors.

[8]   *Remedia Amoris*, in *Ovid*, vols. 1–6, trans. by Grant Showerman, J.H. Mozley, Frank Justus Miller, James George Frazer, and A.L. Wheeler, 2nd revised ed. by G.P. Goold, Cambridge, Massachusetts: Harvard University Press, 1986–89 (*Loeb Classical Library*, vols. 392–7), vol. 2, 178–81 (lines 1–40). Kierkegaard cites the passage with the phrases of the quotation reversed "*quod antea fuit impetus, nunc ratio est*" *SKS* 2, 338 / *EO1*, 349.

[9]   ·   *SKS* 2, 338 / *EO1*, 349.

[10]   *SKS* 2, 363–4 / *EO1*, 375.

has been *eminus*, the more distressing it is, for hand-to-hand combat becomes all the more trifling. Hand-to-hand combat involves a handshake, a touching with the foot—something that Ovid, as is known, recommends just as much as he most jealously rants against it."[11] The reference is to a passage from the *Amores* I.4,[12] one of the more didactic elegies in the collection, in which the poet coaches his beloved on how to flirt surreptitiously with a lover and avoid the erotic advances of her husband while all three are partaking of a banquet in high society.

The second explicit reference to Ovid in "The Diary of a Seducer" is neither as playful nor blatantly erotic, but ridicules the institution of the engagement, which always begins with casual conversation about the couple's love but then only deteriorates from that point on. "This chitchat is also the beginning of the dowry Ovid mentions: *dos est uxoria lites* [the dowry of a wife is quarreling] and the guarantee that their marriage will not lack it."[13] The retort is a witty characterization of the burden of marriage that introduces a description of the more dulcet whispers that should be taken to the bed of the mistress. The allure of the mistress' bed must have resonated strongly with this passage because in the *Papirer* the same line is quoted,[14] followed by a quotation whose source seems to have eluded Kierkegaard in the moment of recording the thought: "What shoulders, what arms did I see—and touch! How suited for caress the form of her breasts! How smooth her body beneath the faultless bosom! What a long and beautiful side! How youthfully fair the thigh."[15] This evocation of feminine beauty is characteristic of Ovid's earliest amorous efforts in the *Amores* that are not directed toward a single unifying female figure who unites the collection—as in the case, perhaps most notably, of Catullus—but rather reveals an appreciation of the charms of any beautiful woman.

Later in "The Diary of a Seducer," he draws on a more extensive passage to illustrate that women are intimidated by the masculine intellect yet precisely that power makes feminine beauty engaging. To rely on masculine beauty and deportment is to abandon the field of erotic conquest to distinctly feminine strategies, which can make some headway but never lead to victory. To achieve that end, manly eloquence is required. "Ulysses was not comely, but he was eloquent; yet he fired two goddesses of the sea with love."[16] In a draft of this passage,[17] Kierkegaard had considered offering a more extended version of the quotation by citing the couplets that precede and follow what in the end was finally chosen: the first advises the cultivation of intellectual power and the last offers a further illustration of Ulysses' verbal dexterity in describing the power his eloquence had on Calypso. Neither of these couplets adds anything substantive that is not contained in the central pair of

---

11   *SKS* 2, 366 / *EO1*, 418.
12   . *Amores*, in *Ovid*, vol. 1, 1977, pp. 329–31 (Book 1.4, lines 1–30).
13   *SKS* 2, 406 / *EO1*, 378. *Ars Amatoria*, in *Ovid*, vol. 2, 1986, pp. 76–7 (Book 2, line 155).
14   *Pap.* III B 162:4.
15   *Amores*, in *Ovid*, vol. 1, 1977, pp. 334–5 (Book 1.5, lines 19–22).
16   *SKS* 2, 351 / *EO1*, 362; *Ars Amatoria*, in *Ovid*, vol. 2, 1986, pp. 74–5 (Book 2, lines 122–3).
17   *Pap.* III B 43.

lines, so their elimination concentrates the power of the observation in the central couplet, thus giving it more arresting power.

Early in his career in a journal entry, Kierkegaard also refers to Ovid in the context of his study of the Provençal troubadours. In an entry dated April 22, 1836, he took notes in a mixture of Danish and German on his reading of the more than 600-page study by Friedrich Christian Diez (1794–1876)[18] entitled *Leben und Werke der Troubadours: Ein Beitrag zur nähern Kenntniss des Mittelalters*. In quoting a passage contrasting the affect of *Naturpoesie* on the one hand and *Kunstpoesie* on the other—not in essence significantly different from the distinction Schiller had famously made between *naive* and *sentimentale Dichtung*—Kierkegaard agrees with Diez that natural and spontaneous poetry has a more powerful impact because artfully constructed poetry lacks a center. He further notes that Ovid was the only classical poet to share that understanding.[19] Diez gives further credence to this conclusion by pointing out that several of the troubadours' characteristic themes could be derived from their "*ars amandi*," a suggestion that invites the conclusion that their works are a continuation of Ovid's *Ars Amatoria*.[20] Kierkegaard's notes are telling in that that they are consistent with Ovid's own highly spirited and intellectually sophisticated early poetry and suggest Kierkegaard's mature understanding of Ovid's early poetic efforts at a relatively young age.

In contrast to the use of passages in praise of love, Kierkegaard also draws on Ovid for imagery suggesting the frustrations and pains of lost love. Rather than coming from Ovid's works on the art of love, Kierkegaard in this regard draws on passages from the *Metamorphoses*. In an excoriating description of his frustration with his relationship with Cordelia, Kierkegaard's narrator Johannes compares her to Paëthon, the son of Helius who wanted to drive the chariot of the sun but was unable to control the spirited horses and scorched some parts of the earth while letting others freeze.[21] In evoking his frustration, Johannes laments, "She likes to drive the sun chariot across the arch of heaven and to come close enough to earth to scorch people a little. But

---

[18]   Friedrich Christian Diez was a prolific scholar with a very broad command of Late Medieval and Renaissance literature of the various romance languages. The volume Kierkegaard was studying (*Die Poesie der Troubadours: Nach gedruckten und handschriftlichen Werken derselben dargestellt von Friedrich Diez*, Zwickau: Gebrüder Schumann 1826; not listed in *ASKB*), was published in a second expanded edition by Karl Bartsch in Leipzig by J.A. Barth in 1882, and that second edition was republished in 1965 (Hildesheim: G. Olms). Among his particularly important scholarly contributions in addition to the volume Kierkegaard was reading are his *Etymologisches Wörterbuch der Romanischen Sprachen*, first published in Bonn by A. Marcus in 1853. It went through several subsequent editions by 1887 including an English version, *An Etymological Dictionary of the Romance Languages; Chiefly from the German of Friedrich Diez*, published by T.C. Donkin in London in 1864 and his *Grammatik der Romanischen Sprachen* published in Bonn by E. Webe between 1836 and 1844 also published in several subsequent editions and translations. See also *Friedrich Diez Centennial Lectures, delivered May 24, 1976*, ed. by Edward F. Tuttle, Berkeley, California: University of California Press 1976.

[19]   *SKS* 17, 62–75, BB:2 / *KJN* 1, 56–68.

[20]   *SKS* 17, 70, BB:2 / *KJN* 1, 64.

[21]   *Metamorphoses*, in *Ovid*, vol. 3, 1966, pp. 54–328 (Book 1, line 747–Book 2, line 328).

she does not trust me; as yet I have prevented every approach even in an intellectual sense."²² The direct reference to this passage ignores the fact that as a punishment Paëthon's father required his life and the transformation—the metamorphosis—of his mourning sister as a result. The reference to this particularly extended narrative episode from the *Metamorphoses* draws only on the fact Paëthon's scorching of the earth is an analogue to Johannes' relationship to Cordelia. In contrast to this negative portrayal of Cordelia based on the *Metamorphoses,* Kierkegaard draws on another episode from the same source but in this case to describe his sense of loss when the bond that had linked Johannes and Cordelia was broken and specifically adduces the metamorphosis at the heart of the episode. To describe this sense of emptiness, he draws on Ovid's portrayal of Pygmalion, the sculptor who, disgusted with women's wantonness, forsakes human affection only to fall in love with a statue he has sculpted that Venus turns into a living woman whom he can love.²³ Kierkegaard, however, reverses the well-known episode in having Johannes opine that the loss of Cordelia would be like having Pygmalion's beloved turned back into stone. "Truly, if this regal flight were a retreat from me, it would pain me very deeply. For me it would be the same as if Pygmalion's beloved were changed to stone again."²⁴ These significant evocations of prominent episodes from the *Metamorphoses* well illustrate the extent to which Kierkegaard saw in Ovid a powerful reference to the influence of love apart from the more immediate descriptions offered specifically in the love poetry.

B. Ovid in Exile

In stark contrast to the playful, sophisticated, and often witty tone of the love poems, which Kierkegaard found particularly congenial for his portrayal of Johannes the Seducer, he also saw in Ovid a great poet who suffered from the humiliating exile he endured during the concluding years of his life. The last years of his life, spent far from home in an extremely harsh and uncongenial setting, became the epitome of suffering that a cruel fate bequeaths. The elegies compiled in the two collections written from exile—the *Tristia* and the *Epistulae ex Ponto*—clearly return to the classical Greek roots of the genre as one of lament, grief, and remorse. Kierkegaard saw in Ovid's suffering the essence of distress resulting from isolation and loss of status.

Kierkegaard refers indirectly to Ovid in *Christian Discourses*, which he wrote as the third installment in a series of religious meditations that began with the *Eighteen Upbuilding Discourses*, continued with the *Upbuilding Discourses in Various Spirits*, and culminated with what formed the third part to which Kierkegaard referred as "The Gospel of Suffering,"²⁵ published under the title *Christian Discourses* in 1848. The first section is entitled "The Cares of the Pagan," and most appropriately, the first reference to Ovid, albeit indirect, is in the chapter "The Cares of Loftiness," which

---

22   *SKS* 2, 349 / *EO1*, 360.
23   *Metamorphoses*, in *Ovid*, vol. 4, 1976, pp. 80–5 (Book 10, lines 243–97).
24   *SKS* 2, 425 / *EO1*, 418.
25   See *SKS* K10, 42–4 for details relating to this designation.

acknowledges that Christianity does not require a person to be lowly. If, though, the person of worldly eminence seeks to be a Christian, he must exercise great caution to be sure no part of his worldly advantage has preempted the possibility that "he could not easily become reconciled to being the lowly person among the people."[26] Ovid had clearly fallen from a lofty social position and, as a pagan, was unable to accommodate himself to his new status and accordingly suffered greatly and therein embodied the care of the pagan under discussion.

Later, in the second part of *Christian Discourses*, Kierkegaard makes another still indirect but more pointed reference to Ovid. In discussing the social and religious advantages of overcoming adversity, he turns his attention directly to poets. Offering his readers some lighter fare than the scriptural assurances that surmounting challenges leads to spiritual prosperity, he asks whether the testimony of poets can be believed? "Do you believe that the poet whose songs delight humankind, do you believe that he could have written these songs if adversity and hard sufferings had not been there to tune his soul! It is precisely in adversity 'when the heart sits in deepest gloom, that the harp of joy is tuned'".[27] This passage also describes to a degree Ovid's situation, and it can certainly be argued that the indignities he suffered late in life brought a profound poignancy to the elegies of the period. The description, though, is broad enough that it evokes the experience of a large company of poets to whose number, however, Ovid surely counts in a prominent way.

C. Frequently Cited Passages

Kierkegaard was intimately familiar with classical mythology from extensive reading in both Latin and Greek, and mythological references as well as verbal echoes of particular stories frequently find their way into his discourse. Given that one of Ovid's purposes in writing the *Metamorphoses* was to provide an epic-like and generally chronological compendium of approximately 250 varied individual mythological or quasi-historical episodes to which he was a particularly sensitive heir, the *Metamorphoses* are an obvious source of a number of important mythological themes that are evoked there but also appear in other classical sources. Kierkegaard could assume that the basic outlines of the stories to which he alludes would also be familiar to his reader and could, thus, often just mention the names of the protagonist or well-known phrases from the narrative sequences he had in mind.

The story of Pyramus and Thisbe—the account of how two young lovers whose parents forbade not only their marriage but also any contact were nonetheless able to converse secretly through a small crack in the brick wall that separated their parental homes—is one such example.[28] Kierkegaard mentions the story twice: once in *Either/Or*'s "Diary of a Seducer"[29] and later in *Stages on Life's Way*.[30] In both cases, the episode is recounted as an elucidating comparison that describes the yearning of lovers for one another though separated by social conventions no less isolating than

---

26   *SKS* 10, 65 / *CD*, 55.
27   *SKS* 10, 165 / *CD*, 157.
28   *Metamorphoses*, in *Ovid* vol. 3, 1966 (Book 4, lines 54–70).
29   *SKS* 2, 413 / *EO1*, 425.
30   *SKS* 6, 77 / *SLW*, 76.

the legendary wall that only let the briefest of affectionate assurances pass through. The rhetorical force of the allusion is to suggest that the potency of the requirements of decorum is no less powerful than the high brick wall precluding all but the most modest and fleeting expressions of affection.

In another allusion, Kierkegaard not only gestures toward a well-known episode from the *Metamorphoses*, but also echoes the precise phrase—in at least one case in the original Latin—that distills the impact of the episode. The recurring Latin phrase is *"pia fraus"* and in Danish *"et fromt Bedrag,"* that is, a pious deception. The expression stems from the *Metamorphoses* 9:711 in the account of Ligdus who so ardently wished his wife Telethusa would bear him a son that he ordained that if the expected child were a daughter, she should be killed. Telethusa, though, bore a girl and in response to the instructions of a goddess announced to her husband that it was a boy—the pious fraud in question—upon whom the father bestowed the non-gender-specific name Iphis.[31] Although raised as a boy, she could not look forward to the fulfillment of her erotic desire in conjugal bliss. Kierkegaard first uses the Latin phrase *"pia fraus"* in *From the Papers of One Still Living* in critiquing Hans Christian Andersen's portrayal of the demise of a character as a pious fraud of education rather than a poetic necessity.[32] The piety of the fraud, however, by no means compensates for the offense to aesthetic standards. The subsequent uses of the phrase are cited in Danish: in its appearance in *A Literary Review* it suggests the pious deception is preferable to the most miserable forms of self-deception.[33] In the first of the *Four Upbuilding Discourses* Kierkegaard then warns against pious deception concerning the nature of God no matter how well-intentioned it may be.[34] In *Stages on Life's Way* he portrays deception as a most serious ethical affront and laments the deceit with which an engagement was broken—however pious its motivation might have been—and the fact that it should have the power that it in the end managed to exercise.[35] Kierkegaard clearly manifests a certain fondness for the simple phrase— perhaps as an engaging oxymoron—in spite of condemning fraud and deception in general. He, though, allowed that the pious fraud—though reprehensible—was preferable to more blatant forms of dissemblance that had no devout sentiments mitigating their patent falsity.

Another Ovidian formulation that had a special appeal for Kierkegaard was *"Bene vixit qui bene latuit"* (He who has well hidden his life has lived well).[36] Ovid made the observation, in which he was quoting an outburst of the well-known Greek philosopher Pythagoras, as warning to a friend that those who live prominently public lives as Ovid had in Rome are often struck down by cruel fate. Everyone should accept, consequently, the position accorded him in life. Kierkegaard quotes the phrase once in Latin in *Stages on Life Way* in the context of his narrator seeking

---

[31]   *Metamorphoses*, in *Ovid*, vol. 4, 1976, pp. 50–61 (Book 9, lines 667–797).
[32]   *SKS* 1, 38 / *EPW*, 83.
[33]   *SKS* 8, 14 / *TA*, 10.
[34]   *SKS* 5, 313 / *EUD*, 322.
[35]   *SKS* 6, 356 / *SLW*, 384.
[36]   *Tristia*, in *Ovid*, vol. 6, 2002, pp. 116–17 (Book 3.4, lines 25–6).

the quiet solitude of an obscure place for contemplation.[37] He concludes that if Ovid's observation is correct, then he has lived well because his secluded spot has been well chosen. Although Kierkegaard does not directly quote the passage again in his published works, he alludes to it on three occasions in his journals. In an entry from 1847, he observes that his frequent appearance on the streets of Copenhagen may well be understood precisely as a means of avoiding anonymity but continues commenting on the demoralizing fact that the thief and the high-born members of society alike seek to live private and indeed hidden lives. The cowardly wretch who anonymously sits and scribbles, though personally lacking the courage to let himself be seen, enjoys the same advantage inherent in the aristocratic privacy.[38] In subsequent journal entries in which Kierkegaard refers to the passage, he does so as an endorsement of living a modest and indeed hidden life, that is, *at leve skjult*.[39] In Kierkegaard's final allusion to the idea in 1849, he asks whether there is not something pharisaical about living opulently especially when holding high ecclesiastical positions.[40] The obvious answer is that the humble and less ostentatious life is more consistent with New Testament teachings.

In the *Metamorphoses* III, 341–401 Ovid narrates the intertwined stories of Narcissus and Echo, which Kierkegaard used as a point of reference on several occasions. Echo was a nymph cursed by Hera because she had frequently detained Hera so that Zeus could escape from dalliances with other nymphs before Hera arrived on the scene. Hera ordained that Echo henceforth would only be able to repeat what she had just heard others say. Narcissus, the son of a nymph and a river god, was an extremely attractive young man who even at the age of sixteen had left a series of rejected lovers of both sexes behind him. Among those who pursued him was Echo, who, though only able to repeat what she heard him say, offered herself to him. Like so many others, though, she too was also rejected. Horrified at what had happened, she spent the rest of her life longing for love until only her voice was left. Narcissus, though, fell passionately in love with his own reflected image in a pure spring from which he was about to drink. Realizing he could never possess the object of his desire, he—joined by Echo—grieved and eventually thrust a dagger into his heart. From the blood-soaked earth, the white narcissus sprang as a memorial to his suffering and death.

In a journal entry from July 20, 1837, Kierkegaard offered a brief commentary on the episode and pointed out that even the ordinary nymph Echo, who from a Romantic perspective is parodistic or even humorous, could be accommodated within the Greeks' harmonious view of life. The force of the observation is to point out the broadly encompassing power of classical Greek civilization. In Kierkegaard's notebook from 1840–1841 he recapitulates the essence of this story identifying Narcissus as a sacrifice for unrequited love.[41] Kierkegaard also takes up the figure of Narcissus in *Either/Or* in discussing the balance between the aesthetic and the

---

37   *SKS* 6, 24 / *SLW*, 17.
38   *SKS* 20, 248, NB3:8.
39   *SKS* 21, 43, NB6:59. *SKS* 21, 331, NB10:147.
40   *SKS* 22, 281, NB13:15.
41   *SKS* 19, 34, Not1:6. *SKS* 19, 214, Not7:34.

ethical. He points out that the individual who has grasped himself in his eternal validity without recognizing flaws has not chosen himself, but "like Narcissus, he has become infatuated with himself. Such a condition has not infrequently ended in suicide."[42] Kierkegaard's point is that the initial perception of oneself with eternal validity is dangerous because it occludes a perception of shortcomings and more importantly of oneself in one's freedom to choose. Such a perception is as flat as Narcissus' reflection on the surface of the still water. In choosing himself as a free act of will, the individual acts and retains his freedom only in so far as he continues to realize it.

All the rest of Kierkegaard's references to the episode are to Echo, and all but one are observations in passing about auditory sensations that the Hongs' translation does not personify by capitalizing the initial letter.[43] In *Works of Love*, however, Echo becomes the veritable embodiment of repetition and specifically divine repetition. After explaining "God's relation to a human being is at every moment to infinitize what is in that human being at that very moment,"[44] Kierkegaard then describes Echo as living in solitude but repeating even the slightest sound back to the hearer, indeed everything that is spoken even inadvertently:

> Echo, as you well know, lives in solitude. Echo pays very close attention, oh, so very close, to every sound, the slightest sound, and renders it exactly, oh, so exactly! If there is a word you would rather not hear said to you, then watch your saying of it; watch lest it slip out of you in solitude, because echo promptly repeats it and says it to *you*. If you have never been solitary, then neither have you discovered that God is; but if you have truly been solitary, then you also learned that God just repeats everything you say and do to other people; he repeats it with the magnification of infinity. God repeats the words of grace or of judgment that you say about another; he says the same thing word for word about you; and these same words are for you grace and judgment.[45]

Ovid's narrative here serves Kierkegaard well as a poetically poignant means of moving from the immediate and readily accessible experience of quotidian life to a glimpse of the infinitely transcendental in a manner that may render it more accessible or fully real.

The final Ovidian figure to which Kierkegaard refers with any notable frequency is Argus (Panoptes), the mythological creature with one hundred eyes of which only two slept at any one time so the others could remain on watch. Juno trusted him to guard Io, whom she had turned into a white cow in an attempt to wrest her from Jove's amorous attention.[46] What attracts Kierkegaard's attention is the fact that Argus never really sleeps, a fact that he mentions in describing Abraham's foes. "He had fought with that crafty power that devises all things, with that vigilant enemy who never dozes, with that old man who outlives everything—he had fought

---

42   *SKS* 3, 221 / *EO2*, 231.
43   *SKS* 6, 258 / *SLW*, 277. *SKS* 4, 469 / *P*, 5.
44   *SKS* 9, 377 / *WL*, 384.
45   *SKS* 9, 377 / *WL*, 384–5.
46   *Metamorphoses*, in *Ovid*, vol. 3, 1966, pp. 46–55 (Book I, lines 62–747).

with time and kept his faith."[47] A description of Abraham in terms of a figure from classical mythology may at first seem jarring, but to the extent that it adduces the many varied forces that Abraham during his long life had combated, it serves as a powerful image and offers a forceful description of Abraham's moral and physical conquests. Kierkegaard makes four other references to the figure, simply mentioning the one hundred eyes as a means of suggesting careful and unflagging observation.[48] The fact that Argus was eventually killed by Mercury, the emissary sent by Jove to fetch Io, and that his one hundred eyes were taken up in the tail of the peacock, plays no role in Kierkegaard's appropriation of the episode.

D. Passages and Episodes Briefly Cited

In addition to the episodes to which Kierkegaard returned on multiple occasions and for which he developed a particular understanding, a number of quotations and events appear as passing citations, allusions, or references. They are quoted as passages that embody particularly poignant ways of making a point. In the chapter of the second issue of *The Moment*, entitled "We Are All Christians," for example, a situation in which someone would be allowed to assert that he is not a Christian would end in everyone declaring himself not to be a Christian. Rejecting that train of thought, Kierkegaard draws from a series of practical precepts that Ovid is rehearsing in the *Remedia Amores* and exclaims "No, no, *principiis obsta*" (resist beginnings) and instead admonishes standing firm on principle.[49] The connection linking Kierkegaard's use to Ovid's is based on the rhetorical force of citing a well-known Latin maxim in rejecting with a dramatic flourish the course that could lead to all espousing atheism. The final fleeting allusion comes in a marginal notation in Kierkegaard's journal (1848) in which he is discussing Feuerbach's polemical relationship to other writers. The note indicates that with regard to Feuerbach one can say "*et ab hoste consilium*" ("and from enemies, wisdom").[50] The Latin passage is not an exact quotation from Ovid but rather an imprecisely remembered paraphrase or allusion to a line from the *Metamorphoses*.[51] The line again seems to be an especially apt encapsulation of a thought not particularly linked to its original context.

Two further passing references to episodes from the *Metamorphoses* in this context also merit mention. The beginning of *Fear and Trembling* evokes the gods' deception of Orpheus in the "Preliminary Expectoration" that resulted because he was "soft, not boldly brave...and a zither player."[52] And later in the same section, Kierkegaard refers to a young girl with faith that all her expectations can be fulfilled, who can "invoke the finite powers of existence and bring the very stones to tears."[53]

---

[47]   *SKS* 4, 115 / *FT*, 19.

[48]   *SKS*, 11, 344 / *SLW* 371. *SKS* 9, 43 / *WL*, 35. *SKS* 21, 32, NB6:38. *SKS* 22, 250, NB12:178.

[49]   *SV1*, XIV, 130 / *M*, 117. *Remedia Amoris*, in *Ovid*, vol. 2, 1966, pp. 184–5 (line 91).

[50]   *SKS* 22, 336, NB13:92b.

[51]   *Metamorphoses*, in *Ovid*, vol. 3, 1966, pp. 208–9 (Book 4, line 428). "*Fas est et ab hoste doceri*" ("It is proper to learn from an enemy").

[52]   *SKS* 4, 123 / *FT*, 27.

[53]   *SKS* 4, 141 / *FT*, 47.

The incident is a recasting of the episode in the *Metamorphoses* in which a stone hurled at Orpheus falls from its trajectory as a result of the sweetness of his song.[54] As with earlier examples, this reference to an Ovidian passage seems motivated not so much by its original context *per se* but by the extent to which it serves as a probably familiar and still powerful example of extraordinary ability. Similarly in *The Sickness unto Death*, Kierkegaard describes the determinist in a comparison to King Midas, who starved after wishing that everything that he touched would turn to gold.[55] Once again, the fleeting veiled reference to an Ovidian account of a metamorphosis is used rhetorically as a convenient and well-known comparison for the lamentable plight that Kierkegaard is evoking in his description of the fatalist for whom everything has become necessity.

An examination of Kierkegaard's citations and allusions to Ovid demonstrates that he was writing from a position of extensive familiarity with the Latin poet. He was, moreover, addressing an implied reader who had a similar knowledge of the works of classical authors. His confidence in the erudition of his readers is suggested by his reference to Ovid simply as "the poet" or unidentified quotations or allusions that suggest readers would have little difficulty in surmising their source. Their shared familiarity with antiquity formed the basis for a kind of communal relationship in which Kierkegaard's more original and often intellectually as well as socially challenging precepts would find something of a congenial hearing.

Kierkegaard's primary use of Ovid that drew on the context from which he excerpted passages is most conspicuously those that appear in the "The Diary of a Seducer." Here Ovid's self-proclaimed role as a *"praeceptor amoris"* is fully acknowledged and even celebrated. His witty and light-hearted observations as well as his commentary on the battles of seduction are integrated in the personality of Johannes the Seducer in such a way as to make him one in a long line of Ovid's only-too-willing students. Although most of the citations and allusions come from the works dealing with love, Kierkegaard occasionally draws on episodes from the *Metamorphoses*, not for the sake of the changes in form or shape they ultimately describe but rather for the aspects of human relations they portray.

The other context in which Kierkegaard aligns his thinking with that of Ovid is in terms of Ovid's endorsement of the hidden life. From his deeply painful exile, he warned of the dangers of a publicly prominent or ebulliently ostentatious existence. It was easy to fall from social visibility to miserable obscurity for reasons that were never to be made entirely clear. The hidden life was thus more likely to be the life well lived. This precept rang true to Kierkegaard in terms of his endorsement of the religious life that was profoundly committed and deeply anchored rather than high ranking ecclesiastical officials parading their pomp and elegance in place of inward piety and humble conviction.

Kierkegaard's many other references to Ovid do not typically have as clear a relationship to the specific context of Ovid's works, be they fictional or autobiographical. The many allusions to the *Metamorphoses*, for example, most

---

[54]   *Metamorphoses*, in *Ovid*, vol. 4, 1976, pp. 120–1 (Book 11, lines 10–13).
[55]   *SKS* 11, 155 / *SUD*, 40. *Metamorphoses*, in *Ovid*, vol. 4, 1976, pp. 126–31 (Book 11, lines 86–146).

typically draw on a segment of an episode as a particularly apt comparison or instantiation of a point that Kierkegaard was endeavoring to make but that is not centered on the process of a metamorphosis that is the theme that unites the fifteen books of the epic-like narrative. Their recontextualization is not so radical that it distorts the original sense beyond recognition, but rather simply finds a new way in which an episode compellingly represents a point.

Ovid served Kierkegaard throughout his career as a writer who offered cogent and memorable formulations of points Kierkegaard was seeking to make both in contexts that paralleled those of the Ovidian source as well as those that displayed the often glittering verbal virtuosity of the Latin poet in a new setting. In both situations, Ovid's intellectual agility and ability to forge the arresting phrase or the potent image provided congenial points of reference that often open an area of shared understanding with readers sensitive to the breadth of his classical understanding.

Bibliography

I. Ovid's Works in The Auction Catalogue *of Kierkegaard's Library*

P. Ovidii Nasonis Quae Supersunt, vols. 1–3, ed. by Anton Richter, Editio Stereotypa, Leipzig: Tauchnitz 1828 (*ASKB* 1265).

Publii Ovidii Nasonis Tristium libri V. et Epistolarum ex Ponto, ed. by Emanuel Sincerum [i.e. Esaias Schneider], Augsburg: Mertz & Mayer 1750 (*ASKB* A I 171).

II. Works in The Auction Catalogue *of Kierkegaard's Library that Discuss Ovid*

Bähr, Johann Christian Felix, *Abriss der Römischen Literatur-Geschichte zum Gebrauch für höhere Lehranstalten*, Heidelberg and Leipzig: Groos 1833 (*ASKB* 975).

Dyck, Johann Gottfried and Georg Schatz (eds.), *Charaktere der vornehmsten Dichter aller Nationen; nebst kritischen und historischen Abhandlungen über Gegenstände der schönen Künste und Wissenschaften, von einer Gesellschaft von Gelehrten*, vols. 1–8, Leipzig: Dyk 1792–1808, vol. 3, pp. 325–94 (*ASKB* 1370–1377).

[Hegel, Georg Wilhelm Friedrich], *Georg Wilhelm Friedrich Hegel's Vorlesungen über die Aesthetik*, vols. 1–3, ed. by von Heinrich Gustav Hotho, Berlin: Verlag von Duncker und Humblot 1835–38 (vols. 10.1–10.3 in *Georg Wilhelm Friedrich Hegel's Werke. Vollständige Ausgabe*, vols. 1–18, ed. by Philipp Marheineke et al., Berlin: Verlag von Duncker und Humblot 1832–45), vol. 1, pp. 506–7; p. 531; vol. 2, pp. 30–4; vol. 3, p. 306 (*ASKB* 1384–1386).

Heiberg, Johan Ludvig, "Om den romantiske Tragedie af Hertz: *Svend Dyrings Huus*. I Forbindelse med en æsthetisk Betragtning af de danske Kæmpeviser," in *Perseus*, vols. 1–2, ed. by Johan Ludvig Heiberg, Copenhagen: C.A. Reitzel 1837–38, vol. 1, pp. 165–264, see p. 219 (*ASKB* 569).

[Longinus, Dionysius], *Dionysius Longin vom Erhabenen Griechisch und Teutsch, Nebst dessen Leben, einer Nachricht von seinen Schriften, und einer Untersuchung, was Longin durch das Erhabene verstehe*, trans. and ed. by Carl Heinrich Heineken, Leipzig and Hamburg: Conrad König 1738, p. 70; p. 144 (*ASKB* 1129).

[Møller, Poul Martin], *Efterladte Skrifter af Poul M. Møller*, vols. 1–3, ed. by Christian Winther, F.C. Olsen and Christen Thaarup, Copenhagen: C.A. Reitzel 1839–43, vol. 3, p. 70 (*ASKB* 1574–1576).

[Montaigne, Michel de], *Michael Montaigne's Gedanken und Meinungen über allerley Gegenstände, ins Deutsche übersetzt*, vols. 1–7, Berlin: F.T. Lagarde 1793–9, vol. 1, pp. 33–4; p. 335; vol. 3, p. 189 (*ASKB* 681–687).

Moréri, Louis, "Ovide," in *Le Grand dictionnaire historique, ou le Mélange curieux de l'histoire sacrée et profane Qui Contient en Abrégé l'Histoire Fabuleuse des Dieux & des Héros de l'Antiquité Payenne*, vols. 1–6, Basel: Jean Brandmuller 1731–32, vol. 5, pp. 642–3.

Schlegel, August Wilhelm, *Ueber dramatische Kunst und Litteratur. Vorlesungen*, vols. 1–2 (vol. 2 in two Parts), Heidelberg: Mohr und Zimmer 1809–11, vol. 2.1, p. 19 (*ASKB* 1392–1394).

Schmidt, W. Adolf, *Geschichte der Denk- und Glaubensfreiheit im ersten Jahrhundert der Kaiserherrschaft und des Christenthums*, Berlin: Verlag von Veit und Comp. 1847, p. 44; p. 49; p. 117; p. 260; p. 262 (*ASKB* 771).

Schopenhauer, Arthur, *Die Welt als Wille und Vorstellung*, vols. 1–2, 2nd revised and enlarged ed., Leipzig: F.A. Brockhaus 1844 [1819], vol. 1, p. 21; pp. 346–7; p. 359; p. 582; vol. 2, p. 409; p. 426 (*ASKB* 773–773a).

Sulzer, Johann Georg, *Allgemeine Theorie der Schönen Künste, in einzeln, nach alphabetischer Ordnung der Kunstwörter auf einander folgenden, Artikeln abgehandelt*, vols. 1–4 and a Register Volume, 2nd revised ed., Leipzig: in der Weidmannschen Buchhandlung 1792–99, vol. 1, p. 109; p. 205; p. 225; p. 407; vol. 2, p. 43; p. 59; p. 123; p. 446; p. 571; vol. 3, p. 182; p. 364 (*ASKB* 1365–1369).

Zeuthen, Ludvig, *Humanitet betragtet fra et christeligt Standpunkt, med stadigt Hensyn til den nærværende Tid*, Copenhagen: Gyldendalske Boghandling 1846, p. 64 (*ASKB* 915).

III. Secondary Literature on Kierkegaard's Relation to Ovid

Downing, Eric, *Artificial I's. The Self as Artwork in Ovid, Kierkegaard, and Thomas Mann*, Tübingen: Max Niemeyer 1993 (*Studien zur deutschen Literatur*, vol. 127).

Sallust:

Kierkegaard's Scarce Use of a Great Roman Historian

Niels W. Bruun

The Roman historian Gaius Sallustius Crispus was born on October 1, 86 BC in the city of Amiternum, today Amatrice, in Abruzzi, and died on May 13 in the year 34. Sallust was a Tribune of the People in 52, and in 50 he was, perhaps for political reasons, expelled from the Senate. During the Civil War he sided with Caesar, and in 46 he became governor of Numidia. Upon his arrival back in Rome, Sallust was accused of economic exploitation of the province, but Caesar prevented him from being condemned. In 44 Caesar was assassinated, and Sallust left political life. He then dedicated himself to writing history, specializing in monographs at the beginning of his authorship.[1]

His first historical monograph is entitled, *Bellum Catilinarium* or *Bellum Catilinae* (*The War against Catiline*) and is a portrayal of the conspiracy, which took place under the leadership of Lucius Sergius Catilina in the years 64–62. The next monograph-length work, *Bellum Jugurthinum* (*The War against Jugurtha*), describes the war which the Romans fought in the years from 111 to 105 BC against Jugurtha, the King of Numidia. Here Sallust exposed the Roman ruling class's corruption and incompetence, while portraying the rise to power of a wholly unknown man, C. Marius.

Sallust's last historical work, *Historiae*, was organized as annals and treated the period from 78 to 67. Since the largest part of this work, however, has been lost, our knowledge of it is quite limited. Sallust's literary model was the Greek historian Thucydides.

Sallust's language is characterized by a preference for archaic words and expressions—here he was under the influence of Cato the Elder (234–149 BC)—and even in antiquity his tendency towards archaicism was criticized. One special archaic feature is his striving for allitteration and paronomasy. With regard to his style, antiquity emphasized its *brevitas* (brevity and succinctness of expression) and *velocitas* (liveliness). In addition, he had a characteristic aversion to balance and harmony.

---

[1]   This is true with the exception of the works *Invectiva in Ciceronem* ("A Pamphlet against Cicero") and *Epistulae ad Caesarem senem* ("Letters to old Caesar"), the authenticity of which continues to be disputed.

His style was criticized at the time and in posterity, but Quintilian compared him favorably to Thucydides.[2] The Roman historian Tacitus (56–115) took him as his model and regarded him as the most outstanding Roman historian.[3]

It is evident from Kierkegaard's reading list that he had read at school "both wars," that is, *Bellum Catilinarium* and *Bellum Jugurthinum*. In his private library he had no less than three editions[4] as well as two Danish translations.[5] It is unclear whether this was due to the fact that Sallust captured his interest or he needed the books since he worked as a Latin teacher at the Borgerdyd School.

The earliest Sallust quotation in Kierkegaard is found in the treatise, *The Concept of Irony*: "Within the system every particular element acquires a meaning different from the one it has outside the system; it has, as it were, *aliud in lingua promtum, aliud pectore clausum*."[6] The quotation is from the *Bellum Catilinarium* 10.5, where one reads: "*Ambitio multos mortalis falsos fieri subegit; aliud clausum in pectore, aliud in lingua promptum habere eqs.*" ("Ambition tempted many to be false, to have one thought hidden in their hearts, another ready on their tongues.")[7] In Kierkegaard's text the formulation and word order of quotation "*in lingua promtum, aliud pectore clausum*" have been changed, which together with Kierkegaard's (and late Latin's) orthography *promtum* for *promptum*, can be taken as evidence that he quotes from memory.

In *Either/Or*, Part One, in the "Rotation of Crops" Kierkegaard writes, "What are the sure signs of friendship? Antiquity answers: *idem velle, idem nolle ea demum firma* amicitia—and is also extremely boring."[8] Kierkegaard here quotes *Bellum Catilinarium* 20.4: "*nam idem velle atque idem nolle, ea demum firma amicitia est.*" ("Identity of likes and dislikes is the one solid foundation of friendship."[9]) It should be noted that *atque* and *est* from the original text are not included, with the result that the statement is made more succinct and takes on the character of a slogan.

---

[2]   *Institutio Oratoria*, 10.1,101: *nec opponere Thucydidi Sallustium verear.*

[3]   *Annales*, 3.30,1: *rerum Romanarum florentissimus auctor.* Cf. Martial 14.191, 2: *primus Romana Crispus in historia.*

[4]   *C. Sallusti Crispi Opera, quæ supersunt*, ed. by Fr. Kritz, vols. 1–2, Leipzig: Lehnhold 1828–34 (*ASKB* 1269–1270); *C. Sallustii Crispi Opera quae extant praeter fragmenta omnia; Textum recognovit et illustravit*, 3rd ed., ed. by Wilhelm Lange, Halle: Hemmerde 1833 (*ASKB* 1271); *C. Sallustii Crispi Opera*, Editio Stereotypa, Leipzig: Tauchnitz 1829 (*ASKB* 1272).

[5]   *Sallusts Catilinariske Krig oversat fra det Latinske. Et Forsøg*, trans. by R. Møller, Copenhagen: Fr. Brummer 1811 (ASKB 1273, cf. ASKB A I 184); *Sallusts Jugurthinske Krig oversat fra det Latinske. Et Forsøg*, trans. by R. Møller, Copenhagen: Fr. Brummer 1812 (ASKB A I 184).

[6]   *SKS* 1, 90, 28–30n. / *CI*, 28n.

[7]   The Latin text from Sallust quoted in this article follows Kritz's edition (see footnote 4); his text has been compared with *C. Sallusti Crispi Catilina. Jugurtha*. Fragmenta ampliora edidit Alphonsus Kurfess, Leipzig: Teubner 1957. English translation quoted from *The Jugurthine War. The Conspiracy of Catiline*, trans. by S.A. Handford, Harmondsworth: Penguin 1963, p. 181.

[8]   *SKS* 2, 284.27–9 / *EO1*, 295.

[9]   *The Jugurthine War. The Conspiracy of Catiline*, p. 189.

In *Either/Or*, Part One, in "The Diary of a Seducer" one reads, "Will you keep this secret? Dare I depend upon you? Tales are told of people who by dreadful crimes initiated each other into mutual silence."[10] It cannot be ruled out that Kierkegaard perhaps has in mind here *Bellum Catilinarium* 22.1–2:

Fuere ea tempestate qui dicerent, Catilinam oratione habita quum ad ius iurandum popularis sceleris sui adigeret, humani corporis sanguinem vino permixtum in pateris circumtulisse; inde quum post exsecrationem omnes degustavissent, sicuti in sollemnibus sacris fieri consuevit, aperuisse consilium suum, atque eo, dictitare, fecisse, quo inter se magis fidi forent, alius alii tanti facinoris conscii. (There was a rumor current at the time that when Catiline, on the conclusion of his speech, called on the associates of his plot to swear an oath, he passed round bowls of human blood mixed with wine; and when all had tasted of it after invoking a curse upon themselves if they broke faith, in accordance with the usual practice at such solemn ceremonies, he revealed the details of his scheme. This he is said to have done in order that the consciousness of having jointly participated in such an abomination might make them more loyal to one another.)[11]

In *Either/Or*, Part Two, in the chapter, "The Balance between the Esthetic and the Ethical," Kierkegaard writes:

The one who has to work will be unfamiliar with the vain joy of being able to have everything; he will not learn to appeal self-confidently to his wealth, to remove every hindrance with money, and to buy every freedom for himself. But then his mind will not be embittered either; he will not be tempted to do what many a rich young man has done, to turn his back contemptuously on existence by saying with Jugurtha: Here is a city that is for sale if it finds a buyer.[12]

This refers to *Bellum Jugurthinum* 35.10, where Jugurtha, following the orders of the Senate, has just left Rome: "*Sed postquam Roma egressus est, fertur saepe eo tacitus respiciens postremo dixisse, urbem venalem et mature perituram, si emptorem invenerit.*" ("After passing through the gates of Rome, it is said that he [sc. Jugurtha] looked back at the city several times in silence, and finally exclaimed.' 'Yonder is a city put up for sale, and its days are numbered if it finds a buyer.' ")[13]

In the Preface to *Philosophical Fragments* the pseudonymous author Johannes Climacus writes of the work at hand: "It is merely a pamphlet and will not become anything more....The accomplishment is, however, in proportion to my talents, for I do not, like that noble Roman, refrain from serving the system *merito magis quam*

10   *SKS* 2, 386.20–5 / *EO1*, 398.
11   *The Jugurthine War. The Conspiracy of Catiline*, p. 191.
12   *SKS* 3, 273.21–8 / *EO2*, 288.
13   *The Jugurthine War. The Conspiracy of Catiline*, p. 73. In *Works of Love* (*SKS* 9, 316.22–8 / *WL*, 319) Kierkegaard returns to this passage in Sallust: "Yet money, money, money! That foreign prince is supposed to have said as he turned his back on mighty Rome, 'Here lies a city for sale and only awaits a buyer.' Ah, how often might not one have been tempted despondently to turn one's back on all existence and say, 'Here lies a world for sale and only awaits a buyer'—provided one does not want to say that the devil has already bought it!"

ignavia, but I am a loafer out of indolence...."[14] Sallust is the one who is respectfully referred to as "that noble Roman." Kierkegaard might here be thinking of the fact that Sallust in the prefaces of his works expounds his characteristic ethical basis for the authorship, never missing an opportunity to distance himself from the ruling class' incompetent and egoistic rule. The quotation is from the *Bellum Jugurthinum* 4.4, where Sallust is giving an account of his decision to abandon Roman politics:

> *Qui si reputaverint et quibus ego temporibus magistratus adeptus sum, et quales viri idem assequi nequiverint, et postea quae genera hominum in senatum pervenerint, profecto existimabunt me magis merito quam ignavia iudicium animi mei mutavisse, maiusque commodum ex otio meo quam ex aliorum negotiis rei publicae venturum.* (But I would ask them to consider what eminent men failed to obtain election to magistracies in the period when I held mine; and, on the other hand, what kinds of men have since gained admission to the Senate. If they will do so, they will surely conclude that I had good reason for altering my opinion about politics, that it was not mere laziness, and that more profit is likely to accrue to the state from my leisured retirement than from the busy activity of others.)[15]

One will note here that the word order of the original text has also been modified or normalized in this quotation.[16]

In view of the fact that Kierkegaard read Sallust at school and, later as a Latin instructor at his old school, presumably used the same texts in his instruction and was thus quite familiar with Sallust's authorship, it is surprising that he refers to, in all, only five passages from Sallust. Kierkegaard's motivation for quoting or referring to Sallust seems to have been a particularly pregnant formulation (*Bellum Catilinarium* 10.5; 20.4; *Bellum Jugurthinum* 4.4) or the desire to recount a dramatic anecdote (*Bellum Catilinarium* 22.1–2; *Bellum Jugurthinum* 35.10).

Translated by Jon Stewart

---

[14]   *SKS* 4, 215.7–13 / *PF*, 5.

[15]   *The Jugurthine War. The Conspiracy of Catiline*, p. 37.

[16]   In a marginal note to the farce, "The Conflict between the Old and the New Soap-Cellar," which is found in the *Journal DD* (*SKS* 17, 281m.16–21, DD:208.g / *KJN* 1, 273) the passage is quoted again, however, this time more correctly and extensively (nonetheless in the original text *mei* after *animi* has been left out): "*profecto existimabunt me magis merito quam ignavia judicium animi mutavisse majusque commodum ex otio meo quam ex aliorum negotiis rei publicæ venturum.*"

Bibliography

I. Sallust's Works in The Auction Catalogue *of Kierkegaard's Library*

C. Sallusti Crispi Opera, quæ supersunt, vols. 1–2, ed. by Fridericus Kritz, Leipzig: Lehnhold 1828–34 (*ASKB* 1269–1270).

C. Sallustii Crispi Opera quae exstant praeter fragmenta omnia; Testum recognovit et illustravit, 3ʳᵈ ed., ed. by Wilhelm Lange, Halle: Hemmerde 1833 (*ASKB* 1271).

C. Sallustii Crispi Opera, Editio Stereotypa, Leipzig: Tauchnitz 1829 (*ASKB* 1272).

Sallusts Catilinariske Krig oversat fra det Latinske. Et Forsøg, trans. by R. Møller, Copenhagen: Fr. Brummer 1811 (*ASKB* 1273, cf. *ASKB* A I 184).

Sallusts Jugurthinske Krig oversat fra det Latinske. Et Forsøg, trans. by R. Møller, Copenhagen: Fr. Brummer 1812 (*ASKB* A I 184).

II. Works in The Auction Catalogue *of Kierkegaard's Library that Discuss Sallust*

[Becker, Karl Friedrich], *Karl Friedrich Beckers Verdenshistorie, omarbeidet af Johan Gottfried Woltmann*, vols. 1–12, trans. by J. Riise, Copenhagen: Fr. Brummers Forlag 1822–29, vol. 3, p. 511; p. 611 (*ASKB* 1972–1983).

Meierotto, Johann Heinrich Ludwig, *Ueber Sitten und Lebensart der Römer in verschiedenen Zeiten der Republik*, vols. 1–2, 3ʳᵈ revised and enlarged ed., Berlin: in der Myliussischen Buchhandlung 1814 (*ASKB* 656).

Meiners, Christoph, *Geschichte des Verfalls der Sitten und der Staatsverfassung der Römer*, Leipzig: bey Weidmanns Erben und Reich 1782 (*ASKB* 660).

[Montaigne, Michel de], *Michael Montaigne's Gedanken und Meinungen über allerley Gegenstände, ins Deutsche übersetzt*, vols. 1–7, Berlin: F.T. Lagarde 1793–99, vol. 3, p. 207 (*ASKB* 681–687).

Schopenhauer, Arthur, *Die Welt als Wille und Vorstellung*, vols. 1–2, 2ⁿᵈ revised and enlarged ed., Leipzig: F.A. Brockhaus 1844 [1819], vol. 2, p. 622 (*ASKB* 773–773a).

III. Secondary Literature on Kierkegaard's Relation to Sallust

None.

Seneca:

Disjecta Membra in Kierkegaard's Writings

Niels W. Bruun

I. Seneca's Life

The philosopher, orator, poet, and politician Lucius Annaeus Seneca was born in the Spanish city Corduba (today Cordoba) between the year 4 BC and AD 1. His father was the well-to-do Roman knight Lucius Annaeus Seneca (55 BC–AD 40), who is today best known under the name Seneca Rhetor.[1]

Seneca was still a young boy when his family, which consisted of his mother Helvia, his little brother Marcus Annaeus Mela, along with his elder brother Lucius Junius Gallio, moved to Rome. There Seneca studied rhetoric and philosophy and went to the lectures of the Stoic Attalus and the philosophers Sotion and Papirius Fabianus. The latter two were both followers of Quintus Sextius, who had developed a special Roman version of Stoicism.[2]

Under the Emperor Tiberius, Seneca became quaestor and senator around the year 33, and in 39 he developed such a great talent for oratory that he attracted the envy of the Emperor Caligula, but he escaped the episode with his life intact. In 41 he was accused of having a relationship with Caligula's sister Julia Livilla. The Emperor Claudius exiled him to Corsica, where he lived until the year 49, when he at the request of Agrippina, the Emperor Claudius' new wife, was called home to Rome and made praetor. Further, he acted as private tutor for the empress' twelve-year-old son from her first marriage, Nero.

With the death of the Emperor Claudius on October 13, 54, Nero came to the throne, and Seneca moved from tutor to political advisor and minister. In the power struggle between Nero and his mother Agrippina, Seneca together with Afranius Burrus, the commander of the praetorian guard, aligned themselves with Nero, and for eight years the two men maintained their influence on him. In 62 Burrus died; Seneca's authority was weakened, and he withdrew from the imperial court. From 62

---

[1]   Seneca Rhetor is the author of the work *Oratorum sententiae divisiones colores* in which he in a lively and detailed manner portrays the talented orators which he heard in his youth. The work comprised ten books devoted to *controversiae* and at least two devoted to *suasoriae*. In our manuscripts only five books of the *controversiae* and one of the *suasoriae* have survived.

[2]   For Seneca and Stoicism, see Rick Anthony Furtak's article on the Stoics in *Kierkegaard and the Greek World*, vol. 2, tome II of this series.

to 65 he lived in retirement on his properties, occupied entirely with his authorship; it can be said of both Cicero and Seneca that their greatest philosophical productivity took place toward the end of their lives, when they lived in inner exile. In 65 Seneca was accused of participation in the so-called Pisonian conspiracy against Nero and was compelled to commit suicide.[3]

II. Seneca's Works

Seneca's literary production, which is very extensive and varied, can be divided into prose and poetry.[4] Of the prose writings one can first name his twelve ethical treatises, which have survived under the designation *Dialogi* [*Dialogues*] because the dialogical element in these treatises is more or less prominent.[5] They consist of *De providentia* [*On Providence*], *De constantia sapientis* [*On the Constancy of the Wise Man*], *De ira* [*On Anger*] in three books, *Ad Marciam de consolatione* [*Consolation to Marcia*], *De vita beata* [*On the Happy Life*], *De otio* [*On Leisure*], *De tranquillitate animi* [*On the Tranquillity of the Mind*], *De brevitate vitae* [*On the Brevity of Life*], *Ad Polybium de consolatione* [*Consolation to Polybius*] together with *Ad Helviam de consolatione* [*Consolation to my Mother Helvia*]. In the works on consolation the point is frequently made that it is not the length of life that counts but rather its depth. The work on the tranquillity of the mind analyzes stress; the constancy of the wise man is tested, among other things, by his ability to resist or ignore insult.

Four other prose works also have survived. The first, entitled *De clementia* [*On Clemency*], is a Mirror of Princes for Nero, emphasizing the ruler's duty to show mercy. The extensive *De beneficiis* [*On Good Deeds*] is a social-psychological study in seven books on the bonds of gratitude. There several examples are given of the conditions of duty and the conflicts of conscience. *Epistulae morales ad Lucilium* [*Moral Letters to Lucilius*] treat the same themes as the *Dialogues*, but endowed with a charming epistolary intimacy. The treatise *Naturales quaestiones* [*Natural Scientific Problems*] in seven books investigates, among other things, natural phenomena such as earthquakes, comets and the flooding of the Nile.

Entirely on its own stands Seneca's *Apocolocyntosis*, which is a brief Menippean satire,[6] which makes a fool of the apotheosis of the Emperor Claudius and at the same time directs a bitter attack on the deceased regent's person and government.

Seneca's main poetic works are his eight tragedies: *Hercules Furens* [*The Angry Hercules*], *Troades* [*The Trojan Women*], *Phoenissae* [*The Phonecian Women*],

---

[3]   The "Pisonian conspiracy" takes its name from Gajus Calpurnius Piso (d. AD 65), who led a conspiracy against the Emperor Nero in AD 65. Piso committed suicide when it was discovered.
[4]   Not all of Seneca's authorship has been preserved. The lost works will not be treated here.
[5]   The genre of dialogue in Seneca's works has more the character of a diatribe than a Platonic dialogue. Seneca's *Dialogi* were, along with his other works, admired by Montaigne and have been an important inspiration for the modern essay.
[6]   That is, a mixture of prose and poetry.

Medea, Phaedra, Oedipus, Agamemnon and *Thyestes.*[7] Both the dramaturgy and the content of thought in these works differ from that of the classical Greek tragedians. Seneca, however, did not reinterpret the ancient myths in the direction of an edifying Stoic belief in providence; it is rather a theatre of cruelty, treating the desire for vengeance and lechery in tyrannical minds.

III. Kierkegaard and Seneca's Works

It is clear from the list of Kierkegaard's Latin readings that he did not read Seneca at school.[8] His own Seneca library was very small and for the first several years limited to two editions: the one was *Annaei Senecae tum rhetoris tum philosophi Opera Omnia, ab Andrea Schotto castigata.*[9] Kierkegaard only had the first volume of this two-volume edition, which is without commentaries. This volume includes, in addition to the writings of Seneca Rhetor, Seneca the Younger's *Dialogi, Naturales quaestiones* and *Apocolocyntosis.* The other edition is *L. Annaei Senecae philosophi Opera omnia. Ad optimorum librorum fidem accurate edita.*[10] This Tauchnitz edition contains all of Seneca's prose writings. Kierkegaard never acquired an edition of the tragedies.

Up until April 1850 Kierkegaard's Seneca quotations are second-hand, like so many of his quotations from the classical authors. But this changed in April 1850. According to the account from the bookseller A.G. Salomon, Kierkegaard purchased "Seneca Abhandl. u. Briefe (Römische Prosaiker)," that is, *Lucius Annäus Seneca des Philosophen Werke.*[11]

With the purchase of this German translation Kierkegaard began to read Seneca's letters. "I have just begun reading Seneca," he admits in the journal entry NB17:94.[12] Kierkegaard's encounter with Seneca was a happy one, and he makes no attempt to hide his enthusiasm: "During this time I am reading Seneca's letters which I find

---

[7]   The tragedies *Hercules Oetaeus* and *Octavia* are not by Seneca.

[8]   An overview of Kierkegaard's Latin and Greek reading at school is printed in Bruce H. Kirmmse (ed.), *Encounters with Kierkegaard: A Life as Seen by His Contemporaries*, Princeton, New Jersey: Princeton University Press 1996, p. 15, which must be supplemented by the account provided on p. 273. For an account of the version which is printed in *B&A*, vol. 1, pp. 4–5, see ibid., p. 273.

[9]   *Annaei Senecae tum rhetoris tum philosophi Opera Omnia, ab Andrea Schotto... castigata*, vol. 1, Geneva: Petrus Chouet 1626 (vol. 2, 1626) (*ASKB* 1274).

[10]   *L. Annaei Senecae philosophi Opera omnia. Ad optimorum librorum fidem accurate edita*, vols. 1–5, Editio Stereotypa, Leipzig: Tauchnitz 1832 (*ASKB* 1275–1279).

[11]   *Lucius Annäus Seneca des Philosophen Werke*, trans. by J.M. Moser, G.H. Moser and A. Pauly, vols. 1–15 (with continuous pagination) (in *Römische Prosaiker in neuen Übersetzungen*, vols. 19–20, vol. 25, vol. 33, vol. 41, vols. 45–6, vol. 50, vols. 53–5, vol. 67, vol. 73, vol. 111 and vol. 115), Stuttgart: Metzler 1828–36 (*ASKB* 1280–1280c). In this edition volumes 12–15 (= *Briefe*, trans. by August Pauly, vols. 1–4, 1832–36) contain Seneca's letters to Lucilius, but only the first 94 letters. The remaining 30 letters only appeared in 1851 in *Werke* vols. 16–17 (= *Briefe*, vols. 5–6), trans. by A. Haakh. Kierkegaard seems not to have purchased these volumes.

[12]   *SKS* 23, 238, NB17:94.

excellent; the incorporated small sentences of Epicurus are superb too."[13] Even though Kierkegaard registers several reservations about Stoicism,[14] this does not diminish his admiration for Seneca: "On the whole Seneca's letters are pithy."[15] As will be made clear below, his reading of the letters was not limited to the German translation. More often he went back to the Latin text, and indeed even tried his hand as translator.[16]

Kierkegaard's intense Seneca studies seem to have lasted a month in the spring of 1850. What Kierkegaard after this time quotes from Seneca's letters is for the most part the after-effect of this reading.

The earliest quotation of Seneca in Kierkegaard appears in the treatise, *The Concept of Irony*, where he writes:

> Even though the world spirit in any process is continually in itself, this is not the case with the generation at a certain time and the given individuals at a certain time in the same generation. For them, a given actuality does not present itself as something that they are able to reject, because the world process leads the person who is willing to go along and sweeps the unwilling one along with it.[17]

The idea of the inevitability of change is presumably taken from Seneca, who in letter 107.11 to Lucilius translates five lines from the Greek philosopher Cleanthes, the last of which runs as follows: *"Ducunt volentem fata, nolentem trahunt."*[18] "For Fate / The willing leads, the unwilling drags along."[19]

In *Fear and Trembling*, Kierkegaard has his pseudonymous author write in "Problema III":

> Everything said here about Sarah, chiefly with regard to poetic presentation and therefore with an imaginary presupposition, has its full meaning when with a psychological interest one explores the meaning of the old saying: *nullum unquam exstitit magnum ingenium sine aliqua dementia.* For such dementia is the suffering of genius in this world, is the expression, if I dare say so, of divine envy, whereas the genius aspect is the expression of preferment.[20]

---

13   *SKS* 23, 239, NB17:98.
14   *SKS* 23, 230–2, NB17:82–3.
15   *SKS* 23, 245, NB17:103.
16   See, for example, *SKS* 23, 245, NB17:104.
17   *SKS* 1, 297 / *CI*, 259.
18   The Latin text is quoted from *L. Annaei Senecae philosophi Opera omnia*. This text has been compared with *Annaei Senecae tum rhetoris tum philosophi Opera Omnia, ab Andrea Schotto castigata.* Kierkegaard is known to have owned the first volume from the 1626 edition, but only a copy of the 1636 edition has been accessible.
19   English translation quoted from *Letters from a Stoic*, trans. by Robin Campbell, Harmondsworth: Penguin 1969, p. 200.
20   *SKS* 4, 195 / *FT*, 106–7. Cf. *SKS* 24, 42.7–18, NB21:57: *"Nullum unquam exstitit magnum ingenium sine aliqua dementia.* The explanation is quite simple. For to truly be a great genius, he would have to be the exceptional. But in order for the exception to have seriousness, he would himself have to be not free, forced into it. Here lies the significance of his madness. It is a fixed point in which he suffers; he cannot come to run with the crowd. This is his torture. This, his madness, perhaps has nothing to do with what is his real genius, but it is

The Latin, which can be translated as follows, "No great genius has ever existed without some touch of madness," is a reworked quotation from Seneca's *De tranquillitate animi* 17.10: *"nullum magnum ingenium sine mixtura fuit."* Seneca himself indicates that he has taken this quotation from Aristotle.[21] In the form *nullum exstitit magnum ingenium sine aliqua dementia* this is also used in the *Journal JJ* with the addition: "this is the worldly way of expressing the religious thesis: The person whom God blesses in the religious sense, He curses *eo ipso* in the worldly sense."[22] In *Notebook 11*, which contains Kierkegaard's notes to Schelling's lecture from 17 January 1842, Kierkegaard ascribes to the philosopher a clear allusion to the aforementioned Seneca passage: "When it is said that there is an element of madness in everything great, this really means that there is a controlled madness; the poetic is precisely an example of such control. The opposite of *Wahnsinn* is *Blödsinn*, in which the understanding lacks inner substance on which it works."[23]

In *The Concept of Anxiety* Kierkegaard writes: "The qualitative leap is enervated; the fall becomes something successive. Nor can it be discerned how the prohibition awakens *concupiscentia*, even though it is certain from pagan as well as from Christian experience that man's desire is for the forbidden."[24] In his draft to "pagan... experience" Kierkegaard added this reminder to himself: "(*above all Seneca is to be quoted*)."[25] It is not known with certainty what Kierkegaard has in mind here since later while making the fair copy he neglects to follow his original plan to introduce quotations from Seneca, which show that human beings are attracted to what is forbidden, but he might have been thinking of *Hercules Oetaeus* 357, *illicita amantur, excidit quidquid licet* or *Phaedra* 699, *fugienda petimus.*

In "Preface VIII" of *Prefaces*, in his polemic with Hegelianism, Kierkegaard writes: "Life is short; would therefore that the art not be made too long for me, above all not longer than life. If it would take an entire life to understand Hegel, then this philosophy would surely contain the most profound contradiction."[26] Here he makes allusion to the popular saying, *vita brevis, ars longa* ("Life is short, the art long"),[27] which originally were the initial words in Hippocrates' first aphorism in the work *Aphorisms*,[28] where he discusses some of the factors which make it difficult to educate oneself to be a doctor and treat patients. The well-known saying, which enjoyed great popularity even in antiquity, was translated by Seneca in *De brevitate* 1.1: *"Inde illa*

---

the pain by means of which he is personally tormented into isolation, and in isolation he must be if he is to become great; and no human being is able to freely keep himself in isolation; he must be forced if it is to be serious."

21   Cf. Pseudo-Aristotle, p. 953a, which refers to *melancholia*.

22   *SKS* 18, 189, JJ:151 /*KJN* 2, 175.

23   *SKS* 19, 346, Not11:28 / *SBL*, 387.

24   *SKS* 4, 346 / *CA*, 40.

25   Manuscript 1.3, see *SKS* K4, 311.

26   *SKS* 4, 516 / *P*, 56.

27   Hippocrates, *Aphorisms*, 1, 1.

28   Cf. [Hippocrates], *Oeuvres complètes d'Hippocrate, traduction nouvelle avec le texte grec en regard, collationné sur les manuscrits et toutes les éditions*, ed. by É. Littre, vols. 1–10, Paris: J.-B. Baillière 1839–61, vol. 4 (1844), p. 458. The word "aphorism" is used here about a medical doctrine.

maximi medicorum exclamatio est, vitam brevem esse, longam artem" ("Therefore the greatest physician, as is known, says that life is short but the art long."). It cannot be determined whether Kierkegaard took the quotation from Seneca or received it from some second-hand source. In *Four Upbuilding Discourses* from 1843 there is a clear allusion to this: "Patience is a poor art, and yet it is very long."[29]

In *Stages on Life's Way* Victor Eremita says, "If Maecenas could not sleep without hearing the splashing of a fountain, then I cannot dine without it."[30] This refers to a story which is told by Seneca in *De providentia* 3.10.[31] According to the story Maecenas was wont to fall asleep to, among other things, "the splashing of spring water" (*aquarum fragoribus*).

In *Stages on Life's Way* one reads further: "Now he strikes an emotional tone and believes he has done something extraordinary by marrying; now he sticks his tail between his legs; now he eulogizes marriage in self-defense—but I wait in vain for the unifying idea that holds these most heterogeneous *disjecta membra* of life-view together."[32] The formulation *disjecta membra* ("scattered members") appears in Seneca's tragedy *Phaedra*, verse 1256, "*disjecta...membra laceri corporis*" ("the scattered members of a body torn to pieces"), but since Kierkegaard apparently never read Seneca's tragedies,[33] he must have received this quotation at second-hand.[34] It is also found in the entry JJ:505, where it functions as a heading for the three following, clearly fragmentarily marked and formulated entries from May 1842.

In *Upbuilding Discourses in Various Spirits* one reads: "The longest school educates for the highest; the school that continues just as long as time can educate only for eternity. The yield of the school for life appears in time, but suffering's life-

---

29   *SKS* 5, 159 / *EUD*, 159.
30   *SKS* 6, 31 / *SLW*, 25.
31   Seneca, *De providentia* 3.10: "*Feliciorem ergo tu Maecenatem putas, cui amoribus anxio et morosae uxoris cotidiana repudia deflenti somnus per symphoniarum cantum ex lonquinquo lene resonantium quaeritur? Mero se licet sopiat et aquarum fragoribus auocet et mille voluptatibus mentem anxiam fallat, tam vigilabit in pluma quam ille in cruce.*" ("Would you count Maecenas more fortunate because, when he was lovesick and bewailing the repulses of his disagreeable wife, he wooed slumber through the strains of music sounding softly in the distance? Though he drug himself with strong wine and divert himself with the rippling of water and beguiled his distraught mind with a thousand delights, he will be as sleepless on his bed of down as Regulus upon his cross.") English translation quoted from *The Stoic Philosophy of Seneca*, trans. by Moses Hadas, Garden City, New York: Doubleday & Company 1958, p. 35.
32   *SKS* 6, 65 / *SLW*, 64.
33   Kierkegaard's small collection of Seneca texts (*ASKB* 1274–1280c) does not include the tragedies. In the *Journal NB16* Kierkegaard again quotes from a tragedy: "A superb saying: *qui timide rogat, docet negare.*" (*SKS* 23, 149.16, NB16:80). This can be translated as follows: "A timid request provokes a refusal." The quotation comes from Seneca's *Phaedra*, verses 593–4. Kierkegaard's source could not be established.
34   One cannot, however, preclude the possibility that the popular quotation perhaps more correctly should be considered a product due to some scholarly ("*bildungssprachlich*") transformation of the well-known line from Horace's *Satires*, 1, 4, 62, *disiecti membra poetae* ("members of a scattered poet ").

school educates for eternity."[35] The idea of a "life-school" is not ancient but is taken from a Latin proverb from a later time: "*non scholae, sed vitae discimus*" ("we do not learn for the school but for life"), which must have been inspired by Seneca's *Epistulae morales* 106.12: "*non vitae sed scholae discimus*" ("we do not learn for life but for the school").[36]

In the *Journal DD* Kierkegaard writes "As far as I can recall, it is Seneca who utters the remarkable words: *Quæ latebra est, in quam non intret metus mortis.*"[37] ("Where does one find a hiding place, where the fear of death does not enter?") Kierkegaard recalls correctly: it is a (literal) quotation from Seneca's *Epistulae morales* 82.4.[38]

In the *Journal JJ* Kierkegaard writes:

> But people need someone like that in any case, if in no other sense, in that of the Stoics when they said: *sapientem nulla re indigere,*[39] *et tamen multis illi rebus opus esse.—Ergo quamvis se ipso contentus sit sapiens,*[40] *amicis illi opus est, non ut habeat, qui sibi ægro assideat, sed ut habeat aliquem, cui ipse assideat, pro quo mori possit.*[41]

The first quotation comes from Seneca's *Epistulae morales* 9.14 and is originally a statement from the Stoic philosopher Chrysippus. The second quotation is a creative montage from Seneca's *Epistulae morales* 9.15, "*Ergo quamvis...opus est*" and 9.8, "*non...ut habeat...assideat*" as well as 9.10, "*pro quo mori possim,*" which Kierkegaard found, along with the first Seneca quotation in Karl Bayer's (1806–83) article "Der Begriff der sittlichen Gemeinschaft."[42] Also in the *Journal JJ* Kierkegaard writes:

---

[35]   *SKS* 8, 358 / *UD*, 261.

[36]   In *The Conflict between the Old and the New Soap-Cellar* (*SKS* 17, 294 / *KJN* 1, 286) Mr. Rushjob says: "...we who have been discharged from school into life...." The statement in *Prefaces* (*SKS* 4, 510 / *P*, 49): "This doubt is overcome not in the system, but in life" leads one perhaps to conceive of it as an allusion to this saying.

[37]   *SKS* 17, 237, DD:46 / *KJN* 1, 228.

[38]   By contrast, Kierkegaard's memory fails him, when in *Either/Or*, Part Two, "The Esthetic Validity of Marriage" (*SKS* 3, 75 / *EO2*, 70) he writes: "An ancient pagan—I believe it is Seneca—has said that when a person has reached his thirtieth year he ought to know his constitution so well that he can be his own physician." The source is in fact Tacitus' *Annals*, Book 6.46, where the Emperor Tiberius is claimed to have said something along these lines. In the *Journal NB25* (*SKS* 24, 519, NB25:107 / *JP* 4, 4939) Kierkegaard writes: "It is the nature of all prudence never to venture more than my understanding tells me I am capable of doing or more than it reckons I will be able to endure in terms of suffering. Seneca correctly stated it thus: I should not venture that which I would be amazed to see accomplished—it is too high." The editors of the *Papirer* edition refer to Seneca' *Epistulae morales* 28.6, but this Seneca text cannot be placed in connection with this passage. Moreover, since the quotation cannot be found in Seneca, this may be another case of faulty memory.

[39]   For *indigere* modern editions now have *egere*.

[40]   Kierkegaard has added "*sapiens.*"

[41]   *SKS* 18, 284–5, JJ:433 / *KJN* 2, 263.

[42]   See *Zeitschrift für Philosophie und speculative Theologie*, vol. 13 (Tübingen: Ludwig Friedrich Fues), 1844, p. 88.

The immediate religious person....surely does not build his salvation on this (then he would be irreligious or he would not know what he was doing), but he is nonetheless happy to be able to do a little to repay God for all that God can do for him (here the Socratic saying is appropriate, when Socrates would not accept the invitation to come to King Archelaus because he could not reciprocate—thus many will not involve themselves with God because they feel that they will become nothing).[43]

This story is told in Seneca's *De beneficiis* 5.6.2: "*Archelaus rex Socratem rogavit, ut ad se veniret: dixisse Socrates traditur, Nolle se ad eum venire, a quo acciperet beneficia, quum reddere illi paria non posset.*" ("King Archelaus invited Socrates to visit him. Socrates is said to have responded that he did not wish to come to a person who showed him favors since he was not able to reciprocate.")

In the *Journal NB10* he writes, "Thomas à Kempis, Book I, Chapter 20: 'Every time I have been with men I always come back less a man.' According to Seneca, Epistle VII, 'I come home again more niggardly, more arrogant, more sensual, more cruel, and more inhuman, because I have been among men.'"[44] The quotation is from Seneca's *Epistulae morales* 7.3: "*avarior redeo, ambitiosior, luxuriosior, immo vero crudelior et inhumanior, quia inter homines fui.*" Kierkegaard's Danish translation is presumably taken from Jens Albrecht Leonhard Holm, who in 1848 translated and published Thomas à Kempis' *On the Imitation of Christ*.[45]

In the *Journal NB11* Kierkegaard writes, "The beginning of Seneca's treatise *De ira* is rhetorically beautiful. To show how inhuman and unworthy of man anger is, he forms a proposition with the antitheses: man is born for mutual support, anger for corruption, etc. (this is in chapter V); thus man—and anger—are placed in opposition to each other."[46] Kierkegaard refers here to *De ira* 1.5.3, which reads, "*Homo in adiutorium mutuum generatus est:*[47] *ira in exitium.*" ("Man is created for mutual help, anger for destruction.")

In the *Journal NB17* he writes:

In this world truth is always suffering and always defenseless. To find coworkers and to secure power are not so difficult, but in choosing coworkers the truth must use truth's infinite caution and therefore require few, perhaps none; thus it is contented with a verification of the words I read yesterday or the day before in one of Seneca's letters (which curiously reminded me of Frater Taciturnus' lines in the first article in *Fædrelandet*, which in a certain sense seem even more felicitous because in addition to a polemical quality they also have a sadness in the expression of inner satisfaction, "I am content with being an author"): I am content with few, with one, with none.[48]

---

[43]   *SKS* 18, 248–9, JJ:336 / *KJN* 2, 229.

[44]   *SKS* 21, 369, NB10:205 / *JP* 2, 2016.

[45]   Thomas à Kempis, *Om Christi Efterfølgelse, fire Bøger*, trans. and ed. by Jens Albrecht Leonhard Holm, introduced by Andreas Gottlob Rudelbach, 3rd ed., Copenhagen: Wahlske Boghandels Forlag 1848 (*ASKB* 273). The Seneca translation is found in the edition, p. 26, note 1.

[46]   *SKS* 22, 114, NB11:191 / *JP* 4, 3905.

[47]   Modern editors read "*genitus est.*"

[48]   *SKS* 23, 238, NB17:94 / *JP* 4, 4868.

The quotation is from Seneca's *Epistulae morales* 7.11: "*Satis sunt, inquit, mihi pauci, satis est unus, satis est nullus.*"

Later in the same journal he writes:

> At present I am reading Seneca's letters and find them excellent, the little quotations from Epicurus which are incorporated are also splendid. In the 22nd letter a passage from Epicurus is quoted, which among other things states: "Even from the most difficult of situations there is hopefully a happy way out, if one does not hurry before it is time or procrastinate when it is time."[49]

The quotation is from Seneca's *Epistulae morales* 22.6, which refers to a letter from Epicurus to his friend Idomeneus: "*...sperat salutarem etiam ex difficillimis exitum, si nec properemus ante tempus, nec cessemus in tempore.*"

Also in the *Journal NB17* he writes, "Seneca's 22nd letter quotes a Stoic: He is not a man of courage if his courage does not increase under difficulties."[50] The passage which Kierkegaard quotes in abbreviated form, is from Seneca's *Epistulae morales* 22.7: "*non est vir fortis ac strenuus, qui laborem fugit; nisi crescit illi animus ipsa rerum difficultate.*" In *Journal NB21* Kierkegaard returns to this passage, which he here reproduces a little more tersely: "Seneca says: It is not really courageous if the courage does not increase with the danger."[51] Again in the *Journal NB17* he writes:

> Seneca's 26th letter. Quoted from Epicurus: "Prepare yourself for death: it is better now that it approaches you, or you it." Thus Seneca is saying that it is a glorious thing to learn to die. You perhaps consider it superfluous to learn something that you can only use once? This is the very reason we must prepare ourselves. That which cannot be experienced in advance must be continuously learned if we want to understand it.[52]

The first quotation is from Seneca's *Epistulae morales* 26.8: "*Meditare utrum commodius sit, vel mortem transire ad nos, vel nos ad eam.*"[53] The second is from Seneca's *Epistulae morales* 26.9: "*Egregia res est mortem condiscere. Supervacuum forsitan putas id discere, quo semel utendum est? Hoc est ipsum quare meditari debeamus: semper discendum est, quod an sciamus, experiri non possumus.*" Also in the *Journal NB17* he writes:

> Seneca's 53rd letter: "Why does nobody admit his mistakes? Because he is still ensnared in them. The person who is awake or waking up tells his dreams—to confess one's mistakes is a sign of healing. Let us wake up, then, in order to be able to convince ourselves or our mistakes."[54]

---

49   *SKS* 23, 239, NB17:98 / *JP* 4, 3906.
50   *SKS* 23, 240, NB17:100 / *JP* 4, 3907.
51   *SKS* 24, 95, NB21:155 / *JP* 4, 3912.
52   *SKS* 23, 244–5, NB17:103 / *JP* 4, 3908.
53   This is the Tauchnitz text which is somewhat in disorder.
54   *SKS* 23, 245, NB17:104 / *JP* 4, 3909. The translation "awake or waking up" reveals that Kierkegaard himself translated the text from Latin and, moreover, had not yet made up his mind about how to translate the Latin *vigilantis*. Consequently he has left both possibilities open in the same manner as he sometimes did when translating the New Testament from

The quotation is from Seneca's *Epistulae morales* 53.8: "*Quare vitia sua nemo confitetur? quia etiamnunc in illis est. Somnium narrare, vigilantis est, et vitia sua confiteri, sanitatis indicium est. Expergiscamur ergo, ut errores nostros coarguere possimus.*"[55]

In *Journal NB18* Kierkegaard writes:

> Seneca tells of a man on whom a king took revenge by having his nose and ears cut off, by having him generally mauled, and then locked up in a cage where he was unable to stand upright—and what does Seneca say further? He relates that after leaving him there amid his own excrement—people finally ceased to have pity on him because he was so loathsome. Wonderful pity![56]

This story is told at Seneca's *De ira* 3.17.3:

> *Nam Telesphorum Rhodium amicum suum undique decurtatum, quum aures illi nasumque abscidisset, in cavea velut novum animal aliquod et inusitatum diu pavit: quum oris detruncati mutilatique deformitas humanam faciem perdidisset. Accedebat fames et squalor et illuvies corporis, in stercore suo destituti, callosis super haec genibus manibusque, quas in usum pedum angustiae loci cogebant; lateribus vero attritu exulceratis, non minus foeda quam terribilis erat forma eius visentibus: factusque poenâ suâ monstrum, misericordiam quoque amiserat.*[57]

Greek into Latin (cf. *SKS* K17, 284). It is worth noting that the Latin *vigilans* does not mean "wake up."

[55] In the entry NB21:39 Kierkegaard returns to this Seneca passage, which he quotes in abbreviated form: "Seneca: *quare vitia sua nemo confitetur? Quia etiam nunc in illis est. Somnium narrare vigilantis est.* (Ep. 55.)."

[56] *SKS* 23, 257–8, NB18:5 / *JP* 3, 3498.

[57] "For Telesphorus the Rhodian, his own friend, he completely mutilated, and when he had cut off his ears and nose, he shut him up in a cage as if he were some strange and unknown animal and for a long time lived in terror of him, since the hideousness of his hacked and mutilated face had destroyed every appearance of a human being; to this were added starvation and squalor and the filth of a body left to wallow in its own dung; furthermore, his hands and knees becoming all calloused—for by the narrowness of his quarters he was forced to use these instead of feet—his sides, too, a mass of sores from rubbing, to those who beheld him his appearance was no less disgusting than terrible, and having been turned by his punishment into a monster he had forfeited even pity." The English translation is quoted from *Seneca, Moral Essays*, trans. by John W. Basore, London and Cambridge, Massachusetts: Harvard University Press 1970, vol. 1, pp. 299–300. In the *Journal NB26* (*Pap.* X–4 A 574 / *JP* 4, 4684) Kierkegaard returns to the story, which he retells as follows: "How jolting the concise, terse truth of Seneca's account (*De ira*, III, Chapter 17) of the cruelty with which Lysimachus had his friend Telesphorus from Rhodus slashed, his nose and ears cut off, and then had him shut up in a cage like a wild animal, and when he became altogether unrecognizable because the cage was never cleansed of filth and because he had so little room that he could not even stand erect or use his arms or legs—now it comes!—then sympathy for him also vanished. This is the way it is. Become really miserable and unfortunate—and compassion stops—at the proper point, no doubt!"

Finally, in *Journal NB21* he writes, "*Plus dolet, quam necesse est, qui ante dolet, quam necesse est.* Seneca's *Epistulae morales* 98."[58] The quotation comes from Seneca's *Epistulae morales* 98.8 and can be translated as follows: "He feels more pain than is necessary who feels pain before it is necessary."

Aside from that month in the spring of 1850 when, inspired by the purchase of a German translation, Kierkegaard read the *Moral Letters to Lucilius* intensively, the rest of his quotations—like in general most all of his quoted passages from the classics—are the fortuitous fruits of reading picked up when he was studying some other subject matter. Also in the case of Seneca his motive for making a quotation or a reference seems to have been the happy or pregnant formulation of a thought or his wish to tell a good anecdote, sometimes with a profound point or a suggestive humanistic message.

Translated by Jon Stewart

Bibliography

I. Seneca's Works in The Auction Catalogue *of Kierkegaard's Library*

*Annaei Senecae tum rhetoris tum philosophi Opera Omnia, ab Andrea Schotto...
castigata,* vol. 1, Geneva: Petrus Chouët 1626 (vol. 2, 1626) (*ASKB* 1274).
*L. Annaei Senecae philosophi Opera omnia. Ad optimorum librorum fidem accurate
edita,* vols. 1–5, Editio Stereotypa, Leipzig: Tauchnitz 1832 (*ASKB* 1275–1279).
Lucius Annäus Seneca des Philosophen Werke, trans. by J.M. Moser, G.H. Moser
and A. Pauly, vols. 1–15 (with continuous pagination) (in *Römische Prosaiker in
neuen Übersetzungen,* vols. 19–20, vol. 25, vol. 33, vol. 41, vols. 45–6, vol. 50,
vols. 53–5, vol. 67, vol. 73, vol. 111 and vol. 115), Stuttgart: Metzler 1828–36
(*ASKB* 1280–1280c).

II. Works in The Auction Catalogue *of Kierkegaard's Library that Discuss Seneca*

Ast, Friedrich, *Grundriss einer Geschichte der Philosophie,* Landshut: Joseph
Thomann 1807, p. 159 (*ASKB* 385).
Bähr, Johann Christian Felix, *Abriss der Römischen Literatur-Geschichte zum
Gebrauch für höhere Lehranstalten,* Heidelberg and Leipzig: Groos 1833 (*ASKB*
975).
[Becker, Karl Friedrich], *Karl Friedrich Beckers Verdenshistorie, omarbeidet
af Johan Gottfried Woltmann,* vols. 1–12, trans. by J. Riise, Copenhagen: Fr.
Brummers Forlag 1822–29, vol. 3, p. 711; p. 718 (*ASKB* 1972–1983).
Buhle, Johann Gottlieb, *Geschichte der neuern Philosophie seit der Epoche
der Wiederherstellung der Wissenschaften,* vols. 1–6 (in 10 tomes), vols. 1–2,
Göttingen: Johann Georg Rosenbusch's Wittwe 1800; vols. 3–6, Göttingen:
Johann Friedrich Röwer 1802–05 (Abtheilung 6 in *Geschichte der Künste
und Wissenschaften seit der Wiederherstellung derselben bis an das Ende des
achtzehnten Jahrhunderts. Von einer Gesellschaft gelehrter Männer ausgearbeitet,*
Abtheilungen 1–11, Göttingen: Röwer and Göttingen: Rosenbusch 1796–1820),
vol. 1, p. 147 (*ASKB* 440–445).
Dyck, Johann Gottfried and Georg Schatz (eds.), *Charaktere der vornehmsten
Dichter aller Nationen; nebst kritischen und historischen Abhandlungen über
Gegenstände der schönen Künste und Wissenschaften, von einer Gesellschaft
von Gelehrten,* vols. 1–8, Leipzig: Dyk 1792–1808, vol. 1, p. 12; p. 32; vol. 4,
pp. 332–408 (*ASKB* 1370–1377).
Flögel, Carl Friedrich, *Geschichte der komischen Litteratur,* vols. 1–4, Liegnitz and
Leipzig: David Siegert 1784–87, vol. 2, pp. 32–7 (*ASKB* 1396–1399).

Hagen, Johan Frederik, *Ægteskabet. Betragtet fra et ethisk-historiskt Standpunct*, Copenhagen: Wahlske Boghandels Forlag 1845, p. 141n; p. 147n (*ASKB* 534).

Hahn, August (ed.), *Lehrbuch des christlichen Glaubens*, Leipzig: Friedrich Christian Wilhelm Vogel 1828, p. 192; p. 199; p. 204; p. 207; p. 359 (*ASKB* 535).

[Hamann, Johann Georg], *Hamann's Schriften*, vols. 1–8, ed. by Friedrich Roth, Berlin: G. Reimer 1821–43, vol. 6, p. 345; vol. 7, p. 397 (*ASKB* 536–544).

[Herder, Johann Gottfried von], *Johann Gottfried von Herder's sämmtliche Werke. Zur Philosophie und Geschichte*, vols. 1–22, Stuttgart and Tübingen: J.G. Cotta'sche Buchhandlung 1827–30, vol. 15, pp. 171–84 (*ASKB* 1695–1705, see also *ASKB* A I 114–24].

Meierotto, Johann Heinrich Ludwig, *Ueber Sitten und Lebensart der Römer in verschiedenen Zeiten der Republik*, vols. 1–2, 3rd revised and enlarged ed., Berlin: in der Myliussischen Buchhandlung 1814 (*ASKB* 656).

Meiners, Christoph, *Geschichte des Verfalls der Sitten, der Wissenschaften und Sprache der Römer, in den ersten Jahrhunderten nach Christi Geburt*, Vienna and Leipzig: Joseph Stahel 1791 (*ASKB* 669).

Michelet, Carl Ludwig, *Vorlesungen über die Persönlichkeit Gottes und Unsterblichkeit der Seele oder die ewige Persönlichkeit des Geistes*, Berlin: Verlag von Ferdinand Dümmler 1841, p. 41 (*ASKB* 680).

[Møller, Poul Martin], *Efterladte Skrifter af Poul M. Møller*, vols. 1–3, ed. by Christian Winther, F.C. Olsen and Christen Thaarup, Copenhagen: C.A. Reitzel 1839–43, vol. 2, p. 527; vol. 3, p. 211 (*ASKB* 1574–1576).

[Montaigne, Michel de], *Michael Montaigne's Gedanken und Meinungen über allerley Gegenstände, ins Deutsche übersetzt*, vols. 1–7, Berlin: F.T. Lagarde 1793–99, vol. 2, p. 133; p. 196; vol. 3, p. 55; p. 197; p. 382; p. 516; vol. 4, p. 118; p. 328; p. 391; pp. 405–22; pp. 473–4; p. 477; p. 481; vol. 5, p. 161; p. 401; vol. 6, p. 272 (*ASKB* 681–687).

Mynster, Jakob Peter, *Den hedenske Verden ved Christendommens Begyndelse*, Copenhagen: Schultz 1850, p. 9; p. 12; p. 20; p. 26; p. 47; p. 49 (*ASKB* 693).

—— *Blandede Skrivter*, vols. 1–3, Copenhagen: Den Gyldendalske Boghandlings Forlag 1852–53 (vols. 4–6, Copenhagen: Den Gyldendalske Boghandlings Forlag 1855–57), vol. 1, p. 240n (*ASKB* 358–363).

[Richter, Johann Paul Friedrich], Jean Paul, *Vorschule der Aesthetik nebst einigen Vorlesungen in Leipzig über die Parteien der Zeit*, vols. 1–3, 2nd revised ed., Stuttgart and Tübingen: J.G. Cotta'sche Buchhandlung 1813, vol. 2, p. 355; vol. 3, p. 929 (*ASKB* 1381–1383).

Ritter, Heinrich, *Geschichte der Philosophie alter Zeit*, vols. 1–4, 2nd revised ed., Hamburg: Friedrich Perthes 1836–39, vol. 4, pp. 189–202 (*ASKB* 735–738).

Ritter, Heinrich and L. Preller, *Historia philosophiae graeco-romanae ex fontium locis contexta*, ed. by L. Preller, Hamburg: Perthes 1838, pp. 437–8 (*ASKB* 726).

Schlegel, August Wilhelm, *Ueber dramatische Kunst und Litteratur. Vorlesungen*, vols. 1–2 (vol. 2 in two Parts), Heidelberg: Mohr und Zimmer 1809–11, vol. 2.1, pp. 25–6 (*ASKB* 1392–1394).

Schmidt, W. Adolf, *Geschichte der Denk-und Glaubensfreiheit im ersten Jahrhundert der Kaiserherrschaft und des Christenthums*, Berlin: Verlag von Veit und Comp.

1847, p. 47; p. 94; p. 101; p. 123; pp. 150–1; p. 182; p. 209; p. 221; p. 223; p. 290; p. 336; pp. 388–91; pp. 412–19 passim; p. 424; p. 433; p. 444 (*ASKB* 771).

Schopenhauer, Arthur, *Die Welt als Wille und Vorstellung*, vols. 1–2, 2nd revised and enlarged ed., Leipzig: F.A. Brockhaus 1844 [1819], vol. 1, p. 9; p. 215; p. 33; p. 338; p. 395; vol. 2, p. 61; pp. 150–1; pp. 156–8; p. 240; p. 629 (*ASKB* 773– 773a).

—— *Parerga und Paralipomena: kleine philosophische Schriften*, vols. 1–2, Berlin: Druck und Verlag von A.W. Hayn 1851, vol. 1, p. 141; p. 175; p. 315; p. 353; p. 396; p. 410; p. 416; p. 428; vol. 2, p. 257 (*ASKB* 774–775).

Stäudlin, Carl Friedrich, *Geschichte und Geist des Skepticismus vorzüglich in Rücksicht auf Moral und Religion*, vols. 1–2, Leipzig: Siegfried Lebrecht Crusius 1794, vol. 1, pp. 358ff. (*ASKB* 791).

[Sulzer, Johann George], *Johann George Sulzers vermischte philosophische Schriften. Aus den Jahrbüchern der Akademie der Wissenschaften zu Berlin gesammelt*, vols. 1–2, Leipzig: bey Weidmanns Erben und Reich 1773–81 [the title of the second volume is modified and reads as follows, *Johann George Sulzers vermischte Schriften. Eine Fortsetzung der vermischten philosophischen Schriften desselben. Nebst einigen Nachrichten von seinem Leben, und seinen sämtlichen Werken*], vol. 1, p. 104 (*ASKB* 807–808).

Tiedemann, Dieterich, *System der stoischen Philosophie*, vols. 1–3, Leipzig: bey Weidmanns Erben und Reich 1776 (*ASKB* 833–835).

Zeuthen, Ludvig, *Humanitet betragtet fra et christeligt Standpunkt, med stadigt Hensyn til den nærværende Tid*, Copenhagen: Gyldendalske Boghandling 1846, p. 44 (*ASKB* 915).

III. Secondary Literature on Kierkegaard's Relation to Seneca

None.

Suetonius:

Exemplars of Truth and Madness: Kierkegaard's Proverbial Uses of Suetonius' *Lives*

Sebastian Høeg Gulmann

Gaius Suetonius Tranquillus (ca. AD 69–ca. 135) is chiefly known as the writer of *The Twelve Caesars* (*De Vita Caesarum*), a work that has been regarded as one of the seminal pieces within the genre of biography ever since antiquity. Given the fact that Kierkegaard only ever makes reference to Suetonius in connection with this work, it is the only one we shall deal with here.

In *The Twelve Caesars* Suetonius writes the *Lives* of the ruling Romans from Julius Caesar (ca. 100–44 BC) to Domitian (AD 51–96). His predominant interest is with what has been called "the rhythm of human biology, reproduction, birth, growth and death" of the first Caesars, and less with the general narrative in which they were involved, a feature which has become a standard difference between the genre of history and biography.[1] He was a polymath, attaining the prestigious posts in the imperial service of *a studiis*, *a bibliothecis* and *ab epistulis* under the reigns of Trajan and Hadrian. Accordingly, his approach can be recognized as scholarly rather than historical.[2] Stylistically, Suetonius appears to lean on classical Roman forebears such as Caesar and Cicero, avoiding the grand style which from Homer onwards had dominated much of antiquity's historical writing.[3]

Suetonius does not appear on Kierkegaard's school curriculum, but at some point in his life he obtained a private copy of the work in the Danish translation by Jacob Baden (1735–1804). Still, it is hard to say what could have drawn him to obtain *The Twelve Caesars*.[4] By way of giving a tentative answer, and at the same time providing a sketch of the main themes included in the pages to come, we may well ask how, on a general level, does Kierkegaard include Suetonius in his own writings?

---

[1]   Andrew Wallace-Hadrill, *Suetonius: The Scholar and his Caesars*, London: Duckworth 1983, p. 11.

[2]   Ibid., p. 10.

[3]   Michael Von Albrecht, *A History of Roman Literature: From Livius Andronicus to Boethius: With Special Regard to Its Influence on World Literature*, London: Brill Academic Publishers 1997, p. 1398.

[4]   Suetonius appears in the auction catalogue of Kierkegaard's library: Caji Svetonii Tranqvilli, *Tolv første romerske Keiseres Levnetsbeskrivelse*, trans. and ed. by Jacob Baden, Copenhagen: Joh. Fred. Schultz 1802 (*ASKB* 1281).

Judging from the mention of the Roman biographer in Kierkegaard's own writings, one can say that he appears to have been used mainly for a reference to an action of a Roman ruler or official as mentioned in *The Twelve Caesars*. Not once does Kierkegaard appear to be specifically interested in Suetonius himself or to articulate admiration for the biographer's literary style. Even where he appears to quote directly from *The Twelve Caesars*, it is often difficult to tell if he is merely citing a *bon mot* whose connection to the original context would remain vague even, perhaps, to Kierkegaard himself. That said, there appears to be a certain affinity in the interests of the two authors: a love of the curious and the heightened drama pertaining to a great man at a decisive moment in life.

Suetonius primarily functions as a source of examples for Kierkegaard. The biographical anecdotes of the different emperors are a well from which he can draw parallels that will sufficiently strengthen the momentum of his own text—especially in cases where eccentric behavior or a fateful decision will illuminate his own argument. This procedure, of course, is very old—a stable ingredient from ancient rhetoric and onwards. Petrarch, who is only one out of many later major writers on whom Suetonius has been an influence, describes the latter not only as *auctor certissimus rerum scriptor*, but also as *curiosissimus* which in Latin can be taken to mean both most *thorough* and most *curious*—but not, seemingly, *odd* as is possible in English.[5] It would appear, as the following pages will hopefully show, that Kierkegaard favors exactly this last aspect of the word in regards to the content of Suetonius' *Lives*.

Because Kierkegaard, with a few intriguing exceptions, only ever refers to Suetonius in Danish and, as stated, he probably only owned *The Twelve Caesars* in Danish translation, I have found no reason to delve too much into the Latin in which it was originally written. As regards the English quotations, I make grateful use of Robert Graves' translation.[6]

In the following section I shall proceed by describing Kierkegaard's uses of Suetonius, first, where Suetonius' name is mentioned, whether or not there is any accompanying quotation. Then I will proceed to quotations that seem to be from Suetonius (directly or indirectly), though his name is not mentioned.

I.

There are four direct mentions of Suetonius in Kierkegaard's works. The first known use is to be found in *Notebook 1* where Suetonius' name crops up in a marginal note. The context is a series of notes taken from theology professor Henrik Nicolai Clausen's (1793–1877) *Lectures on Dogmatics*, which Kierkegaard attended during his theology studies in 1833. Here Suetonius is credited, probably by Clausen, but not impossibly later on by Kierkegaard, as one of several sources portraying the Messiah. After mentioning several prophets who make reference to the Messiah, Kierkegaard's notes add the remark, "This is also seen from...Suetonius and Tacitus."[7] In fact, the

5   Von Albrecht, *A History of Roman Literature*, p. 1407.
6   Suetonius, *The Twelve Caesars*, trans. by Robert Graves, London: Cassel 1962.
7   *SKS* 19, 39, Not 1:7.c.

Life of Claudius has "Because the Jews at Rome caused continuous disturbances at the instigation of Chrestus, he [Claudius] expelled them from the city."[8] Kierkegaard does not quote this passage. But since this is the only reference in the *Lives* on this subject, we can be fairly certain that this is the place alluded to. Kierkegaard's use of Suetonius here is, as can be seen, very limited; especially because the marginal note appears to be nothing more than the jotting down of words from a lecture. What more than his own phrasing could Kierkegaard possibly have added?

The second direct quotation involving Suetonius' name is from the *Journal DD* and is almost the same story. This entry, dated the June 8, 1837, goes under the heading "*Eine Parallele zur Religionsphilosophie von Carl Rosenkranz*" and refers to an article to be found in the *Zeitschrift für spekulative Theologie*, a publication which appears in Kierkegaard's private library. Johann Karl Friedrich Rosenkranz (1805–79) was a German Hegelian philosopher and theologian who served for many years as a professor at the University of Königsberg. The entry consists of little more than Kierkegaard's paraphrasing and partial translation of said article with very little personal input involved.[9] Kierkegaard boils down Rosenkranz's main argument, namely, that the different forms of religion ("*Religions-Skikkelser*") can be reduced to "the simplest expression" by laying down three propositions: "*1) der Mensch ist Gott, 2) Gott ist Gott, 3) Gott ist Mensch.*"[10] The brief direct reference to Suetonius crops up when Kierkegaard through Rosenkranz, having described the different faces of "man is God" throughout the ages, comes to compare pagan religion with monotheism. He concludes that the heathen religions consummated themselves in madness because of the negative aspect of their individuality. The deified emperor exemplifies the special brand of madness, which is attributed to Roman civilization, and it is then stated that "Suetonius' *Vitae Imperatorum* gives examples of this."[11] One could have expected Rosenkranz to follow up by giving us just one such example, but instead Kierkegaard's pen continues to quote him quoting Hegel on the nature of the deified Roman emperor. We are thus left to speculate as to what Rosenkranz could have meant by citing Suetonius. The reason is so obvious that the learned reader, not to mention Kierkegaard himself, would very well know that Suetonius offers several examples of the apotheosis of Roman emperors. Of the twelve emperors covered in the *Lives*, no less than five were deified after their death: Julius Caesar, Augustus, Claudius, Vespasian, and Titus.

The third direct reference is yet another quotation of a quotation. In a short entry from the *Journal JJ*, written at some point in 1842, Kierkegaard writes:

> No orthodoxy has ever indulged as extravagantly in idolatry as was done in the imperial period with the image of the emperor: a man was convicted of high treason for striking his slave who had a silver drachma stamped with the emperor's image. (See Philostratus, *Leben des Apollonius v. Tyana*, p. 185. Annotation cited by Suetonius, *vita Tiberii*, 58.)[12]

---

8   Suetonius, "Claudius," 25, p. 177.
9   *Zeitschrift für spekulative Theologie*, ed. by Bruno Bauer, vols. 1–3, Berlin: bei Ferdinand Dümmler 1836–38 (*ASKB* 354–357).
10   *SKS* 17, 219, DD:10 / *KJN* 1, 211.
11   *SKS* 17, 221, DD:10 / *KJN* 1, 213.
12   *SKS* 18, 149, JJ:19 / *KJN* 2, 138–9.

As can be seen, Suetonius appears as yet another source to which the above-
mentioned story can be referred. Philostratus (ca. 170–247) was a sophist and
rhetorician who wrote a *Life* of the neo-Pythagorean Apollonius who lived in the
first century AD. Kierkegaard owned Philostratus' work in a German translation.[13]
According to Philostratus, Apollonius during his travels came to the town of
Aspendus in Pamphylia where the governor tried to avoid getting burned alive by
the people by clinging to the statue of the Roman Emperor Tiberius.[14] The reference
to Suetonius, as cited by Kierkegaard, appears in the editor's footnote, where the
practice of seeking protection from the statues of the emperors is explained:

> *Schutz bei den Standbildern der Herrscher zu suchen, war, wie es scheint, unter den*
> *Ptolemäern gebräuchlich geworden; in Rom kam es unter August auf. Antoninus Pius*
> *verbot es. Von der tyrannischen Ausdehnung, mit der unter Tiberius das Majestätsgesetz*
> *gehandhabt wurde, gibt Suetonius (vita Tiber. 58.) Beispiele, welche den hier erwähnten*
> *nicht nachstehen.*[15]

The mentioned paragraph 58 in Suetonius' *Life* of Tiberius gives several examples of
the consequences of lese-majesty:

> One man was accused of decapitating an image of Augustus with a view of substituting
> another head; his case was tried before the senate, and finding a conflict of evidence,
> Tiberius had the witness examined under torture. The offender was sentenced to death,
> which provided a precedent for far-fetched accusations: people could now be executed for
> beating a slave, or changing their clothes, close to an image of Augustus, or for carrying a
> ring or a coin, bearing Augustus' head, into a privy or a brothel; or for criticizing anything
> Augustus had ever said or done. The climax came when a man died merely for letting an
> honor be voted him by his native town council on the same day that honors had once been
> voted to Augustus.[16]

Nowhere in paragraph 58 do we hear of a man who was condemned because he hit
a slave carrying a coin with the emperor's stamp on it. But this story does lie within
the bounds of what could reasonably be adduced from the text: if someone could
be executed for "carrying a ring or a coin, bearing Augustus' head, into a privy or a
brothel," then it would seem likely that a master could be punished also for beating
a slave carrying a coin with the same head on it.

Kierkegaard, far from being interested in the historical accuracy of his source,
merely wants to procure an extreme example of idolatry with which to compare
religious orthodoxy. The *Journal JJ* is virtually crammed with similar short entries,
in which Kierkegaard duly makes reference to the source in question. The entry JJ:13,

---

[13]   *Flavius Philostratus Werke*, tomes 1–5, in one volume, trans. by Friedr. Jacobs,
Stuttgart 1828 (*ASKB* 1143).
[14]   *Leben des Apollonius von Tyana*, Book 1, Chapter 15, in *Flavius Philostratus, des
Aeltern, Werke*, trans. by Jacobs, tome 2, 1829, p. 185.
[15]   *Leben des Apollonius von Tyana*, Book 1, Chapter 15, in *Flavius Philostratus, des
Aeltern, Werke*, trans. by Jacobs, tome 2, 1829, p. 185.
[16]   Suetonius, "Tiberius," 58, p. 122.

for example, quotes directly in Latin from Descartes; JJ:17 quotes or paraphrases Aristotle's *Ethics*.

The fourth and last direct mention of Suetonius is from *Stages on Life's Way* published in 1845. Here at last we are treated to more than the quotation of a quotation or some other weakening of the connection between Kierkegaard and Suetonius. Near the end of *" 'Guilty?' / 'Not Guilty'"* it says:

> Nor does it follow that everyone who has a distended belly is about to give birth—it could also be a flatulence. Likewise, neither does it follow that everyone who has an obstructed abdomen is about to give birth, since it could be something completely different, as Suetonius reminds us when he says of one of the Roman emperors: *vultus erat nitentis* [the face was that of one who is straining].[17]

This sentence exemplifies a case that will soon become familiar: Kierkegaard's juxtaposing of two texts unrelated in terms of historical relevance, but brought together into a common theme which will clarify or drive home some point he is making. The context here is the endnote "A Concluding Word" of the said work by the pseudonym Frater Taciturnus, which continues the theme of the work as a whole: the different life-views—aesthetic, ethical, religious—and the implications for the person having them.

This is where the Suetonius quotation comes into the picture when in the *Life* of Vespasian (Titus Flavius Vespasianus, AD 9–79) he describes the said emperor as "square-shouldered, with strong, well-formed limbs," who "always *wore a strained expression on his face*."[18] Kierkegaard chose to quote the sentence in Latin (*"vultu veluti nitentis"*), which probably means that he is quoting a *bon mot* from some other text available to him or ever referring to an orally transmitted version of the wording.

The contextual meaning is clear: to have "a flatulence" is a common denominator for all sicknesses where the abdomen is tightened to the point of being like a drum by something from the inside.[19] By quoting the passage from Suetonius, Kierkegaard avoids falling into a language too improper, but nonetheless alluding to such things, because the very next sentence in the *Life* of Vespasian points the fact that the emperor's strained expression is connected with defecation: "so that once, when he [Vespasian] asked a well-known wit who always used to make jokes about people: 'why not make one about me?' the answer came: 'I will, when you have at last finished relieving yourself.' "[20] So when Kierkegaard with his knowledge of Latin in the above cited quotation writes, "it could be something completely different," he could mean nothing other than what is given birth here is feces. Kierkegaard's use of Suetonius can here be described as a rhetorical *concealment*. This means the encryption of what is for one reason or another personally or socially improper into another language in order to avoid saying what is improper but still including it. Further, the passage mentioned is not even explicit in itself, but only so when read

---

17	*SKS* 6, 454 / *SLW*, 439.
18	Suetonius, "Vespasian," 20, p. 259. My emphasis.
19	See *SKS* K6, 401.
20	Suetonius, "Vespasian," 20, p. 159.

in connection with the next passage in Suetonius, which is quoted. Lastly, reverting to Latin is reverting from the vernacular to a classical language. It is not unlikely that this in itself at Kierkegaard's time could still have had the effect of connoting something highbrow and thus creating the paradoxical effect of turning what is lowbrow in content into something magisterial looking to the untrained eye.

II.

From quotations where Suetonius is named explicitly, I shall now proceed with the quotations that do not mention him, but where it is more or less certain he is the one referred to. Whereas the direct quotations were introduced chronologically, this section will be divided thematically after the emperor in question. Within these subsections I shall proceed chronologically, except for the cases where Kierkegaard makes use of the same passage several times, in which case these texts will be examined as a whole.

A. Caesar

Probably the first known use by Kierkegaard of Suetonius is to be found in the *Journal AA*. The status of entry AA:12 in which the reference appears is controversial since it is disputed whether the text is a commentary to a letter possibly addressed to the brother of his brother-in-law, Peter Wilhelm Lund (1801–80), or whether it is a piece of fiction.[21] The entry is dated by Kierkegaard as August 1, 1835 and is supposedly written in Gilleleje, a small town on the north coast of Zealand where Kierkegaard spent the summer that year studying and rambling. The content of the entry, at least in its main aspects, is a sustained meditation on the different sciences and their merits according to the young Kierkegaard.[22] But now he turns to a more personal discussion about what he is to do with himself: "I shall now try to look calmly at myself and begin to act inwardly; for only in this way will I be able, as a child in its first consciously undertaken act refers to itself as 'I,' to call myself 'I' in a profounder sense."[23] But in order to find this "I," Kierkegaard grants that patience is needed:

> Just as one does not begin a feast with the rising of the sun but with its setting, so also in the spiritual world one must first work ahead for a time before the sun can really shine for us and rise in all its glory. For although it is said that God lets his sun rise upon both the good and evil, and the rain fall on the just and the unjust, that isn't so in the spiritual world. So let the lot be cast—I am crossing the Rubicon! This road no doubt leads me *into battle*, but I will not give up.[24]

With the wording "So let the die be cast—I am crossing the Rubicon!" we most likely encounter a reference to Suetonius' *Life* of Caesar. In paragraph 32 Suetonius

---

21   For a discussion of this question, see *SKS* K17, 18–21.
22   *SKS* 17, 18–23, AA:12 / *KJN* 1, 13–25.
23   *SKS* 17, 29–30, AA:12 / *KJN* 1, 24. Translation slightly modified.
24   *SKS* 17, 30, AA:12 / *KJN* 1, 24–5.

portrays Caesar in doubt about whether he should defy the senate and cross the river Rubicon in Northern Italy with his army. He finally decided to do so with the words "the die is cast," by which he indicated that the crossing was a point of no return.[25] An irreversible move has been made. Kierkegaard uses the expression "Let the lot be cast," not "...the die..." This would not, in my opinion, warrant a change in the interpretation, and considering his mention of the Rubicon at such close proximity in the text, it is more likely that the use of the word "lot" was a variation used during Kierkegaard's time.

It is quite possible that Kierkegaard could have used this passage about Caesar's crossing the Rubicon without having looked it up in Suetonius' text. Johan Ludvig Heiberg (1791–1860), for example, with whom Kierkegaard was soon to be temporarily affiliated, used a rewriting of the line in his famous *Elves' Hill*, letting King Christian IV cross a Danish river, saying: "I may not be Caesar, and these waves not the Rubicon, / but still I say: *Jacta est alea*." [26] Rather than any specific ancient source, it is much more likely that Kierkegaard here draws on a whole tradition, which in time turned this statement into a proverb.

The text as a whole portrays Kierkegaard's remarkable mastery of language even at the age of 22 when this was written down. It also shows that his eagerness to find his own style at times makes him go over the top and flirt dangerously with the hyperbolic. Comparing the result of his decision to turn inwards upon himself in order to find an original "I" with Caesar's knowledge that a civil war is about to be unleashed may be just such an example. But on the other hand, and at the risk of anachronism, this trope would fit well for a person who, as Kierkegaard later was to stress, wishes to give all importance to "that single individual" as opposed to the matters of the world at large.

The very same dictum crops up later in Kierkegaard's works; this time it figures quite prominently as it is used at a, perhaps *the*, crucial turning point in "The Seducer's Diary" from *Either/Or* (1843). This is the passage where the seducer Johannes decides to call off the engagement with the innocent Cordelia. The entry, taking the form of a diary entry, begins: "*Jacta est alea*. Now the turn must be made."[27] Here the use of Caesar's supposed wording appears more in line with the text than in the former example since this is a place of heightened importance in *Either/Or*. Rather than emphasizing some youthful aspiration applicable to Kierkegaard only, the words convey a dramatic underlining of a shift in a situation of which the reader is aware. If Kierkegaard's use of Suetonius in AA:12 had taken the form of a personal note only, this would hardly matter. But as has been frequently pointed out, Kierkegaard's early journal entries often take the form of writing exercises. This probably includes imagining an audience of some kind, and if this is the case, it would be fair to say that Kierkegaard makes much better use of Caesar's quotation in *Either/Or* than in AA:12, where the statement is about as dramatic as it would have been had Caesar been a shepherd deciding to cross the Rubicon in search of better pastures.

---

25   Suetonius, "Caesar," 32, p. 15.

26   Johan Ludvig Heiberg, *Elverhöi*, Copenhagen: Jens Hostrup Schultz 1828, p. 94: "*Vel er jeg ikke Cæsar, / Og disse Bølger ikke Rubicon; / Men dog jeg siger: Jacta est alea!*"

27   *SKS* 2, 408 / *EO1*, 420.

A reference to Caesar's crossing of the Rubicon is mentioned a third and last time in *Christian Discourses* (1848). In one of the many chapters under the heading "Prayer" Kierkegaard chooses to discuss 1 Corinthians 11:23 and the sentence beginning "the Lord Jesus, on the night when he was betrayed."[28] He conjures up the night of Jesus' death and urges the people not to regret not being there to re-witness this dark hour "for truly that person chose the better part who first and foremost prays that the terror might stand vividly before him."[29] This is the night of his betrayal. After summing up all of Jesus' worldly successes, Kierkegaard turns his attention to his fall: "he is now as if cast put of the world; he is sitting apart in a room with the twelve. But the die has been cast; his fate has been decided by the decree of the Father and the high priests."[30] If the first use of Caesar's famous dice throw was to serve a mainly personal purpose and the second a public but fictitious one, this last mention serves yet another kind of public purpose, namely, the age-old tradition of oral Bible commentary. Kierkegaard himself was aware of the idea that especially historical commentary could much enhance the personal relationship between the faithful and the Bible; so it is only natural that his own oration on the Last Supper should serve to heighten the listener or reader's attention to what is already there in the text. This strategy lends itself well to the use of a rhetoric that heightens the drama of the situation—and in this case maybe the juxtaposition of yet another ancient source with the Bible is meant by Kierkegaard to produce a similar "flavor" to the one in the text in question. In any case, there really is no turning back for Jesus at this point since this betrayal and later, the painful death, of course, were meant to happen. It could be ventured that this ought to imply that the whole of Jesus' life also was meant to happen in the way that it did—that his fate must have been sealed from the very beginning—and thus there ought to be no throw of the dice at around the time of the Last Supper, but this is perhaps making a bit much out of the use of a Caesar quotation.

The last mention of Caesar where Suetonius is a plausible source is to be found in *A Literary Review* (1846). In his critique of Thomasine Gyllembourg's (1773–1856) novel *Two Ages*, Kierkegaard writes of one of the characters, Mariane, that she does not possess enough of "love's exulting courage to take feminine charge of the holy expedition of marriage when the beloved loses self-possession."[31] What she does have is *inwardness* (*Inderlighed*) which, according to Kierkegaard, is "with essentially the same strength but manifesting itself in an essentially different way."[32] She may be willing to give up the man, Bergland, but she will not return the ring— for that to her would be giving up the *being in love* which she still feels. This being in love is identified as a recalling of a suffering inwardness, which befalls the girl preoccupied with the "quiet virtues," and it is the last blow to a girl with little sense of reality.[33]

---

28   *SKS* 10, 296–300 / *CD*, 276–81.
29   *SKS* 10, 296 / *CD*, 276.
30   *SKS* 10, 296 / *CD*, 276.
31   *SKS* 8, 50 / *TA*, 51.
32   *SKS* 8, 50 / *TA*, 51.
33   *SKS* 8, 50 / *TA*, 51.

Here Kierkegaard evokes the killing of Caesar: "So also Caesar remained erect when the conspirators plunged their daggers into him, but when he saw that Brutus was a party to it, he wrapped his cloak about him and gave himself up to death with these words: You, too, my son Brutus!"[34] The intent of the inclusion of this famous incident appears to be that Mariane, by turning from outside matters to the noble suffering associated with inward fervor, resigns just as Caesar is supposed to have resigned himself to his death at the moment he saw a loved one as part of the conspiracy. What would seem to be implied in Caesar's example is the use of fighting when one's beloved turns against one, and what, in Mariane's case, is the use of fighting when one's last contact with the world is cut off? It is somewhat uncertain whether Kierkegaard here alludes to Suetonius, Plutarch, both, or neither. In Suetonius, Caesar covers and resigns himself when confronted with "a ring of drawn daggers." It is not stated when he sees Brutus. On the other hand, the famous words *"et tu, Brute?,"* which Suetonius offers as an alternative to a silent Caesar, rendered in Greek as Καὶ σὺ τέκνον, meaning "you too, child" are not mentioned by Plutarch who claims that Caesar died without a word.[35] Here, as elsewhere, Kierkegaard uses a famous historical moment to highlight a certain action in the world of a person he is portraying. Suetonius here functions as a mere conveyer of what Kierkegaard wants to use. His comparative example would be much less appropriate in the given situation if he had to rely on a strict rendering of the sources.

B. Augustus

Kierkegaard mentions Augustus several times, but we can be certain of a connection to Suetonius only once. The context is the witty reminiscence of the Kierkegaardian pseudonym William Afham, who at an early point in "In vino veritas" in *Stages on Life's Way* describes a place in Zealand—Grib Forest. No one comes to this place called "the Nook of the Eight Paths," except for a certain insect:

> The eight paths—heavy traffic is only a possibility, a possibility for thought, because no one travels this path except a tiny insect that hurries across *lente festinans* [hastening at leisure]. No one travels it except that fugitive traveler that is constantly looking around, not in order to find someone but in order to avoid everyone.[36]

What Kierkegaard brings to life is a scene of utter desolation—and making an insect move *lente festinans* (hastening at leisure) gives the impression of nature moving at its own pace with no real care for the dealings of man. The original context is Suetonius' *Life* of Augustus, Chapter 25, where Augustus' dislike of "haste" and "recklessness" in a military commander is described. Suetonius writes that Augustus "constantly quoted such Greek proverbs as σπεῦδε βραδέως ("hastening at leisure," better known in Latin as *festina lente*), and "Better a safe commander than a rash one."[37] Again, Kierkegaard favors the use of a proverb purged of its historical

---

34   *SKS* 8, 51 / *TA*, 51.
35   Suetonius, "Caesar," 82, p. 36.
36   *SKS* 6, 23–4 / *SLW*, 16.
37   Suetonius, "Augustus," 25, p. 51.

context, and this is another situation where Suetonius is pretty clearly not the direct source. Further, the wording is not central to this passage, but ancillary to "hurries across" and could even be deemed tautological, were it not for the notion of slowness supplied by the Latin *lente*. .

C. Tiberius

There appears to be no specific reference to Tiberius as related by Suetonius in Kierkegaard's works; but in the early journal entry, AA:12, which we have dealt with in relation to Caesar, Kierkegaard refers to a Roman consul from the time of the Punic Wars, mentioned in Suetonius' *Life* of Tiberius.[38] In a part of this possibly fictitious letter under the heading "Theology" Kierkegaard turns to the relations between Christianity and rationalism.[39] The latter is described as subordinated, but also at times indifferent, to Christianity. It uses whatever it can from it for its purposes, and what it cannot use—it discards. Kierkegaard pictures the willingness to do so by use of yet another historical analogy. He writes that the rationalists, "just like the Roman consul...are also prepared to throw the sacred hens overboard if they will not eat."[40] This sentence could possibly refer to the historian Valerius Maximus, but mention of this story is also made in *The Twelve Caesars*.[41] In the *Life* of Tiberius, Suetonius mentions an ancestor of an emperor in the Claudian line named Publius Claudius Pulcher, a Roman consul and naval commander who lost a battle against the Carthaginians because he refused to follow the auspices before the battle: "Claudius the Fair who, as Consul, took the auspices before a naval battle off Sicily and, finding that the sacred hens had refused their feed, cried: 'if they will not eat, let them drink!' He threw them into the sea, fought the battle in defiance of their warning and lost it."[42] The meaning in Kierkegaard's context seems fairly plain: that the rationalists easily and even haughtily would be willing to sacrifice Christian principles if these did not match those of their own beliefs. Kierkegaard concludes, "The error lies thus in the fact that when they find themselves in agreement with Scripture, they use it as the foundation, but otherwise not, and thus they rest on two incongruous positions."[43]

Kierkegaard's interest in sacred hens does not stop here. A reference to the same story is also be found in journal entry EE:153 written on August 7, 1839:

> Philosophers treat the dogmas, the sacred utterances of Scripture, in short the whole consciousness of holy things, as Appius Pulcher treated the sacred hens; one consults them and if they bode ill, one says as that general said: if the sacred hens won't eat, let them drink, and thereupon threw them overboard.[44]

---

[38]   See Suetonius, "Tiberius," 9–12, pp. 100–102.

[39]   For a short background on the rationalists and Kierkegaard's relation to them, see *SKS*, K17, 56-7.

[40]   *SKS* 17, 22, AA:12 / *KJN* 1, 17.

[41]   See *SKS* K17, 59.

[42]   Suetonius, "Tiberius," 2, p. 96.

[43]   *SKS* 17, 22, AA:12 / *KJN* 1, 17.

[44]   *SKS* 18, 54, EE:153 / *KJN* 2, 49.

Here is an almost exact copy of both the primary content (the rationalists) and the secondary (Pulcher) as in AA:12. Only now a few years later, Kierkegaard compresses the intended meaning into one of his many aphoristic entries, making the general meaning shine through in an instant. The example, possibly from Suetonius, must have stuck with him over the years, or he could have found the comparison too good to remain buried in the middle of a youthful letter, thus writing EE:153 after having reread the old entry.

D. Caligula

Along with Caesar and Domitian, Gaius Iulius Caesar Germanicus (AD 12–41), known as "Caligula" ("Bootee"), is the Roman emperor most frequently mentioned by Kierkegaard.

In a journal entry Kierkegaard mounts a scathing attack on people who would expect to find redemption in nature. No particular members of this group are mentioned, but it could be assumed that Kierkegaard is referring to the Romantics following in the footsteps of Rousseau. Whoever the target, these worshippers are described as "drivel-heads" [*Vrøvlehoveder*], and they are put in a most unfavorable light.[45] Kierkegaard hears no wisdom coming from the trees—only the repeated nonsense of the nature lovers, causing the anguished trees to beg to be chopped down in order be relieved of this drivel. This leads Kierkegaard to wish "all these drivel-heads sat upon a single neck," and to proceed by proclaiming that "like Caligula, I would know what to do."[46] Kierkegaard here refers to a quotation in *The Twelve Caesars* where, according to Suetonius, Caligula is supposed to have scolded the Roman people for their behavior at the Games: "On one occasion the people cheered the wrong team; he cried angrily: 'I wish the Romans had only one neck!'"[47] For Kierkegaard the general point must be that the group of nature lovers is so sizable that he considers himself unable, or only with great difficulty, to keep them all in check. How much easier it would be if they could all somehow be counted into one—and as the analogy would imply—be dealt with severely.

In another journal entry dated May 4, 1839, Kierkegaard returns to the theme of Caligula and the many heads on a single neck. This time he reflects on the actual message in Suetonius' rendition of the emperor's words: "Caligula's idea of wanting to have all heads put on one neck is nothing but an attempted, cowardly suicide. It is the counterimage of a suicide, they are two similarly despairing worldviews.—"[48]

The entry ends with a dash and is presumably continued on May 5—as this entry begins with a punctuated line; "...and especially in our times," it begins, "when the ideas are so confused, when the world is so busy with its affairs, so loud, when the selfish pleasure that is in a human being has broken its chains asunder in so many ways; especially in our time it is so easy for us to put ourselves in a wrong relation to Christianity, it is so easy."[49]

---

[45]   *SKS* 17, 205–6, CC:15 / *KJN* 1, 197.
[46]   *SKS* 17, 205, CC:15 / *KJN* 1, 197.
[47]   Suetonius, "Caligula" 30, p. 146.
[48]   *SKS* 18, 24–5, EE:55 / *KJN* 2, 20.
[49]   *SKS* 18, 25, EE:56 / *KJN* 2, 20.

This relationship can end in a state of offense (*Forargelse*) on the part of man, and God will have to "stop us in our tracks, as he stopped Paul," or God will call out "Like a father who watches in pain as his son goes his own way, I have left nothing untried in order to call you to me; how often have I not wanted to gather you as a mother hen gathers her chicks under her wings."[50] If we bring the two entries together, a certain coherence appears: the first entry turns Caligula's wish for the beheading of the whole crowd of the arena into a symbolization of the wish of one man for the rest of mankind to perish. This is a kind of early variation on Sartre's "*L'enfer, c'est les autres*," but it stresses that this wish—to be all alone in the world—is not much different from not being there at all. The next day's entry tries to come to grips with the cause of such an unhealthy disposition. Caligula is left behind as a direct reference, but Kierkegaard keeps the theme of estrangement, elaborating on it so as not only to make it pertain to man's failing relationship with man—but also to man's estrangement from God. The example at the end of EE:56 with God, wishing to gather estranged man "as a mother hen gathers her chicks under her wings," could be interpreted as a conclusion upon what began in the entry the day before; Caligula's idea is a turning away from the world and from God—a cowardly reaction from someone who, as it says in the second entry, will not be "warmed by the love with which I [sc. God] have loved you since before the foundations of the world were laid."[51]

Kierkegaard also makes use of the example of "multiple heads on one neck" in *Either/Or*, where the ever-reasonable Assessor Wilhelm attempts to guide his young friend A towards a more stable existence. At a point in his long letter under the heading "The Esthetic Validity of Marriage" the Assessor introduces the idea of the congregation, which he believes will pose a problem for A as a part of marital life. He presupposes that A's response will be as follows: "The congregation, the blessed parish, which despite its plurality still is a moral character—yes, even if it had just as it has all the boring qualities of moral characters, also the good quality of having only one head on the neck...I know very well what I would do."[52] Perelman and Olbrechts-Tyteca have described the typical tendency in Romantic thought to turn a *locus* (a premise of a general nature) of quantity into a locus of quality: "When the Romanticist contrasts the will of the multitude and the individual will, the former may be conceived as a manifestation of a superior will, that of the group, which will be described as a unique being."[53] In the Assessor's interpretation of what he believes to be A's viewpoint, the congregation's individual members are transformed into to a single moral (and thus to A, by definition, boring) person whom he would gladly behead. As with Caligula, the case is presented as irreal, but probably for a different reason. Judging from Suetonius' portrait of Caligula the wish to have the crowd beheaded would not have to have been mere words; his inability to do so

50 *SKS* 18, 25, EE:56 / *KJN* 2, 21.
51 Ibid.
52 *SKS* 3, 101 / *EO2*, 99.
53 Chaïm Perelman and Lucie Olbrechts-Tyteca, *The New Rhetoric: A Treatise on Argumentation*, trans. by Hohn Wilkinson and Purcell Weaver, Notre Dame, Indiana: University of Notre Dame Press 1969, pp. 98–9.

probably has more to do with the pragmatics involved in such a slaughter. With A the words are supposed to be understood as a figure of speech—to be at a distance from reality. The wish to kill the congregation probably means nothing more than the expression of a great dislike for and a wish to "get rid of" the congregation. This is a good example of how proverbs often lose contact, not only with their historical context, but also with semantics of the language.

It seems that Kierkegaard had this motif running in his head like a jingle: only a little later in *Either/Or* he turns once more to Caligula and beheading. In "The Balance Between the Esthetic and the Ethical in the Development of Personality" as a part of the large portrait of Nero (to which I shall return shortly) it is stated about the latter:

> If he were not the Roman emperor, he perhaps would end his life with suicide, for, indeed, they are just different expressions of the same thing when Caligula wishes that the heads of all people were on one neck so that the whole world could be annihilated with one stroke and when a person takes his own life.[54]

Kierkegaard here returns precisely to the theme of EE:55—how being alone in the world would be like non-existence. This is another case of borrowing from his own archives.

The last time Kierkegaard finds use for quoting Caligula's unusual wishes is in the *Concluding Unscientific Postscript* published in 1846. This time the use is far from the original meaning. In Johannes Climacus' treatment of the interpretation of the Holy Writ it is stated that "even if the heads of all the critics were mounted on a single neck, one would never arrive at anything more than an approximation, and that there is an essential misrelation between that and a personal, infinite interestedness in one's eternal happiness."[55] The many heads on one neck would imply an accumulation of knowledge of many learned men in the mind of a single person. According to Climacus, this would not bring the critic to an ultimate truth on the subject. The point is that such an accumulation would normally be regarded as a *good thing* in itself, and not, as with the other examples, as a pernicious device by means of which someone might decapitate a number of people more easily. Suetonius' story completely loses its inner logic; Kierkegaard retains only a textual ornament, which will effectively help underscore his particular point.

Jumping backwards in time but forwards to a new theme, *Either/Or* makes use of a well-known Suetonius quotation. Opening a new diary entry with the words, "*Oderint, dum metuant*, as if only fear and hate belong together, whereas fear and love have nothing to do with each other, as if it were not fear that makes love interesting."[56] According to Suetonius,[57] Caligula utters the Latin words at the beginning of the sentence, meaning "Let them hate me, so long as they fear me," as a kind of motto justifying, or rather—plainly explaining, his atrocities towards guilty and innocent alike. Suetonius attributes the quotation to a certain Roman tragic poet

54   *SKS* 3, 182 / *EO2*, 187.
55   *SKS* 7, 31 / *CUP1*, 24.
56   *SKS* 2, 411 / *EO1*, 424.
57   Suetonius, "Caligula," 30, p. 146.

(*tragicum illud*), and, as with several other proverbs earlier mentioned, it is hard to say from where Kierkegaard got the words. Once again, we notice his use of the original Latin wording; this could suggest that the proverb was obtained on loan through daily conversation, or, less convincingly, he could have found it written in some other work. Kierkegaard's protagonist Johannes ponders the meaning of the saying and suggests that the fear–love relationship is just as natural. For love to be interesting, there needs to be fear: "Behind it ought to brood the deep, anxious night from which springs the flower of love."[58]

E. Nero

The next Roman emperor about whom Kierkegaard has something to say is Claudius Caesar Augustus Germanicus (AD 37–68), better known as Nero. This emperor has gone down in history, perhaps somewhat undeservedly, as a bloodthirsty maniac, and it is in this picture Kierkegaard portrays him. *Either/Or* has a special place for this emperor. In the "Rotation of Crops" we hear of the restless drive for change, described as a "the rotation of crops that depends upon the boundless infinity of change, its extensive dimension."[59] This type, described as "vulgar," is embodied in the person tired of life in the country who now moves to the city, or in a fit of "*Europamüdigkeit*" moves to America. "Or," as it says, "there is another direction, but still extensive. One is weary of eating on porcelain and eats on silver; weary of that, one eats gold; one burns down half of Rome in order to visualize the Trojan conflagration."[60] The writer then asks rhetorically: "What, after all, did Nero achieve?" and through this particular example highlights the possibly enormous consequences of a decision made from one man's wish for mere diversion. Although the Great Fire of Rome on July 18, AD 64 is mentioned by both Dio Cassius and Tacitus, the source here is probably Suetonius since he is the only one who draws a connection with the fall of Troy. According to Suetonius, it was Nero who instigated the fire:

> pretending to be disgusted by the drab old buildings and narrow, winding streets of Rome, he brazenly set fire to the City; and though a group of ex-consuls caught his attendants, armed with oakum and blazing torches trespassing on their property, they dared not interfere. The fire lasted for six days and seven nights, causing many people to take shelter in the tombs.[61]

Kierkegaard's mention of the "Trojan conflagration" refers to the following quotation from Suetonius: "Nero watched the conflagration from the tower of Maecenas, enraptured by what he called 'the beauty of the flames'; he put on his tragedian's costume and sang *The Fall of Ilium* from beginning to end."[62] Kierkegaard follows the gist of Suetonius' text fairly closely. Suetonius' text, though, does not state that Nero set Rome on fire *in order* to recreate the scene of the burning Troy; rather,

---

[58]   *SKS* 2, 411 / *EO1*, 424.
[59]   *SKS* 2, 281 / *EO1*, 291.
[60]   *SKS* 2, 281 / *EO1*, 291–2.
[61]   Suetonius, "Nero," 38, pp. 209–10.
[62]   Ibid., p. 208.

it would appear that he was inspired to make this connection upon seeing the gruesome spectacle. But the biographer is not very clear on this point, and so it could be said that Kierkegaard in this instance stays within something like a reasonably "conventional" interpretation.

This same understanding of Nero's intention comes to the fore in "The Balance Between the Esthetic and the Ethical in the Development of Personality," where we hear of people tired of a prosaic life who "would like to fling themselves into all the wildness into which desire can spin a person."[63] This longing is only rarely made reality because only very few people possess the means to make the dream come true. But, as it says:

> In history, however, we find an occasional example of this, and since I believe there may be some benefit in seeing where this life-view leads when everything is in its favor, I shall present such a character, and to that end I choose that omnipotent man, the emperor Nero, before whom a whole world bowed, who was perpetually surrounded by a countless host of the accommodating messengers of desire.[64]

From this general description of a Roman emperor—one of the few men on earth for whom every wish really is someone else's command—Kierkegaard goes on to refer to the fire of Rome. Addressing his friend A, the pseudonymous B quotes the former for having claimed "with your usual rashness" that "Nero could hardly be blamed for burning Rome in order to get an idea of the conflagration of Troy, but one might question whether he actually had enough artistry to understand how to enjoy it."[65] B thinks that A in some sense wishes to defend Nero "in fixing one's gaze not on what he does but on the *how*."[66] This aesthetic approach to a fire killing thousands, but vividly recreating a scene famous from literature, is very much in line with B's general interpretation of A's disposition. He writes off his friend's attitude as youthful recklessness and seems sure that even Nero himself flinches "at such ferociousness, and yet I should never advise enough anyone to attribute to himself, in the strictest sense, strength enough not to become a Nero."[67] Nero's nature is, according to B, melancholy (*Tungsind*), a trait he deems the old church considered a cardinal sin and something for which the person under its sway can only hold himself responsible.

B then creates a life portrait of an emperor, who could be Nero or Caligula, and how it came to be that he, with all goods in the world at his disposal, in time turned into this melancholy person. In a scenario of an almost archetypal character, Nero is portrayed as a person unable to satiate his desire. One desire only leads to another and this to yet another—with satisfaction always out of sight. "Spirit" (*Aanden*) tries to break through, but he is constantly reminded of something new that he has to possess and is returned to the world and its capricious temptations. This unhappy situation creates in the emperor an inner anger, which he at first appeases by, for example, setting fire to Rome. But now even such a bombast bores him: he turns instead to the

63   *SKS* 3, 179 / *EO2*, 184.
64   Ibid.
65   Ibid.
66   *SKS* 3, 180 / *EO2*, 185.
67   Ibid.

pleasures involved in creating fear. "There is a still greater pleasure; he will make people anxious. He is a riddle to himself, and anxiety is his nature; now he will be a riddle to everybody and rejoice over their anxiety."[68] But now he has lost pleasure in anything this world has to offer: "But what the world has is exhausted, and yet he cannot breathe if this is silenced."[69] This could well, B states, end in suicide, had he not been the emperor. B ends this little story by proclaiming that "even after his death Nero causes anxiety."[70] On a more general level he diagnoses melancholy as a "hysteria of spirit,"[71] a predicate open to anyone who, like our emperor, stays within the bounds of "immediacy" and never moves on to a situation "when spirit requires a higher form, when it wants to lay hold of itself as spirit."[72]

Much of Kierkegaard's portrait appears to rest on a very general idea of certain Roman emperors that could have had as their source Tacitus, Dio Cassius, Suetonius, or even authors of the later tradition. That said, there is a certain Suetonian flavor to the writing, perhaps detectable in the portrait form and maybe pertinent in the primarily psychological description of the emperor. What, of course, has nothing to do with Suetonius is B's interest in the (lack of) spiritual advancement on behalf of the emperor. Suetonius *is* highly preoccupied with the emperor's different vices and virtues, but most of the time his is a descriptive approach—not didactic. Von Albrecht aligns him methodically with Academic skepticism and states that "if Suetonius had any principle at all, it was doubt."[73] Kierkegaard thus reacts to the (Suetonian) text by use of a certain interpretative freedom when it comes to what is implicated by it, but keeps close in his description to the overall construct of the ancient biographers. In other words, he uses the *dicta* for his own purposes.

F. Vespasian

The Suetonian biographies of the short reigns of Galba, Otho, and Vitellius go unnoticed in Kierkegaard's *oeuvre*—enter Emperor Vespasian. In an example in *Works of Love* Kierkegaard compares "a pagan emperor" with Christianity's attitude towards money. Kierkegaard cites this emperor for supposedly having said that "one should not sniff at money."[74] As the commentary in *Søren Kierkegaards Skrifter* points out,[75] this is an imprecise reference to Suetonius' *Life* of Vespasian:

> Titus [Vespasian's son and emperor to be] complained of the tax which Vespasian had imposed on the contents of the City urinals (used by the fullers to clean woolens). Vespasian handed him a coin, which had been a part of the first day's proceeds: "Does it smell bad, my son?" he asked. "No, Father!" "That's odd: it comes straight from the urinal!"[76]

---

68   *SKS* 3, 181 / *EO2*, 187.
69   Ibid.
70   *SKS* 3, 183 / *EO2*, 188.
71   Ibid.
72   Ibid.
73   Von Albrecht, *A History of Roman Literature*, p. 1400.
74   *SKS* 9, 318 / *WL*, 321.
75   *SKS* K9, 242.
76   Suetonius, "Vespasian," 23, p. 261.

As can be seen, the meaning here would be that money is of equal value no matter where it comes from, and this is exactly what Kierkegaard means to infer in the above mentioned example. Of this we can be fairly sure because of his rendition of Christianity's attitude towards money, which is mentioned next in the text as the opposite attitude to that of the emperor: "Christianity, however, teaches quite rightly to sniff at money. It teaches that money itself smells bad."[77] Here Kierkegaard appears to have the specifics of Suetonius' biography far from sight: the emperor, unlike many of the other examples, is nameless, which more than suggests that a version of the *Lives* was not at hand at the time of writing and that Kierkegaard did not want his discourse to be mixed with too much distracting historical detail. On the other hand, the use of the *Life* of Vespasian involves little of the creative rewriting as was the case with many of the more literally close examples mentioned above.

G. Domitian

As Kierkegaard makes no mention of Titus, we move on to the last of the twelve emperors mentioned by Suetonius, Domitian, a man of whom Kierkegaard has something to say.

In *Either/Or* right after one of the aforementioned treatments of Caligula's craving for beheadings, Kierkegaard mentions

> the insane man who had the fixed idea that his apartment was full of flies, so that he was in danger of being smothered by them. In the anxiety of despair and with the rage of despair, he fought for his life. In the same way you, too, seem to be fighting for your life against a similar imaginary swarm of flies, against what you call "the congregation."[78]

The theme of this statement is a continuation of the ethically inclined Assessor Wilhelm's attempt to promote the idea of the congregation in connection with marriage.[79] The crazy man in question can be none other than Domitian as described by Suetonius in the said emperor's *Life*, chapter 3: "At the beginning of his reign Domitian would spend hours alone every day catching flies—believe it or not!—and stabbing them with a needle-sharp pen. Once, on being asked whether anyone was closeted with the emperor, Vibius Crispus answered wittily: 'No, not even a fly.' "[80] Kierkegaard's rendition is easily recognizable in Suetonius' story, but the meaning is different from that found in the original. With Kierkegaard we find the crazy man's craziness exemplified in an *idée fixe*, in the belief that his room is swarming with flies, a belief, it must be understood, that does not reflect reality. Furthermore, this man is presented as being in great inner turmoil. None of this is apparent in Suetonius' text. Here the anecdote portrays the emperor as an eccentric sadist whose mind, it may be implied, is not entirely in order, but who goes about his business without any mentioned existential qualms.

---

[77]   *SKS* 9, 318 / *WL*, 321.
[78]   *SKS* 3, 101 / *EO2*, 99.
[79]   For Kierkegaard's treatment of Caligula in relation to the same theme, see above, pp. 136f.
[80]   Suetonius, "Domitian," 3, p. 273.

As was the case with Caligula's wish for many heads to be collected on a single neck, this particular story is one to which Kierkegaard returns several times. In an almost bizarre manner, Kierkegaard each time adds something new to his narrative loan that was not there before. *Repetition* from 1843 offers a good example. The pseudonym Constantin Constantius, after having wittily described the method by which he attains something akin to the "repeatable" in life—walking in a straight line back and forth in the same room and making sure to take each step at an equal length—elaborates:

> To maintain this established and enduring order, I made use of every possible expedient. At certain times, like Emperor Domitian, I even walked around the room armed with a flyswatter, pursuing every revolutionary fly. Three flies, however, were preserved to fly buzzing through the room at specified times.[81]

At first sight it might seem that Constantius' walking around with his flyswatter and the three flies kept alive reflects Suetonius; but, as it turns out, the only allusion in sight is the mere fact that Domitian spent a lot of time killing flies. The rest is entirely of Kierkegaard's own making.

Domitian, the flies, and Kierkegaard's powerful imagination make a final return in *Works of Love* where Kierkegaard speaks of "the rigid and domineering person":

> Whether the rigid and domineering person is assigned a large sphere of activity or a small one, whether he is a tyrant in an empire or a domestic tyrant in a little attic room essentially makes no difference; the nature is the same: domineeringly refusing to go out of oneself, domineeringly wanting to crush the other person's distinctiveness or torment it to death. The nature is the same—the worst tyrant who ever lived and had a world to tyrannize became bored with it and ended up tyrannizing flies, but he really remained the same![82]

Kierkegaard's use of Domitian in the text appears to serve two ends: one, the portrayal of a person with the maximum potential for tyrannizing, two, an apt anecdote with which to exemplify how such a person's *urge* to tyrannize is no bigger or smaller than that of the next person. Suetonius' story of Domitian and the flies, in vividly picturing a sadistic personality whose hatred for even the tiniest living things makes him use several hours of the day for their extermination, serves Kierkegaard well. But, as has been pointed out so many times as to risk the reader's impatience, he parts company with Suetonius when it suits him. There is no hint in the *Life* of Domitian that the emperor turns to the killing of flies when he has grown tired of greater atrocities. It is even stated by Suetonius that this habit took place "at the beginning of his reign," which can mean little else than that Domitian's daily craving for fly-extermination waned later on. What leads Kierkegaard to reverse the causality of this anecdote is anybody's guess, but I would be tempted to think that he is here quoting very loosely from Suetonius' text—most probably resorting to memory.

It should now have become evident that Kierkegaard's relation to Suetonius the person and the author is slight. The fact that he owned a copy of his book, does not,

---

81   *SKS* 4, 50 / *R*, 179.
82   *SKS* 9, 269 / *WL*, 207–8.

in this case, change much. On the other hand, Kierkegaard's interest in the narratives mentioned by Suetonius is indisputable: the often explicit nature of the descriptions found in *The Twelve Caesars* has served as excellent material for Kierkegaard to work on and adopt into his own scheme of things. Not least because several of the Caesars in the *Lives* are portrayed as both extreme personalities and very powerful people, traits which Kierkegaard often and to different ends chose to write about.

As has hopefully been stated strongly enough, it is often difficult to tell which sources Kierkegaard used when citing the actions of the Roman Caesars. Many of the above-mentioned examples most probably do not derive from Kierkegaard's reading of *The Twelve Caesars*, but have instead found their way into his works by way of oral transmission in the form of proverbs circulating at his time or in written form, possibly through *Adagia* collections.[83] This makes Suetonius a somewhat shadowy but in the end quite well-represented character in Kierkegaard's writings—a source whose importance as such can be disputed but which nevertheless, even in its indirect state, has served Kierkegaard with many exemplars of truth and madness.

---

[83]   For this suggestion, as well as many others concerning the Kierkegaard-Suetonius connection, I am exceedingly grateful to Fritz S. Pedersen.

Bibliography

I. Suetonius' Works in The Auction Catalogue *of Kierkegaard's Library*

Tolv første romerske Keiseres Levnetsbeskrivelse, trans. and ed. by Jacob Baden, Copenhagen: Joh. Fred. Schultz 1802 (*ASKB* 1281).

II. Works in The Auction Catalogue *of Kierkegaard's Library
that Discuss Suetonius*

[Becker, Karl Friedrich], *Karl Friedrich Beckers Verdenshistorie, omarbeidet af Johan Gottfried Woltmann*, vols. 1–12, trans. by J. Riise, Copenhagen: Fr. Brummers Forlag 1822–29, vol. 3, p. 741 (*ASKB* 1972–1983).

Dyck, Johann Gottfried and Georg Schatz (eds.), *Charaktere der vornehmsten Dichter aller Nationen; nebst kritischen und historischen Abhandlungen über Gegenstände der schönen Künste und Wissenschaften, von einer Gesellschaft von Gelehrten*, vols. 1–8, Leipzig: Dyk 1792–1808, vol. 1, p. 33 (*ASKB* 1370–1377).

Hagen, Johan Frederik, *Ægteskabet. Betragtet fra et ethisk-historiskt Standpunct*, Copenhagen: Wahlske Boghandels Forlag 1845, p. 137n; p. 149n (*ASKB* 534).

Meierotto, Johann Heinrich Ludwig, *Ueber Sitten und Lebensart der Römer in verschiedenen Zeiten der Republik*, vols. 1–2, 3rd revised and enlarged ed., Berlin: in der Myliussischen Buchhandlung 1814 (*ASKB* 656).

Meiners, Christoph, *Geschichte des Verfalls der Sitten und der Staatsverfassung der Römer*, Leipzig: bey Weidmanns Erben und Reich 1782, p. 171; p. 177; p. 179; p. 190; p. 195; p. 203; p. 216; p. 218; p. 246; p. 276; p. 284 (*ASKB* 660).

—— *Geschichte des Verfalls der Sitten, der Wissenschaften und Sprache der Römer, in den ersten Jahrhunderten nach Christi Geburt*, Vienna and Leipzig: Joseph Stahel 1791 (*ASKB* 669).

[Montaigne, Michel de], *Michael Montaigne's Gedanken und Meinungen über allerley Gegenstände, ins Deutsche übersetzt*, vols. 1–7, Berlin: F.T. Lagarde 1793–99, vol. 2, p. 312 (*ASKB* 681–687).

Mynster, Jakob Peter, *Den hedenske Verden ved Christendommens Begyndelse*, Copenhagen: Schultz 1850, p. 7; p. 10; p. 48 (*ASKB* 693).

—— *Blandede Skrivter*, vols. 1–3, Copenhagen: Den Gyldendalske Boghandlings Forlag 1852–53 (vols. 4–6, Copenhagen: Den Gyldendalske Boghandlings Forlag 1855–57), vol. 1, p. 161n; p. 167n (*ASKB* 358–363).

Schopenhauer, Arthur, *Die Welt als Wille und Vorstellung*, vols. 1–2, 2nd revised and enlarged ed., Leipzig: F.A. Brockhaus 1844 [1819], vol. 2, pp. 521–2 (*ASKB* 773–773a).

Schmidt, W. Adolf, *Geschichte der Denk- und Glaubensfreiheit im ersten Jahrhundert der Kaiserherrschaft und des Christenthums*, Berlin: Verlag von Veit und Comp. 1847, passim (*ASKB* 771).

III. Secondary Literature on Kierkegaard's Relation to Suetonius

None.

Tacitus:

Christianity as *odium generis humani*

Jon Stewart

Although Tacitus was a profoundly influential historian who has been read throughout the ages, he is not generally considered an important part of Kierkegaard's universe of thought. Indeed, he is usually not even counted among the group of Kierkegaard's most important ancient sources, where names like Plato, Aristotle, Cicero, and Seneca figure prominently. Further, most Kierkegaard scholars would regard it as outright preposterous to turn to Tacitus as a source for Kierkegaard's conception of Christianity.

In this article, I wish to re-examine some of these intuitions. I hope to demonstrate that Kierkegaard in fact had an active interest in Tacitus' writings throughout his authorship. In addition to a number of scattered references to different passages in Tacitus' texts, Kierkegaard also repeatedly returns to a single motif in Tacitus' description of early Christianity, specifically his characterization of Christianity as a doctrine which teaches an "*odium generis humani*" or "hatred of the human race." Somewhat surprisingly, I wish to argue, Kierkegaard finds information in Tacitus that he uses to form his own view of Christianity. Thus, paradoxically, this pagan author ultimately proves to be an important source for Kierkegaard's Christian thinking.

I. The Life and Work of Tacitus

Cornelius Tacitus is generally recognized the greatest historian of imperial Rome. He was born presumably in Gaul or in northern Italy around AD 56, although the exact place is uncertain. In 77 he married the daughter of Agricola, the Roman governor in Britain. He had political career, beginning as praetor in 88, and subsequently passing through a series of important positions. He was consul in 97 and became proconsul of Asia in 112. Tacitus was apparently well known in Roman literary circles. He was close to Pliny the Younger, with whom he corresponded.[1] He is thought to have died sometime around 117. Tacitus is, however, better known for his historical writings than for his political career. It is through his surviving texts that we obtain the most detailed picture of the first century of Imperial Rome.

---

[1] See Ronald Syme, "Tacitus and Pliny" in his *Tacitus*, vols. 1–2, Oxford: Oxford University Press 1958, vol. 1, pp. 59–131.

The work often considered Tacitus' first is the *Dialogus de Oratoribus* or *Dialogue on the Orators*. (Its dating is, however, uncertain, and some scholars place it after the *Germania* and before the *Histories* in the chronology of Tacitus' works.) This treatise portrays a dialogue, which purportedly took place in 74–75, in which the interlocutors address themselves to the question of why Roman oratory had declined under the empire after so many flourishing centuries. This text is modeled on Cicero's famous accounts of the art of oratory such as *De Oratore*.

Tacitus penned two other short early works, which were both published in AD 98. The first, *De vita Iulii Agricolae* or simply the *Agricola*, is a eulogy for Tacitus' father-in-law, Gnaeus Julius Agricola. This brief biography lauds Agricola's management of Britain, where he was governor from AD 70 to 74 and again from 78 to 84, and Aquitania, where he held the same post in the intervening period from 74 to 77. This work also contains a famous and charming description of early Britain (Chapters 10–12).

The other work is *De origine et situ Germanorum* or *On the Origin and Geography of Germany*, generally referred to simply as the *Germania*. This is a short book that describes the nature and customs of the German tribes that the Romans encountered in their conquests. It follows in the tradition of Julius Caesar's observations on the Germans in Book VI of his *Gallic War*. The *Germania* was particularly topical at the time due to the fact that Trajan, in 97, a year before becoming emperor, had been made governor of Upper Germany, where he had previously waged many campaigns. Tacitus is remarkably sympathetic in his portrayal of the German tribes who are painted as simple and innocent savages, free from the corruption and decadence of the civilized world in Rome. Both of these works are interesting ethnographical studies of foreign peoples, which occasion Tacitus to reflect on the mission and destiny of Roman power.

Tacitus' two masterpieces are clearly the *Annals* and the *Histories*. These works rank among the most important sources for the history of the early empire. The *Annals* cover the period from AD 14, from the death of Augustus, until the death of Nero in 68, thus portraying in detail the reigns of Tiberius, Gaius (better known as Caligula), Claudius, and Nero. This work originally consisted of 16 or 18 books, of which only some survive. (We have Books I–IV, parts of V and VI, Books XII–XV, and parts of XI and XVI.)

The *Histories* takes up the narrative on January 1, AD 69 and runs until the death of Domitian in 96, providing a fascinating overview of imperial power, civil wars, assassinations, and political intrigue. The work originally consisted of at least twelve books, of which four survive *in toto* and a large part of a fifth. Here Tacitus covers the brief and chaotic reigns of Galba, Otho, and Vitellius in the troubled year of 69, and then moves to the longer, more stable reigns of Vespasian, Titus, and Domitian.

In the pages of these works, Tacitus' criticism of his contemporary age comes out clearly. In the *Annals*, Tacitus explains his view of the task of history: "It seems to me a historian's foremost duty is to ensure that merit is recorded, and to confront evil deeds and words with the fear of posterity's denunciations."[2] Tacitus was thus keen

2   Tacitus, *Annales*, Book III, 65; English translation quoted from *The Annals of Imperial Rome*, trans. by Michael Grant, Harmondsworth: Penguin 1971, p. 150.

to praise virtue and censure vice, but his history writing contains much more of the latter than the former. Like other Roman historians, he was critical of the institution of the Principate and had a nostalgic longing for the Republic. He believed that the early emperors had forgotten the traditional Roman military virtues and had thus made the state weak and corrupt. Tacitus is not sensational and does not dwell on moral vice and corruption in the same way as Suetonius. He is more concerned with giving a sound historical overview of the events. He is generally acknowledged to be a careful and accurate historian in contrast to, for example, Livy or Nepos. Famous for his conciseness and precision, he is also known as a remarkable stylist and ranked among the best writers of the imperial period.

Tacitus' influence was slow in coming. He was apparently little read during the Middle Ages, and only a single medieval manuscript of his works, which dates from the eleventh century, survives. He was, however, widely read in the Renaissance and modern period. Today there are several editions of his texts and numerous commentaries. In addition, there is an extensive body of secondary literature on his works.[3] His vivid accounts of power, intrigue, and loyalty betrayed have captivated many generations and continue to do so.

II. Kierkegaard's Knowledge of Tacitus

In his extensive Latin studies at the Borgerdyd School in Copenhagen, Kierkegaard as a young man seems not to have read Tacitus. Tacitus' writings were not a part of the fixed Latin curriculum at the school.[4] Moreover, in the account of the readings that he presented for his examination, one finds other Roman historians, specifically, Livy, Caesar, Sallust, and Nepos, but no mention is made of Tacitus.[5]

However, there can be no doubt that Kierkegaard later developed a clear interest in Tacitus since he owned four different editions of his works. In the *Auction Catalogue* one finds that he had a Latin edition of Tacitus' works: *C. Cornelii Taciti Opera ex recensione Ernestiana*, edited by the famous German philologist and classicist

---

3   See, for example, Clarence W. Mendell, *Tacitus, the Man and His Work*, New Haven: Yale University Press; Toronto: Oxford University Press 1957; Syme, *Tacitus*; Richard Reitzenstein, *Aufsätze zu Tacitus*, Darmstadt: Wissenschaftliche Buchgesellschaft 1967; Donald R. Dudley, *The World of Tacitus*, London: Secker & Warburg 1968; Ronald Syme, *Ten Studies in Tacitus*, Oxford: Clarendon Press 1970; F.R.D. Goodyear, *Tacitus*, Oxford: Clarendon Press 1970; Herbert W. Benario, *An Introduction to Tacitus*, Athens, Georgia: University of Georgia Press 1975; Harold Y. McCulloch Jr., *Narrative Cause in the Annals of Tacitus*, Königstein/Ts.: Verlag Anton Hain 1984; Judith Ginsburg, *Tradition and Theme in the Annals of Tacitus*, Salem, New Hampshire: The Ayer Company 1984; Etienne Aubrion, *Rhétorique et histoire chez Tacite*, Metz: Centre de recherché "Littérature et spiritualité" de l'Université de Metz 1985; Ellen O'Gorman, *Irony and Misreading in the Annals of Tacitus*, Cambridge: Cambridge University Press 2000.
4   See Per Krarup, *Søren Kierkegaard og Borgerdydskolen*, Copenhagen: Gyldendal 1977, pp. 25–6.
5   *B&A*, vol 1, pp. 4–5 / *LD*, 5, Document V. (See also Bruce H. Kirmmse (ed.), *Encounters with Kierkegaard*, Princeton: Princeton University Press 1996, p. 273.)

August Immanuel Bekker (1785–1871) and published in Berlin in 1825.[6] In addition
to this, he also owned an older German translation entitled *Des C. Cornelius Tacitus
Sämmtliche Werke*. This work was translated in three volumes by Johann Samuel
Müller (1701–73) and published in Hamburg from 1765 to 1766.[7]

   In addition to these works, Kierkegaard owned two different Danish translations.
The first of these is a three-volume edition entitled simply *Cajus Cornelius
Tacitus*, which was translated by the critic and linguist Jacob Baden (1735–1804)
and published in Copenhagen from 1773 to 1797.[8] A professor at the University
of Copenhagen, Baden published a series of Danish translations of various Latin
authors: Quintilian, Horace, Suetonius, Cicero, and others. The second translation
is a Danish edition of the *Dialogue on the Orators*, entitled *Dialog om Talerne eller
om Aarsagerne til Veltalenhedens Fordærvelse*.[9] This work, published in 1802, was
also from the hand of Baden. The fact that Kierkegaard owned these four different
works, totaling in all eight separate volumes, clearly suggests a serious interest in
the Roman historian.

   Kierkegaard, of course, also owned a number of books that discuss Tacitus, either
briefly or extensively. Many of these were by German authors, for example, Christoph
Meiners' (1747–1810) *Geschichte des Verfalls der Sitten, der Wissenschaften und
Sprache der Römer, in den ersten Jahrhunderten nach Christi Geburt*, from 1791.[10]
In this work Tacitus is used throughout as a source text. Another important work is
Wilhelm Adolf Schmidt's (1812–87) *Geschichte der Denk- und Glaubensfreiheit im
ersten Jahrhundert der Kaiserherrschaft und des Christenthums*, published in Berlin
in 1847.[11] This book likewise uses Tacitus extensively throughout.

   Kierkegaard also owned a number of Danish works, where Tacitus' writings
play some role. Johan Frederik Hagen's (1817–59) treatise on the concept and
development of marriage contains references to Tacitus in the context of an analysis
of the legal institution of marriage in the Roman world.[12] Kierkegaard also owned
works by Jakob Peter Mynster (1775–1854) and Frederik Ludvig Bang Zeuthen

---

[6]   *C. Cornelii Taciti Opera ex recensione Ernestiana*, ed. by Immanuel Bekker, Berlin:
G. Reimer 1825 (*ASKB* 1282).
[7]   *Des C. Cornelius Tacitus Sämmtliche Werke*, trans. by Johann Samuel Müller, vols.
1–3, Hamburg: Johann Carl Bohn 1765–66 (*ASKB* 1283–1285).
[8]   *Cajus Cornelius Tacitus*, vols. 1–3, trans. and ed. by Jacob Baden, vols. 1–3,
Copenhagen: trykt hos Morten Hallager 1773–97 (*ASKB* 1286–1288).
[9]   *Dialog om Talerne eller om Aarsagerne til Veltalenhedens Fordærvelse*, trans. by
Jacob Baden, Copenhagen: Johan Frederik Schultz 1802 (*ASKB* 1289).
[10]   Christoph Meiners, *Geschichte des Verfalls der Sitten, der Wissenschaften und
Sprache der Römer, in den ersten Jahrhunderten nach Christi Geburt*, Vienna and Leipzig:
Joseph Stahel 1791 (*ASKB* 669). Tacitus is also mentioned in Meiners' *Geschichte der Verfalls
der Sitten und der Staatsverfassung der Römer*, Leipzig: bey Weidmanns Erben und Reich
1782, p. 25; p. 78; p. 85 (*ASKB* 660).
[11]   W. Adolf Schmidt, *Geschichte der Denk- und Glaubensfreiheit im ersten Jahrhundert
der Kaiserherrschaft und des Christenthums*, Berlin: Verlag von Veit und Comp. 1847 (*ASKB*
771).
[12]   Johan Frederik Hagen, *Ægteskabet. Betragtet fra et ethisk-historiskt Standpunct*,
Copenhagen: Wahlske Boghandels Forlag 1845, p. 134n; p. 149n; p. 172n (*ASKB* 534).

(1805–74) on the historical development of early Christianity, both of which use Tacitus as a central source.[13] Kierkegaard's library was thus well stocked for the pursuit of an interest in Tacitus, in the form of both the primary texts and modern studies which made use of them for different purposes.

III. Scattered References to Tacitus in Kierkegaard's Writings

This first reference to Tacitus in Kierkegaard's *corpus* appears in his *Notebook 1* from 1833–34. The passage in question comes from Kierkegaard's notes to the theologian, Henrik Nicolai Clausen's (1793–1877) "Lectures on Christian Dogmatics" which were given at the University of Copenhagen during Winter Semester 1833–34.[14] In these entries Kierkegaard adds a number of marginal notes at a later period of time, presumably when Clausen repeated the lectures in Winter Semester 1839–40.[15] There, in one of these notes, Kierkegaard records Clausen as listing a number of sources for various portrayals of the Messiah. After listing the sources from the Old Testament and the Apocrypha, Clausen, according to Kierkegaard's notes, says, "This is also seen from Mth: 2:2, Luc. 2:26, also from Suetonius and Tacitus—about a predecessor for the Messiah."[16]

The commentators of *Søren Kierkegaards Skrifter* claim that the passage Clausen has in mind is Tacitus' *Annals*, Book XV, 44.[17] This conclusion seems sound since this is the only place where Tacitus mentions Christ. In the passage in question Tacitus recounts how a great fire ravaged Rome in AD 64. As a consequence, serious efforts were made to appease the gods so that such an event would not happen again. Rumors abounded that a criminal element was responsible for starting the blaze, and the inevitable search for scapegoats began, with the blame quickly falling on the Christians. In this context, Tacitus writes:

> But neither human resources, nor imperial munificence, nor appeasement of the gods, eliminated sinister suspicions that the fire had been instigated. To suppress this rumor, Nero fabricated scapegoats—and punished with every refinement the notoriously depraved Christians (as they were popularly called). Their originator, Christ, had been executed in Tiberius' reign by the governor of Judea, Pontius Pilatus. But in spite of this temporary setback the deadly superstition had broken out afresh, not only in Judea (where the mischief had started) but even in Rome. All degraded and shameful practices collect and flourish in the capital.[18]

---

[13] Jakob Peter Mynster, *Den hedenske Verden ved Christendommens Begyndelse*, Copenhagen: Schultz 1850, p. 8n, p. 12n, p. 23n, p. 47n, p. 48n (*ASKB* 693). Ludvig Zeuthen, *Om den christelige Tro i dens Betydning for Verdenshistorien. Et Forsøg*, Copenhagen: Gyldendalske Boghandels Forlag 1838, p. 18, p. 37, p. 48, p. 51 (*ASKB* 259).
[14] *SKS* 19, 7–74, Not1:1–8.
[15] See Niels W. Bruun and Steen Tullberg, "Tekstredegørelse" to *Notesbog 1*, in *SKS* K19, 8ff.
[16] *SKS* 19, 39m, Not1:7.
[17] *SKS* K19, 49.
[18] Tacitus, *Annales*, Book XV, 44; *The Annals of Imperial Rome*, trans. by Grant, p. 365.

This passage from Tacitus is of course very different from the biblical references to the Messiah that Clausen lists first. This is rather an account, through the eyes of a skeptical Roman, of the problems arising from Christ and his followers and not a portrayal of a Messiah from the pen of a religious believer. In any case, this is, for obvious reasons, a well-known *passus* in the *Annals*. While the statement in Kierkegaard's notebook should probably be attributed to Clausen and not Kierkegaard himself, nonetheless this passage in Tacitus did make its mark on the young student, who, as we shall see, returned to it much later. This passage is also important in tracing Kierkegaard's exposure to Tacitus. Although, as was seen above, he did not read Tacitus in school, nonetheless from this passage it is clear he learned about him in his first years at university.

As is well known, after defending his dissertation, Kierkegaard left for Berlin in the fall of 1841 in order to attend the lectures of Schelling on "The Philosophy of Revelation." In his lecture notes, which he wrote down in *Notebook 11*, Kierkegaard records Schelling as making an allusion to Tacitus. In the lecture held on February 2, 1842, Kierkegaard writes the following:

> Sabianism is always where there are no fixed buildings; Tacitus describes the Germans in this way. Since man turns away from the universal god, from the boundless, he demands limitation, but when he has experienced the deficiencies of civic life, he longs again for the infinite, for the vast dome of heaven.[19]

In this lecture Schelling continues an analysis from his previous lectures on Indian, Egyptian, and Greek mythology. Here he refers to the religion of the Sabians, who worshiped the heavenly bodies such as the sun and the moon. The point is that it was natural to worship these kinds of deities outdoors and not in a closed temple or church.

Here Schelling has in mind a passage from Tacitus' *Germania*, where the historian describes the religious beliefs of the ancient Germans. There the Roman historian writes: "The Germans do not think it in keeping with the divine majesty to confine gods within walls or to portray them in the likeness of any human countenance. Their holy places are woods and groves, and they apply the names of deities to that hidden presence which is seen only by the eye of reverence."[20] Tacitus observes that the German tribes do not have temples like the Romans but instead have certain holy places outdoors in nature. For Schelling this indicates a desire for the infinite.

While he was in Berlin attending these lectures, Kierkegaard was also busy writing *Either/Or*. In this work there is a hidden reference to Tacitus. In Part Two, in "The Esthetic Validity of Marriage" Judge William says, "An ancient pagan—I believe it is Seneca—has said that when a person has reached his thirtieth year he ought to know his constitution so well that he can be his own physician. I likewise believe that when a person has reached a certain age he ought to be able to be his own

[19]   *SKS* 19, 365, Not11:38 / *SBL*, 410.
[20]   Tacitus, *Germania*, IX; English translation quoted from *The Agricola and the Germania*, trans. by H. Mattingly, translation revised by S.A. Handford, Harmondsworth: Penguin 1970, p. 109.

pastor."[21] The reference to Seneca has thrown commentators off. In fact, Kierkegaard apparently remembers incorrectly or intentionally has Judge William do so.[22]

The reference is instead to Tacitus' *Annals*. There the story is told of the ailing emperor Tiberius, who, in AD 37, had difficulty appointing a successor. After a series of predictions about what fates will befall the immediate candidates, Tiberius was all but ready to give up the attempt. Tacitus writes, "However, despite failing health, Tiberius did not ration his sensualities. He was making a show of vigor to conceal his illness; and he kept up his habitual jokes against the medical profession, declaring that no man over thirty ought to need advice about what was good or bad for him."[23] In the context of *Either/Or* the use of this story seems to be little more than anecdotal. In any case, nothing more seems to be made of it or its disguised source in this context.

Tacitus appears again in 1846 in a draft of a polemical article in connection with Kierkegaard's well-known conflict with the *Corsair*. This time the reference is somewhat more cryptic. In the draft Kierkegaard writes:

What if contemptibleness is feared and has power? To be sure, the elder has said that it has never reached that point in the world. But I may, after all, imagine the worst without in the remotest manner worrying about any actual situation that might keep me from thinking the thought through and even though I am glad that such a thing can never happen. Would power in the remotest way alter the dialectic of contemptibleness? By no means, for when suppressed and downtrodden, contemptibleness is in a way almost defended; when it has power, it is completely defenseless.[24]

In the margin to this, Kierkegaard then writes, "and just as Tacitus detected the contemptible slave mind in the Jewish King Agrippa, because he exercised tyrannical power, so contemptibleness is always seen most readily when it possesses power."[25]

The Hongs take this as a reference to Book V, Chapter 8 of the *Histories*,[26] where Tacitus describes the conquest of Judaea and the destruction of Jerusalem by Titus Caesar in AD 70. As a prelude to this account, he explains to his Roman readers the history of the Jews:

While the Assyrian, Median and Persian Empires dominated the East, the Jews were slaves regarded as the lowest of the low. In the Hellenistic period, King Antiochus made an effort to get rid of their primitive cult and Hellenize them, but his would-be reform of this degraded nation was foiled by the outbreak of war with Parthia, for this was the moment of Arsaces' insurrection. Then, since the Hellenistic rulers were weak and the Parthians had not yet developed into a great power (Rome, too, was still far away), the Jews established a dynasty of their own. These kings were expelled by the fickle mob,

21 *SKS* 3, 75 / *EO2*, 70.
22 See *SKS* K2–3, 272.
23 Tacitus, *Annales*, Book VI, 46; *The Annals of Imperial Rome*, trans. by Michael Grant, op. cit., p. 224.
24 *Pap.* VII–1 B 11, p. 175 / COR, 164.
25 *Pap.* VII–1 B 11, p. 175 / COR, 164n.
26 *COR*, 297, note 278.

but regained control by force, setting up a reign of terror which embraced, among other typical acts of despotism, the banishment of fellow-citizens, the destruction of cities, and the murder of brothers, wives and parents. The kings encouraged the superstitious Jewish religion, for they assumed the office of High Priest in order to buttress their regime.[27]

While there is here a reference to "acts of despotism," there is no mention of the Jewish King Agrippa as in Kierkegaard's text. While Tacitus does mention King Agrippa elsewhere both here in the *Histories*[28] and in the *Annals*,[29] he is not referred to anywhere as a tyrant. Similarly, the editors of the *Papirer* edition of Kierkegaard's *Nachlaß* refer to the following chapter, that is, Book V, Chapter 9 of the *Histories*,[30] but this passage is no more plausible since it, too, fails to mention King Agrippa. It should be noted that Agrippa appears in Acts 25–26, where he hears Paul's case. There as well he does not make any particularly tyrannical or contemptible impression. Given that this reference cannot be localized, it is difficult to know what conclusions can be drawn from Kierkegaard's allusion.

In 1849 in the *Journal NB14*, Kierkegaard alludes to another motif about the early Christians. Here he refers to Tacitus' description of the terrifying forms of punishment exacted on the Christians:

> During the persecution of Christians there was also the cruel practice of smearing the martyrs with pitch and the like, igniting them as torches, and using them to illuminate the festivities. Basically the same thing is always repeated in Christendom—the unbloody martyrs in particular have had to burn slowly—and their suffering has thus been the light in the Church.[31]

Kierkegaard thus draws a parallel between Christianity's early martyrs and the "unbloody martyrs" of later Christendom. Since, according to Kierkegaard, the age of passion is past, modern Christians are not persecuted in the same way with torture and execution, but rather with public scorn and derision. These are thus the modern "unbloody martyrs" with whom he identifies his own efforts. The image that he paints here concerns the "light," which was literal in the sense of the light of the flames that burnt the ancient martyrs but can be understood metaphorically as symbol of hope in the sense of "the light in the Church." So also the modern martyrs, although they are not subject to flames, nonetheless "have had to burn slowly." They too represent a positive light for true Christianity insofar as they refuse to capitulate to corruption and compromise despite all the criticism and mockery that they are made the object of. Kierkegaard thus finds here a useful image that he can apply in a metaphorical manner to the modern situation.

---

[27]   Tacitus, *Histories*, Book V, 8; English translation quoted from *The Histories*, trans. by Kenneth Wellesley, Harmondsworth: Penguin 1972, p. 276.

[28]   Tacitus, *Histories*, Book II, 81; *The Histories*, p. 130. *Histories*, Book V, 1; *The Histories*, p. 271.

[29]   Tacitus, *Annales*, Book XIII, 7; *The Annals of Imperial Rome*, trans. by Grant, p. 287.

[30]   See the footnote in *Pap.* VII–1 B 11, p. 175.

[31]   *SKS* 22, 411, NB14:111 / *JP*, 3, 2657.

The source of Kierkegaard's information is presumably Tacitus' *Annals*, Book XV, 44. In his account of how the Christians were made scapegoats for the aforementioned fire in Rome in 64, Tacitus writes:

> First, Nero had self-acknowledged Christians arrested. Then, on their information, large numbers of others were condemned....Their deaths were made farcical. Dressed in wild animals' skins, they were torn to pieces by dogs, or crucified, or made into torches to be ignited after dark as substitutes for daylight.[32]

The commentators of *Søren Kierkegaards Skrifter* also refer to a passage in Karl Friedrich Becker's (1776–1806) *Verdenshistorie*, which refers to the same incident.[33] Thus the source is either Tacitus directly or via Becker indirectly. In any case it is clear that Kierkegaard is primarily interested in Tacitus' depiction of the treatment of the early Christians. He uses this as a parallel to what he regards as the corrupt state of Christianity in his own day.

IV. References to Tacitus' "sine ira atque studio"

In addition to these scattered references to Tacitus' works, there are also a couple of others which recur in Kierkegaard's authorship. The first of these is the phrase "*sine ira atque studio.*" In his master's thesis *The Concept of Irony*, from 1841, Kierkegaard begins his treatment of the condemnation of Socrates by noting that the trial and execution of Socrates were factual events. Thus here, Kierkegaard speculates, it may be possible to obtain a degree of objectivity, which might otherwise have been lacking in the accounts given by those who had vested interests since they knew him. At the beginning of the section on this topic, he writes:

> Everyone will promptly perceive that here we are dealing with something factual, and therefore the issue cannot be a view as with Xenophon, Plato, and Aristophanes, for whom the actuality of Socrates was the occasion for and a factor in a presentation that sought to round off and to transfigure his person ideally—something that the solemnity of the state could not possibly enter into, and therefore its conception is *sine ira atque studio.*[34]

At first glance the Latin phrase "*sine ira atque studio,*" meaning "without indignation or partisanship," seems unmotivated.

It is in fact a quotation from Tacitus' prefatory statements in his *Annals*. There Tacitus notes that the history of the Roman Republic has already been treated by distinguished historians, and even the Augustan period has been well recorded. By contrast, however, the post-Augustan age has not been adequately treated due to the fact that the historians during this period had to bow to the pressure and coercion

---

[32]   Tacitus, *Annales*, Book XV, 44; *The Annals of Imperial Rome*, trans. by Grant, p. 365.

[33]   *Karl Friedrich Beckers Verdenshistorie, omarbeidet af Johan Gottfried Woltmann*, vols. 1–12, trans. by J. Riise, Copenhagen: Fr. Brummers Forlag 1822–29, vol. 3, p. 716 (*ASKB* 1972–1983). See *SKS* K22, 523.

[34]   *SKS* 1, 215 / *CI*, 167.

of tyrannical emperors. Tacitus thus proposes to undertake an account of this period that will be objective and impartial. The passage reads:

> Famous writers have recorded Rome's early glories and disasters. The Augustan Age, too, had its distinguished historians. But then the rising tide of flattery exercised a deterrent effect. The reigns of Tiberius, Gaius, Claudius, and Nero were described during their lifetimes in ficticious terms, for fear of the consequences; whereas the accounts written after their deaths were influenced by still raging animosities. So I have decided to say a little about Augustus, with special attention to his last period, and then go on to the reign of Tiberius and what followed. I shall write without indignation or partisanship [*sine ira atque studio*]: in my case the customary incentives to these are lacking.[35]

Tacitus makes a similar claim in his introductory remarks to his *Histories*, where he refers to writing "*neque amore et sine odio*" or "without partiality and without hatred."[36] There he goes out of his way to demonstrate that he is a neutral and objective historian since he is beholden to no one.[37] In any case, the statement "*sine ira atque studio*" seems simply to have become proverbial for anyone claiming objectivity in the treatment of his or her subject matter. In the context in which Kierkegaard invokes it, this phrase is thus perfectly appropriate.

In *Stages on Life's Way*, from 1845, Kierkegaard returns to the same expression. In the "Letter to the Reader" by Frater Taciturnus, the expression "*sine ira et studio*" is used in the discussion of Quidam and Quaedam. Of Quidam we read:

> His sympathetic nature must be illuminated from all sides, and therefore I had to have a female character who can make the whole thing as dialectical as possible for him and among other things can bring him into the anguish of seeing her break with the idea, as he calls it, even if she does nothing else (if she does that) than that she, *sine ira et studio* without losing her feminine lovableness, acquires for herself a new partner in the dance of life—in other words, if a person cannot have the one, then take the other, unembarrassed by prolixity of ideas, and precisely for that reason lovable.[38]

Given that the statement "*sine ira et studio*" was originally a part of Tacitus' description of his impartiality as a historian, in *Stages on Life's Way* it seems far removed from its original context and is simply reduced to a general *bon mot*. It should be noted that this frequent use of foreign words or phrases is a fixed element in Frater Taciturnus' style. It is difficult to make much more of the use of Tacitus in this context.

---

[35]   Tacitus, *Annales*, Book I, 1; *The Annals of Imperial Rome*, trans. by Grant, pp. 31–2.
[36]   Tacitus, *Histories*, Book I, 1; *The Histories*, trans. by Wellesley, p. 21. Wellesley translates this passage as follows: "But partiality and hatred towards any man are equally inappropriate in a writer who claims to be honest and reliable."
[37]   See Herbert W. Benario, "Historical Integrity," in his *An Introduction to Tacitus*, Athens, Georgia: University of Georgia Press 1975, pp. 148–65.
[38]   *SKS* 6, 421 / *SLW*, 456.

V. References to Tacitus' "odium generis humani"

Another slogan from Tacitus that Kierkegaard uses more than once is the phrase "*odium generis humani*" literally "hatred of the human race." This appears repeatedly in his later writings from 1849 onward. In the *Journal NB10*, for example, Kierkegaard quotes this passage in Latin without mentioning a source. He writes, "Humanly speaking Christianity is, however, a hostility towards the human; humanly speaking paganism was indeed correct to call it the *odium generis humani*. And even Christianity itself says this: that it is hatred of the world."[39]

This is a slightly modified quotation from Tacitus' *Annals*, which was presumably quoted from memory. This is in fact a quotation from the same general passage, referred to previously in Clausen's lectures and in the *Journal NB14*, where Tacitus reports on the persecutions of the Christians on occasion of the fire in Rome. Again, it reads: "First, Nero had self-acknowledged Christians arrested. Then, on their information, large numbers of others were condemned—not so much for incendiarism as for their hatred of the human race [*otio humani generis*]."[40] Here although the wording is not exact, it is clearly close enough for us to infer that Tacitus is the source.

At this time, Kierkegaard returned to this same formulation again and again in his attempt to understand the strict demands of true Christianity. In his *Journal NB11*, also from 1849, Kierkegaard begins his criticism of the corrupt version of Christianity in his day. In the entry in question he begins with the claim, "The situation is neither more nor less than that Christianity has been abolished in Christendom, and that Christendom nevertheless will still not give up the claim of being Christian."[41] He then continues:

> Christendom has repeated the parable of the vineyard workers who killed the lord's messengers and finally also his son, "because this is our vineyard." We think we might just as well be a Christian—who knows, it might be prudent. But there is no ear for what Christianity requires regarding self-denial, renunciation, and seeking *first* the Kingdom of God. And then once in a while someone comes along who either is a true Christian or is so concerned for the truth that he makes no secret of what is understood by being a true Christian. He is shouted down as a traitor, an *odium totius christianitatis* (*ad modum odium generis humani*), as the earliest Christians were called, and killed.[42]

Here it is the true Christian of modern times who is rejected for his "*odium totius christianitatis*" or "hatred of all Christendom" in the sense of a hatred of the human race, "*ad modum odium generis humani*." The ancient pagan description of the early Christians given by Tacitus is used, in Kierkegaard's eyes, as a perfectly fitting description of the true Christian in modern times. However, the change in the social-political status of Christianity renders it ironic. While the ancient Christians were persecuted for, among other things, their hatred for humanity, the true Christian of

---

[39]   *SKS* 21, 297, NB10:77.
[40]   Tacitus, *Annales*, Book XV, 44; *The Annals of Imperial Rome*, trans. by Grant, p. 365. Translation slightly modified.
[41]   *SKS* 22, 95, NB11:160 / *JP*, 1, 383.
[42]   *SKS* 22, 95, NB11:160 / *JP*, 1, 383.

the nineteenth century is subject to a similar kind of persecution at the hands not of the pagans but of self-proclaimed Christians. The point is clearly that the modern complacent Christians do not realize the difficult demands of Christianity, which require them to reject the world in a way that looks like misanthropy. Kierkegaard thus refers to the same passage as previously from Tacitus' *Annals*. He notes that the designation of the Christians as having a hatred for human beings is in a sense wholly correct since they do not lose sight of these difficult demands.

This same quotation appears in *Journal NB12*, from the same year. There Kierkegaard writes:

> To the natural man the Christian view of life must seem to be a hatred toward life, and the pagans were justified as pagans in calling Christians: *odium generis humani*. "Established Christendom" has messed the whole thing up with human sympathy, and therefore the natural man is almost highly pleased with—yes, with Christendom, which, of course, is not Christianity.[43]

This passage can in a sense be seen as an explanation of the previous one. The same parallel is drawn between the ancient Christian and the modern one. The critical parallel between Christendom and paganism is also present as before. The irony is that Christendom criticizes and persecutes true Christianity for its hatred of humanity in the same way paganism did in the Roman world.

The passage then finally appears in printed form in *Practice in Christianity*, from 1850. Kierkegaard has his pseudonym write the following, as if a commentary to the previously quoted passages from his journals: "For a pagan to think himself to be doing his god a service by killing an apostle is not as mad as the persecution of the 'true Christian' in 'Christendom'—and that 'the Christians' then consider this a service to God and 'Christ.' "[44] Here the parallel in the previous passages is made explicit. Kierkegaard's pseudonymous author then continues:

> Here one also sees the connection between this and a frequently made objection to Christianity that in a certain sense is quite correct and in any case has more point to it than the silly defense of Christianity usually made in this regard. The objection is that Christianity is misanthropic, as indeed the early Christians were called *otium totius generis humani*.[45]

So far, this appears to be more or less what was said in the previously quoted journal entries, which make use of this quotation from Tacitus' *Annals*. Now, however, Kierkegaard's pseudonymous author explains explicitly what he takes this to mean:

> The connection is this. In relation to what the natural man, who loves himself selfishly or loves himself in a womanly way, regards as love, friendship, and the like, Christianity resembles a hatred of what it is to be a human being, the greatest curse and torment upon what it is to be human. Indeed, even the more profound person can have many weaker moments when to him it is as if Christianity were misanthropy, because in the weaker

---

[43]   *SKS* 22, 150, NB12:8 / *JP*, 1, 507.
[44]   *SKS* 12, 123 / *PC*, 116.
[45]   *SKS* 12, 124 / *PC*, 117.

moments he wants to coddle himself, whimper, have an easy life in the world, live in rather quiet enjoyment.[46]

True Christianity must, according to this view, resist this impulse towards comfort. It requires that one reject things such as friendship and love and, instead, embrace suffering and persecution. This is something that Christendom has forgotten, while it has eliminated the possibility of offense.

There can be no doubt that the portrayal of the early Christians in the *Annals* XV, 44, 2–5 was what interested Kierkegaard most in Tacitus' writings. He returns to different aspects of this passage on several occasions. He is fascinated by the pagan perspective of Christianity, which represents a kind of common-sense response. By bringing this out, Kierkegaard wishes to make clear that Christianity is not something that is obvious or straightforward, although this is what it has become in Christendom. He wishes to indicate that there is an important insight in the pagan perspective. Tacitus' shock at Christianity is precisely what has been lost in Christendom, where everything has been reduced to bourgeois pleasantries and there is nothing frightening or offensive left. In a sense Kierkegaard enjoins his readers to look at Christianity again through the eyes of Tacitus and to come to terms with the hard demands that it issues. We should resist the urge to domesticate and soften the radicality of the Christian message.

From this, it is only a short step to other aspects of Christianity that the later Kierkegaard wants to emphasize. Thus this same passage also interests him for its account of the persecutions of the early Christians. This is useful for him as he develops his own concept of martyrdom and its role in Christian faith and practice. As a Christian, one should be prepared to be mocked and cast out. The true Christian cannot expect to enjoy a comfortable or pleasant life; this is the province of the hypocrite and the corrupt Christian in Christendom.

Given all this, there can be no doubt that Kierkegaard, somewhat paradoxically, finds inspiration for different aspects of his conception of Christianity in this pagan historian. Beginning with the notion of Christianity as a hatred of humanity, Kierkegaard can then move on to the whole constellation of Christian concepts that he wishes to sketch and contrast to the corrupt and complacent Christianity of Christendom.

---

[46]   Ibid.

Bibliography

I. Tacitus' Works in The Auction Catalogue *of Kierkegaard's Library*

C. Cornelii Taciti Opera ex recensione Ernestiana, ed. by Immanuel Bekker, Berlin: G. Reimer 1825 (*ASKB* 1282).

Des C. Cornelius Tacitus Sämmtliche Werke, trans. by Johann Samuel Müller, vols. 1–3, Hamburg: Johann Carl Bohn 1765–66 (*ASKB* 1283–1285).

Cajus Cornelius Tacitus, vols. 1–3, trans. and ed. by Jacob Baden, vols. 1–3, Copenhagen: trykt hos Morten Hallager 1773–97 (*ASKB* 1286–1288).

Dialog om Talerne eller om Aarsagerne til Veltalenhedens Fordærvelse, trans. by Jacob Baden, Copenhagen: Johan Frederik Schultz 1802 (*ASKB* 1289).

II. Works in The Auction Catalogue *of Kierkegaard's Library that Discuss Tacitus*

[Becker, Karl Friedrich], *Karl Friedrich Beckers Verdenshistorie, omarbeidet af Johan Gottfried Woltmann*, vols. 1–12, trans. by J. Riise, Copenhagen: Fr. Brummers Forlag 1822–29, vol. 3, p. 613; p. 732 (*ASKB* 1972–1983).

Buhle, Johann Gottlieb, *Geschichte der neuern Philosophie seit der Epoche der Wiederherstellung der Wissenschaften*, vols. 1–6 (in 10 tomes), vols. 1–2, Göttingen: Johann Georg Rosenbusch's Wittwe 1800; vols. 3–6, Göttingen: Johann Friedrich Röwer 1802–05 (Abtheilung 6 in *Geschichte der Künste und Wissenschaften seit der Wiederherstellung derselben bis an das Ende des achtzehnten Jahrhunderts. Von einer Gesellschaft gelehrter Männer ausgearbeitet*, Abtheilungen 1–11, Göttingen: Röwer and Göttingen: Rosenbusch 1796–1820), vol. 1, p. 590 (*ASKB* 440–445).

Hagen, Johan Frederik, *Ægteskabet. Betragtet fra et ethisk–historiskt Standpunct*, Copenhagen: Wahlske Boghandels Forlag 1845, p. 134n; p. 149n; p. 172n (*ASKB* 534).

Meiners, Christoph, *Geschichte der Verfalls der Sitten und der Staatsverfassung der Römer*, Leipzig: bey Weidmanns Erben und Reich 1782, p. 25; p. 78; p. 85 (*ASKB* 660).

—— *Geschichte des Verfalls der Sitten, der Wissenschaften und Sprache der Römer, in den ersten Jahrhunderten nach Christi Geburt*, Vienna and Leipzig: Joseph Stahel 1791 (*ASKB* 669).

[Montaigne, Michel de], *Michael Montaigne's Gedanken und Meinungen über allerley Gegenstände, ins Deutsche übersetzt*, vols. 1–7, Berlin: F.T. Lagarde 1793–99, vol. 3, p. 178; vol. 4, p. 277, p. 322, p. 407; vol. 5, pp. 400–405 (*ASKB* 681–687).

Mynster, Jakob Peter, *Den hedenske Verden ved Christendommens Begyndelse*, Copenhagen: Schultz 1850, p. 8n, p. 12n, p. 23n, p. 47n, p. 48n (*ASKB* 693).

Ritter, Heinrich and L. Preller, *Historia philosophiae graeco-romanae ex fontium locis contexta*, ed. by L. Preller, Hamburg: Perthes 1838, p. 436, p. 438 (*ASKB* 726).

Schmidt, W. Adolf, *Geschichte der Denk- und Glaubensfreiheit im ersten Jahrhundert der Kaiserherrschaft und des Christenthums*, Berlin: Verlag von Veit und Comp. 1847 (*ASKB* 771).

Sulzer, Johann Georg, *Allgemeine Theorie der Schönen Künste, in einzeln, nach alphabetischer Ordnung der Kunstwörter auf einander folgenden, Artikeln abgehandelt*, vols. 1–4 and a Register Volume, 2nd revised ed., Leipzig: in der Weidmannschen Buchhandlung 1792–99, vol. 1, p. 101; p. 221; vol. 3, p. 268 (*ASKB* 1365–1369).

Tennemann, Wilhelm Gottlieb, *Geschichte der Philosophie*, vols. 1–11, Leipzig: Johann Ambrosius Barth 1798–1819, vol. 5, p. 22 (*ASKB* 815–826).

Zeuthen, Ludvig, *Om den christelige Tro i dens Betydning for Verdenshistorien. Et Forsøg*, Copenhagen: Gyldendalske Boghandels Forlag 1838, p. 18, p. 37, p. 48, p. 51 (*ASKB* 259).

—— *Humanitet betragtet fra et christeligt Standpunkt, med stadigt Hensyn til den nærværende Tid*, Copenhagen: Gyldendalske Boghandling 1846, pp. 44–5 (*ASKB* 915).

III. Secondary Literature on Kierkegaard's Relation to Tacitus

None.

Terence:

Traces of Roman Comedy in Kierkegaard's Writings

Mikkel Larsen

I. Introduction: Terence and the Seriousness of Comedy

Sources quoted by the historian Suetonius in his short biography on Terence tell us that the Roman comedy writer died at a young age from a profound depression.[1] On a study trip to Greece, Terence had collected and adapted a large number of comedies by Menander, the greatest representative of Greek New Comedy.[2] When he sent them on ahead to Rome, the ship that carried them was wrecked, and the manuscripts sank to the bottom of the sea with it. The loss caused Terence to wither away and die of grief shortly after in the year 159 BC.[3]

This touching anecdote is, quite probably, an example of Suetonius repeating earlier inventions based on inferences from the works of the playwright.[4] After all, shipwrecks play quite a significant role in the plays of Terence. But the tale also gives us a kind of ancient profile of the comedy writer. It not only reveals his way of working, but it also indicates his affection for Greek comedy and Menander in particular. And it suggests his more serious approach to comedy as a way of portraying life compared to his predecessor, the more playful Plautus,[5] an approach that would leave an indelible mark not just on Latin comedy but on later literature, education, and the dramatic tradition in Europe as a whole.

---

[1]   The biography by Suetonius, the *Life of Terence* (*Vita Terentii*), hereafter referred to as the *Life*, was written around AD 100. It can be found in the second volume of the Loeb edition of the works of Suetonius, translated by J.C. Rolfe, Cambridge, Massachusetts: Harvard University Press 1914 or later, pp. 452ff.

[2]   Menander (342–ca. 292 BC) is said to have written almost a hundred comedies, many of which exercised great influence on the subsequent comic tradition at Rome.

[3]   The *Life* also gives an alternative version according to which Terence himself went down with the ship and drowned.

[4]   This was a far from uncommon practice among ancient biographers. See George E. Duckworth, *The Nature of Roman Comedy: A Study in Popular Entertainment*, 2nd ed., Norman: University of Oklahoma Press 1994, p. 57.

[5]   Titus Maccius Plautus (ca. 250–184 BC) is the only other Roman writer of comedies preserved in more than just fragmentary form. Twenty of the 130 comedies ascribed to him have survived.

Publius Terentius Afer, as was his full name, was the only pre-classical Roman author to have a biography written about him. Even so, the details concerning his life are sparse, often contradictory, and give only a blurry picture of the course of his existence. Most probably he was born in the North African city of Carthage around the year 195 BC. This origin is the likeliest explanation for his cognomen, Afer, which literally means "African." He seems to owe the rest of his name to the fact that he, at a young age, was brought to Rome as a slave and entered the household of the senator Terentius Lucanus. According to the *Life*, he got a liberal education there, and, to judge from his works, this must have comprised a broad selection of both Latin and Greek literature. Reaching a mature age, he was manumitted—due to his wits and handsome figure, says Suetonius—and, as was custom in ancient Rome, he took the name of his former master.[6]

We do not know when Terence started his career as a comedy writer. The six comedies that have survived from his hand—*Andria, Hecyra, Heaton Timorumenos, Eunuchus, Phormio,* and *Adelphoe*—were all staged in the short span of years from 166 to 160. No testimony of other titles has been handed down to us, and these were, most probably, his entire production before his career was cut short by his untimely death at an age of only 36 years.[7]

The comedies of Terence formed part of a young Roman tradition that depended heavily on Greek models.[8] The Roman plays were usually adaptations of comedies from the New Greek Comedy, now all but lost. They were situation comedies peopled by stock characters where the action, typically, took place in Greece; in a city street in front of a couple of houses where the main characters lived. The plots were dominated by domestic concerns and family conflicts, mostly between fathers, sons, and slaves over love, marriage, idleness, and money. These stereotyped, but generally realistic, confrontations led to seemingly endless entanglements and, ultimately, a solution and a happy ending.

Four of the six comedies of Terence were based on plays by his Greek idol, Menander, but the Roman playwright was not just content to produce uninspired translations.[9] The Greek traits were to some degree adapted to the new context,

---

[6]   For discussions of the facts of Terence's life see Duckworth, *The Nature of Roman Comedy*, pp. 56ff. and Michael von Albrecht, *A History of Roman Literature: From Livius Andronicus to Boethius: With special regard to its Influence on World Literature*, vols. 1–2, Leiden and New York: E.J. Brill 1997, vol. 1, pp. 214–15.

[7]   Duckworth, *The Nature of Roman Comedy*, pp. 59 ff.; Von Albrecht, *A History of Roman Literature*, vol. 1, p. 215.

[8]   The first Roman comedy was written around 240 BC by Livius Andronicus, probably a freed slave of Greek descent. The genre did not pick up speed, however, until it consolidated its position with the programs of the traditional religious festivals and Plautus arrived on the scene. Both coincided with the last days of the Second Punic War at the end of the century. For more on the early history of Roman comedy, see Duckworth, *The Nature of Roman Comedy*, pp. 39ff. and W. Beare, *The Roman Stage*, 3rd ed., London: Methuen 1968, pp. 25ff.

[9]   This can be deduced from the prologue to the *Eunuch,* where Terence talks about an adversary who, *translating well* (*bene vortendo*) but *writing badly* (*scribendo male*), turns good Greek plays into bad Roman ones, *Eunuch*, vv. 6–7. Cf. also the Roman concept of *imitatio et aemulatio*.

and the characters were Romanized. This gave the Latin comedy a different *tone*. Furthermore, Terence added his personal touch.[10] Hence, while the plays of Plautus have been called farcical and compared to *Commedia dell'Arte*, Terence can be said to have written comedies that were not just intended as entertainment. As opposed to the guffaw of Plautine comedy, the jokes of Terence, in general, provoke "thoughtful laughter."[11] This can be seen, for example, in his frequent preference for moral *sententiae*, maxims, over more crude efforts to amuse.[12]

The clever intrigue and profound characters of the Terentian plays give us an insight into the complexities of human nature; in particular, he is famed for his sympathetic descriptions of the anguish of young lovers, which foreshadowed the works of the later Roman love poets. This picture gets even clearer when one takes a look at the plots he chose to adapt. Most of Terence's plays deal sensitively with problems that have ethical dimensions: generational differences, how to raise children, the role of women, the meaning of citizenship, and the like.

This moral inclination and his alleged affiliation to the philhellenic literary circle of the nobleman Scipio Aemilianus gave rise early on to the idea of a particular Terentian *humanitas*, a distinctive sympathetic understanding of human nature well ahead of his time. However, this concept, first coined by Cicero a century later, must be applied to Terence with great care. There is no doubt about the playwright's sensibility and seriousness, but it should not be exaggerated.[13]

Even though in his later comedies he made a greater effort to accommodate the public's desires, his seriousness and lack of *action* cost Terence some popularity with the volatile Roman audience. He experienced great successes, especially with *Eunuchus* (the *Eunuch*), but also saw his *Hecyra* (*The Mother-in-Law*) fail twice, only to be completed in the third attempt of staging it.[14]

After Terence's death his popularity on stage declined rapidly. Not until a century later was he brought back to the forefront of literary life, and this time, mostly, due to his style. Terence had developed a language characterized by "reserve, reticence, and restraint,"[15] that suited his new comedies better than the uproarious style of Plautus. It has been called elitist, but at the same time this more refined language was

---

[10]   It is the only reasonable explanation for the great differences that exist between the works of Terence and Plautus, after all. This, in turn, is also the most solid argument against the, not uncommon, view that Roman comedy lacked all originality. For more, see Duckworth, *The Nature of Roman Comedy*, pp. 384ff.

[11]   Duckworth, *The Nature of Roman Comedy*, p. 392.

[12]   These maxims were not only used to communicate moral concepts to the audience but also to connect with the spectators by appealing to everyday experience and commonplace wisdom. Moreover, they helped to characterize the personages and put emphasis on situations in the play, a technique he inherited from Menander. See Von Albrecht, *A History of Roman Literature*, vol. 1, p. 223.

[13]   See Sander M. Goldberg, *Understanding Terence*, Princeton, New Jersey: Princeton University Press 1986, pp. 9ff.

[14]   In the preserved prologue to the play Terence himself tells us how the audience interrupted the play because a riot broke out and, in the second case, someone announced a gladiatorial combat. *Hecyra*, vv. 29ff.

[15]   Leonard R. Palmer, *The Latin Language*, London: Faber & Faber 1999, p. 89.

a closer approximation to natural speech than earlier writers had sought. In the first century BC the great stylist Cicero praised him for his lucid and graceful Latin.[16] His language, thus, became a model for elegant spoken Latin for future generations, and his comedies were undisputed school texts for more than 1,800 years.[17]

Another reason for the proliferation of the works of Terence was his fame as a great humanist, propagated by, among others, the Stoic philosopher Seneca. Terence, as a consequence, became a significant influence on the later European humanists and moralists like Petrarch and Michel de Montaigne.[18] Moreover, many of his *sententiae* became traditional proverbs and common sayings that have been used by writers—as intentional or unwitting references—up to this very day.

However, his most notable literary influence was in the world of the theater, where in time he rose to form part of the triumvirate of ancient Roman playwrights together with Plautus and the tragedy-writing Seneca. From the end of antiquity the Terentian plays were no longer staged, but during the Middle Ages they were by far the most read comedies. At the beginning of the fifteenth century, chiefly due to humanist scholars, and subsequently helped by the invention of printing, the Roman comedies began to circulate widely, and performances began to take place again. Renaissance comedy in the vernacular languages was born almost exclusively on the basis of this heritage, and Terence played an essential part in the poetics of the time where, above all, his refined techniques and style were imitated. He later became an important model for such diverse playwrights as Shakespeare, Molière, and Ludvig Holberg.

The fame of the plays of Terence and Plautus lasted well into the nineteenth century. The Terentian comedies were still read in school, but the Roman plays were no longer admired without reserve. Scholarly opinion was changing in favor of the—mostly imagined—wonders of the Greek models, rarely preserved as they were, and only in very fragmentary form.[19] New tastes had emerged on the stage as

---

[16] Cicero, *Ad Atticum* 7, 3, 10 and in the lost work *Limo* quoted in Suetonius, *Vita Terentii* V. In the latter text we also find Caesar praising Terence's style, although at the same time he censured him for his lack of *force* (*vis*), and called him *half a Menander* (*dimidiate Menander*).

[17] Even Church Fathers, such as Jerome, Ambrose, and Augustine, recommended the reading of the pagan Terence, although Augustine did issue a warning that young people, instead of learning Latin, might learn to misbehave by reading about the scandalous behavior of the characters (Augustine, *Confessiones*, I, 16, 26).

[18] Montaigne, for example, rated the gentlemanly Terence among his favorite poets. See Gilbert Highet, *The Classical Tradition—Greek and Roman Influences on Western Literature*, Oxford: Oxford University Press 1985, p. 188.

[19] One of the earliest and most famous formulations of this view is found in August Wilhelm Schlegel's *Lectures on Dramatic Art and Literature*, trans. by John Black, Lenox, Massachusetts: Hard Press 2006, lecture XIV, pp. 137–144. However, the first collection of fragments by Menander was not published until 1855, the year Kierkegaard died. Our knowledge of the Greek comedy writer's work has since been supplemented by several findings of fragments. In 1958 the *editio princeps* of the only completely preserved play by Menander, the *Dyskolos* (*The Grouch*), was published after it had been recovered from a

well; especially, the melancholy Scribian plays, with their ideal of *la pièce bien faite*, now dominated the theaters.[20]

II. Terence at the Borgerdyd School and in Kierkegaard's Library

At the time when Søren Kierkegaard went to the Borgerdyd School in Copenhagen (1821–30)[21] the instruction in Latin was still one of the basic pillars of the preparation for university. Kierkegaard therefore received extensive tutoring in both the Latin language and the classics of Latin literature. According to the list of readings he submitted for his entrance examination to the University of Copenhagen—dated July 29, 1830 and signed by headmaster Michael Nielsen (1776–1846)—Kierkegaard had read more than 11,000 verses of Latin poetry and some 1,250 pages of prose during his school years. This extensive syllabus included works by Cicero, Horace, Virgil, Caesar, Livy, Sallust, Cornelius Nepos, and Terence. Two plays by the latter are found on the list: *Andria* and *Phormio*.[22]

In " 'Guilty'/'Not-Guilty' " from *Stages on Life's Way* (1845), Kierkegaard makes the character Quidam tell a story about a class reading the *Phormio* with their Latin teacher. This, most likely, reflects his own experiences at the Borgerdyd School:

> When I attended grammar school as a boy I had a Latin teacher whom I frequently recall. He was very capable, and by no means was it the case that we learned nothing from him, but at times he was somewhat strange or, if you choose to look at it that way, somewhat absented-minded. Yet his absentmindedness was a matter not of losing himself in thought, falling asleep, etc., but of occasionally speaking suddenly in a completely different voice and from a completely different world. One of the books we read with him was Terence's *Phormio*. It tells of Phaedria, who fell in love with a cither player and was reduced to following her to and from school. The poet then says:
>
> > *ex advorsum ei loco*
> > *Tonstrina erat quædam; hic solebamus fere*
> > *plerumque eam opperiri, dum inde rediret domum.*[23]
>
> With pedagogic gravity the teacher asked the pupil why *dum* in this instance takes the subjunctive. The pupil answered: because it means the same as *dummodo*. Correct, replied

---

papyrus manuscript dug up in the Egyptian desert. It is not, however, the model for any of the surviving Roman plays.

[20]   For a modern treatment of the differences between the theater of Augustin Eugène Scribe and the ancient tradition, see the chapter "The Well-Made Play" in Goldberg, *Understanding Terence*, pp. 61–90. For more on the historical influence of Terence, see, for example, Von Albrecht, *A History of Roman Literature*, pp. 231–6.

[21]   The full name of the school was *Borgerdydskolen i Kjøbenhavn*, which literally means *The School of Civic Virtue in Copenhagen*. It was founded in 1787.

[22]   The complete syllabus of Kierkegaard can be found in Bruce H. Kirmmse (ed.), *Encounters with Kierkegaard: A Life as Seen by His Contemporaries*, Princeton, New Jersey: Princeton University Press 1996, p. 273.

[23]   *Phormio*, vv. 88–90. The Oxford edition of Terence's plays (Robert Kauer and Wallace M. Lindsay (ed.), *P. Terenti Afri Comoediae*, 2nd ed., Oxford: Clarendon Press 1953),

the teacher, but thereupon began to explain that we were not to regard the subjunctive mood in an external way as if it were the particle as such that took the subjunctive. It was the internal and the psychical that determined the mood, and in the case at hand it was the optative passion, the impatient longing, the soul's emotion of expectancy. Thereupon his voice changed completely, and he went on to say: the person sitting and waiting there in that barbershop as if it were a café or a public place such as that is not an indifferent man but a man in love waiting for his beloved. In fact, if he had been a porter, a chair carrier, a messenger, or cabdriver who was waiting there, then the waiting could be thought of as occupying the time while the girl was at her music and singing lesson, which is not to be considered subjunctive but indicative, unless it was the case that these gentlemen were waiting to be paid, which is a very mediocre passion. Language really ought not to be allowed to express that kind of expectation in the subjunctive mood. But it is Phaedria who is waiting, and he is waiting in a mood of: if only she, if she would only, would that she might only soon, soon come back; and all this is appropriately the subjunctive mood. There was a solemnity and a passion in his voice that made his pupils sit as if they were listening to a spectral voice. He fell silent, then cleared his throat, and said with the usual pedagogical gravity of teaching: Next.

This was a recollection from my school days. Now it is clear to me that my unforgettable Latin teacher, although he concerned himself only with Latin, could have taken on other subjects as well as Latin.[24]

The teacher has been identified as Ernst Bojesen (1803–64), one of the three Latin teachers Kierkegaard had at the Borgerdyd School.[25] The scene suggests that the focus in the instruction of Terence was generally on the stylistic and grammatical problems, although not always without sensibility to the content. It also suggests the interest young Kierkegaard himself had in Latin and the "many lovely little secrets of the subjunctive."[26]

Kierkegaard never comments on the fact that he studied the *Andria* at school, but we know from other sources that is was a popular play in the Danish school system at the time and widely read. In a short story from the year 1834, titled "The Christmas Holidays," the Danish author Steen Steensen Blicher (1782–1848) makes the narrator, a headmaster of a school in a small town in Jutland, tell us about one of the Latin teachers in the following terms: "Thus I remember, among other things,

---

which I have taken as standard for all quotations in this article, reads: "*...exadvorsum ilico / tonstrina erat quaedam: hic solebamus fere / plerumque eam opperiri dum inde iret domum.*" All translations are from *The Comedies of Terence*, trans. by Frederick W. Clayton, Exeter: University of Exeter Press 2006. In this case Clayton translates (p. 158): "...vis-à-vis / There was a barber's shop. So as a rule / We waited there for her coming home from school."

[24]	*SKS* 6, 191–2 / *SLW*, 204–5.
[25]	For convincing arguments for the identification of Boisen, see Per Krarup, *Søren Kierkegaard og Borgerdydskolen*, Copenhagen: Gyldendal 1977, pp. 61–3. Kierkegaard's other two Latin teachers were headmaster Michael Nielsen and Carl Scharling.
[26]	*SKS* 20, 98 NB: 146 / *JP* 5, 5981. We know from several sources that Kierkegaard had a keen interest in Latin and was a competent student of this subject. In his later years at school and the first years at university he acted as assistant teacher to headmaster Michael Nielsen, correcting the papers of other students. See the headmaster's statement from November 1840 about Kierkegaard's knowledge of Latin in Kirmmse, *Encounters with Kierkegaard*, pp. 28–9. For further testimony on this, see also ibid., p. 7; pp. 12–3; pp. 272–3.

that one of the first days I was at the school I heard him go through a scene from Terence, where you find the phrase: '*ira amantium amoris est integratio.*' "[27] The quoted phrase is a vulgarized rendering of *Andria*, verse 555: "*amantium irae amoris integratiost.*"[28] The fact that Blicher does not mention the name of the play shows that it was expected that the reader would know the origin of the phrase.[29]

According to the *Auction Catalogue* of Kierkegaard's library, which was drawn up after his death, Kierkegaard owned several Latin editions and two different translations into Danish of the comedies of Terence.[30] One of the latter was a copy of *Andria, Selvplageren og Formio, tre latinske Lystspil* by Mathias Rathje. As we shall see in the following, these three plays, *Andria, Heauton Timorumenos,* and *Phormio,* were the works Kierkegaard would later refer to and quote from.

III. Kierkegaard's Use of Terence

Terence's name appears only once in the writings of Kierkegaard, namely, in the above-mentioned passage in *Stages on Life's Way,* where Quidam tells us about his Latin teacher.[31]

Apart from this single named quotation, all the references to the Roman playwright dispersed throughout the works of Kierkegaard are anonymous. In the following survey, these occurrences will be treated in relation to the three Terentian comedies from which they were taken. To round off the inquiry, I will deal with a possible but dubious reference to the comedy writer, and with a couple of more general references to ancient comedy and thus to Terence.

---

[27]   The Danish title of the short story is "Juleferierne." The translation into English is my own from the text found in Steen Steensen Blicher, *Noveller,* ed. by Esther Kielberg, Copenhagen: Borgen/DSL 1999, pp. 152–3.

[28]   This is the reading in all the known manuscripts of the text. In Clayton's words (*The Comedies of Terence* , p. 26) it translates "nothing renews love like a lover's quarrel." However, the final part of the quotation could be translated more closely "lovers' quarrel." The modifications in word order in Blicher's rendering indicate that the meter was not considered of any real importance at the time, or, at least, that the text was memorized by the pupils in proverbial form.

[29]   Further testimony for knowledge of the *Andria* in contemporary Danish society can be found in an exercise book in which the influential Danish theologian Nicolai Frederik Severin Grundtvig (1783–1872), a generation earlier, as a pupil at the vicarage of Tyregod (ca. 1798), had begun a translation of the Terentian play. The exercise book is today part of the Grundtvig Archive at the Royal Library of Copenhagen (fasc. 483, 32–9). That the play was generally well-known in the intellectual circles of Danish society at the beginning of the nineteenth century is also suggested by the fact that the artist Nicolai Abildgaard (1743–1809), who never attended grammar school, completed four large paintings with motives from the *Andria* during the years 1801–04.

[30]   For more details, see the bibliography at the end of this article (I. Terence's Works in *The Auction Catalogue* of Kierkegaard's Library).

[31]   *SKS* 6, 191 / *SLW*, 204: "One of the books we read with him was Terence's *Phormio.*"

A. Andria

The Woman from Andros was the first comedy to spring from the Roman playwright's hand. It was produced at Rome in April 166 BC. The play is mainly based on a comedy by the same name written by Menander, now lost, but it also contains bits from another lost play by the Greek dramatist called *Perinthia* (*The Girl from Perinthos*).[32]

Andria has quite a simple, traditional plot based on conflicts, deceit, and misunderstandings across the generation gap: the old Athenian gentleman Simo wants his son Pamphilus to marry Philumena, the daughter of his neighbor Chremes. But Pamphilus has fallen head over heels in love with the Glycerium, who is thought to be the sister of a deceased courtesan from the island of Andros. When Chremes finds out about Pamphilus' infatuation with Glycerium, the wedding with Philumena is called off. Simo now tries to trick his son to agree to marry, and the complications begin. In the end, however, it is revealed that Glycerium was shipwrecked at Andros as a child. The circumstances of the wreck reveal that she is, in fact, the daughter of Chremes. The impediments to the wedding are now gone, and all ends happily.

Although Kierkegaard never explicitly refers to the play in his later writings, he does quote several phrases from this comedy, which have an especially proverbial character. In *Stages on Life's Way* he writes:

> Thereupon Johannes the Seducer spoke as follows:
> Esteemed drinking companions, are you possessed by the devil? You certainly are talking like undertakers; your eyes are red with tears and not from wine. You are almost moving even me to tears, for an unhappy lover endures a most miserable role in life. *Hinc illae lacrymae.*[33]

This Latin phrase, derived from the opening scene of the *Andria*,[34] literally means "hence those tears." In the play the words are spoken by Simo. The scheming father is telling his trusted freedman Sosia how he realized that the tears his son Pamphilus was shedding at the funeral of the courtesan from Andros were not for the courtesan herself but for her supposed sister.[35]

Having read the comedy, Kierkegaard might have remembered the origin of the phrase, and in the quoted passage he uses it to refer to tears, thus playing on the original meaning of the words. However, the most common use of the phrase was in its proverbial sense; to describe any (surprising) revelation even when there were no tears involved. The meaning was then more or less just "hence the trouble."[36] This is

---

[32]   *Andria*, vv. 9ff.
[33]   *SKS* 6, 71 / *SLW*, 71.
[34]   *Andria*, v. 126.
[35]   The whole sentence reads "*Attat hoc illud est, / hinc illae lacrumae, haec illast misericordia.*" Clayton translates it (p. 7): "There, there's the source / Of all our tears and sympathy—of course!"
[36]   The phrase already acquires its character of proverb in antiquity. It is attested as such in Cicero's speech *Pro Caelio* (25, 61) and in Horace's *Epistles* (1, 19, 41). The proverbial character of the Latin phrase in Danish at Kierkegaard's time is supported by its use in a letter dated February 27, 1846 from Edvard Collin to his friend Hans Christian Andersen,

the case, for example, in the first part of *Either/Or* (1843) when Kierkegaard makes the character "A" review the comedy *The First Love* by his contemporary Augustin Eugène Scribe (1791–1861): "Let him have seduced ten girls, she will take him, take him *à tout prix*, but if he is married, she cannot take him. *Hinc illae Lacrymae.*"[37] In the *Concluding Unscientific Postscript* (1846) we find a reference to another phrase from the *Andria* that was already a maxim at the time of Terence:

> It is well know that over the temple at Delphi there was also the inscription: *ne quid nimis*. This motto is the *summa summarum* of all finite wordly wisdom. If it is supposed to be the maximum, Christianity should immediately be revoked as a juvenile and immature whim. Just try to apply this *ne quid nimis* to the god who allows himself to be crucified, and you will immediately conjure up mockery of religion as witty as is seldom heard in this world, since mockers of religion are ordinarily hotheaded and obtuse....That maxim, *ne quid nimis*, may be valid in many life relationships, but applied to the absolute passionate rerlationship, to the absolute τελος it is nonsense.[38]

As can be deduced from this passage, *ne quid nimis* is the Latin translation of the Greek μηδὲν ἄγαν, meaning "nothing in excess." This was just one of several proverbial ways of expressing the common idea of the mean found throughout ancient Greek literature, most notably in the Aristotelian idea of the "golden mean."[39]

In the *Andria* we once again find the phrase in the opening scene.[40] The *ne quid nimis* is Sosia's ingratiating comment to Simo's speech about how his son has tried many different hobbies—horse keeping, hunting dogs, and courses in higher thought—but, unlike other youngsters, he has not become fanatic about any of them.[41]

---

the famous fairy tale writer: "For basically you and Denmark agree splendidly, and would agree even better if there were no theater in Denmark; *hinc illæ lacrymæ!*" My translation from the text found in *H.C. Andersens Brevveksling med Edvard og Henriette Collin*, ed. by C. Behrend and H. Topsøe-Jensen, Copenhagen: Levin & Munksgaard 1933–37, vol. 2, no. 4, letter no. 322, pp. 72–5.

[37]   *SKS* 2, 267 / *EO1*, 275. Emmeline gets furious when she finds out that Charles is married, but she sheds no tears. In *SKS* 17, 131n, BB:37 (note 10) / *KJN* 1, 124n, *hinc illæ lacrymæ* is found in an even more obviously proverbial manner when, in a footnote, Kierkegaard comments on the dangers arising when the storyteller does not himself believe the stories he is telling to children.

[38]   *SKS* 7, 368 / *CUP1*, 404.

[39]   Due to the fact that the μηδὲν ἄγαν was attributed to one of the Seven Sages, usually to Solon or to Chilon, and was inscribed on the temple of Apollo at Delphi, it became a revered aphorism early on. For more, see Eliza G. Wilkins, "Μηδὲν ἄγαν in Greek and Latin Literature," *Classical Philology*, vol. 21, no. 2, 1926, pp. 132–148.

[40]   *Andria*, vv. 60–1.

[41]   The whole sentence reads: "*Nam id arbitror / adprime in vita esse utile, ut nequid nimis.*" Clayton translates it (p. 5): "The Golden rule, I say, / Is 'Nothing in excess.'" In his commentary on these lines G.P. Shipp writes: "Menander's fragments show a great fondness for the maxims of everyday philosophy. It has been pointed out that Terence sometimes omits them in his adaptations. Here instead of doing so he makes a neat use of the saying by putting it in the mouth of the somewhat tedious Sosia, who has the partiality of many half-educated folk for proverbs and quotations." G.P. Shipp, *P. Terenti Afri Andria—with Introduction and Commentary*, 2nd ed., Oxford: Oxford University Press 1960.

This opinion and the philosophical tidbit from Sosia's mouth has a particularly ironic effect when just a little later we find out that Pamphilus is like any other teenager, only having eyes for his beloved Glycerium.

Despite the context, the Terentian passage became, already in antiquity, the *locus classicus* for expressing the idea of the mean in Latin.[42] And it is as such that Kierkegaard uses the phrase, as a Latin translation of the Greek pagan idea that he is attacking.[43] Again, the Terentian wording cannot, then, be seen as a conscious reference to Terence, although Kierkegaard was in a position to recognize its origin.

The last reference to the *Andria* is found in the "Preface" to *Prefaces* (1844): "One day after we had threshed through our differences and the conflict as usual had resolved itself in a *redintegratio amoris* [re-establishment of love], she finally took me intimately by the arm, looked as winsomely as possible at me, and said: 'My dear....' "[44] *Redintegratio amoris* is a further corruption of the quotation we saw earlier in the piece from Blicher's short story.[45] In *Andria* we find the phrase uttered by Chremes in a conversation with Simo. The latter is pleading with Chremes to let the marriage between their children take place. After all, Simo says, Pamphilus and his mistress Glycerium have had a row, and he has hopes of parting them. Chremes' objection to this is that "nothing renews love like a lovers' quarrel," and he is not willing to take the risk and put his daughter's happiness at stake.[46]

This corruption—together with the changed word order, as we saw in the case of Blicher—is again a good indication of the proverbial status of the phrase.[47]

---

[42]   Terence also expressed the idea in *Heauton Timorumenos,* where he uses the words *nil nimis* (v. 519). Both formulations appear frequently in later Latin literature, especially in the works of Cicero and Seneca. See Wilkins, "Μηδὲν ἄγαν in Greek and Latin Literature," pp. 144ff.

[43]   In *SKS* 22, 157, NB12:24 / *JP* 2, 2121 we see the same attack on the pagan maxim as the opposition of Christianity. *Ne quid nimis* appears three times in this passage, most notably in the first instance: "*Ne quid nimis*—if this is true, then Christianity is a lie, every line in Holy Scripture madness and confusion." In *SKS* 21, 209, NB9:22 / *JP* 4, 4372 he plays on the expression in a similar context when he writes only *quid nimis*, "something in excess."

[44]   *SKS* 4, 475 / *P*, 11.

[45]   *Andria*, v. 555: "*amantium irae amoris integratiost.*"

[46]   Terence also expresses this idea in *The Eunuch*, vv. 59ff. Clayton translates it (p. 105): "Love is a tale of discord, loud and long, / Suspicion, outright rage, outrageous wrong, / truces, treatises, war and peace."

[47]   The use of *redintegratio* in this passage is documented already in some of the manuscripts containing the commentaries on Virgil by the grammarian Servius (in the early fifth century AD), relating to Vergil, *Eclogues*, II, 14. See J.D. Craig, "Terence Quotations in Servius," *The Classical Quarterly*, vol. 24, nos. 3–4, 1930, p. 183. Once again we are dealing with a maxim, or at least an idea taken over from the Greeks, cf. Alfredus Koerte and Andreas Thierfelder (eds.), *Menandri quae supersunt*, 2nd ed., Leipzig: B.G. Teubner 1959, fragment 567 of Menander: ὀργὴ φιλούντων ὀλίγον ἰσχύει χρόνον ("The anger of lovers is short-lived").

B. Heauton Timorumenos

The Self-Tormentor was the third comedy written by Terence. It was presented for the first time in the spring of 163 BC. Again it is an adaptation of a Menandrian play, keeping the original Greek title.

The story line is tightly knit along the traditional lines: the severity and incomprehension of the old Athenian Menedemus has forced his son Clinia, who is madly in love with Antiphila, a young supposed orphan girl of scant means, to secretly abandon home and enlist as a mercenary in Asia. The father now regrets his harshness and punishes himself by renouncing all commodities and working hard in the family's fields until his beloved son returns. What Menedemus does not know, though, is that Clinia has returned to Athens after only a few months. Fearing his father's reaction, he has moved into the house of his friend Clitipho, the son of Chremes. Clitipho, at the same time, is spending horrendous sums of money on *his* beloved, the extravagant courtesan Bacchis, without his father's knowledge. Thus the troubles begin. In the end, the wife of Chremes discovers that Antiphila is actually their long lost daughter. As a respectable Athenian citizen, she can now marry Clinia, and all are contented.

In *Stages on Life's Way,* we find one of the most famous and at the same time most debated Terentian quotations, which is derived from the *Heauton Timorumenos*:

> From this standpoint of self-understanding, I am well aware that as a human being I am very far from being a paradigm; if anything, I am a sample human being. With a fair degree of accuracy, I give the temperature of every mood and passion, and when I am generating my own inwardness, I understand these words: *homo sum, nil humani a me alienum puto* [I am a human being; I hold that nothing human is alien to me]. But humanly no one can model himself on me, and historically I am even less a prototype for any human being.[48]

The *homo sum* phrase is found in the dialogue between Menedemus and Chremes that opens the play. Menedemus is reluctant to speak about his problems with his nosy neighbor, who then uses this sentence to justify his curiosity.[49] In spite of this contextual twist, the phrase has often been seen as the prime example of the aforementioned *humanitas* of Terence and as expressing the Stoic doctrine of the brotherhood of man.[50] This interpretation was questioned already in antiquity, most notably by Cicero, who discussed the motives of the self-righteous busybody Chremes in one of his philosophical treatises.[51] Nevertheless, the phrase was handed

---

[48]   *SKS* 6, 339 / *SLW*, 365.

[49]   *Heauton Timorumenos*, v. 77: "*Homo sum: humani nil a me alienum puto.*" Clayton translates it (p. 55): "But I'm a man, and what any human being / Does or experiences I can't help seeing / As my concern." See Duckworth, *The Nature of Roman Comedy*, p. 304.

[50]   See, for example, Seneca, *Epistulae morales*, 95, 53.

[51]   *De officiis*, I, 9, 30. Cicero also alludes to the passage in other works: *De finibus*, I, 1, 3 and III, 19, 64 and *De legibus*, I, 12, 33.

down to posterity with the moral gravity of a maxim, and it is as such that Kierkegaard receives it and adapts it to his thinking about what is common for mankind.[52]

Kierkegaard does not quote any more from *The Self-Tormentor*. Twice, however, he refers to the title of the play. In the second part of *Either/Or* he writes: "I have also felt that there are moments when the only salvation is to let duty speak, that it is sound and healthful to let it carry its own punishment, not with the gloomy unmanliness of a *Heautontimorumenos* [self-tormentor], but in all earnestness and firmness."[53] The brief description in this passage fits the character of Menedemus quite well. Kierkegaard could have been thinking specifically of him when he wrote it. The use of the Greek title gives us a hint of this. As we have seen, he did not read this comedy at school, but he had the text in his library in both Latin editions and Danish translations. Just as likely, however, he could have been thinking of any "man who torments himself," which is the literal translation of the Greek words. As such, it is a synonym for "self-tormentor," and it is used to develop an important concept in the philosophy of Kierkegaard.

This more generic use is clearly seen the second time we encounter the Greek term. In the first line of the appendix called "Self-Inflicted Sufferings—Self-Torment" in " 'Guilty?'/'Not-Guilty?,' " Kierkegaard writes, "From the point of view of the esthetic, every *heautontimorumenos* is comic."[54] Just a little later he adds: "Precisely because it is esthetically correct that all self-torment is comic, one is psychologically wise in an actual situation to use the comic explorer before dealing with self-torment another way."[55] Further on in the same chapter he goes on to treat self-tormenting religiously and designates it as "a sin like other sins."[56] He analyzes this more thoroughly in *Works of Love* (1847):

> When someone self-tormentingly thinks to do God a service by torturing himself, what is his sin except not willing to love himself in the right way? And if, alas, a person presumptuously lays violent hands upon himself, is not his sin precisely this, that he does not rightly love himself in the sense in which a person *ought* to love himself?...is it not therefore all the more important that Christianity's doctrine should be brought to mind again and again, that a person shall love his neighbor as himself, that is, as he ought to love himself.[57]

A man who does not love himself does not accept himself as he is, and he demands too much of himself. This, in turn, influences his relationship with God.[58]

---

[52]   A couple of years earlier, in 1841–42, Kierkegaard had commented on the same saying in a similar way in one of his notebooks (*SKS* 19, 260, Not9:1): "It applies to evil as well that: *homo sum, nil humani a me alienum puto.*"

[53]   *SKS* 3, 150 / *EO2*, 152–3.

[54]   *SKS* 6, 429 / *SLW*, 465.

[55]   *SKS* 6, 429–30 / *SLW*, 466.

[56]   *SKS* 6, 431 / *SLW*, 468.

[57]   *SKS* 9, 31 / *WL*, 23. See also *SKS* 4, 253 / *PF*, 70–1.

[58]   See *SKS* 5, 330 / *EUD*, 342. *SKS* 7, 421 / *CUP1*, 354. *SKS* 19, 194–5., Not6:10. *SKS* 20, 159–60, NB2:49. *SKS* 22, 89, NB11:152. Self-torment can sometimes be seen as useful in this aspect, as well, for example when taken as a Christian contrast to the pagan "freedom from care." *SKS* 21, 153, NB8:18.

In *Christian Discourses* (1847), in the chapter "The Care of Self-Torment," Kierkegaard extends his analysis by saying that self-torment is not just being content with the torments of today: "But care about the next day is precisely self-torment, and therefore the bird does not have the care of self-torment."[59] A few pages later he writes, "...who indeed would be as cruel as the self-tormenter is toward himself. But all his torments, all these cruelly devised and cruelly practiced torturing agonies are comprehended in this one phrase, 'the next day.' "[60] The solution for Kierkegaard is to be a Christian believer and to live according to the dictum *carpe diem*.[61] However, despite all his warnings, he was quite prone to self-torment himself, as can be seen in several places. "Self-tormenting, as I have always been, I invented this task in sadness and probably also with an addition of pride to torment me."[62] And that the reason for the self-torment was not always the worries for "the next day," can be inferred from a passage in a journal from 1849. Here he talks about how he broke the engagement to Regine Olsen for the second time, and in the following paragraph, under the title "About 'her' " he writes:

> Now I must not, except at certain times, think more about that, or else I will be in full swing with the self-torment....Maybe there will come a day when she has completely forgotten me, maybe; in any case it is a free matter. She once threw herself onto my relationship with God in such a way that I carry her with me all my life. Yet I must be careful that I do not indulge in self-torment.[63]

C. Phormio

Phormio was the fifth play presented by Terence. It was performed for the first time in 161 BC. Unlike the majority of his comedies, it is not based on a play by Menander but on a comedy called *Epidikazomenos* (*The Claimant*) by Apollodorus of Carystus,[64] another then famous but today practically unknown third-century BC Greek playwright.

The plot is traditional but a bit more complex this time: While the brothers Demipho and Chremes are out of town, their sons, the young Athenians Antipho and Phaedria, fall hopelessly in love with two girls. The resourceful parasite Phormio thinks up a plan to help Demipho get the poor orphan girl he has fallen for: by pretending that Antipho is the girl's nearest relative, he obtains a court order saying

---

[59]   *SKS* 10, 80 / *CD*, 70.

[60]   *SKS* 10, 84 / *CD*, 75.

[61]   See also *SKS* 5, 456–7 / *TD*, 84–5. *SKS* 6, 418 / *SLW*, 352.

[62]   *SKS* 21, 367, NB10:200. See also *SKS* 19, 440, Not15:9 and *SKS* 22, 116n, NB11:193. *SKS* 22, 127a, NB11:204.

[63]   *SKS* 22, 217, NB12:123. A similar situation is found in *Stages on Life's Way*, where we hear how the narrator meets "her" outside the King's Garden in Copenhagen. Here Kierkegaard uses the concept of self-torment more narrowly to compare himself to a flagellant, the medieval religious ascetics who used physical torment as penitence and to please God. *SKS* 6, 312 / *SLW*, pp. 258–9. This narrow use is also seen in *SKS* 4, 330 / *CA,* 17; *SKS* 7, 421 / *CUP1*, 354. For self-torment in relation to the past and remorse, see also *SKS* 5, 327 / *EUD*, 338–9 and *SKS* 5, 330 / *EUD*, 342.

[64]   *Phormio*, vv. 25–6.

that he must marry her according to Athenian law. At the same time, Phaedria unfortunately has no money to buy the lute-playing slave-girl he loves from her master. At this point the two fathers return from their respective journeys, and when they find out what has happened, they get furious. Demipho tries to annul the marriage of Antipho, but the action takes a turn when it is revealed that his young orphan wife is in reality the illegitimate daughter of Chremes. The two fathers now agree to let the marriage stand so that the legitimate wife of Chremes does not find out about his extramarital relationship to the girl's mother. But Phormio reveals the truth. The wife of Chremes in the end forgives her husband—though she gives him to understand that his infidelity will not be forgotten—and all ends well.

The passage about the Latin teacher in " 'Guilty'/'Not Guilty' "[65] mentioned earlier is by far the longest of all passages in the works of Kierkegaard dealing with Terence. It has already been analyzed, but I will add a few comments on it here regarding Kierkegaard's use of Terentian quotations and passages. The scene is about the love affair between Phaedria and the young lute-playing slave girl.[66] As we have seen, the analysis of the situation that Quidam ascribes to his Latin teacher gives a sensitive picture of the young lover's tormenting situation—an analysis that seems in keeping with Kierkegaard's own views on the subjunctive. In the play, however, the words are spoken by the slave Geta who is in charge of the two teenagers while their fathers are away. Although the comment is not without the sympathy for the young lover so characteristic of Terence, it should rather be read as a complaint about the impossibility of controlling the hormonally disturbed youngsters.

Once more Kierkegaard's rendering of the quotation varies from the text of Terence. In the last line Kierkegaard has *rediret domum* instead of *iret domum,* that is, *return home* instead of *go home*. This can be seen just as a clarification of the meaning, but, again, it disrupts the meter.[67]

Later in the same book Kierkegaard mentions *Phaedria* again. In the diary entry dated "April 7th. Midnight." the narrator compares himself to the young Athenian by saying: "...for actually it is only with the breaking of the engagement that I can say of myself in every sense and every respect what is said of Phaedria: *amare coepit perdite* [she fell desperately in love]."[68] This line is found at the beginning of Geta's speech, where he tells his fellow slave Davus how Phaedria met the lute-playing girl.[69] Quidam, on the other hand, is talking about the burning passion he feels for his now ex-fiancée. Kierkegaard thus, knowingly, gives the quotation an ironic twist

---

[65]   *SKS* 6, 191–2 / *SLW*, 204–5.

[66]   *Phormio*, vv. 88–90.

[67]   Except for this, his rendering of the text is quite close to that of the editions of his own time, such as *P. Terentii Afri Comoediae sex*, ed. by M.B.F. Schmieder and F. Schmieder, 2nd enlarged edition, Halle: Hemmerde & Schwetschke 1819, p. 419.

[68]   *SKS* 6, 274 / *SLW*, 295.

[69]   *Phormio*, v. 82. In the edition of Schmieder and Schmieder the line reads "*hanc amare coepit perdite.*" Clayton translates it (p. 158): "...and fall / Madly in love with her." The preserved manuscripts of Terence unanimously present *amare* in this verse. However, Kauer and Lindsay, on the basis of other ancient testimonies, have chosen to write *ardere*, i.e., *burn*, instead. Cf. W.M. Lindsay, "Gleanings from Glossaries and Scholia," *Classical Quarterly*, vol. 20, no. 2, 1926, pp. 104–5.

by applying it to a situation where a relationship has ended unhappily rather than to the beginning of a love affair, as is the case of Phaedria. For Quidam, the reason for the burning love is now the impossibility of getting his beloved back. Significantly, the adverb *perdite* can also be translated "hopelessly."

In *The Concept of Anxiety* (1844) we find another significant reference to the *Phormio*. In the main text we read, "And this is the wonder of life, that each man who is mindful of himself knows what no science knows, since he knows who he himself is, and that is the profundity of the Greek saying γνῶθι σεαυτόν [*know yourself*]...."[70] Then in a footnote to this he writes, "The Latin saying *unum noris omnes* [if you know one, you know all] light-mindedly expresses the same and actually expresses the same, if by *unum* is understood the observer himself, and one does not inquisitively look for an *omnes*, but earnestly holds fast to the one that actually is all."[71] The Latin phrase used by Kierkegaard is an abbreviated version of the sentence found in the Terentian play: *unum quom noris omnis noris*.[72] The words are spoken by Demipho when he is scolding his nephew Phaedria for trying to cover up for his cousin Antipho, who has married without his father's consent.[73]

The phrase, which Kierkegaard himself denotes as a "Latin saying" without any reference to the origin, is not a translation of the Greek "know yourself," as he suggests.[74] It is rather a rendering of other Greek sayings expressing the idea of one person taken as a standard for all, and it became the Latin maxim for expressing this idea.[75]

In Niels Thulstrup's words, Kierkegaard adapts the phrase to mean that "since the one is neither better nor worse than the other, it is sufficient to know *one*."[76] And this *one*, of course, is *oneself*. Kresten Nordentoft calls the phrase "one of Kierkegaard's favorite expressions, a key principle in his psychological method,"[77] a method that, according to Nordentoft, is based on self-observation and self-understanding. The ultimate meaning of Kierkegaard's use is, thus, that to know oneself is the decisive

---

[70]   *SKS* 4, 381–2 / *CA*, 78–9. Γνῶθι σεαυτόν, in Greek, was the other famous proverb ascribed to the Seven Sages, traditionally, Thales from Miletus or the Spartan Chilon, and inscribed on the front of the temple of Apollo at Delphi. The original meaning of the maxim was that we humans must know that we are only weak mortals in contrast with the powerful immortal Gods.

[71]   *SKS* 4, 382n / *CA*, 79n.

[72]   *Phormio*, v. 265. Schmieder and Schmieder have "*unum cognoris, omnes noris*."

[73]   The whole sentence (vv. 265–6) reads: "*ecce autem similia omnia! Omnes congruont: / unum quom noris omnis noris.*" Clayton translates it (p. 166): "Birds of a feather, singing the same song! / Know one and know the lot!"

[74]   The traditional Latin translation of this maxim is *nosce te ipsum*.

[75]   See, for example, *Appendix Proverbiorum*, centuria II, no. 69: ἐξ ἑνὸς τὰ πάντ᾽ ὁρᾶν (to see everything from one thing). (Leutsch & Schneidewin, *Corpus Paroemiographorum Graecorum, Paroemiographi Graeci*, vol. I, 1839, p. 407.) Echoes in later Latin literature can be found in Virgil's *Aeneid* 2, 65 "*et crimine ab uno disce omnes.*"

[76]   Niels Thulstrup, *Commentary on Kierkegaard's Concluding Unscientific Postscript*, trans. by Robert J. Widenmann, Princeton, New Jersey: Princeton University Press 1984, p. 325.

[77]   Kresten Nordentoft, *Kierkegaard's Psychology*, trans. by Bruce H. Kirmmse, Pittsburgh: Duquesne University Press 1978, p. 6.

precondition for knowing others and understanding the surrounding world, not just on the basis of "mere introspective familiarity with life, but it is, also, and especially, an ethical self-reflection."[78]

Kierkegaard himself writes the following in a draft to *The Concept of Anxiety*: "Therefore, it is important to maintain with profound psychological decisiveness: *unum noris omnes* [if you know one, you know all]. When the possibility of sin appears in one man, it has appeared in all...."[79] He later uses the same phrase with a slightly different content when he discusses the individual in relation to different types of collective: "In community the single individual is the microcosm who qualitatively reproduces the cosmos; here, in a good sense, it holds true that *unum noris omnes* [If you know one, you know all]. In a public there is no single individual, and the whole is nothing; here it is impossible to say *unum noris omnes*, for here there is no one."[80]

The next possible allusion to the *Phormio* is found in *Stages on Life's Way*, where we read, "I could have left it at that, but in order to throw light on him I had the thought enter his mind, and actuality seemed to encourage it, that it would nevertheless all end in a completely natural way with her being quite free and unrestrained again through a *restitutio in integrum* [restitution to the original state]."[81] At the end of the second act of the Terentian play we find the formulation *restitui in integrum*.[82] The sentence is part of a discussion where Demipho is consulting with some friends as to what he can do to invalidate his son's inopportune marriage. One of the friends suggests that he should go back to court, where he will undoubtedly win the suit.[83] As can be seen from the context, the phrase was already a well-known legal term, at least in the middle Roman Republic. It has been passed on to posterity as part of Roman Law.[84] Kierkegaard uses the legal term in a more general, figurative sense where it denotes the natural, inevitable break-up of the relationship between the

---

[78]   Ibid., p. 4. See also *SKS* 7, 323 / *CUP1*, 353: "In a certain sense, the subjective thinker speaks just as abstractly as the abstract thinker, because the latter speaks about humanity in general, subjectivity in general, the other about one human being (*unum omnes noris* [if you know one, you know all]). But this one human being is an existing human being, and the difficulty is not left out."

[79]   *Pap.* V B 49:15 / *CA*, Supplement, 183. See *SKS* 19, 260, Not9:1 and what has been said above about the *homo sum* phrase from the *Heauton Timorumenos*.

[80]   *SKS* 23, 40, NB15:60 / *JP* 3, 2952. A similar use is found in *SKS* 18, 299, JJ:478 / *KJN* 2, 275 where he writes: "What is so splendid with Plato's *Republic* is that he does not make the state higher than the individual, least of all in the sense of the Hegelian nonsense. In order to describe the individual, he describes the state; he describes a democrat and to do so he describes democracy; he constructs a state for the individual, *unum noris omnes*—this is the proper human ideality; otherwise we get the confusion about many producing, by being many, something quite [different] from what each is individually."

[81]   *SKS* 6, 401 / *SLW*, 433–4.

[82]   *Phormio*, v. 451.

[83]   The whole sentence (vv. 450ff.): "*quod te absente hic filius / egit, restitui in integrum aequomst et bonum, / et id impetrabis.*" Clayton translates it (p. 173): "And I would suggest / It's right and fair that any act of your son done / While you were absent should be legally undone. / The court'll agree."

[84]   Through Justinian's *Digests* (46, 3, 95, 3), first written down by Aemilianus Papianus around AD 206–12.

"sympathetic" man and the woman who is "in the sense of immediacy innocently self-loving."[85]

The last parallel to the *Phormio* in Kierkegaard's writings is found in the *Journal HH*:

> *fortes fortuna* [Fortune (favors) the brave] is the pagan position; God is mighty in the weak is the Christian position; one sees immediately that the former is a category of immediacy, since happiness in this case is merely a reflection of the given immediate genius of the individual, the immediate *harmonia præstabilita* [predestinate harmony]: the latter is a category of reflection, arrived at through the annihilation of the individual.[86]

In the play the words are spoken by the slave Geta, this time in conversation with the two young men Phaedria and Antipho. He is trying to encourage them after they have found out that their fathers have returned from their respective business trips.[87] Again we are dealing with an idea taken over from Greek everyday philosophy whose Terentian wording became the standard expression in Latin. It is one of the most repeated Terentian phrases of them all.[88] As in other cases, Kierkegaard uses the Latin proverbial expression to highlight a contrast between paganism and Christianity.

D. The Latin Poet?

In *The Concept of Anxiety* we find a passage that has caused some confusion: "The present is the eternal, or rather, the eternal is the present, and the present is full. In this sense the Latin poet said of the deity that he is *praesens* (*praesentes dii* [the presence of the gods]), by which expression, when used about the deity, he also signified the powerful assistance of the deity."[89] Some have chosen to see the "Latin poet" (*Latineren*) as a reference to Terence.[90] This identification is dubious at best. Terence does not use the exact phrase *praesentes dii* anywhere, and, even though he does talk about a *praesentem deum* in the *Phormio*,[91] he is not likely to be the one referred to. Leaving aside the ironic tone in the Terentian context, Kierkegaard could be quoting from memory or adapting it to his needs. But why, then, refer to a plural form when the phrase is in the singular in Terence and Kierkegaard himself is talking about a single deity?

---

85   *SKS* 6, 400 / *SLW*, 432.
86   *SKS* 18, 125a, HH:2 / *KJN* 2, 117.
87   *Phormio*, v. 203. The whole phrase reads "*fortis fortuna adiuvat.*"
88   Greek parallels can be found in Menander and other Greek writers (οὐ τοῖς ἀτίμοις ἡ τύχη συλλαμβάνει). Donatus calls it a "proverb" (*paroimia*) in his commentary to the *Phormio*. The idea was already known in Rome at the time of Plautus (*Poenulus* 972). Echoes of the Terentian wording are abundant in later writers such as Cicero, Virgil, Seneca, and others.
89   *SKS* 4, 390 / *CA*, 86.
90   See, for example, Jane Chamberlain and Jonathan Rée (eds.), *The Kierkegaard Reader*, Oxford: Blackwell 2001, p. 197 note 16.
91   *Phormio*, v. 345: "*ea qui praebet, non tu hunc habeas plane praesentem deum?*" Clayton translates it (p. 169): " 'Our host's a god on earth,' you say, 'A saint he is!' "

The idea of the gods who vouchsafe their presence to help the humans was a popular theme in Latin literature, especially among the Augustan age poets. And a phrase closer to the wording in *The Concept of Anxiety* and maybe also to the meaning Kierkegaard was looking for, is found in the *praesentis divos* from the first *Eclogue* by Virgil.[92] This poet is, most certainly, also the one referred to when Kierkegaard again uses the ambiguous term in the "Diary of the Seducer."[93]

All this, however, does not mean that the term is just to be understood as an alternative way to denote Virgil. It is rather to be seen as a reference to a Latin poet or writer to be recognized from the context. This is supported by an even more general use in *The Concept of Anxiety* where Kierkegaard uses the term "*Latineren*" about anyone speaking Latin.[94]

E. General References

Having analyzed all the possible allusions to Terence in the works of Kierkegaard, it is now time to take a brief look at a few more general references that could be relevant in a discussion of Kierkegaard's relationship to Roman comedy and, thus, to Terence.

In "The First Love" in *Either/Or,* Kierkegaard writes about the merits of what he calls "the modern comedy (especially Scribe's)" in comparison with the "older comedy."[95] The latter term almost certainly refers to the ancient tradition represented by Plautus and Terence and their later successors, such as Molière and Kierkegaard's compatriot Holberg. From the following passage, where he talks about the modern theater, it is possible to deduce to some degree what Kierkegaard thought about this tradition:

> No information is necessary in order to orient the spectator; no pause in the drama is required in order to give clues and accounts. So it is in life, where one always needs explanatory notes, but it ought not to be so in poetry. Then the spectator, free from care, can enjoy, can absorb undisturbed, the dramatic life. Although modern drama seems to require less self-activity on the part of the spectator, it perhaps nevertheless requires more in another way or, more correctly, does not require it but takes revenge on the forgetting of it. The less perfect the dramatic form or the structure of the drama, the more frequently the spectator is provoked out of his sleep, insofar as he is sleeping.[96]

---

[92]   *Eclogues*, I, 41. Kierkegaard did not read this text at school, but we know that he had several copies of it in his library (*ASKB* I 192–3, 194, 195 and *ASKB* II 29–30). Cf. also the similar phrase, *praesentia numina*, in the *Georgics*, I, 10. The Latin term *numina* means "divine or supernatural powers." In poetic language it is often synonymous with "gods."

[93]   *SKS* 2, 405 / *EO1*, 418: "My Cordelia, The Latinist says of an attentive pupil that he hangs on the teacher's lips. For love, everything is a symbol; in recompense, the symbol in turn is actuality. Am I not a diligent, attentive pupil? But you do not say a word. Your Johannes." The phrase "hangs on the teacher's lips" is very close to a famous line from the *Aeneid* where we read *"pendetque iterum narrantis ab ore"* (*Aeneid*, 4, 79).

[94]   *SKS* 4, 364n / *CA*, 59n. Here it is used in the same general sense as "Frenchman" (*Franskmanden*) in a discussion of the use of the word "alteration." See also Kierkegaard's manuscript for the text: *Pap.* V B 53, 19.

[95]   *SKS* 2, 240 / *EO1*, 247.

[96]   *SKS* 2, 241 / *EO1*, 247–8.

He goes on to compare watching a traditional comedy with a rough trip on a bumpy highway, whereas modern comedy is seen as a road where driving is comfortable and enjoyable—and allows one to sleep. This view is in accordance with the new tastes of his time, when the Roman plays were no longer admired unconditionally.[97]

That Kierkegaard had abundant knowledge of ancient Greek comedy, particularly Aristophanes, is well documented.[98] However, only one reference to the New Greek Comedy, which was the direct model for the later Roman tradition, is found in his works. In an entry in a notebook from 1842, containing a succinct discussion of the history and subject of Greek comedy, he writes: "With Menander the new comedy begins in 333. (See Curtius p. 110.)"[99]

The main reason for this scarce treatment is, as we have seen, that Menander, at the time of Kierkegaard, was still only known from a few fragments, apart from the adaptations of his works by the Roman comedy writers.

The parallels to Terence in the works of Søren Kierkegaard are relatively numerous, but mostly limited to phrases of proverbial character. They appear throughout his writings, but predominantly in the mid-1840s, and most frequently in *Stages on Life's Way*. In general, Kierkegaard does not refer to the Roman comedy writer or his plays. We know that he studied the *Andria* and the *Phormio* at school. In the *Auction Catalogue* we can see that the philosopher owned several editions of the works of the Roman comedy writer, both in Latin and in translations into Danish. Apart from that, he could easily have encountered the more proverbial sayings in other works or in everyday speech, where they were recurrently quoted. A few references show that he was aware of the provenance of, at least, some of the phrases and possibly most of them. His use of the *Heaton Timorumenos* in relation to his own thoughts about self-tormenting shows that, not surprisingly, he knew about this comedy, even though he never mentions that he has read it. This is also a good example of how, in some cases, Kierkegaard uses the allusions to denote or explain key concepts in his thinking, occasionally changing the quotations to fit his needs.

Kierkegaard never really reveals his opinion of Terence as a playwright. A hint about his more general, less than appreciative, views of the ancient comical tradition is found, however, in a few comments on the merits of contemporary drama in contrast to the traditional theater.

---

[97]   An early example of this attitude in a Danish context is found in Grundtvig's *Verdens Krønike* (1812), where he explicitly mentions Terence and Plautus as illustrations of the fact that Roman art and literature was just a simple (and poor) imitation of Greek art. See *Nikolaj Frederik Severin Grundtvigs Udvalgte Skrifter*, vols. 1–10, ed. by Holger Begtrup, Copenhagen: Gyldendal 1904–06, vol. 2, p. 208.

[98]   See the article on Kierkegaard's relationship to Aristophanes in the preceding volume in this series, *Kierkegaard and the Greek World*.

[99]   *SKS* 19, 377, Not12:12 / *JP* 4, 4836. The work by Curtius that Kierkegaard refers to is *Aristoteles, Dichtkunst ins Deutsche übersetzt, mit Anmerkungen und besondern Abhandlungen versehen*, translated and commented by Michael Conrad Curtius, Hannover: Joh. Chr. Richter 1753 (*ASKB* 1094).

Bibliography

I. Terence's Works in The Auction Catalogue *of Kierkegaard's Library*

P. Terentii Afri Comoediae, ed. by Richard Bentley, annotated by Gabriello Faerno, Leipzig: Schwickert 1791 (*ASKB* 1290).

P. Terentii afri comoediae sex, ed. by M. Beni. Frid. Schmieder and Fridericus Schmieder, 2nd revised ed., Halle: Schwetschke 1819 (*ASKB* 1291).

P. Terentii Phormio, ed. by Carolus Guil. Elberling, Copenhagen: Gyldendal 1833 (*ASKB* 1292).

Terentses Skuespil, trans. and ed. by Frederik Høegh Guldberg, vols. 1–2, Copenhagen: Johan Frederik Schultz 1805 (*ASKB* 1293–1294, cf. also *ASKB* A I 189–190).

Andria Selvplageren og Formio, tre latinske Lystspil, trans. by Mathias Rathje, Copenhagen: P.M. Liunges Forlag paa Børsen 1797 (*ASKB* 1295).

Publii Terentii Afri Comoediae sex, ed. by Johannes Minellius, Stockholm 1699 (*ASKB* A I 187).

Publii Terentii Afri Comoediae sex, ed. by Johannes Minellius, Copenhagen: Frid. Christian Pelt 1771 (*ASKB* A I 188).

Terentii Comoediae, vols. 1–2, opera et studio Gudmundi Magaei, Copenhagen 1789 (*ASKB* A II 33–34).

II. Works in The Auction Catalogue *of Kierkegaard's Library that Discuss Terence*

Bähr, Johann Christian Felix, *Abriss der Römischen Literatur-Geschichte zum Gebrauch für höhere Lehranstalten*, Heidelberg and Leipzig: Groos 1833 (*ASKB* 975).

Dyck, Johann Gottfried and Georg Schatz (eds.), *Charaktere der vornehmsten Dichter aller Nationen; nebst kritischen und historischen Abhandlungen über Gegenstände der schönen Künste und Wissenschaften, von einer Gesellschaft von Gelehrten*, vols. 1–8, Leipzig: Dyk 1792–1808, vol. 1, p. 11 (*ASKB* 1370–1377).

Flögel, Carl Friedrich, *Geschichte der komischen Litteratur*, vols. 1–4, Liegnitz and Leipzig: David Siegert 1784–87, vol. 4, p. 72; pp. 111–15 (*ASKB* 1396–1399).

Hagen, Johan Frederik, *Ægteskabet. Betragtet fra et ethisk-historiskt Standpunct*, Copenhagen: Wahlske Boghandels Forlag 1845, p. 104n (*ASKB* 534).

Meierotto, Johann Heinrich Ludwig, *Ueber Sitten und Lebensart der Römer in verschiedenen Zeiten der Republik*, vols. 1–2, 3rd revised and enlarged ed., Berlin: in der Myliussischen Buchhandlung 1814 (*ASKB* 656).

[Montaigne, Michel de], *Michael Montaigne's Gedanken und Meinungen über allerley Gegenstände, ins Deutsche übersetzt*, vols. 1–7, Berlin: F.T. Lagarde 1793–99, vol. 2, p. 201; p. 402; vol. 3, pp. 192–3; vol. 4, p. 316 (*ASKB* 681–687).

Mynster, Jakob Peter, *Den hedenske Verden ved Christendommens Begyndelse*, Copenhagen: Schultz 1850, p. 17 (*ASKB* 693).

[Richter, Johann Paul Friedrich], Jean Paul, *Vorschule der Aesthetik nebst einigen Vorlesungen in Leipzig über die Parteien der Zeit*, vols. 1–3, 2nd revised ed., Stuttgart and Tübingen: J.G. Cotta'sche Buchhandlung 1813, vol. 3, p. 929 (*ASKB* 1381–1383).

Schlegel, August Wilhelm, *Ueber dramatische Kunst und Litteratur. Vorlesungen*, vols. 1–2 (vol. 2 in two Parts), Heidelberg: Mohr und Zimmer 1809–11, vol. 1, pp. 357ff.; vol. 2.1, pp. 4ff.; (*ASKB* 1392–1394).

Schopenhauer, Arthur, *Die Welt als Wille und Vorstellung*, vols. 1–2, 2nd revised and enlarged ed., Leipzig: F.A. Brockhaus 1844 [1819], vol. 2, p. 336 (*ASKB* 773–773a).

—— *Parerga und Paralipomena: kleine philosophische Schriften*, vols. 1–2, Berlin: Druck und Verlag von A.W. Hayn 1851, vol. 1, p. 441 (*ASKB* 774–775).

Sulzer, Johann Georg, *Allgemeine Theorie der Schönen Künste, in einzeln, nach alphabetischer Ordnung der Kunstwörter auf einander folgenden, Artikeln abgehandelt*, vols. 1–4 and a Register Volume, 2nd revised ed., Leipzig: in der Weidmannschen Buchhandlung 1792–99, vol. 1, p. 490; vol. 2, p. 58; vol. 3, p. 129; vol. 4, p. 147; p. 522 (*ASKB* 1365–1369).

Zeuthen, Ludvig, *Humanitet betragtet fra et christeligt Standpunkt, med stadigt Hensyn til den nærværende Tid*, Copenhagen: Gyldendalske Boghandling 1846, pp. 43–4; p. 72 (*ASKB* 915).

III. Secondary Literature on Kierkegaard's Relation to Terence

Kresten Nordentoft, *Kierkegaard's Psychology*, trans. by Bruce H. Kirmmse, Pittsburgh: Duquesne University Press 1978, pp. 6ff.

Valerius Maximus:

Moral *Exempla* in Kierkegaard's Writings

Nataliya Vorobyova

In the footnotes to some of Kierkegaard's compositions one can stumble upon the name of Valerius Maximus, a crafty and for that reason popular Roman storyteller. A contemporary reader might associate the name with moral punch lines, memorable anecdotes, or aphorisms such as, for instance: "the divine wrath is slow indeed in vengeance, but it makes up for its tardiness by the severity of the punishment."[1] This and similar statements originate from the book *Factorum et dictorum memorabilium libri IX* or *The Memorable Deeds and Saying in 9 Books*. This is the only written text produced by Valerius. Unfortunately, not much is known about his personal history.

I.

It is most likely that Valerius Maximus comes from an insignificant and maybe even poor family. One certain fact about his life, according to researchers, is that he owed everything to Sextus Pompeius, an influential Roman magistrate and a consul in AD 14. It is possible to gather bits and pieces of information about Valerius' life from his own work, which he wrote during the rule of Tiberius, who led the country from AD 14 until his death in 37. With this fact in mind, it is rather striking that most of the sources used by Valerius belong to the times of Augustus, Tiberius' predecessor, the emperor famous for establishing the *Pax Augusta*. For a long time the work of Valerius Maximus was not fully appreciated by scholars. It was considered a plagiarism, and the author himself was regarded as a mere collector of particularly remarkable historical anecdotes. Nevertheless, there have recently appeared some

---

[1]   Valerius Maximus, *Factorum et dictorum memorabilium libri IX*, I, 1, 3: "*Lento quidem gradu ad vindictam divina procedit ira, sed tarditatem supplicii gravitate compensat.*" English translation here and below quoted from Valerius Maximus, *Memorable Doings and Sayings*, vols. 1–2, ed. and trans. by D.R. Shackleton Bailey, Cambridge, Massachusetts: Harvard University Press, London: William Heinemann 2000 (*Loeb Classical Library*).

detailed studies of this extravagant and highly rhetorical text,[2] and a new English translation of *The Memorable Deeds* has been published.[3]

Valerius gave his work a clear structure: every book is divided into smaller chapters each of which has a catchy title praising moral values. One can, for instance, come across chapters entitled "Paternal Love," "Constancy," "Moderation," "Friendship," and "Justice"; he also introduces as chapter titles two terms, as it were, binary pairs, such as "Love and Lust." There are also more descriptive titles which present the reversal of good luck or fortune, such as "The Lowborn Who Tried Through Deceit to Enter Others' Families," and "The Mutability of Customs and Fortune." Each chapter has, moreover, a strict structural division. First, there are examples originating from Roman history or of Roman origin. These are usually followed up by foreign stories, mostly Greek. As one Valerius scholar comments: "the individual story has most often been taken from a classical Latin author, placed under a heading, and stylistically reworked so as to be suitable for insertion into a declamation."[4] Such an organizational principle of the books makes it clear that Valerius' predecessor was Cicero and his *Orator*, even though a rather substantial number of the Valerius' examples come from Livy's *The History of Rome from its Foundation*.

These conclusions clarify the purpose of Valerius' composition: to collect and combine examples which could be easily contextualized and used in oratorical practice, allowing the speaker to elaborate eloquently on various topics mentioned during the speech. There are also scholars who argue that the organization of Valerius' book may suggest its pedagogical purpose, for it praises true Roman virtues. Yet, the most significant feature of the work is the manner in which the examples are collected and the combinations in which they occur, for the known source texts normally suggest a different emphasis or lack specific details introduced by Valerius, which were most likely taken from a different source text. This observation has led scholars to conclude that Valerius was jumping from one source text to the other, while summarizing and probably dictating the stories he had chosen to include in his collection.[5] In this manner he not only reworked every anecdote stylistically, but made a story more complete and shifted its accents, focusing not on an accurate historical report but on ethical side of the narrative.

Bloomer in his elaborate study on Valerius vividly presents a reconstruction of the manner in which the ancient researcher worked. He briefly characterizes the way of conducting the work as not at all "flattering": "our picture of research methods remains hazy, and skeptical; it is most influenced by two criteria: the supposed difficulty of reading and the alleged preference of reading to any form of autopsy."[6]

---

2   W. Martin Bloomer, *Valerius Maximus and the Rhetoric of the New Nobility*, Chapel Hill: University of North Carolina Press 1992. Clive Skidmore, *Practical Ethics for Roman Gentlemen: The Work of Valerius Maximus*, Exeter: University of Exeter Press 1996. Hans-Friedrich Mueller, *Roman Religion in Valerius Maximus*, London and New York: Routledge 2002.

3   Valerius Maximus, *Memorable Deeds and Sayings: One Thousand Tales from Ancient Rome*, ed. and trans. by Henry John Walker, Indianapolis: Hackett 2004.

4   Bloomer, *Valerius Maximus and the Rhetoric of the New Nobility*, p. 17.

5   Ibid., p. 32.

6   Ibid., p. 57.

This method implied a lot of reading without particular attention to noting the source of the information. In the case of an especially interesting story, there was always a slave nearby to note down all the details. This, as Bloomer stresses, could easily explain the fact that some of Valerius' examples include several sources. He also underlines the specificity of the sources and the form in which they appeared:

> Reynolds and Wilson...describe the difficulty of the ancient papyrus roll (minimal punctuation, no indices, scribal errors, the task of covering and uncovering a particular passage). Notably, Cicero only complained (to Atticus) of the copyist's errors. These alone slaves' labour could not easily mitigate, though the learned Tiro must have been considerable help.[7]

Obviously the method used by Valerius will remain a matter of conjecture. He surely did not read every single source he quotes from; however, it is impossible to deny that he is well read in Latin prose. For as Bloomer reminds is: "with no index a reader could not easily find the passage that interested him."[8] Furthermore, the researcher calls attention to the fact that such a massive work as Valerius' was in fact the outcome of the effort of many people, as the Roman historian always had slaves to write out relevant passages.[9] This supposition can explain a combination of various sources in one example and a simultaneous stylistic reorganization of the text.

After close textual analysis, scholars have concluded that Valerius used Livy's *History* and some works by Cicero, Seneca, Sallust, and Pompeius Trogus. However, Valerius' originality is hidden exactly in his skillful interpretations and ability to combine different narrative strands. Besides referring to Roman classical authors, the historian also definitely used Greek sources, "for that he knew and read Greek and traveled through Greece is beyond doubt."[10] All the so-called "foreign" examples, which appear in *The Memorable Deeds and Sayings*, originate from Diodorus Siculus, Dionysius of Halicarnassus, Celsus, Manilius, and others.

All in all, what seems to be the greatest merit of Valerius' work, namely, retelling an event of ancient history by adding numerous details from sources which do not survive, has today become the greatest curse for commentators. They can hardly ever be sure if in a particular case they are dealing with Valerius' own interpretation of the account or whether he is merely summarizing his source. Yet, the work already had a certain value in the time when it was created since the historian's collection of stories served a specific purpose which guaranteed its popularity:

> The work was clearly meant for specific audiences and uses; a collection of anecdotes organized under general rubrics was of most service for students and practitioners of declamation, a form of oral performance that constitutes both the final stage in Roman education and, for the professional performer and the Romans who thronged the recital halls, the pre-eminent public art form of the early Principate.[11]

---

[7]   Ibid., p. 59.
[8]   Ibid., p. 60.
[9]   Ibid.
[10]   Ibid., p. 79.
[11]   Ibid., p. 4.

In any case, from a historical point of view, the work is by no means without value, for its author succeeded in preserving accounts of many curious events which cannot be found elsewhere.

At the same time, scholars have detected a large number of errors in those cases where it was possible to compare Valerius' account with collateral testimony. Accuracy was not Valerius' main goal; he made an attempt to impress both the potential reader and listener with the story itself. This might also be the reason why the opening book of his work is dedicated to the subject of religion and the supernatural. The stories recount various instances of miracles and prophetic dreams; for instance, there is an account of Calpurnia's dream vision, which preceded the death of her husband, Julius Caesar. Regardless of the topic of each particular book, the purpose of Valerius' work can be summarized as a tribute to Cicero's idea of a great orator, who should have a vast knowledge of history and literature in order to properly illustrate his speech with relevant examples.

II.

At this point we should turn our attention to Kierkegaard's works and the contexts in which he refers to the texts of Valerius Maximus. Even though Kierkegaard's commentators mention the text of Valerius as a possible source of allusion in the philosopher's writings, it is rather difficult to prove or disprove the actual use of this particular source. In the *Auction Catalogue* of the books which belonged to Kierkegaard there is listed a German copy of the text: *Sammlung merkwürdiger Reden und Thaten* (1828), translated by Friedrich Hoffmann.[12] However, Valerius is not listed among the authors which were a part of the obligatory studies at the Borgerdyd School: Horace, Virgil, Terence, Cicero, Livy, Caesar, Sallust, Cornelius Nepos.[13] Since the book he owned was a German translation of the Latin original, one might be tempted to assume that Kierkegaard either bought it during his trip to Berlin or right afterwards. However, it is also possible that he acquired the book in Copenhagen where German books were widely available. In any case, this translated volume would not be something that would have been used in the classroom instruction at the Borgerdyd School.

One fact which seems to speak for the idea that the Danish philosopher did not use Valerius Maximus extensively as a source text is that there are only three known references to the work in Kierkegaard's entire authorship. Additionally, Kierkegaard never mentions Valerius' name, which may only strengthen the belief that he never read the original. The passages which allude to *The Memorable Deeds* occur in the books published one after another: *Either/Or* (February 20, 1843), *Fear and Trembling* (May 5, 1843) and *Philosophical Fragments* (June 1844).

---

[12]   Valerius Maximus, *Sammlung merkwürdiger Reden und Thaten*, vols. 1–3, trans. by Friedrich Hoffmann, Stuttgart: Verlag der J.B. Metzler'schen Buchhandlung 1828 (*Römische Prosaiker in neuen Uebersetzungen*, ed. by G.L.F. Tafel, E.N. Osiander and G. Schwab) (*ASKB* 1296).

[13]   Bruce H. Kirmmse (ed.), *Encounters with Kierkegaard: A Life as Seen by his Contemporaries*, Princeton, New Jersey: Princeton University Press 1996, p. 273.

Commentators have found an illustrative passage in the *Journal AA*. In the entry dated June 1, 1835, while discussing theology Kierkegaard confronts the profundity of Christian belief with "rationalism," accentuating that the latter frequently undertakes the task of "giving an account of the relation between God and the world"[14] and overlooks Christian spirituality. Rationalism does not attempt to associate itself with Christianity through faith, but rather "bases its expositions on Scripture, and sends out chapter-and-verse by the legion in advance of every single point, but the exposition itself is not penetrated by it."[15] This is followed by an obscure remark: the rationalists "conduct themselves like Cambyses, who in his campaign against Egypt sent the sacred hens and cats ahead, but just like the Roman Consul they are also prepared to throw the sacred hens overboard if they will not eat."[16]

The story of Cambyses can be found in Valerius' Book VI in the chapter entitled "Of Severity." Its location in the collection indicates that this particular account is of foreign origin; further, Herodotus has been identified as its source.[17] Here is the account offered by Valerius:

> Cambyses' severity was unusual. He flayed the skin from a certain corrupt judge and had it stretched over a chair on which he ordered the man's son to sit when passing judgment. He was a king and a barbarian and by the horrible and novel punishment of a judge he sought to make sure that no judge could be bribed in the future.[18]

Even though the passage explains the nature of Cambyses, stressing his severity, it does not disclose where Kierkegaard might have found the account about the sacrifice of the animals before the battle, which he refers to.

Yet, there remains the question of who was that "Roman Consul"? Most likely Kierkegaard alludes to Claudius Pulcher and his action before the sea battle near Drepanum in 249 BC. As Valerius reports in the chapter "Of Augury":

> *Paris.* In the First Punic War P. Claudius, wanting to join battle at sea, sought the auspices in the traditional fashion. When the keeper of the chickens reported that the chickens did not leave their coop, he ordered them flung into the sea, saying, "Since they won't eat, let them drink."

---

14   *SKS* 17, 22, AA:12 / *KJN*, 1, 17.
15   Ibid.
16   Ibid.
17   Herodotus, *The Histories*, trans. by Aubrey de Sélincourt, Harmondsworth: Penguin 1954, Book V, 25, p. 349: "Darius then left for Susa and made Histiaeus accompany him. Before he went he appointed Artaphernes, his brother by the same father, as governor of Sardis, and gave Otanes the command of the coast. Otanes' father Sisames had been put to death by Cambyses: he was one of the royal judges, and as a punishment for taking a bribe and perverting justice Cambyses had him flayed; all his skin was torn off and cut into strips, and the strips stretched across the seat of the chair which he used to sit on in Court. Cambyses then appointed his son to be judge in his place, and told him not to forget what his chair was made of, when he gave his judgments."
18   Valerius Maximus, *Factorum et dictorum memorabilium*, Book VI, 3, ext. 3; *Memorable Doings and Sayings*, vol. 2, p. 43.

Nepotianus. P. Claudius, a man of impulse, consulted a chicken-keeper in the First Punic War. On his reporting that the chickens were not eating, which is a bad omen, Claudius said, "Let them drink," and ordered them thrown into the sea. Soon afterwards he lost his fleet off the Aegates islands with great damage to the commonwealth and his own destruction.[19]

This account is accurately summarized by Kierkegaard, whose attention was caught by a curious paradox: people believe only when it is comfortable to believe; however as soon as the prediction, sign or omen is not comfortable and does not match the grand human plan, the belief is thrown overboard and easily forgotten. This is the crucial feature of the "rationalists," who, as the philosopher ironically observes, "when they find themselves in agreement with Scripture, they use it as the foundation, but otherwise not."[20] With the help of cross-historical parallels, Kierkegaard addresses the universality of the problem of human faith and its rationalization. However, the problem of the source of this particular reference remains unsolved, for the passage in Valerius' work has multiple sources, and one of them is Cicero's *De Natura Deorum*, which might have been a part of obligatory school reading during Kierkegaard's times. Nevertheless, the parallel provided by the philosopher and its accuracy once again show the suitability of ancient texts for such topics.

The next reference to Valerius' work was found in the epigraph to *Fear and Trembling*: "*Was Tarquinius Superbus in seinem Garten mit den Mohnköpfen sprach, verstand der Sohn, aber nicht der Bote* [What Tarquinius Superbus said in the garden by means of the poppies, the son understood but the messenger did not.] Hamann."[21] Valerius' Book VII has a Greek title "Stratagems," and the author claims that "examples of this category have virtually no satisfactory expression in our language; in Greek they are called Stratagems."[22] As the title suggests, the collected examples focus on deceit and outwitting of the enemy. Here, we find the story of Periander:

> And not to leave our kings just yet, Sex. Tarquinius, son of Tarquin, took it hard that Gabii could not be stormed by his father's power. So he thought of a method stronger than arms whereby to capture the town and add it to the Roman empire. He suddenly betook himself to the Gabii as though fleeing from his parent's cruelty and stripes, which he had suffered of his own accord. Step by step, with false, manufactured blandishments he won the good will of each individual so as to become highly influential with them all. He then sent a comrade to his father to tell him how he had everything in his own hands and to ask what he wished done. The old man's astuteness matched the young man's cunning. Tarquin was highly delighted by the message, but not altogether trusting the honesty of the messenger he gave no answer but drew him aside into the garden and there with his

---

[19]   Valerius Maximus, *Factorum et dictorum memorabilium*, Book I, 4.3; *Memorable Doings and Sayings*, vol. 1, p. 51. There is a cross-reference to the passage in Cicero's *De Natura deorum*, Book II, 7. (English translation: *The Nature of the Gods*, trans. by Horace C.P. McGregor, Harmondsworth: Penguin 1972, p. 126.)

[20]   *SKS* 17, 22, AA:12 / *KJN*, 1, 17.

[21]   *SKS* 4, 100 / *FT*, 3.

[22]   Valerius Maximus, *Factorum et dictorum memorabilium*, Book VII, 4.2: "*appellatione nostra vix apte exprimi possunt, Graeca pronuntiatione Strategemata dicuntur*"; *Memorable Doings and Sayings*, vol. 2, p. 149.

stick struck down the heads of the largest and tallest poppies. Young Sextus, hearing of his father's silence and of what he did, understood the reason for the one and the meaning of the other, not failing to realize that he was being advised to get rid of the most prominent citizens of Gabii by banishment or liquidate them by death. So he virtually handed over the community with hands bound to Tarquin, stripped of its loyal defenders.[23]

The commentators of *Fear and Trembling* call attention to the fact that a similar story can be found in Aristotle's *Politics*.[24] Moreover, commentators to Valerius suggest Livy's *History* as the source of the story. In Livy we read:

At last he [Sextus] was able to feel that he had the town, as it were, in his hip pocket, and was ready for anything. Accordingly he sent a confidential messenger to Rome, to ask his father what step he should take, his power in Gabii being, by God's grace, by this time absolute. Tarquin, I suppose, was not sure of the messenger's good faith: in any case, he said not a word in reply to his question, but with a thoughtful air went out into the garden. The man followed him, and Tarquin, strolling up and down in silence, began knocking off poppy-heads with his stick. The messenger at last wearied of putting his question and waiting for the reply, so he returned to Gabii supposing his mission to have failed. He told Sextus what he had said and what he had seen his father do: the king, he declared, whether from anger, or hatred, or natural arrogance, had not uttered a single word. Sextus realized that though his father had not spoken he had, by his action, indirectly expressed his meaning clearly enough; so he proceeded at once to act upon his murderous instructions. All the influential men in Gabii were got rid of—some being brought to public trial, others executed for no better reason than that they were generally disliked.[25]

It is easy to observe that Kierkegaard was familiar with the story, yet it is impossible to conclude which account he read and remembered. But the suggested origin, even though correct, does not explain or justify the appearance of this particular epigraph as the opening of *Fear and Trembling*. The only possible conclusion in this case might be that this historical account, which in Valerius' summary is transformed into a moral fable, was well known in the nineteenth century.

The identification of the source of the epigraph is rendered even more difficult due to the fact that it was quoted originally by Kierkegaard from Herder, as an entry in the *Journal JJ* suggests.[26] In addition, the commentators of the English edition of *Fear and Trembling* point out that this epigraph was discussed by Lessing in his *Abhandlung über die Äsopische Fabel*.[27] The Hongs write:

---

[23]   Valerius Maximus, *Factorum et dictorum memorabilium*, Book VII, 4.2: "*Tarquinius, fidei autem nuntii parum credens, nihil respondit, sed seducto eo in hortum maxima et altissima papaverum capita baculo decussit. Cognito adulescens silentio simul ac patris facto, causam alterius, alterius argumentum pervidit, nec ignoravit praecipi sibi ut excellentissimum quemque Gabinorum aut exsilio summoveret aut morte consumeret*"; *Memorable Doings and Sayings*, vol. 2, p. 149.
[24]   Aristotle, *Politics*, 1284 a. See *FT*, 339 notes.
[25]   Livy, *The Early History of Rome*, trans. by Aubrey de Sélincourt, Harmondsworth: Penguin 1960, Book I, 54, p. 94.
[26]   *SKS* 18, 146, JJ:7 / *KJN* 2, 16. *SKS* 18, 183, JJ:133 / *KJN* 2, 170.
[27]   Gotthold Ephraim Lessing, *Abhandlung über die Äsopische Fabel*, in *Gotthold Ephraim Lessing's sämmtliche Schriften*, vols. 1–32, vols. 1–28, Berlin: Vossische

Lessing's treatise (1759) antedates the Hamann source by four years. Kierkegaard was a reader of Lessing's works also in the years 1842–43, when he was writing *Fear and Trembling*. A later entry (*Pap.* X–1 A 363) indicates that Kierkegaard was familiar with Lessing's essay on fable. It is therefore not unlikely that he drew on Lessing's allegorical interpretation of the Tarquinius story in the essay.[28]

Kierkegaard's irony is present even here: the philosopher obscures the trail of the origin of his thought, leaving behind only a deleted passage from the epigraph, which brings a smile to the reader's face. The passage, which Kierkegaard quotes in German, reads as follows:

> A layman and unbeliever can explain my manner of writing in no other way than as nonsense, since I express myself in various tongues and speak the language of sophists, of puns, of Cretans and Arabians, of whites and Moors and Creoles, and babble a confusion of criticism, mythology, rebus, and axioms, and argue now in a human way and now in an extraordinary way. Hamann.[29]

Therefore, in this case Kierkegaard is clearly not referring to Valerius Maximus' text. The reason that Maximus' oratorical interpretation of Livy's historical account was not able to provide Kierkegaard with any attention-grabbing examples was that his contemporaries had already developed up-to-date critical theories of this historical account, thus opening new possibilities for further intertextual references.

The next time the name of Valerius Maximus is mentioned is in the commentary to *Repetition*. Constantine Constantius finishes the first part of his report with a passionate and eloquent passage, which confronts death with life:

> Why has no one returned from the dead? Because life does not know how to captivate as death does, because life does not have the persuasiveness that death has. Yes, death is very persuasive if only one does not contradict it but lets it do the talking; then it is instantly convincing, so that no one has ever had an objection to make or has longed for the eloquence of life. O death! Great is your persuasiveness, and next to you there is no one who can speak as beautifully as the man whose eloquence gave him the name πεισιθάνατος [persuader to death], because with his power of persuasion he talked about you![30]

The author has in mind Hegesias, the Cyrenaic philosopher, who was so eloquent and spoke so highly about death that some of his followers and listeners committed suicide. The only reason why a reference to Valerius Maximus seems relevant in this case is that in Chapter 9 of Book VIII, entitled "How Great is the Force of Eloquence," Valerius admires Hegesias' skills:

> What power do we imagine was in the eloquence of the Cyrenian philosopher Hegesias? He made the evils of life so vivid that when their pitiful image was thrust into the hearts

---

Buchhandlung 1825–27; vols. 29–32, Berlin and Stettin: Nicolaische Buchhandlung 1828 (*ASKB* 1747–1762), vol. 18, pp. 164–5.

[28]   *FT*, 339 notes.

[29]   *Pap.* IV B 96:4 / *JP* 2, 1551.

[30]   *SKS* 4, 49 / *R*, 176.

of his hearers he generated in many the desire for suicide. And on that account he was forbidden by king Ptolemy to discourse any further on the subject.[31]

However, this quotation does not have any direct parallels with Kierkegaard's text, since the key notion there is a Greek term, πεισιθάνατος, translated as "persuader to death," something that is absent in Valerius. Thus, the commentators of the Roman historian have identified the sources of this account, suggesting, among others, Diogenes Laertius, a biographer of the Greek philosophers, who mentions the fact that Hegesias was called πεισιθάνατος.[32] Yet, it is most likely that the only source of this reference in the case of Kierkegaard is Wilhelm Gottlieb Tennemann's *Geschichte der Philosophie*, which, according to the *Auction Catalogue*, was in Kierkegaard's possession.[33] As Kierkegaard's commentators note,[34] Tennemann cites both Cicero's *Tusculanae Disputationes* and Diogenes Laertius, but does not mention Valerius.

The final illustration which might refer to *The Memorable Deeds* can be found in the Preface to *Philosophical Fragments*:

> It is not given to everyone to have his intellectual pursuits coincide happily with the interests of the public, so happily that it almost becomes difficult to decide to what extent he is concerned for his own good or for that of the public. Did not Archimedes sit undisturbed, contemplating his circles while Syracuse was being occupied, and was it not to the Roman soldier who murdered him that he said those beautiful words: *Nolite perturbare circulos meos* [Do not disturb my circles]?[35] But one who is not that fortunate should look for another prototype.[36]

This passage could be inspired by Valerius' account in Book VII, entitled "On Study and Diligence," where he reports the story of Archimedes, who was murdered by mistake right after Syracuse were taken by the Romans:

---

[31]   Valerius Maximus, *Factorum et dictorum memorabilium*, Book VIII, C. 9; *Memorable Doings and Sayings*, vol. 2, p. 249.

[32]   Diogenes Laertius, Book II, 86. In English as *Lives of Eminent Philosophers*, vols. 1–2, trans. by R.D. Hicks, Cambridge, Massachusetts: Harvard University Press, London: William Heinemann 1980 (*Loeb Classical Library*), vol. 1, p. 217. In this English translation πεισιθάνατος is rendered "the prompter of suicide."

[33]   Wilhelm Gottlieb Tennemann, *Geschichte der Philosophie*, vols. 1–11, Leipzig: Johann Ambrosius Barth 1798–1819, see vol. 2, p. 106 (*ASKB* 815–826).

[34]   See *FT*, 369 notes.

[35]   This is the Latin/English translation of the Greek: "μή μου τοὺς κύκλους τάραττε," a legendary phrase, which is believed to have been uttered by Archimedes' right before he died. None of the sources which report Archimedes' death or the seige of Syracuse quote the above-mentioned sentence. See Livy, *The War with Hannibal*, trans. by Aubrey de Sélincourt, ed. by Betty Radice, Harmondsworth: Penguin 1965, Book XXV, 31, p. 338; Plutarch, *Makers of Rome. Nine Lives by Plutarch*, trans. by Ian Scott-Kilvert, Harmondsworth: Penguin 1965, "Marcellus," 19, pp. 104–5; Cicero, *The Verrine Orations: Against Verres*, trans. by L.H.G. Greenwood, Cambridge, Massachusetts: Harvard University Press, London: William Heinemann 1970 (*Loeb Classical Library*), II, 4.131.

[36]   *SKS* 4, 215 / *PF*, 5.

I should say that Archimedes' diligence also bore fruit if it had not both given him life and taken it away. At the capture of Syracuse Marcellus had been aware that his victory had been held up much and long by Archimedes' machines. However, pleased with the man's exceptional skill, he gave out that his life was to be spared, putting almost as much glory in saving Archimedes as in crushing Syracuse. But as Archimedes was drawing diagrams with mind and eyes fixed on the ground, a soldier who had broken into the house in quest of loot with sword drawn over his head asked him who he was. Too much absorbed in tracking down his objective, Archimedes could not give his name but said, protecting the dust with his hands, "I beg you, don't disturb this," and was slaughtered as neglectful of the victor's command; with his blood he confused the lines of his art. So it fell out that he was first granted his life and then stripped of it by reason of the same pursuit.[37]

As the Latin text suggests, Archimedes says, "*'noli' inquit, 'obsecto, istum disturbare,'*"[38] which corresponds to the general meaning of the quotation used by Johannes Climacus. But the fact that Archimedes' last words have acquired the status of an adage, make the task of identification of the source rather doubtful, undermining the idea that the Danish philosopher used Valerius as a source of this particular piece of information.

Clearly, identifying direct intertextual connections between the work of Valerius Maximus, which is itself based on numerous sources, and Kierkegaard's philosophical works is almost impossible. It seems unlikely that Kierkegaard used *The Memorable Deeds and Sayings* as a reference book. Valerius' narrative combines a number of features which could have captivated the Danish philosopher: the stories are short, but very vivid, the language is highly eloquent and the selection of topics rather inspiring. If Kierkegaard had ever read Valerius' work, it would have made a great impact on the sensitive and imaginative side of his nature and inspired him to use the source rather extensively. However, the Danish philosopher may have had only partial knowledge of the Latin work and the events it reports.

---

[37]   Valerius Maximus, *Factorum et dictorum memorabilium*, Book VII, 7, ex. 7; *Memorable Doings and Sayings*, vol. 2, p. 235.
[38]   Valerius Maximus, *Factorum et dictorum memorabilium*, Book VII, 7, ex. 7; *Memorable Doings and Sayings*, vol. 2, p. 236.

Bibliography

I. Valerius Maximus' Works in The Auction Catalogue *of Kierkegaard's Library*

Sammlung merkwürdiger Reden und Thaten, vols. 1–3, trans. by Friedrich Hoffmann, Stuttgart: Verlag der J.B. Metzler'schen Buchhandlung 1828 (*Römische Prosaiker in neuen Uebersetzungen*, ed. by G.L.F. Tafel, E.N. Osiander and G. Schwab) (*ASKB* 1296).

II. Works in The Auction Catalogue *of Kierkegaard's Library*
that Discuss Valerius Maximus

Bähr, Johann Christian Felix, *Abriss der Römischen Literatur-Geschichte zum Gebrauch für höhere Lehranstalten*, Heidelberg and Leipzig: Groos 1833 (*ASKB* 975).

Meierotto, Johann Heinrich Ludwig, *Ueber Sitten und Lebensart der Römer in verschiedenen Zeiten der Republik*, vols. 1–2, 3rd revised and enlarged ed., Berlin: in der Myliussischen Buchhandlung 1814 (*ASKB* 656).

Meiners, Christoph, *Geschichte des Verfalls der Sitten und der Staatsverfassung der Römer*, Leipzig: bey Weidmanns Erben und Reich 1782, p. 25; p. 57; p. 65; p. 116; pp. 120–1; p. 160; p. 164; p. 185, pp. 191–2; p. 281 (*ASKB* 660).

Rötscher, Heinrich Theodor, *Die Kunst der dramatischen Darstellung. In ihrem organischen Zusammenhange*, vols. 1–3, Berlin: Verlag von Wilhelm Thome 1841–46, vol. 1 (1841), p. 142n (*ASKB* 1391; for vols. 2–3, also entitled *Cyclus dramatischer Charaktere. Nebst einer einleitenden Abhandlung über das Wesen dramatischer Charaktergestaltung*, cf. *ASKB* 1802–1803).

Schmidt, W. Adolf, *Geschichte der Denk-und Glaubensfreiheit im ersten Jahrhundert der Kaiserherrschaft und des Christenthums*, Berlin: Verlag von Veit und Comp. 1847, pp. 331–4 (*ASKB* 771).

Schopenhauer, Arthur, *Parerga und Paralipomena: kleine philosophische Schriften*, vols. 1–2, Berlin: Druck und Verlag von A.W. Hayn 1851, vol. 2, p. 257 (*ASKB* 774–775).

Sulzer, Johann George, *Allgemeine Theorie der Schönen Künste, in einzeln, nach alphabetischer Ordnung der Kunstwörter auf einander folgenden, Artikeln abgehandelt*, vols. 1–4 and a Register Volume, 2nd revised ed., Leipzig: in der Weidmannschen Buchhandlung 1792–99, vol. 1, p. 205; p. 290; p. 518 (*ASKB* 1365–1369).

III. Secondary Literature on Kierkegaard's Relation to Valerius Maximus

None.

Virgil:

From Farms to Empire: Kierkegaard's Understanding of a Roman Poet

Steven P. Sondrup

At least in part as a result of Virgil's works—particularly the *Aeneid*—having traditionally been read as justifying Rome's imperial aspirations and supporting the claims to political authority of Caesar Augustus, he has enjoyed an unparalleled prominence among Roman poets from the unauthorized publication of the *Aeneid* by his literary executors shortly after his death to the present.[1] That such a reputation and renown should rest on such a small corpus consisting of only a few minor poems, the *Eclogues*, the *Georgics*, and the *Aeneid* speaks eloquently of both their collective importance and their considerable cultural capital. He brought to his poetry and most conspicuously to his epic a significant and unparalleled degree of lyric flexibility while at the same time remarkably never losing sight of a strict sense of overall structure. His career began with works of a smaller scale but ended with a masterpiece that was almost immediately seen as a reflection of the destiny of the nation and shortly after its publication was already widely quoted by contemporary poets. Just as those whose exposure to Latin literature may be rather modest have typically read the prose of Caesar and Cicero, their experience with poetry has most often been with that of Virgil, a fact which assures a broader audience than other classical authors can readily claim.

---

[1]   Recent readings of Virgil have stressed that the poet's support for the political agenda of Caesar Augustus may not have been as straightforward as has been previously believed but rather involved a conspicuous endorsement of the emperor but also a more subtle critique and subversion or his policies. See Adam Parry, "The Two Voices of Virgil's *Aeneid*," *Arion*, vol. 2. no. 4, 1963, pp. 66–80 (also published in *Virgil: A Collection of Critical Essays*, ed. by Steele Commager, Englewood Cliffs, New Jersey: Prentice-Hall 1966, pp. 107–23). For a similar reading of Virgil see also W.R. Johnson, *Darkness Visible: A Study of Vergil's Aeneid*, Berkeley, California: University of California Press 1976 and C.J. Putnam, *The Poetry of the Aeneid*, Ithaca, New York: Cornell University Press 1988.

I. Survey of Virgil's Life and Works

Publius Vergilius Maro, the son of small land-owners, was born near Mantua on October 15, 70 BC.[2] Although the details of his youth are far from certain, it appears that his father provided for his education in Rome and Naples under the tutelage of Siro, a prominent Epicurean philosopher. Traces of the influence of Epicureanism resonate in his earliest major work, the *Bucolics* or the *Eclogues* as they are perhaps better known. These ten brief poems were written between 42 and 39 BC and consist of hexameters ranging in length from the shortest of just 63 lines to longest extending to 111 lines. Their dating is in part based on an allusion to the considerable unrest in the area around Mantua having to do with the expropriation of farms for the compensation of participants in the battle of Philippi. The poems allude to the profound sense of loss of the small-scale farmers whose land was confiscated. A tradition of unclear veracity arose over the years that Virgil himself may have lost his land but was later able to reclaim it. Through Virgil's thorough familiarity with and great sympathy for Theocritus' *Idylls*, he saw aesthetic possibilities of dealing with the lives and more specifically the dialogues of rural shepherds. Though clearly drawing on the work of Theocritus, Virgil's poem—the work of a strong poet—is considerably more than an imitation of Theocritus or his Hellenistic predecessors, especially in terms of the significant degree to which he brings history to bear on the otherwise largely atemporal pastoral world. They exhibit in many ways a very complex relationship with their antecedents that has prompted their frequent consideration as equals rather than derivatives.

Following the completion of the *Ecologues* around 38 BC, Virgil associated himself with the prominent circle around Maecenas, which shortly thereafter came to include Horace as well. This affiliation brought the two poets into the sphere of influence of Octavian, who by the middle of the decade had consolidated his rule and had become the sole political power in Italy. The social and intellectual ambience that the company of his new patron afforded provided him the context in which he could devote himself for nearly ten years to what would eventually be recognized as Virgil's most polished work, the *Georgics*. These poems reveal a staggering command of both Greek and Latin literature as well as philosophical and historical texts. Biographers have been quick to point out that Virgil scrupulously attended to every detail, frequently made corrections and revisions, and consequently invested not only considerable effort but an extensive amount of time in the poems. The time that the composition required is also reflected in the historical allusions appearing throughout the poem from the suffering occasioned by the civil wars to those reflecting Octavian as triumphantly bringing peace, albeit at the cost of great suffering. Inspired to a degree by Hesiod's *Works and Days*, Varro's *De Re Rustica*,

---

[2]   The number of biographies of Virgil is vast. Among the most recent are Peter Levi, *Virgil: His Life and Times*, New York: St Martin's Press 1999; Pierre Grimal, *Virgile, ou, La seconde naissance de Rome*, Paris: Arthaud 1985; Alexander Gordon McKay, *Vergil's Italy*, Greenwich, Connecticut: New York Graphic Society 1970; Friedrich Klingner, *Virgil. Bucolica, Georgica, Aeneis*, Zürich: Artemis Verlag 1967; W.F. Jackson Knight, *Roman Vergil*, 2nd ed., Harmondsworth: Penguin 1966; Otis Brooks, *A Study in Civilized Poetry*, Oxford: Oxford University Press 1964.

and more specifically by Lucretius, the *Georgics* are a didactic poem grounded in a loose Augustan agenda of agrarian reform that looked more to the past than to the realities of rural life during the period. The four books deal very selectively with various aspects of the agricultural economy: tilling the fields, the cultivation of trees, raising livestock, and beekeeping. The structure of the poem moves from large to small—from the expanse of the fields to be plowed to the narrow constraints of the hive—and from labor intensive endeavors to those that are more passive—from the cultivation and nurturing of the fields to the collection of honey. The poem was at long last complete by 29 BC and was recited to Octavian during his return to Rome after the victory over Antony and Cleopatra.

The dawning sense of a *pax Augusti* brought with it the expectation of a new epoch that would in fact prove not so much to be a continuation of the familiar Ennian tradition, but would replace it. As early as the third book of the *Georgics*, Virgil had declared his willingness to sing the praise of the accomplishments of Augustus and in so doing confront Homer head on. Like the *Odyssey*, the first six books of the *Aeneid* recount Aeneas' perilous journey from Troy by way of Carthage to the Latium shores; like the *Iliad*, the second six books portray the battles that do not come to an end until the death of Turnus in literally the last line of the poem with the once vanquished Trojans now victorious.

In received readings of the *Aeneid*, the final victory of Aeneas serves to legitimate the end of the Roman Republic and the beginning of Rome's new imperial power by providing it with antecedent necessities and deep historical precedents while simultaneously praising Augustus by celebrating his legendary ancestors. The enshrinement of now triumphal Trojan culture, which had once been defeated by the Greeks, as the fountainhead of Latin civilization allowed Rome to assert a cultural parity with Greece at a time when its political and military power was clearly on the ascendancy throughout the Mediterranean.

In 19 BC Virgil left Rome, planning to travel to Greece and the eastern Mediterranean with the anticipation of revising the poem. In Athens, however, he met Augustus, who was returning home and was persuaded by the emperor to return to Italy with him. At Megara he was taken ill and grew worse during the course of the ensuing voyage. A few days after arriving in Brundisium, Virgil died on September 22, 19 BC. He had been acutely aware of what he considered faults and shortcomings in his poem that his untimely death had not allowed him to amend. He had begged Varius, one of his literary executors, to burn the epic he considered unfinished if he died before being able to make the final corrections. Augustus, however, ordered that the poem should be published and charged Virgil's executors with removing certain unsatisfactory passages but not adding anything to it. Fortunately Augustus' order was followed.

II. Virgil in Kierkegaard's Library

Kierkegaard's educational background with its clear emphasis on the Greek and Latin classics would have provided the precocious young man with a knowledge of the entire Virgilian corpus even at an early age.³ Although the works of Virgil are traditionally a central part of the compulsory classical curriculum, the number of copies of Virgil's works in various editions in Kierkegaard's library suggests that Virgil may also have been a particular favorite.⁴ *The Auctioneer's Sales Record*

---

³   For a general introduction to Kierkegaard's relationship to classical antiquity see *Kierkegaard's Classical Tradition*, ed. by Niels Thulstrup and Marie Mikulová Thulstrup, Copenhagen: C.A. Reitzel 1985 (*Bibliotheca Kierkegaardiana*, vol. 14). Although it deals exclusively with Greek topics, it is nonetheless useful in understanding the broad importance of classical antiquity for Kierkegaard from his school days on.

⁴   The number of studies of Virgil's influence is vast. A highly selective list of recent book-length studies includes Geoffrey Atherton, *The Decline and Fall of Virgil in Eighteenth-Century Germany: The Repressed Muse*, Rochester, New York: Camden House 2006; Richard F. Thomas, *Virgil and the Augustan Reception*, Cambridge: Cambridge University Press 2001; Richard Morton, *John Dryden's Aeneas: A Hero in Enlightenment Mode*, Victoria, British Columbia: University of Victoria 2000; Fiona Cox, *Aeneas Takes the Metro: The Presence of Virgil in Twentieth-Century French Literature*, Oxford: European Humanities Research Centre and British Comparative Literature Association 1999; Philippe Logié, *L'Enéas, une traduction au risque de l'invention*, Paris: Champion 1999; Craig Kallendorf, *Virgil and the Myth of Venice: Books and Readers in the Italian Renaissance*, Oxford: Clarendon Press 1999; Margaret Tudeau-Clayton, *Jonson, Shakespeare and Early Modern Virgil*, New York: Cambridge University Press 1998; Sabine MacCormack, *The Shadows of Poetry: Vergil in the Mind of Augustine*, Berkeley: University of California Press 1998; Bruce E. Graver, *Translations of Chaucer and Virgil*, Ithaca, New York: Cornell University Press 1998; Richard Waswo, *The Founding Legend of Western Civilization: From Virgil to Vietnam*, Hanover, New Hampshire: University Press of New England for Wesleyan University Press 1997; James J. O'Hara, *True Names: Vergil and the Alexandrian Tradition of Etymological Wordplay*, Ann Arbor, Michigan: University of Michigan Press 1996; John Watkins, *The Specter of Dido: Spenser and Virgilian Epic*, New Haven, Connecticut: Yale University Press 1995; Christopher Baswell, *Virgil in Medieval England: Figuring the Aeneid from the Twelfth Century to Chaucer*, Cambridge: Cambridge University Press 1995; Judith Haber, *Pastoral and the Poetics of Self-Contradiction: Theocritus to Marvell*, Cambridge: Cambridge University Press 1994; Niall Rudd, *The Classical Tradition in Operation: Chaucer/Virgil, Shakespeare/Plautus, Pope/Horace, Tennyson/Lucretius, Pound/Propertius*, Toronto: University of Toronto Press 1994; David Quint, *Epic and Empire: Politics and Generic Form from Virgil to Milton*, Princeton, New Jersey: Princeton University Press 1993; Judith Weissman, *Of Two Minds: Poets Who Hear Voices*, Hanover, New Hampshire: University Press of New England for Wesleyan University Press 1993; Theodore Ziolkowski, *Virgil and the Moderns*, Princeton, New Jersey: Princeton University Press 1993; Susan Lindgren Wofford, *The Choice of Achilles: The Ideology of Figure in the Epic*, Stanford, California: Stanford University Press 1992; Elizabeth J. Bellamy, *Translations of Power: Narcissism and the Unconscious in Epic History*, Ithaca, New York: Cornell University Press 1992; James H. McGregor, *The Shades of Aeneas: The Imitation of Vergil and the History of Paganism in Boccaccio's Filostrato, Filocolo, and Teseida*, Athens, Georgia: University of Georgia Press 1991; Edward Peter Nolan, *Now through a Glass Darkly: Specular Images of Being and Knowing from Virgil to Chaucer*, Ann Arbor, Michigan: University of Michigan Press 1990; Donna B. Hamilton, *Virgil and The Tempest: The Politics of Imitation*, Columbus, Ohio: Ohio State University Press 1990; Mihoko Suzuki, *Metamorphoses of Helen: Authority, Difference, and the Epic*, Ithaca, New York: Cornell University Press 1989; Annabel Patterson, *Pastoral and Ideology: Virgil to Valéry*, Berkeley, California: University of California Press 1988; Sarah Spence,

lists two copies of the same two-volume edition of Virgil's works, albeit in the appendices, *P. Virgilii Maronis Opera: Perpetua Adnotatione Illustrata in Vsum Scholarum Daniae et Norvagiae.* This school edition was edited by the philologian Jacob Baden (1735–1804) and published in Copenhagen in 1778–80.[5] Having been prepared for school use, it is far from a critical edition even by the standards of the day. Again if we count the appendices in the *Auction Catalogue*, he also possessed the two-volume octavio edition of *P. Virgilii Maronis Opera* edited by Ernst Karl Friedrich Wunderlich (1783–1816) based on the edition of Christian Gottlob Heyne and published in Hannover in 1816.[6] Heyne (1729–1812) was a distinguished scholar, who published numerous critical editions of Greek and Roman classics and was in close contact with many of the best minds of the late eighteenth and early nineteenth centuries. His prodigious scholarly production and intellectual acumen are still of considerable scholarly interest today.[7] His edition of Virgil—albeit only the first of two volumes—would have served Kierkegaard well. In addition to these editions in Latin, Kierkegaard's library presumably also included a translation into

---

Rhetorics of Reason and Desire: Vergil, Augustine, and the Troubadours, Ithaca, New York: Cornell University Press 1988; Ronald R. Macdonald, *The Burial-Places of Memory: Epic Underworlds in Vergil, Dante, and Milton*, Amherst, Massachusetts: University of Massachusetts Press 1987; Barbara J. Bono, *Literary Transvaluation: From Vergilian Epic to Shakespearean Tragicomedy*, Berkeley, California: University of California Press 1984; Robert Hollander, *Il Virgilio dantesco: Tragedia nella Commedia*, Florence: Olschki 1983; Andrew Fichte, *Poets Historical: Dynastic Epic in the Renaissance*, New Haven, Connecticut: Yale University Press 1982; Donald M. Rosenberg, *Oaten Reeds and Trumpets: Pastoral and Epic in Virgil, Spenser, and Milton*, Lewisburg: Bucknell University Press 1981; Theodore M. Andersson, *Early Epic Scenery: Homer, Virgil, and the Medieval Legacy*, Ithaca, New York: Cornell University Press 1976; Raymond J. Cormier, *One Heart One Mind. The Rebirth of Virgil's Hero in Medieval French Romance*, University, Mississippi: Romance Monographs Inc. 1973 (*Romance Monographs*, vol. 3); Charles Roden Buxton, *Prophets of Heaven and Hell: Virgil, Dante, Milton and Goethe. An Introductory Essay*, New York: Russell and Russell 1969; Sir Cecil Maurice Bowra, *From Virgil to Milton*, London and New York: Macmillan, St Martin's 1963.

⁵   *P. Virgilii Maronis Opera: Perpetua adnotatione Illustrata*, vols. 1–2, ed. by Jacob Baden, Copenhagen: Gyldendal 1778–80 (*ASKB* A I 192–193; *ASKB* A II 29–30).

⁶   *P. Virgilii Maronis opera in tironum gratiam perpetua annotatione illustrata a Chr. Gottl. Heyne, edidit et sua animadversiones adiecit Ern. Car. Frid. Wunderlich* [ed. by Ernst Karl Friedrich Wunderlich], Hannover: Sumtibus Librariae Hahnianae 1816 (*ASKB* A I 194).

⁷   The extent of appreciation for Heyne's work and interest in it is suggested by the number of books by and about him published in just the last ten years: Marianne Heidenreich, *Christian Gottlob Heyne und die Alte Geschichte*, Munich: Saur 2006 (*Beiträge zur Altertumskunde*, vol. 229); Sotera Fornaro, *I greci senza lumi: L'antropologia della Grecia antica in Christian Gottlob Heyne (1729–1812) e nel suo tempo*, Göttingen: Vandenhoeck & Ruprecht 2004; Fee Alexandra Haase, *Christian Gottlob Heyne (1729–1812): Bibliographie zu Leben und Werk: Gedruckte Veröffentlichungen, Zeitgenössische Schriften zu seiner Rezeption, Forschungsliteratur*, Heidelberg: Palatina 2002; Irene Polke, *Selbstreflexion im Spiegel des Anderen: Eine wirkungsgeschichtliche Studie zum Hellenismusbild Heynes und Herders*, Würzburg: Königshausen & Neumann 1999; Christian Gottlob Heyne (ed.), *Opuscula academica collecta*, vols. 1–6, facsimile reprint, Hildesheim: Olms 1997 [Göttingen: Dieterich 1785–1812].

German by Johann Heinrich Voß (1751–1826) in three volumes, published in 1800,[8] and a parody, *Virgils Aeneide travestirt* published in 1844 in Schwäbisch Hall of whose use there is no clear evidence.[9]

In addition to these primary texts, Kierkegaard was also well supplied with useful reference works. He owned two important guides to classical mythology that would have provided him with ample information about the classical past in general and details relating to figures Virgil mentions in particular. The first is a second, revised and enlarged edition of the important early nineteenth-century two-volume guide to classical mythology by Paul Friedrich Achat Nitsch (1754–94), the *Neues mythologisches Wörterbuch für studirende Jünglinge, angehende Künstler und jeden Gebildeten überhaupt*.[10] While his editions of Virgil and this guide to classical mythology are standard early nineteenth-century publications, Louis Moréri's (1643–80) *Le Grand dictionnaire historique* has a much longer history extending back to 1674 when the first edition was published in Basel by Pierre Roques (1685–1748) and a second important edition in Lyon in 1681. The work was widely disseminated and went through several editions with corrections and additions during the late seventeenth and eighteenth centuries. Kierkegaard's edition was published in Basel in 1731–32 in six folio volumes.[11]

III. Direct Quotations from Virgil

A particularly prominent passage frequently cited by Kierkegaard comes from the sixth book of the *Aeneid* at the point after which appropriate sacrifices had been offered and Aeneas is prepared to enter into the underworld. Those assembled call upon Hecate, who is supreme in both heaven and on earth (*vocans Hecaten caeloque Ereboque potentem* [l. 247]).[12] Upon her arrival, the ground shook and the ridge trembled, and as was typical at Roman rituals, the uninitiated were dismissed with the sibyl's shrieks: "*Procul, O procul este profani*" (6.258) ("Away! away! unhallowed ones"). In *Either/Or* in his discussion of the aesthetic validity of marriage, the narrator expresses his willingness to submit to the wishes of his wife but bans the intrusion of any alien authority with that Latin citation of the command to depart.[13]

---

[8]   *Werke Des Publius Virgilius Maro Werke*, vols. 1–3, trans. by J.H. Voß, Vienna and Prague: Haas 1800 (*ASKB* A I 195).

[9]   *Virgils Aeneide travestirt*, trans. by Aloys Blumauer, Schwäbisch Hall 1844 [1783] (*ASKB* 1298).

[10]   Paul Friedrich Achat Nitsch, *Neues mythologisches Wörterbuch für studirende Jünglinge, angehende Künstler und jeden Gebildeten überhaupt*, 2nd revised edition by Friedrich Gotthilf Klopfer, vols. 1–2, Leipzig and Soran: Friedrich Fleischer 1821 (*ASKB* 1944–1945).

[11]   Louis Moréri [ed. by Pierre Roques], *Le Grand Dictionnaire historique, ou le Mélange curieux de l'histoire sacrée et profane, Qui Contient en Abregé l'Histoire Fabuleuse des Dieux & des Héros de l'Antiquité Payenne*, vols. 1–6, Basel: Jean Brandmuller 1731–32 (*ASKB* 1965–1969).

[12]   *Virgil*, vols. 1–2, trans. by H. Rushton Fairclough, revised ed., Cambridge, Massachusetts: Harvard University Press 1967, p. 522.

[13]   *SKS* 3, 59 / *EO1*, 53.

The citation is used in a purely secular sense with no indication of the ritual or religious context from which it emerged but rhetorically connotes a powerful and binding dismissal. Kierkegaard, however, uses the phrase laden with considerable Christian sentiment in *The Moment 10*, an article written in 1855 shortly before he died, which with irony and occasionally humorous satire laments the tepid state of Christianity in a way that could only be done after the demise of his father's pastor, Bishop Mynster. "Christianity is so high that what it understands by grace is what all the profane (*procul, o procul este profani*) will of all things most decline with 'Thanks for nothing.' "[14] Kierkegaard's dismissal of those less ardently engaged with Christianity than he would advocate certainly has its parallels *mutatis mutandis* with the sibyl's dismissal of the uninitiated and, thus, the unworthy Trojans from the sacred grove. The phrase is used again in the same context but in a particularly prominent position rather than as the former parenthetical interjection. On the title page of the chapter "Come Here All You Who Labor and Are Burdened, and I Will Give You Rest" from *Practice in Christianity*, Kierkegaard cites the passage as an epigraph for the work.[15] As such, it sets the tone for the work to follow and as early drafts reveal had long been part of Kierkegaard's conception of the work.[16]

Kierkegaard uses an expression from the mouth of Neptune that appears in the first book of the *Aeneid*. The seas were tossing and turbulent and the winds were scattering the Trojan fleet in every direction to the extent that they were almost overwhelmed by the fury of the storm. Neptune summons the east wind and the west wind to reproach them for raising such confusion without his command and concludes his chastisement with the interjection "*quos ego—*!"[17] Literally the Latin means "Whom I—!" and appears to be the beginning of a threat that was withdrawn in mid-sentence with the resolve that the simple advice that it is better to be calm would be sufficient. Kierkegaard's use of the phrase is in a journalistic bellicose context centering on the *Corsair* affair. In a letter emerging from the fracas, Kierkegaard writes, "How did they study their law, if they do not know such a simple thing, and as vigilant and zealous policemen should they not, as is becoming and suitable to zealous and vigilant police, know in advance whether this was *dolus* or *culpa* or merely *casus*? *Quos ego!*"[18] Here the translation provided by the Hong edition is "I will teach them." The phrase in both cases is used for humorous effect that would not be lost on those who recognized its origin in the *Aeneid*.

A number of passages are cited only once and often represent particularly well-turned phrases to express an idea that is relatively independent of the context from which it is drawn. Frequently individual expressions are used as well-turned phrases. In *Either/Or*'s discussion of the immediate erotic stage in terms of Mozart's operas, he notes that desire vanishes "*et apparet sublimis*" [and is seen aloft], quoting Book

---

[14]   *SV1* XIV, 356 / *M*, 345.
[15]   *SKS* 12, [9] / *PC*, [5].
[16]   *Pap.* IX B 29 / *PC*, Supplement, p. 309.
[17]   *Virgil*, trans. by Fairclough, vol. 1, pp. 250–1.
[18]   *SV1* XIII, 465 / *COR*, 68. The authenticity of the letter with this citation is disputed. See *COR*, XXXV, footnote 134 for a discussion of the issue.

1, line 404 of the *Georgics*;[19] and in "The Seducer's Diary" the narrator describes how the enthralling beauty of a mother and child can be destroyed: "The father is visible—a huge defect, since that cancels the myth, the charm. The earnest chorus of sponsors is visible—*horrenda refero* [I report dreadful things]—and one sees nothing at all."[20] The original (*horresco referens*) comes from Book 2, line 204 of the *Aeneid*[21] in Aeneas' description of the how two endlessly long snakes arise and coil themselves around Laokoön (to whom Virgil returns in other contexts), a tale that certainly was terrible to relate in amusing contrast to the compromising of the Seducer's vision of feminine beauty. In recognizing the diversity of people and their abilities, Kierkegaard paraphrases Book 8, line 63 of the *Eclogues* "*Non omnes omnia possumus* [We cannot all do everything]" but with little resonance of the Latin context or any particular disparity with it.[22] In terms of yet another quotation, Kierkegaard contemplates the emptiness that one day might befall him as a result of the loss of the beloved and follows Aeneas' speech of comforting his company as they are shipwrecked shortly after leaving Troy in flames by projecting present woes into the future as pleasant memories (2.198–207):[23]

> And finally, this I know, I will be a recollection of her when death one day separates us—oh, that my memory will be faithful, that it will preserve everything when it is lost, an annuity of recollection for my remaining days, that it will give me even the most minor details again and that I may say with the poet when I am anxious about today: *et haec meminisse juvat* [and it is pleasant to recollect these things], and when I am troubled about tomorrow: *et haec meminisse juvabit* [and it will be pleasant to recollect the things].[24]

Kierkegaard's quotation and elaboration of the phrases retain the same high-minded solemnity that the words had originally had in the mouth of Aeneas and indeed may in that regard achieve heightened power by force of the context from which they were taken.

IV. Allusions to Virgilian Episodes and Characters

Kierkegaard frequently alludes—both directly and indirectly—to episodes or characters that Virgil describes. One of the most frequent is from the *Aeneid*, Book 6, lines 424–9, where Aeneas is described as leaving the River Styx and hearing wailing voices. These are the voices of "the souls of infants weeping, whom...the black day swept off and plunged into bitter death."[25] Kierkegaard first refers to the episode in the "Diapsalmata" of *Either/Or*. After a meditation on the nature of time and eternity, the narrator contrasts his age with antiquity in wondering why he had not died as child so that he could be buried by his father. He concludes with the arresting

---

19   *SKS* 2, 82 / *EO1*, 76; *Virgil*, vol. 1, pp. 108–9.
20   *SKS* 2, 422 / *EO1*, 435.
21   *Virgil*, vol. 1, pp. 308–9.
22   *SKS* 7, 319 / *CUP1*, 349.
23   *Virgil*, vol. 1, pp. 254–5.
24   *SKS* 6, 92 / *SLW*, 94–5.
25   *Virgil*, vol. 1, pp. 535–6.

observation: "Only in the happy days of yore could people have the idea of babies weeping in Elysium because they died so prematurely."[26] The next reference to the scene is again staged as an assertion that those who believe that all the difficulty of life is removed if a child dies shortly after being baptized have completely failed to grasp the essence of Christianity and do not even understand the pagan belief of small children weeping in Elysium.[27] Kierkegaard adduces the situation for a final time in the *Concluding Unscientific Postscript*:

> But then a child dies and a funeral oration is delivered, or in a sermon one alludes to the troubled parents who have lost a child, and one is humoristically above all the vanity of temporality. Mention is made of the seventy years as toil and as spiritual wear and tear, of all the rivers running into the sea without its ever becoming full. Thus the Romans were more consistent in letting these infants weep in Elysium because they were not permitted to live.[28]

Although Kierkegaard is clearly not endorsing the pagan view, he sees in it a consistency of cultural values that is more palatable and ultimately more logically defensible than the superficial Christian view that conceives of life as endless turmoil only to be endured before escaping into a happier estate. The Roman conception of infants weeping for having died too soon, thus, becomes a point of reference for an implied critique of facile Christianity.

As one might expect, among the figures to whom Kierkegaard frequently alludes or mentions directly is Dido, whose tragic love affair with Aeneas and eventual death is related in Book 4 of the *Aeneid*. In *Either/Or*, for example, Elvira's contempt for Don Giovanni, who has seduced and abandoned her and killed her father, is compared to that of Dido for Aeneas, who deserted her, feeling duty-bound by his vocation to establish Rome:

> Even if his [Don Giovanni's] voice were more insinuating than his own voice, his advances craftier than his own advances, he would not move her; even if the angels pleaded for him, even if the Mother of God were to be the bridesmaid at the wedding, it would be futile. Just as in the underworld Dido herself turns away from Aeneas, who was unfaithful to her, so she certainly will not turn away from him but will face him even more coldly than Dido.[29]

Although the motives for the abandonment of the two women are entirely different and Aeneas' fated mission to reestablish a center of Trojan culture may be construed as a mitigating circumstance, the scorn of the abandoned women nonetheless remains the same. By linking Elvira's fate to that of Dido, Kierkegaard elevates it to the mythic, archetypical level and to a kind of universal response. Kierkegaard's second allusion to Dido in *Stages on Life's Way*, however, is more indirect and highlights a far more obscure aspect of Dido's story. In describing the binding and constraining power of marriage, Kierkegaard notes that it spans a lifetime and encircles every

---

[26]   *SKS* 2, 49 / *EO1*, 40.
[27]   *SKS* 7, 267 / *CUP1*, 293.
[28]   *SKS* 6, 161 / *SLW*, 173.
[29]   *SKS* 2, 193 / *EO1*, 197.

moment. This encircling power is compared to the "hide that measures out the circumference of Carthage."[30] The allusion is to a passage in the first book of the *Aeneid* (lines 365–9) in which Dido explains to Aeneas that the Phoenicians entered into a contract with the Libyans for as much land as could be covered by the hide of a bull. According to legend, the hide was then cut into narrow strips so that it ultimately circumscribed a considerable tract. The parenthetical comparison of marriage's encompassing potential to the craftiness of the Phoenicians injects an element of levity into the description, but is at the same time to be taken seriously in suggesting the way Kierkegaard saw marriage delineating the perimeter of activity of both parties.

In his journals and notebooks, Kierkegaard quotes lines referring to Dido that have not only a literary resonance, but a potentially much deeper and more directly personal meaning as well. In a notebook under the heading *"Min Pige"* (My Girl) and dating from 1840–41—precisely the period of Kierkegaard's troubled relationship to Regine—Kierkegaard cites a passage from the *Aeneid* describing how Dido hung on every word of Aeneas' narration of the fall of Troy (4.79).[31] In contrast to Virgil's description of Dido's rapt attention that captures what is said with her attentive ears, Kierkegaard is a diligent listener even though his attention is not always attuned to what is said because he hears the heart even when nothing is verbally communicated.

An even more specific connection of Dido to Regine Olsen appears in a journal entry in which he notes that he could elevate the words of the poet (Virgil) to a motto for part of his life's suffering. He then paraphrases Aeneas' words to Dido in response to her request that he tell of the unspeakable pain associated with the sacking of Troy (2.3):[32] *"Infandum me jubes* Regina *renovare dolorem"*[33] ("You command me, *O Queen*, to renew unspeakable pain"). It may well be something of a hyperbole for Kierkegaard to compare his suffering—profound though it was—to that of the loss of home and native land experienced by the Trojans, but *double entendre* is here at play. In referring to Dido as the queen (Regina), Kierkegaard is surely alluding as well to his troubled and still troubling engagement to Regine Olsen, who by the time of the journal entry (1847) was happily married. The paraphrase returns specifically associated with Regine Olsen in *Notebook 15*, which is entitled *"Mit Forhold til 'hende'"* (My Relationship to "her"), and dates from "25 Aug[ust] [18]49." On the verso of the title page the passage about recalling pain is again paraphrased precisely as before and positioned on the page so as to align with a description of their first meeting on the recto of the next page.[34] There can be no doubt that Kierkegaard linked his continuing pain over the failed relationship to that which Aeneas felt in recounting the fall of Troy. But his identification of Regine Olsen with Dido—two women abandoned by men they loved even though their ultimate fates were quite different—suggests that Kierkegaard may have seen his breaking the engagement as

---

30   *SKS* 6, 108 / *SLW*, 114.
31   *SKS* 19, 217, Not7:46; *Virgil*, vol. 1, pp. 400–1.
32   *Virgil*, vol. 1, pp. 294–5.
33   *SKS* 20, 268, NB3:43.
34   *SKS* 19, 431–3, Not15:1–4.

a parallel to Aeneas' departure from Carthage in order to accomplish a higher and divinely mandated mission. Whether such a train of thought is best regarded as a compelling psychological explanation, a groundless self-justification, or something in between can only be a matter of speculation. What is clear is that Kierkegaard interpreted his own life's experience in terms of a powerful literary model offered by Virgil.

Another Virgilian figure—though mentioned in numerous other ancient sources—is Laokoön, who thrust his spear into the Trojan horse and as punishment—at least from the point of view of the invading Greeks—was with his sons cruelly bitten but more graphically surrounded and suffocated by the entwining coils of the snakes (2.199–227).[35] In his "Reflection on Marriage" from *Stages on Life's Way*, Kierkegaard's narrator, a married man, compares marriage to Laokoön's plight if his concept of being bound by marriage were to change:

> Suppose everything were to change for me—my God, if that were possible!—suppose I were to feel tied down by being married—what would Laocoön's misery be compared to mine, for no snake, no ten snakes, would be able to wind themselves as alarmingly and tightly around a person's body and squeeze as does the marriage that ties me down in hundreds of ways and consequently would fetter me with a hundred chains.[36]

Although the reference is couched in terms that might arise if the married narrator's attitudes toward marriage were to change, the question still emerges as to whether the hypothetical description offered by the married narrator may not reflect at least in part some of Kierkegaard's own apprehension emanating from his failed engagement. In quite a different context in a marginal note to a brief commentary on 1 Peter 5:7 ("Casting all your care upon him; for he careth for you."), Kierkegaard observes that cares represent a very elastic and flexible concept that, if conceived with any artificiality or insincerity, will coil themselves around the individual like the snakes about Laokoön.[37] Though not as dramatic as equating the bonds of marriage with the snakes, the brief observation suggests the strangulating and ultimately suffocating force of a sophistic lack of integrity.

Kierkegaard's thesis *On the Concept of Irony* contains three different allusions to Virgilian descriptions of mythological figures. In an early footnote commenting on the role of history with regard to the temporal and the eternal, Kierkegaard notes that according to the ancient view "eternal life began when one drank of the river Lethe in order to forget the past."[38] The allusion is to the passage in the *Aeneid* (6.713–15), where Anchises explains to his son, Aeneas, during his sojourn in the

---

[35]   *Virgil*, vol. 1, pp. 308–9. The reference to Laokoön may also have been motivated in part by Kierkegaard's extensive familiarity with Lessing in general—his personal library included *Gotthold Ephraim Lessing's sämmtliche Schriften* (vols. 1–32, vols. 1–28, Berlin: Vossische Buchhandlung 1825–27; vols. 29–32, Berlin and Stettin: Nicolaische Buchhandlung 1828, *ASKB* 1747–1762)—and with Lessing's essay "Laokoön oder über die Grenzen der Malerei und Poesie" to which he refers in the first part of *Either/ Or*. *SKS* 1, 167 / *EO1*, 169.
[36]   *SKS* 6, 89 / *SLW*, 91.
[37]   *SKS* 19, 216, Not7:41a.
[38]   *SKS* 1, 72–3 / *CI*, 10.

underworld the power of the waters of Lethe. Later, in describing irony's changing appearances, Kierkegaard evokes the figure of Proteus (*proteusagtigt*) as one who similarly could change his appearance at will.[39] The mythological story of Proteus is related by Homer in the *Odyssey* 4.414–24 but as well by Virgil in a slightly different way in the *Georgics* 4.387–414.[40] It is impossible to know which account Kierkegaard had in mind, but either links the ever-changing face of irony to a well-known mythological referent in such a way that it rhetorically strengthens the force of the argument. Kierkegaard's final reference to Virgil in his thesis is more extended and complex. He explains that just as Charon in ferrying souls across the river Styx had them divest themselves of all signs of worldly honor or glory lest the boat prove inadequate to carry the load, so Socrates transported individuals from reality to ideality.[41] As with other mythological references, the figure of Charon appears in many ancient sources, but of particular interest in this context is his description in the *Aeneid* 6.295–330.[42]

In *Either/Or* and *Repetition*, Kierkegaard makes a passing and relatively straightforward reference to Cerberus and Proserpine respectively. With regard to the former, he explains that for those skilled in the art of forgetting no adversity is so uncongenial that it cannot be flattered into disappearing from memory just as even Cerberus, who guards the entrance to the underworld, could be drugged and accordingly fall asleep so that Aeneas could enter (6.417–25).[43] In the latter, Kierkegaard describes the detailed memory of the narrator of *Repetition* concerning the nightly details in a restaurant. And to stress his point he adds, "No one escaped my attention: Like Proserpine, I plucked a hair from every head."[44] The allusion is to the *Aeneid* 4.693–9 that explains that Dido could not die until Proserpine had plucked a hair from her head.[45]

These single passing references bear testimony to Kierkegaard's intimate and extensive familiarity with Virgil, but play only a minor role in the exposition of the ideas in question. They provide for a rhetorical intensification of what is being argued and suggest a broader context to understand the point that is being made, indeed that it might be understood as a single instantiation of a mythic pattern.

V. Direct References to Virgil

Although the great majority of Kierkegaard's references to Virgil are to his works, he occasionally mentions him directly as an individual. In a note in which he is exploring the modern as opposed to the classical use of metaphor, he notes that the Romans and the Greeks are given to lengthy expansion of the figure to the extent

---

39   *SKS* 1, 109 / *CI*, 48.
40   *Virgil*, vol. 1, pp. 222–5.
41   *SKS* 1, 277 / *CI*, 226.
42   *Virgil*, vol. 1, pp. 526–9.
43   *SKS* 2, 284 / *EO1*, 294; *Virgil*, vol. 1, pp. 534–5.
44   *SKS* 4, 44 / *R*, 170.
45   *Virgil*, vol. 1, pp. 442–3.

that the central idea can be lost. The particular author he cites is "Virgil, for example, 'Like a wanderer who suddenly plunges' etc."[46]

On four occasions—once in *Either/Or*,[47] twice in his journals,[48] and once in the notebooks[49]—Virgil is referred to the sorcerer or magician (*Troldmanden* or *Troldkarlen*). The appellation harks back to a medieval legend concerning Virgil. His works—especially the *Aeneid*—were conceived of as not just unparalleled literary masterpieces, but also so remarkably prophetic, profound, and presciently allegorical that no mere human could have been their author. From that perception developed the folk belief that he was capable of miracles of every sort, and he entered into the European collective literary consciousness as a kind of Faustian figure and was eventually taken up in that sense in a Dutch folk book.[50] The part of the legend that most interested Kierkegaard was that he allowed himself to be cut into pieces and a cooked in a cauldron for the sake of regaining his youth.

As one of the writers of the most enduring interest and influence from classical antiquity, Virgil also loomed large in Kierkegaard's literary consciousness. The late medieval tradition of Virgil as a magician with formidable power was noted, but naturally his works—most especially the *Aeneid* and to a lesser extent the *Georgics*—were of paramount importance. He drew from the references that served to illustrate points he was making with Virgilian examples that would have been well-known and appreciated by his contemporaries.

Two narrative episodes stand out as having commanded particular attention: the sections of Books 2 and 4 of the *Aeneid* that deal with Aeneas' relationship with and response to Dido and the parts of Book 6 that center on Aeneas' visit to the underworld before making his way in earnest to the shore of Latium. The figure of Dido as someone courted but later abandoned for the sake of a higher calling is too obvious a parallel not to be considered as a possible basis for the attraction, the general popularity of the episode notwithstanding. The coincidence of the given name of his erstwhile fiancée—Regine—and Dido's title of *regina Carthoginis* and the similarities of their situation were not lost on Kierkegaard.

The references he drew from the sixth book's account of the underworld—the allusions to the rivers Lethe and Styx, to Charon, Cerberus, and weeping children—served to illustrate many arguments but perhaps most tellingly to highlight the

---

46   *Pap.* I A 251 / *JP* 3, 2305.

47   *SKS* 2, 35 / *EO1*, 27.

48   *SKS* 17, 104, BB:13 / *KJN* 1, 96. *SKS* 17, 237, DD:45 / *KJN* 1, 228.

49   *SKS* 19, 116, Not3:16.

50   See *SKS* K19, 167. Virgil as a Faustian figure has recently attracted critical attention. Among the most important articles are Leander Petzoldt, "Virgilius Magus: Der Zauberer Virgil in der literarischen Tradition des Mittelalters," in *Hören-Sagen-Lesen-Lernen: Bausteine zu einer Geschichte der kommunikativen Kultur*, ed. by Ursula Brunold-Bigler and Hermann Bausinger, Bern: Peter Lang 1995, pp. 549–68; David Flusser, "Virgil the Magician in an Early Hebrew Tale," *Florilegium: Papers on Late Antiquity and the Middle Ages*, vol. 7, 1985, pp. 145–4; Juliette Wood, "Virgil and Taliesin: The Concept of the Magician in Medieval Folklore," *Folklore*, vol. 94, 1983, pp. 91–104: George L. Frost, "Caesar and Virgil's Magic in England," *Modern Language Notes*, vol. 51, 1936, pp. 431–3: Rupert Hänni, "Der Vergilische und der Faustische Mensch," *Schweizerische Rundschau*, vol. 32, 1932, pp. 53–66.

difference between pagan beliefs and the Christian doctrines he was endeavoring to explicate with new clarity and force.

Virgil's widely held reputation as a poet of unusual allegorical and moral power lent credibility and substance to Kierkegaard's arguments and situated them in a broader and more universal context than the immediate day-to-day reality of nineteenth-century Copenhagen. In associating his thought from clearly articulated principles to informal reflections and ruminations with Virgilian *topoi*, characters, or episodes, Kierkegaard reaches beyond his quotidian experience to more universal frames of reference. This rhetorical strategy may be used to lend authority and wisdom of ages to his points or may also invite humor or slightly ironic readings. On the whole, however, the high-minded seriousness of Virgil's thought and the near perfection of his Latin verse served Kierkegaard well in providing compelling points of reference and convincing illustrations that cast him in the role of the heir to one of the great traditions in Western literary history.

Bibliography

I. Virgil's Works in The Auction Catalogue *of Kierkegaard's Library*

Virgils Aeneide travestirt, trans. by Aloys Blumauer, Schwäbisch Hall 1844 [1783] (*ASKB* 1298).

P. *Virgilii Maronis Opera: Perpetua adnotatione Illustrata*, vols. 1–2, ed. by Jacob Baden, Copenhagen: Gyldendal 1778–80 (*ASKB* A I 192–193; Cf. also *ASKB* A II 29–30).

P. *Virgilii Maronis opera in tironum gratiam perpetua annotatione illustrata a Chr. Gottl. Heyne, edidit et sua animadversiones adiecit Ern. Car. Frid. Wunderlich*, Hannover: Sumtibus Librariae Hahnianae 1816 (*ASKB* A I 194).

Des Publius Virgilius Maro Werke, vols. 1–3, trans. by J.H. Voß, Vienna and Prague: Haas 1800 (*ASKB* A I 195).

II. Works in The Auction Catalogue *of Kierkegaard's Library that Discuss Virgil*

Adler, Adolph Peter, *Optegnelser fra en Reise*, Copenhagen: C.A. Reitzel 1849, p. 111 (*ASKB* 2041).

—— *Theologiske Studier*, Copenhagen: Trykt paa Forfatterens Forlag hos Louis Klein. I Commission hos Universitets-Boghandler C.A. Reitzel 1846, p. 44 (*ASKB* U 12).

Bähr, Johann Christian Felix, *Abriss der Römischen Literatur-Geschichte zum Gebrauch für höhere Lehranstalten*, Heidelberg and Leipzig: Groos 1833 (*ASKB* 975).

Dyck, Johann Gottfried and Georg Schatz (eds.), *Charaktere der vornehmsten Dichter aller Nationen; nebst kritischen und historischen Abhandlungen über Gegenstände der schönen Künste und Wissenschaften, von einer Gesellschaft von Gelehrten*, vols. 1–8, Leipzig: Dyk 1792–1808, vol. 1, p. 24; vol. 7, pp. 241–309 (*ASKB* 1370–1377).

Fichte, Immanuel Hermann, *Sätze zur Vorschule der Theologie*, Stuttgart and Tübingen: J.G. Cotta'sche Buchhandlung 1826, p. 225n (*ASKB* 501).

[Hegel, Georg Wilhelm Friedrich], *Georg Wilhelm Friedrich Hegel's Vorlesungen über die Aesthetik*, vols. 1–3, ed. by von Heinrich Gustav Hotho, Berlin: Verlag von Duncker und Humblot 1835–38 (vols. 10.1–10.3 in *Georg Wilhelm Friedrich Hegel's Werke. Vollständige Ausgabe*, vols. 1–18, ed. by Philipp Marheineke et al., Berlin: Verlag von Duncker und Humblot 1832–45), vol. 1, p. 520; p. 544; vol. 2, p. 250; p. 438; vol. 3, p. 107; p. 287; p. 328; p. 365; pp. 368–71; p. 382; p. 387; p. 394; p. 404; p. 415 (*ASKB* 1384–1386).

[Montaigne, Michel de], *Michael Montaigne's Gedanken und Meinungen über allerley Gegenstände, ins Deutsche übersetzt*, vols. 1–7, Berlin: F.T. Lagarde 1793–99, vol. 2, p. 162; p. 164; vol. 3, pp. 191–2; vol. 4, p. 484; vol. 5, pp. 139–287 (*ASKB* 681–687).

Moréri, Louis, "Virgile," in *Le Grand Dictionnaire historique, ou le Mélange curieux de l'histoire sacrée et profane, Qui Contient en Abregé l'Histoire Fabuleuse des Dieux & des Héros de l'Antiquité Payenne*, vols. 1–6, ed. by Pierre Roques, Basel: Jean Brandmuller 1731–32, vol. 6, p. 952 (*ASKB* 1965–1969).

Mynster, Jakob Peter, *Blandede Skrivter*, vols. 1–3, Copenhagen: Den Gyldendalske Boghandlings Forlag 1852–53 (vols. 4–6, Copenhagen: Den Gyldendalske Boghandlings Forlag 1855–57), vol. 2, p. 360 (*ASKB* 358–363).

[Richter, Johann Paul Friedrich], Jean Paul, *Vorschule der Aesthetik nebst einigen Vorlesungen in Leipzig über die Parteien der Zeit*, vols. 1–3, 2nd revised ed., Stuttgart and Tübingen: J.G. Cotta'sche Buchhandlung 1813, vol. 2, p. 521 (*ASKB* 1381–1383).

Schopenhauer, Arthur, *Die Welt als Wille und Vorstellung*, vols. 1–2, 2nd revised and enlarged ed., Leipzig: F.A. Brockhaus 1844 [1819], vol. 1, p. 259; vol. 2, p. 409 (*ASKB* 773–773a).

Sulzer, Johann George, *Johann George Sulzers vermischte philosophische Schriften. Aus den Jahrbüchern der Akademie der Wissenschaften zu Berlin gesammelt*, vols. 1–2, Leipzig: bey Weidmanns Erben und Reich 1773–81 [the title of the second volume is modified and read as follows, *Johann George Sulzers vermischte Schriften. Eine Fortsetzung der vermischten philosophischen Schriften desselben. Nebst einigen Nachrichten von seinem Leben, und seinen sämtlichen Werken*], vol. 2, Vorbericht, p. 101; main text, p. 233 (*ASKB* 807–808).

—— *Allgemeine Theorie der Schönen Künste, in einzeln, nach alphabetischer Ordnung der Kunstwörter auf einander folgenden, Artikeln abgehandelt*, vols. 1–4 and a Register Volume, 2nd revised ed., Leipzig: in der Weidmannschen Buchhandlung 1792–99, vol. 1, p. 30; p. 75; p. 150; p. 206; p. 295; p. 414; vol. 2, p. 509; pp. 590ff.; vol. 3, p. 181; vol. 4, p. 274 (*ASKB* 1365–1369).

Thiersch, Friedrich, *Allgemeine Aesthetik in akademischen Lehrvorträgen*, Berlin: G. Reimer 1846, p. 75; p. 147; p. 409 (*ASKB* 1378).

Thomsen, Grimur, *Om den nyfranske Poesie, et Forsøg til Besvarelse af Universitetets æsthetiske Priisspørgsmaal for 1841: "Har Smag og Sands for Poesi gjort Frem- eller Tilbageskridt i Frankrig i de sidste Tider og hvilken Aarsagen?,"* Copenhagen: Paa den Wahlske Boghandlings Forlag 1843, p. 120; p. 155 (*ASKB* 1390).

Zeuthen, Ludvig, *Humanitet betragtet fra et christeligt Standpunkt, med stadigt Hensyn til den nærværende Tid*, Copenhagen: Gyldendalske Boghandling 1846, p. 69 (*ASKB* 915).

III. Secondary Literature on Kierkegaard's Relation to Virgil

None.

Index of Persons

Abildgaard, Nicolai (1743–1809), Danish painter, 169.

Abraham, 5, 46, 60, 61, 98, 99.

Agamemnon, 60.

Agricola, i.e., Gnaeus Julius Agricola (AD 40–93), Roman general, 148.

Agrippa I (10 BC–AD 44), king of the Jews, 153, 154.

Alexander the Great, 81.

Amor, 1, 4.

Anaxagoras, 16, 18, 19.

Andersen, Hans Christian (1805–75), Danish poet, novelist and writer of fairy tales, x, 42, 58, 96.

Antigone, 82–4.

Antoninus Pius, i.e., Titus Aurelius Fulvus Boionius Arrius Antoninus (86–161), Roman emperor, 128.

Apollodorus of Carystus, 175.

Apollonius of Tyana (ca. AD 15–ca. 100), Greek Neopythagorean philosopher, 128.

Apuleius, i.e., Lucius Apuleius Platonicus (ca. 125–ca. 180), Romanized Berber author, xi–xiii, 1–9.

Archelaus, 16, 118.

Archimedes, 193, 194.

Argus, 98, 99.

Aristophanes, 155, 181.

Aristotle, ix, 2, 12, 17, 19, 29, 115, 129, 147, 171, 191.

Assessor Wilhelm, see "Judge William."

Ast, Friedrich (1778–1841), German philologist, 16.

Attrup, Martin, 57.

Atticus, Titus Pomponius (ca. 110 BC–ca. 35 BC), Roman patron of letters, friend of Cicero, 76, 77.

Augustine of Hippo (354–430), church father, 1, 12.

Augustus, i.e., Gaius Julius Caesar Octavianus (63 BC–AD 14), Roman emperor, 39, 40, 53, 76, 87, 88, 127, 128, 133–5, 138, 148, 156, 185, 197–9.

Aulus Gellius (ca. AD 125–ca. 180), Roman writer, 76.

Baden, Jacob (1735–1804), 125, 150, 201.

Baiter, Johann Georg (1801–77), Swiss philologist, 3.

Barfod, Hans Peter (1834–92), Danish jurist and newspaper editor, editor of Kierkegaard's *Efterladte Papirer*, 41, 79.

Bayer, Karl (1806–83), German philosopher, 117.

Becker, Karl Friedrich (1776–1806), German historian, 155.

Bekker, August Immanuel (1785–1871), German philologist and classicist, 150.

Blicher, Steen Steensen (1782–1848), Danish author, 168, 169, 172.

Boccaccio, Giovanni (1313–75), Italian author and poet, 2.

Bojsen, Ernst (1803–64), teacher at the Borgerdyd School in Copenhagen, 168.

Brandes, Georg (1842–1927), Danish author and literary critic, 13.

Brutus, Marcus Junius (85 BC–42 BC), Roman senator, 39, 60, 133.

Caesar, Gaius Julius (100 BC–44 BC), Roman military and political leader, xi, xii, 11, 39, 78, 87, 88, 105, 125, 127, 130–5, 148, 149, 153, 167, 188, 197.

Caligula, i.e., Gaius Julius Caesar Augustus Germanicus (AD 12–41), Roman emperor, 111, 135–8, 141, 142, 148, 156.

Calvin, John (1509–64), French theologian, 24.

Index of Subjects